# ILLIBERAL
# EDUCATION

# ILLIBERAL EDUCATION

### The Politics of Race and Sex on Campus

## Dinesh D'Souza

THE FREE PRESS
*A Division of Macmillan, Inc.*
NEW YORK

Collier Macmillan Canada
TORONTO

Maxwell Macmillan International
NEW YORK   OXFORD   SINGAPORE   SYDNEY

The Free Press
A Division of Macmillan, Inc.
866 Third Avenue, New York, N.Y. 10022

Collier Macmillan Canada, Inc.
1200 Eglinton Avenue East
Suite 200
Don Mills, Ontario M3C 3N1

Printed in the United States of America

printing number
 2 3 4 5 6 7 8 9 10

*Library of Congress Cataloging-in-Publication Data*

D'Souza, Dinesh
    Illiberal education : the politics of race and sex on campus /
Dinesh D'Souza.
        p.   cm.
    Includes bibliographical references (p.    ) and index.
    ISBN: 978-0-6848-6384-9
    1. Educational equalization—United States—Case studies.
    2. Discrimination in education—United States—Case studies.
    3. Minorities—Education (Higher)—United States—Case studies.
    I. Title.
    LC213.2.D78   1991
    370.19'342—dc20                                              90-47055
                                                                  CIP

*For Laura A. Ingraham*

# Contents

# Acknowledgments

The information in this book was assembled from a wide array of firsthand sources, whose cooperation and support made this study possible. My research assistants Kyra Larkin of Georgetown University and Wendy Adams of the University of Virginia Law School were indispensable in assembling much of these data, setting up interviews, preparing questions, checking facts, and offering suggestions at every stage. Numerous university officials, faculty, and students helped with references, background information, press clippings, internal documents, and interviews. I cannot individually list these persons, but with the exception of press spokesmen and those who requested anonymity, they appear in the text of the manuscript. I am indebted to Stephen Balch, John Bunzel, Joseph Calihan, Leslie Carbone, Chester Finn, Morton Kondracke, Les Lenkowsky, William Raspberry, Richard Samuelson, and Thomas Short for valuable leads and suggestions. Among those who read my drafts and offered helpful criticism were: Jay Aragones, Stephan Bates, Harmeet Dhillon, Anthony Dolan, Mary Eberstadt, Carole Goldberg, Yaakov Hammer, Keeney Jones, Elizabeth Lurie, Ken Masugi, Adam Meyerson, Michael Novak, Joseph Obering, Nita Parekh, Jeremy Rabkin, Jonathan Rauch, Sue Reichel, Harold Ripley, Hilary Ryan, Mark Schmitt, Gregory and Melinda Sidak, Scott Walter, Wilcomb Washburn, and Ben Wildavsky. I wish to thank the American Enterprise Institute and its president, Christopher DeMuth, for giving me the time and research facilities to complete this book, as well as the John Olin Foundation, and its president William Simon and executive director Jim Piereson, for research support. I deeply appreciate the confidence of The Free Press and its publisher Erwin Glikes in entrusting me with this challenging project. My editor, Adam Bellow, guided my thoughts and my prose at every stage. Raphael Sagalyn, my agent, helped shape my proposal and defended my pecuniary interests. Finally, I owe more than I can express to my college teachers, especially Jeffrey Hart, Henry Terrie, and Donald Pease of Dartmouth; Robert Hollander of Princeton; and Harry V. Jaffa of Claremont McKenna College.

DINESH D'SOUZA
*Washington, D.C.*

# 1

# The Victim's Revolution
# on Campus

There are few places as serene and opulent as an American university campus. The students move in small groups, heading for class, the library, or the dining hall, greeting their friends and apparently conscious of being part of a community. At the major universities, gigantic auditoriums, dormitories, and gymnasiums sprawl across the landscape, advertising a tremendous investment of resources. At the prestige schools, such as those of the Ivy League, impressive domes and arches give off a distinct aroma of old money and tradition. Across the lawns the scholars come and go, talking of Proust and Michelangelo. Tributes to the largesse of democratic capitalism, American universities are nevertheless intellectual and social enclaves, by design somewhat aloof from the pressures of the "real world."

For the last decade or so, the larger society has not heard much from the university, certainly little of the truculence and disruption that seemed a campus staple in the late 1960s and early 1970s. The reason for the taciturn university atmosphere of the eighties, commentators generally agree, is that the current generation of young people lacks social consciousness, and cares mainly about careers and making money. Yet in the past few years, the American campus appears to be stirring again. University outsiders have been shocked to hear of a proliferation of bigotry on campus; at the University of Michigan, for example, someone put up posters which said, "A mind is a terrible thing to waste—especially on a nigger." Typically these ugly incidents are accompanied by noisy protests and seizures of administration buildings by minority activists, who denounce the university as "institutionally racist." Both bewildered and horrified, the university leadership adopts a series of measures to detoxify the atmosphere, ranging from pledges to reform the "white male curriculum" to censorship of offensive speech.

Both university insiders as well as informed off-campus observers

1

know that the recent incidents of bigotry have produced a good deal of excess on all sides. Responding to several cases of insensitivity or flagrant bigotry at Michigan, student and faculty activists demanded that all black professors be given immediate tenure, that admissions requirements such as standardized test scores be abolished, and that female and minority students be permitted to conduct hearings to penalize white students whom they find guilty of making racially and sexually "stigmatizing" remarks. In this case, the university administration took each of these demands seriously and partially acquiesced in them, agreeing to give preferential treatment to minority student and faculty applicants over non-minorities with stronger qualifications, and to adopt censorship regulations outlawing speech offensive to "persons of color," as well as women and homosexuals.

It is not always obvious, in these disputes, whose side a reasonable person should take, or whether it is possible, in good conscience, to endorse any side at all. The middle ground seems to have disappeared as a consequence of ideological fracas and polarization; whether it can be restored is an open question. But for those who visit any American campus, peruse the student newspaper, enter the student union and talk with some of the undergraduates, or examine the lectures and workshops listed on the bulletin board, it is clear that the heavily publicized racial confrontations on campus are mere symptoms of much deeper changes that are rapidly under way, with far-reaching consequences for American society.

These are changes in the intellectual and moral infrastructure of the American university, not in its outer trappings. Within the tall gates and old buildings, a new worldview is consolidating itself. The transformation of American campuses is so sweeping that it is no exaggeration to call it an academic revolution. The distinctive insignia of this revolution can be witnessed on any major campus in America today, and in all major aspects of university life.

## ADMISSIONS POLICY

Virtually all American universities have changed their admissions rules so that they now fill a sizable portion of their freshman class each year with students from certified minority groups—mainly blacks and Hispanics—who have considerably lower grade point averages and standardized test scores than white and Asian American applicants who are refused admission. Since it is often difficult for minorities admitted on the basis of preferential treatment to compete, most universities offer an array of programs and incentives, including cash grants, to encourage these students to pass their courses and stay in school. The coveted perks of so-called affirmative action policies have sometimes been extended to other groups claiming deprivation and discrimination, such as American Indians, natives of Third World countries, women, Vietnam veterans, the physically disabled (now sometimes called the "differently abled"), homosexuals, and lesbians.

• At the University of California at Berkeley, black and Hispanic student applicants are up to twenty times (or 2,000 percent) more likely to be accepted for admission than Asian American applicants who have the same academic qualifications. Ernest Koenigsburg, a Berkeley professor of business who has served on several admissions committees, asks us to imagine a student applicant with a high school grade point average of 3.5 (out of a possible 4.0) and a Scholastic Aptitude Test (SAT) score of 1,200 (out of a possible 1,600). "For a black student," Koenigsburg says, "the probability of admission to Berkeley is 100 percent." But if the same student is Asian American, he calculates, "the probability of admission is less than 5 percent." Koenigsburg, one of the architects of the policy, is satisfied with this outcome. "I suppose it's unjust, in a way, but all rules are unjust."[1]

• At Ivy League colleges, which are among the most competitive in the nation, incoming freshmen have average grade scores close to 4.0 and average SATs of 1,250 to 1,300. According to admissions officials, however, several of these schools admit black, Hispanic, and American Indian students with grade averages as low at 2.5 and SAT aggregates "in the 700 to 800 range."[2]

• A similar pattern can also be found at state schools. Over the past five years, the University of Virginia has virtually doubled its black enrollment by accepting more than 50 percent of blacks who apply, and fewer than 25 percent of whites, even though white students generally have much better academic credentials. In 1988, for example, the average white freshman at the university scored 240 points higher on the SAT than the average black freshman. An admissions dean told the *Washington Post,* "We take in more from the groups with weaker credentials and make it harder for those with stronger credentials."[3]

• At Pennsylvania State University, preferential treatment for black students extends beyond admissions; the university offers financial incentives to induce blacks to maintain minimum grades and graduate.

All black students who maintain a grade average of C to C+ during the course of a year get checks from the school for $580; for anything better than that, they get $1,160. This official policy endures for all four years of college; it is not connected with financial aid; it applies regardless of economic need. White and other minority students are ineligible for the cash awards.[4]

• Financial subsidies are also offered elsewhere. Starting in the fall of 1990, as part of a program to increase black enrollment by 50 percent, Florida Atlantic University is offering free tuition to every black student who is admitted, regardless of financial need. President Anthony Catanese said the measure is necessary to demonstrate that FAU is "serious about recruiting."[5] Miami-Dade Community College recruits minority students by promising that, if they do not find jobs in their fields of study after graduation, the college will refund their tuition money. No other students qualify for this money-back guarantee.[6] Earlham College in Indiana has a standing offer restricted to black, Hispanic, and American Indian residents of the state: if they choose to attend, the school will replace their student loans with grants.[7] And the University of Nebraska uses state money to fund special scholarships of $1,500 to $3,995 which Vice Chancellor James Griesen maintains are essential "to correct a documented under-representation of specified minorities in our student population."[8]

• Sometimes university leaders offer justifications for these preferences. Erdman Palmore, a Duke University professor who serves as chairman of the Committee on Black Faculty, maintains that financial inducements are essential for minority students and faculty whose social contributions have been historically undervalued. "By bidding up the price of blacks," says Palmore, "we are hoping to increase their value."[9] Michael Harris, professor of religious studies at the University of Tennessee, argues for greater preferential treatment for minorities and suspension of academic requirements because "when you see the word 'qualifications' used, remember that this is the new code word for whites."[10]

• Although they are stipulated as the prime beneficiaries, not all blacks feel honored by preferential treatment awards. When Stephen Carter, a graduate of Stanford, applied to the Harvard Law School, he received a letter of rejection. Then, a few days later, two Harvard officials telephoned him to apologize for their "error." One explained, "We assumed from your record that you were white." The other noted that the school had recently obtained "additional information that should have been counted in your favor," namely the fact that Carter is black.

Carter recalled:

> Naturally I was insulted by this. Stephen Carter, the white male,
> was not good enough for the Harvard Law School. Stephen Carter,
> the black male, not only was good enough, but rated agonized
> telephone calls urging him to attend. And Stephen Carter, color
> unknown, must have been white: how else would he have achieved
> what he did in college? In other words, my academic record sounded
> too good for a black Stanford undergraduate, but not good enough
> for a white Harvard Law student. Because I was black, however,
> Harvard was quite happy to scrape me from what it apparently
> considered the bottom of the barrel.[11]

• Favorable recruitment and hiring policies are not limited to racial
minorities at Columbia University. In 1989, the *Columbia Law Review*
announced a recruitment program offering preferential treatment for
homosexuals and lesbians. The journal added five extra seats to its
editorial board to promote "diversity," including special consideration
for "sexual orientation."[12]

## IN THE CLASSROOM

Most American universities have diluted or displaced their "core
curriculum" in the great works of Western civilization to make room
for new course requirements stressing non-Western cultures, Afro-
American Studies, and Women's Studies. Since race and gender issues
are so sensitive, the university leadership often discourages faculty
from presenting factual material that may provoke or irritate minority
students. Several professors who cross the academic parameters of
what may be said in the classroom have found themselves the object
of organized vilification and administrative penalties. Again, these intellectual curbs do not apply to professors who are viewed as the champions
of minority interests—they are permitted overtly ideological scholarship,
and are immune from criticism even when they make excessive or
outlandish claims with racial connotations. This dogmatism extends to
the official policy of academic organizations such as the Modern Language
Association.

• In the winter of 1989, at the University of Virginia Law School,
Professor Thomas Bergin was conducting his usually sprightly class
on property. As students responded to his queries, he shot back rebut-
tals and jibes, egging them on to more thoughtful answers. It is Bergin's

style to employ colloquial jargon; thus when one black student stumbled over a question, Bergin said, "Can you dig it, man?" Some students laughed, the class went on, the bell rang.

The next class day, Bergin entered the room visibly shaken. "I have never been so lacerated," he said. He read from an anonymous note calling him a "racist" and a "white supremacist" on account of his remark to the black student.

Bergin did not ask who wrote the note. He did not explain his intentions, and move on with the class material. Rather, he gave the class a lengthy recital of his racial resume: he did *pro bono* work for the civil rights movement, he was a member of Klanwatch which monitors hate groups, he was active in recruiting minorities to the university, and so on. Eventually Bergin's eyes filled with tears. "I can't go on," he said. He rushed out of the classroom, unable to control himself.[13]

• When Princeton University in the early 1980s debated whether to introduce a Women's Studies program, which would study "gender scholarship" outside the traditional departments, Dante scholar Robert Hollander expressed reservations at the faculty meeting. "I did not like the fact that this was not a debate about academic issues but about political sensitivity," Hollander says. "My colleagues were telling me that they didn't think much of the program, but would vote for it anyway. I spoke out because I did not want to respond cynically."

When he criticized the proposed program for its stated political objectives, however, Hollander remembers being subjected to a barrage of personal attacks. "I achieved instant notoriety. Even now, years later, my speech is the thing that most people remember about me." Hollander was surprised to discover that "colleagues I had worked with for a long time, with whom I got on extremely well, turned on me with incredible savagery. I wanted to say, hey, this is your friend, this is Bob Hollander. But nothing I could say would hold them back."

When the motion to establish Women's Studies passed, Hollander remembers, "Women were embracing and kissing on the floor. This struck me as odd. Was this an academic discussion or a political rally? Were we discussing ideas or feelings? It confirmed what I had feared about the program."

• New approaches to teaching now enjoy prominence and acclaim on campus. Speaking at an October 1989 conference in Washington, Houston Baker of the University of Pennsylvania argued that the American university suffers from a crisis of too much reading and writing. "Reading and writing are merely technologies of control," Baker alleged.

They are systems of "martial law made academic." Instead of "valorizing old power relations," universities should listen to the "voices of newly emerging peoples." Baker emphasized the oral tradition, extolling the virtues of rap music and holding up as an exemplar such groups as Public Enemy and NWA.[14] NWA stands for Niggers With Attitude. The group, among other things, sings about the desirability of violence against white people.[15] Baker himself is regarded as one of the most promising black intellectuals in the country, and a leader of the movement to transform the American academy.

• African American scholar Leonard Jeffries claims that whites are biologically inferior to blacks, that the "ultimate culmination" of the "white value system" is Nazi Germany, and that wealthy Jews were responsible for financing the slave trade. Adopting an evolutionary perspective, Jeffries told his class that whites suffer from an inadequate supply of melanin, making them unable to function as effectively as other groups. One reason that whites have perpetrated so many crimes and atrocities, Jeffries argues, is that the Ice Ages caused the deformation of white genes, while black genes were enhanced by "the value system of the sun."[16] Jeffries is no academic eccentric; he is chairman of the Afro-American Studies department at City College of New York (CCNY), and coauthor of a controversial multicultural curriculum outline for all public schools in New York State. Moreover, such extreme views are now frequently expressed by black scholars and activists.

• Many white students graduate from college with similar ideas. Reflecting several themes now promoted on the American campus, a recent graduate from two of the nation's top universities commented in a national magazine:

> I am a male WASP who attended and succeeded at Choate preparatory school, Yale College, Yale Law School, and Princeton Graduate School. Slowly but surely, my lifelong habit of looking, listening, feeling, and thinking as honestly as possible has led me to see that white, male-dominated, Western, European culture is the most destructive phenomenon in the known history of the planet. . . . It is deeply hateful of life and committed to death; therefore, it is moving rapidly toward the destruction of itself and most other life forms on earth. And truly, it deserves to die. . . . We're going to have to bite the bullet of truth. We have to face our own individual and collective responsibility for what is happening— our greed, brutality, indifference, militarism, racism, sexism, blindness. . . . Meanwhile, everything we have put into motion continues to endanger us more every day.[17]

• Frequently the sources of such sentiments are minority studies courses. In a manual for race and gender education, distributed by the American Sociological Association, Brandeis University Women's Studies professor Becky Thompson acknowledges the ideological pre-suppositions of her basic teaching methodology: "I begin the course with the basic feminist principle that in a racist, classist and sexist society we have all swallowed oppressive ways of being, whether inten-tionally or not. Specifically, this means that it is not open to debate whether a white student is racist or a male student is sexist. He/she simply is. Rather, the focus is on the social forces that keep these distortions in place."[18]

• It is now familiar practice for professional associations of scholars to adopt political positions to which they lend their academic credibility. In 1987, the Modern Language Association, whose members include humanities scholars from universities across the country, passed the following resolution: "Be it therefore resolved that the MLA will refrain from locating future conventions, not already scheduled, in any state that has criminalized acts of sodomy through legislation, unless that legislation, though still on the books, has been found to be unconstitu-tional, or the state has been enjoined from enforcing it through decisions rendered by the courts."[19]

## LIFE ON CAMPUS

Most universities seek to promote "pluralism" and "diversity" on campus by setting up and funding separate institutions for minority groups; thus one finds black student unions, black dormitories and "theme houses," black fraternities and sororities, black cultural centers, black dining sections, even a black yearbook. Universities also seek to protect minority sensitivities by imposing administrative sanctions, ranging from forced apologies to expulsion, for remarks that criticize individuals or policies based on race, gender, and sexual orientation stereotypes. Since blacks, feminists, and homosexuals are regarded as oppressed victims, they are usually exempt from these restrictions and permitted considerable license in their conduct.

• For example, graduate student Jerome Pinn checked into his dormitory at the University of Michigan to discover that his roommate had covered the walls with posters of nude men. When the young man told Pinn he was an active homosexual who expected to have partners over, Pinn approached the Michigan housing office and asked to be transferred to another room. "They were outraged by this," Pinn says. "They asked me what was wrong with me—what *my* problem was. I said that I had a religious and moral objection to homosexual conduct. They were surprised; they couldn't believe it. Finally they agreed to assign me to another room, but they warned me that if I told anyone of the reason, I would face university charges of discrimination on the basis of sexual orientation."

• In 1988 the law school faculty of the State University of New York at Buffalo adopted a resolution which warned students not to make "remarks directed at another's race, sex, religion, national origin, age or sexual preference," including "ethnically derogatory statements, as well as other remarks based on prejudice or group stereotype." Students who violate this rule should not expect protection under the First Amendment, the faculty rule says, because "our intellectual community shares values that go beyond a mere standardized commitment to open and unrestrained debate." The faculty agrees to take "strong and immediate steps" to prosecute offending students through the university judiciary process, but it will "not be limited solely to the use of ordinary university procedures." The faculty also resolves to write to "any bar to which such a student applies," offering "where appropriate, our conclusion that the student should not be admitted to practice law."[20]

• Censorship regulations at several colleges today are restrictive enough that a typical policy at the University of Connecticut interprets as "harassment" all remarks that offend or stigmatize women or minorities. Examples of violations of the University President's Policy on Harassment, for which the penalty ranges from a reprimand to expulsion, include "the use of derogatory names," "inconsiderate jokes," and even "misdirected laughter" and "conspicuous exclusion from conversation." At the same time, and in apparent contradiction with this policy, U-Conn places no restrictions on the sexual conduct of students; the handbook notes that "the university shall not regard itself as the arbiter or enforcer of the morals of its students."[21]

• When the University of Pennsylvania recently announced mandatory "racism seminars" for students, one member of the University Planning Committee voiced her concerns about the coercion involved. She expressed her "deep regard for the individual and my desire to protect the freedoms of *all* members of society." A university administrator sent her note back, with the word "individual" circled and the comment, "This is a RED FLAG phrase today, which is considered by many to be RACIST. Arguments that champion the individual over the group ultimately privilege the 'individuals' who belong to the largest or dominant group."[22]

• Although male white students are expected, on pain of punishment, to demonstrate tolerance and acceptance of minority sentiments, Gayatri Spivak, Andrew Mellon Professor of English and cultural studies at the University of Pittsburgh, argues that such qualities as tolerance cannot reasonably be expected of minority victims. "Tolerance is a loaded virtue," said Spivak, "because you have to have a base of power to practice it. You cannot ask a certain people to 'tolerate' a culture that has historically ignored them at the same time that their children are being indoctrinated into it."[23]

• A student newspaper funded by Vassar College termed black activist Anthony Grate "hypocrite of the month" for espousing anti-Semitic views while publicly denouncing bigotry on campus. In an acrimonious debate, Grate reportedly referred to "dirty Jews" and added, "I hate Jews." Grate later apologized for his remarks. Meanwhile, outraged that the *Spectator* had dared to criticize a black person, the Vassar Student Association first attempted to ban the issue of the publication, and when that failed it withdrew its $3,800 funding. The newspaper "unnecessarily jeopardizes an educational community based on mutual understanding," the VSA explained.[24]

• Some black students have noticed that the campus environment permits and even encourages a double standard on issues affecting race. Rachael Hammer, a bright and attractive young student at Columbia University, said that a black campus activist accused her of being a racist for refusing to date him. "He said: you are going to go out with me," Hammer recalls. "I said no. He then said I was a racist."

Hammer said that the only overt racism she has encountered at Columbia involves hostility directed against whites. "I am told that as a person of color and a member of a historically persecuted group, I cannot be racist against whites," Hammer said. "But blacks can say anything about whites and Jews." Of her prospective suitor, Hammer said, "I knew him since freshman year. Nobody ever heard of him until he got into a fight with a white guy. He turned it into a racial issue that rocked the campus for weeks." Pretty soon, Hammer said, "he started organizing rallies, writing articles in the student paper. His language changed into a kind of ghetto slang. He got into writing poetry—basically a string of epithets about what it felt like to be a black male."

• Among many young blacks on campus, there are hints of profound estrangement and suspicion toward the larger culture. In early 1989, Howard University's campus newspaper, *The Hilltop*, published an article which advanced an argument not infrequently heard on the campus. In "The White Conspiracy," undergraduate Malcolm Carson writes that "black males are specifically programmed for self-destruction by this society. . . . Hundreds of thousands of U.S. military troops are called on to wage urban warfare on our people. . . . An avalanche of cheap heroin was unleashed into our communities to lull our people to sleep. . . . African Americans are beginning to realize that the real enemy is not the brother standing across the street, but the white man in the top floor of the downtown high rise."[25]

• Feminists are capable of equally stern sentiments. Commenting on the problem of sexual harassment in late October 1989, University of Colorado graduate student Kristen Asmus observed, "Let's just face it. The men in our society cannot control themselves." Her solution? "Women will start fighting back. Women will begin to react with as much violence as men have mustered against them. Women will begin to stop talking about castration, and make it a reality. Women will begin to abandon their life-giving, caring inner nature and start carrying guns. Women will begin to kill men if they have to."[26]

• University administrators are not always sure how to deal with minority grievance and protest. In May 1989, thirty-one black and Hispanic students barricaded themselves in the office of Stanford president Donald Kennedy, demanding further action on minority issues. Kennedy issued a statement saying "the university will not negotiate on issues of substance in response to unlawful coercion."[27] The next day, Kennedy broke down under pressure, went on to negotiate with the students, and committed the university to hiring thirty minority professors over the next decade and doubling the number of minority doctoral students within the next five years.[28]

• When minority students forcibly occupied the office of the president of the University of Vermont, Lattie Coor, he agreed to sign a seventeen-point agreement, including the provision that "in no case will the number of minorities hired for faculty positions be less than four each year." Coor explained how he came to negotiate with the students. "When it became clear that the minority students with whom I had been discussing these issues wished to pursue negotiations in the context of occupied offices, I agreed to enter negotiation with them."[29]

• One way in which universities appease minority protesters is by setting up and funding distinctive black, Hispanic, or Third World organizations. For example, although its handbook advocates racial integration, Cornell University supports a host of ethnic and minority institutions, most of which do not admit, and none of which encourage, white students as members: Cornell Black Women's Support Network; Ethos Minority Yearbook; Black Biomedical and Technical Association; Gays, Bisexuals and Lesbians of Color; La Asociaciòn Latina; La Organizaciòn de Latinas Universitarias; Le Club Haitien; Mexican-American Student Association; Minority Business Students Association; Minority Industrial and Labor Relation Student Organization; Minority Undergraduate Law Society; National Society of Black Engineers; Pamojani Gospel Choir; Society of Hispanic Professional Engineers; Society of Minority Hoteliers; Students of African Descent United; Uhuru Kuumba; Washanga Simba. In addition, there are nine black and Hispanic fraternities and sororities.[30]

• In some quarters not just whites, but also heterosexuals, are suspect. The University of California at Los Angeles (UCLA) recently granted official recognition to Lambda Delta Lambda, a lesbian sorority. UCLA officials emphasized, however, that the sorority may not ban heterosexual women from joining.[31]

• The difficulties encountered by universities in their effort to define and promote "diversity" are evident in an incident at Yale University a few years ago. In August 1987, taking account of the extremely well-attended and vocal activism of homosexuals at Yale, the *Wall Street Journal* reported that the place was getting a gay reputation.[32] Yale has no less than five gay and lesbian groups, including one just for Chicano lesbians.[33] More than a thousand students attend Yale's annual gay-lesbian ball, and gay activist Sara Cohen asks, "What's wrong with a little bestiality?"[34] Concerned that this flagrancy would upset alumni donors, President Benno Schmidt of Yale promptly sent a letter to two thousand volunteer fund-raisers, denying that Yale was a "gay school" and concluding, "If I thought there were any truth to the article, I would be concerned too."[35] Schmidt's statement caused an eruption at the university. A graduate student announced that he was cancelling his course in homosexual rights. Gay activist groups beseiged Schmidt and demanded to know: what was wrong with 25 or even 70 percent of Yale students being homosexual? What was wrong with Yale being a gay school?[36] Somewhat chagrined, Schmidt responded that, no, there wouldn't be anything wrong with that, but Yale needed to have a proportionate number of heterosexuals too—for the sake of diversity.[37]

* * *

As these examples suggest, an academic and cultural revolution is under way at American universities. It is revising the rules by which students are admitted to college, and by which they pay for college. It is changing what students learn in the classroom, and how they are taught. It is altering the structure of life on the campus, including the habits and attitudes of the students in residence. It is aimed at what University of Wisconsin chancellor Donna Shalala calls "a basic transformation of American higher education in the name of multiculturalism and diversity." Leon Botstein, the president of Bard College, goes further in observing that "the fundamental premises of liberal education are under challenge. Nothing is going to be the same any more."

This revolution is conducted in the name of those who suffer from the effects of Western colonialism in the Third World, as well as race and gender discrimination in America. It is a revolution on behalf of minority victims. Its mission is to put an end to bigoted attitudes which permit perceived social injustice to continue, to rectify past and present inequities, and to advance the interests of the previously disenfranchised. Since the revolutionaries view xenophobia, racism, sexism, and other prejudices to be endemic and culturally sanctioned, their project seeks a fundamental restructuring of American society. It involves basic changes in the way economic rewards are distributed, in the way cultural and political power are exercised, and also in privately held and publicly expressed opinions.

The American university is the birthplace and testing ground for this enterprise in social transformation.

There are two reasons why such changes are worthy of close and careful examination. The first is that universities are facing questions that will soon confront the rest of the country. America is very rapidly becoming a multiracial, multicultural society. Immigration from Asia, Latin America, and the Caribbean has changed the landscape with an array of yellow, brown, and black faces.[38] Meanwhile, European immigration has shrunk from 50 percent of all arrivals between 1955 and 1964 to around 7 percent between 1975 and the present.[39] The recolorization of America is further enhanced by domestic minority birth rates, which exceed that of whites.[40]

The result is a new diversity of pigments and lifestyles. When America loses her predominantly white stamp, what impact will that have on her Western cultural traditions? On what terms will the evanescent majority and the emerging minorities, both foreign and domestic, relate to each other? How should society cope with the agenda of increasingly powerful minority groups, which claim to speak for blacks, Hispanics, women, and homosexuals? These challenges are currently being faced by the leadership of institutions of higher education.

Universities are a microcosm of society. But they are more than a reflection or mirror; they are a leading indicator. In universities, an environment where students live, eat, and study together, racial and cultural differences come together in the closest possible way. Of all American institutions, perhaps only the military brings people of such different backgrounds into more intimate contact. With coeducation now a reality in colleges, and with the confident emergence of homosexual groups, the American campus is now sexually democratized as well. University leaders see it as a useful laboratory experiment in training young people for a multicultural habitat. Michael Sovern, president of Columbia, observes, "I like to think that we are leading society by grappling earnestly and creatively with the challenges posed by diversity."[41]

Since the victim's revolution is transforming what is taught, both inside and outside the American university classroom, the second major reason to examine the changes is to discover what young people are learning these days, particularly on questions of race and gender, and the likely consequences for their future and that of their country.

Numerous books, studies, and surveys have documented the alarming scientific and cultural illiteracy of American students.

• A 1989 survey commissioned by the National Endowment for the Humanities showed that 25 percent of college seniors have no idea when Columbus discovered America; the same percentage confuse Churchill's words with Stalin's, and Karl Marx's ideas with those in the U.S. Constitution. A majority of students were ignorant of the Magna Carta, the Missouri Compromise, and Reconstruction. Most could not link Dante, Shakespeare, and Milton with their major works.[42]

• A recent survey of five thousand faculty members by the Carnegie Foundation for the Advancement of Teaching found general agreement about the "widespread lowering of academic standards at their institutions," a deterioration that was only partially camouflaged by an equally "widespread grade inflation."[43]

• A review of twenty-five thousand student transcripts by Professor Robert Zemsky of the University of Pennsylvania showed broad neglect of mathematics and science courses, especially at the advanced level, and an overall "lack of depth and structure" in what undergraduates study.[44]

• Research indicates that it is possible to graduate from 37 percent of American colleges without taking any courses in history, from 45 percent without taking a course in American or English literature, from 62 percent without studying any philosophy, and from 77 percent without studying a foreign language.[45]

Parents, alumni, and civic leaders all invest substantial resources of time and money in American higher education. They are justifiably anxious about whether the new changes in universities will remedy these problems, or exacerbate them. Will the new policies in academia improve, or damage, the prospects for American political and economic competitiveness in the world? Will they enrich, or debase, the minds and souls of students? Will they enhance, or diminish, the prospects for harmony among different groups? In short, how well will the new project prepare the nation's young people for leadership in the multicultural society of the future?

\* \* \*

The current academic revolution is being conducted at the highest levels of the university establishment. It is what Donald Kagan, dean of arts and sciences at Yale University, calls a "revolution from the top down." This fact distinguishes the contemporary period from the 1960s, when student activists applied pressure to a reluctant and recalcitrant administration. Today's university officials are generally sympathetic and often actively engaged in the victim's revolution. In some cases, they sponsor the changes without any student or faculty demands. These revolutionaries inhabit the offices of presidents, provosts, deans, and other administrators. Thus it is possible to alter the basic character of liberal education without very much commotion; as Kagan says, "Few outside the university have any idea what is going on."

Most university presidents and deans cooperate with the project to transform liberal education in the name of minority victims. This group includes an overwhelming majority of presidents of state universities, and all the presidents of the Ivy League schools. Only two or three college heads in the country have voiced public reservations about the course of the academic revolution.[46]

Here, for instance, are the presidents of four major universities voicing support for the minority agenda. While their statements vary in stridency, all of them diagnose the same underlying inequities, and seek the structural reform of higher education as a solution. Further, they all employ the characteristic vocabulary of the revolution, which we must learn to recognize as a kind of code language for the changes to which they point.

"We can create a model here of how a more diverse and pluralistic community can work for our society," University of Michigan president James Duderstadt said in a letter to students and faculty.[47] He added, "Our university has a moral imperative to address the underrepresentation of racial and ethnic groups. . . . The insights and erudition of hitherto excluded groups can enrich our scholarly enterprise; indeed, it seems apparent that we cannot sustain the distinction of our university in the pluralistic world that is our future without the diversity that sustains excellence."[48]

Stanford president Donald Kennedy told the Academic Council in May 1989 that, "we accept the basic design of the multicultural community, and commit ourselves to the encouragement and preservation of these minority groups. We confirm that many minority issues and concerns are not the special pleadings of interest groups, but are Stanford issues—ones that engage all of us."[49]

Keith Brodie, president of Duke University, said in his convocation address to the freshman class in 1989, "We have come to realize that the naturally broadening and civilizing process of a liberal arts education is not enough, by itself, to accomplish the goals of community we have set before us. We must engage intolerance . . . openly and publicly, as a community, at every opportunity."[50]

Donna Shalala of the University of Wisconsin remarked, "I would plead guilty to both racism and sexism. The university is institutionally racist. American society is racist and sexist. Covert racism is just as bad today as overt racism was thirty years ago. In the 1960s we were frustrated about all this. But now, we are in a position to do something about it."

These statements are not mere rhetoric. Several colleges have issued internal blueprints outlining a basic transformation of the campus over the next few years. In March 1989 Smith College published its *Smith Design for Institutional Diversity*, endorsed by President Mary Dunn and the board of trustees, which includes a pledge for Smith to more than quadruple minority representation on the faculty to 20 percent.[51] The Stanford administration has accepted most of the 132 provisions of the *Final Report of the University Committee on Minority Issues*, which calls for compulsory ethnic studies, graduate programs in Afro-American Studies, further expansion of preferential treatment, and funding for "ethnic theme houses" for blacks, Hispanics, and American Indians.[52] Ohio State operates under the *Ohio State University Action Plan*, which seeks to more than double minority student and faculty recruitment by 1994, regardless of the available pool of qualified applicants.[53] The University of Wisconsin has issued *The Madison Plan*, initiated by the chancellor and now official policy, which includes a timetable for special scholarships for minority students, a minority cultural center, an ethnic studies requirement, sensitivity education in race and gender, and the hiring of at least seventy minority faculty in three years.[54] The University of Michigan in early 1990 issued its *Michigan Mandate*, claiming credit for hiring seventy-six minority faculty through affirmative action efforts in two years, for multiplying black and Hispanic scholarships and fellowships, for establishing a multimillion-dollar Afro-American studies center, and for allocating $27 million for various minority-related programs.[55]

Other colleges such as Arizona State, Berkeley, Columbia, Cornell, Florida State, Harvard, Miami University of Ohio, Penn State, Princeton, Rutgers, the State University of New York at Albany, Stockton State, Temple, Tufts, Vassar, Wayne State University, the University of Arizona, UCLA, University of Massachusetts at Amherst, University of North Carolina at Chapel Hill, and the University of Pennsylvania have announced ambitious projects to rearrange admissions and curricular requirements to foster such values as "tolerance" and "diversity." Over the past few years, presidents and deans on most campuses have assembled task forces to set their agenda for "multiculturalism" or "pluralism," and have then incorporated several of their recommendations into official policy. Diversity, tolerance, multiculturalism, pluralism—these phrases are perennially on the lips of university administrators. They are the principles and slogans of the victim's revolution.

Among university professors, there are many qualms about the academic revolution under way because it challenges traditional norms of scholarship and debate. But these doubts are dissipating with time, as the composition of the body of American faculty rapidly changes. Older, traditionally liberal professors are retiring and making way for a new generation, weaned on the assorted ideologies of the late 1960s: the civil rights movement, the protest movement against U.S. involvement in Vietnam, and the burgeoning causes of feminism and gay rights. Many of these scholars in the humanities and social sciences have now invested their energies in what sociologist David Riesman of Harvard University calls "domestic liberation movements"; in fact, at a recent conference on liberal education, the *New York Times* found the young academics in agreement that "just about everything . . . is an expression of race, class or gender."[56]

Speaking with the typical frankness of these newly ascendant activists, black scholar Henry Louis Gates of Duke University remarks, "Ours was the generation that took over buildings in the late 1960s and demanded the creation of Black and Women's Studies programs and now, like the return of the repressed, we have come back to challenge the traditional curriculum."[57] Middlebury English professor Jay Parini writes, "After the Vietnam War, a lot of us didn't just crawl back into our library cubicles; we stepped into academic positions. With the war over, our visibility was lost and it seemed for a while— to the unobservant—that we had disappeared. Now we have tenure, and the work of reshaping the universities has begun in earnest."[58] Annette Kolodny, dean of the humanities at the University of Arizona, says that she was ideologically trained as a leader of the Berkeley protests of the 1960s. "I see my scholarship as an extention of my political activism," she says. As a former worker for Caesar Chavez's United Farm Workers, Kolodny maintains that her scholarship is designed to expose "the myths the U.S. has always put forward about itself as an egalitarian nation." In fact, she argues, the United States has "taken this incredibly fertile continent and utterly destroyed it with a ravaging hatred."[59]

These younger professors are now the bellwethers of the victim's revolution. Already their influence is dominant; soon they will entirely displace the old guard. As it is, most of the senior humanities and social science faculty acquiesce in the changes, and mildly protest only when the issue engages obvious faculty concerns such as intellectual freedom or the preservation of academic standards. Outside the mainstream of the academy, the National Association of Scholars, a small group of faculty crusaders, is launching a bold but somewhat quixotic effort to arrest the pace of the revolution.[60]

Although it began in the humanities and social sciences, the reverberations of the revolution are now being felt in law schools, medical schools, and the departments of the hard sciences which previously considered themselves exempt from campus agitation. Many law school and medical school deans and faculty are already reconciled to routinely extending admission to minority students who are academically less prepared than other applicants who are refused admission. Professor Bernard Davis of Harvard Medical School says that faculty face enormous pressure from the administration to pass black and Hispanic students even when they fail the same exam repeatedly.[61] For the first time, undergraduate and graduate professors in physics, chemistry, and biology are accused by minority activists of practicing "white male science" and operating "institutionally racist" departments. While many continue to resist pressures for preferential minority hiring and the inclusion of minority and especially female "perspectives" in the hard sciences, they seem bewildered about, and mute in responding to, accusations of systematic and methodological racism and sexism; consequently, with administrative and activist pressure, the victim's revolution is beginning its siege of the final bastion of "pure scholarship."

Many students are unable to recognize the scope of the revolution, because it is a force larger than themselves, acting upon them. Thus they are like twigs carried by a fast current. They are well aware that something is going on around them, and they might even squirm and complain, but for the most part students do not shape the rules that govern their academic and social lives in the university. Rather, those rules are intended to shape them. There are, on virtually every campus, organized alliances of minority, feminist, and homosexual students, who generally form the youth corps of the revolution. But they are not its prime movers: their numbers are too small, and they have no power to make the fundamental decisions that change the basic structure and atmosphere of the university.

Iconoclastic student newspapers at a number of universities mount spirited attacks on the revolution. Of the fifty or so publications, perhaps the most famous is the *Dartmouth Review* at my own alma mater. As a former editor of the *Review,* I witnessed first-hand engagement with the administration, although I had graduated long before the newspaper's most notorious showdowns—the 1986 sacking of anti-apartheid shanties by conservative students on the Dartmouth green, and the bitter confrontation between *Review* reporters and a black music professor in 1988.

While these recent episodes are not representative of the content of the *Review* or other papers, they illustrate the temptations to which overzealous undergraduate activists sometimes succumb. No doubt some of these antics are sophomoric, but we must remember that they are largely carried out by sophomores. The result, however, is that the influence of the "alternative student papers" is generally limited to confounding a few professors and deans, offering a therapeutic outlet for a small group of students, and in some cases informing and mobilizing a part of the alumni body. These undergraduate renegades are not powerful enough to stall the victim's revolution; perhaps for this reason, some of their attacks are reflexive, ill-considered, unkind, and lacking in historical perspective; thus they become further symptoms, rather than remedies, for campus maladies. Much of the time, they serve as a kind of journalistic tripwire, kicking up issues larger than they are equipped to handle.

Consequently, the current academic revolution on behalf of minor-

ity victims moves at a swift pace. Nothing interrupts it or gives it
pause; changes are proposed, accepted, and implemented in broad,
continuous strokes. It is not that the changes are indefensible, but
simply that they are seldom if ever subjected to criticism; thus there
is never any need to offer an explanation.

Nevertheless, it is crucial that the arguments for the revolution
be made, objections to them offered, and the two sides weighed against
one another. Such an approach will ensure that universities define and
defend their objectives, that mechanisms are developed to carry out
worthy objectives, and that both the ends and the means serve the
students for whom the universities exist in the first place.

* * *

In this book, I dramatize the transformation in academia through
an examination of six episodes at different universities—Berkeley, Stanford, Howard, Michigan, Duke, and Harvard—which are in the vanguard
of the revolution of minority victims. These colleges are leaders in
the academy whose policies smaller schools often emulate. In every
instance, I supply examples to show that the phenomena I describe
are widely experienced on other campuses. Each case study exposes
the conflicts and challenges which the revolution must face, and reveals
kernels of principle upon which priorities have been established and
those challenges resolved. Through narrative and firsthand interviews,
I seek to give the reader an inside look into how the controversial
claims of the new politics of race and sex assert themselves in all
areas of campus life, and are debated and adjudicated within the govern-
ing framework of the university.

Three basic issues are addressed:

## Who Is Admitted?

How are preferential treatment policies justified which treat racial
groups differently and admit some students based on academic merit,
and others largely or exclusively based on their skin color? Is there
such a thing as good discrimination? What effect does "affirmative action"
have in the classroom and on campus? What becomes of students
who benefit from preferential admissions? What are the arguments of
justice and of expediency that warrant such programs?

## What Is Studied?

Why are universities expelling Homer, Aristotle, Shakespeare,
and other "white males" from their required reading list? Is it true

that a study of non-Western and minority cultures will liberate students from ethnocentrism, racism, sexism, and homophobia? What are the merits of overtly ideological scholarship in Afro-American Studies and Women's Studies programs? What totems and taboos attend the teaching of sensitive material in race and gender scholarship? What do students learn from the new curriculum that prepares them for life after college?

## Life on Campus

Should universities promote integration or separatism? Why do minority students attack exclusivity, yet seem to prefer segregated institutions for themselves? Should universities encourage or allow corresponding all-white groups, and if not, why? Is there a case for university censorship of opinions that trespass on the feelings of blacks, feminists, and homosexuals? Should universities subject students to "sensitivity education" aimed at raising their consciousness of race and gender? Why are there so many racial incidents on campuses in recent years, and why do they happen most frequently at universities which are most resolute in their campaigns to combat bigotry?

While in each case I show what internal and external forces generate the conflicts that universities must face, my emphasis throughout is on how the university leadership deals with its challenges. It is here, after all, that social responsibility for establishing a healthy educational and cultural environment ultimately rests, and it is those in charge who make the rules that either solve problems or make them worse. Since I uncover and document many areas where our current university leadership seems to fall short, in my final chapter I suggest ways in which these issues could be handled more responsibly, so that the revolution of minority victims may more effectively achieve its legitimate aspirations, and all students may be better prepared for the challenges of career and citizenship in the society in which they will find themselves after graduation.

* * *

During my research for this book I discovered a tremendous curiosity, on the part of my sources, about my own background and where I was "coming from." Issues of race and sex are inevitably personal, and detachment is considered difficult, if not impossible. I am usually credited with a "Third World perspective," a term I find unclear and problematic. For readers who are interested, however, I offer a few personal comments which may be helpful in establishing my own interest and viewpoint.

I am a native of India who came to the United States in 1978. India is a democratic country struggling to accommodate enormous religious, tribal, and cultural heterogeneity. From my childhood I have experienced, and wondered about, this struggle, which is a subject of ongoing conversation and debate among Indians. America affords me a rare opportunity to examine questions of ethnocentricity, race, and gender, but from a unique cultural perspective. On questions that are so close to our daily lives, that engage us on both a conscious and subconscious level, I think that an element of critical distance may be helpful and illuminating. It makes possible observations that are more difficult to make when one is too close to, or engulfed by, an issue.

A personal anecdote may clarify why I believe this is so. A month or so after I arrived in the United States and enrolled, as a Rotary exchange student, in a public high school in Arizona, my host parents urged me to take someone from my class to the Homecoming dance. At first I was reluctant, but finally agreed. I approached a pretty young woman who said that she would have to ask her parents but would let me know tomorrow.

The next day I asked, "What did they say?"

She looked at me, "Who?"

"Your parents," I said.

"Say about what?"

At first I was simply astounded, but then I realized, with a sinking feeling, that I had approached *the wrong girl*. It was only later that I realized what my problem was: I thought all white women looked alike.

Later, when I was at Dartmouth and heard a student in the Afro-American Society charge that it was "grossly racist" that she was mistaken for someone else by a white student, I was sympathetic but could not be totally outraged. My own experience helped me understand that, no matter what our skin color or background, it is not easy to transcend our cultural particularity. Provincialism is a universal problem which all groups must confront; it is not a moral deformity confined to whites.

I enrolled as a freshman at Dartmouth in 1979, and graduated in 1983. I spent the next two years at Princeton University, where I edited an alumni magazine. Since then, I have continued to observe and follow goings-on in the American academy. For the past two years I have researched and studied the revolution of minority victims, spending a great deal of time on various campuses, attending classes and interviewing administrators, faculty, and students. As a student, I developed hypotheses that subsequent research has systematized or, in some cases, invalidated. Although I now write from a position more informed, and I hope more mature, than that of my undergraduate days, I believe that my close contact with the university over the past decade has given me a valuable eyewitness position to observe the sweeping changes going on around me.

I found, during my recent campus travels, that I can still pass for a student. I feel a bond with the new generation of young people, and do not agree with those who say that today's students are only interested in personal aggrandizement. Everywhere I observed a strong idealism, a search for principles that transcend expediency and self-interest. I admire this youthful quest and believe that universities should sustain and encourage it.

I especially empathize with minority students, who seek to discover principles of equality and justice that go considerably beyond the acquisition of vocational skill. Acutely conscious of America's history of exclusion and prejudice, they know that their past victories have not come without a struggle, and they yearn to find their place in the university and in society, to discover who they are, individually and as a people. These are challenges I faced very recently in college, and continue to face as a first-generation immigrant. Thus I feel a special kinship with minority students, and believe that the university is the right location for them to undertake their project of self-discovery.

I believe, as John Henry Newman writes in *The Idea of a University,* that the goal of liberal learning is "that true enlargement of mind which is the power of viewing many things at once as one whole, of referring them severally to their true place in the universal system, of understanding their respective values, and determining their mutual dependence." This knowledge of ourselves, and of the geographic and intellectual universe we inhabit, is ultimately what liberates and prepares us for a rich and full life as members of society. The term *liberal* derives from the term *liberalis,* which refers to the free person, as distinguished from the slave. It is in liberal education, properly devised and understood, that minorities and indeed all students will find the means for their true and permanent emancipation.

# 2

# More Equal Than Others
## Admissions Policy at Berkeley

It is thought that justice is equality, and so it
is, but not for all persons, only those who
are equal.

— *Aristotle*

When high school senior Yat-pang Au received his rejection
letter from the University of California at Berkeley in 1987, he was
incredulous. "I read it again and again," he said, "because I thought
maybe I had misunderstood or that it wasn't addressed to me. I had
my mind and my heart set on Berkeley. I worked hard in high school
to get into Berkeley. I couldn't believe I'd been turned down."[1] Yat-
pang's family was equally perplexed. When he heard the news, remarked
Sik-kee Au, Yat-pang's father who is a Berkeley alumnus, "I thought
my son was joking."

Yat-pang's credentials were not in question. He graduated first
in his class at San Jose's Gunderson High School with a straight A
average; his SAT scores were 1,340, which places him in the 98th
percentile, considerably above the Berkeley average; he ran a Junior
Achievement company; won varsity letters in cross country and track;
was elected to the student council and school Supreme Court. Yat-
pang won seven scholarships, including prizes from the National Society
of Professional Engineers, Bank of America Laboratory Science, and
Santa Clara County Young Businessman of the Year Club. Popular
with teachers and students alike, Yat-pang was described by his school
vice principal as "one of the finest students I've ever encountered,
and a real gentleman too."

At first, Yat-pang thought that Berkeley would not admit him because the university's admission standards were too high; excellent though his credentials were, perhaps other students were better. Then Yat-pang discovered that ten other students from Gunderson High were accepted to Berkeley, and none of them had Yat-pang's roster of achievements. "We knew of other students, with lower test scores and grades, who were admitted," Sik-kee Au told the *Los Angeles Times Magazine*.

Against their inclinations, the Au family began to suspect discrimination. As immigrants from Hong Kong, Yat-pang's mother Mandy said, "We've felt discrimination before, but I really hate to see it affecting education. Education is special. Every child should have an equal chance." Although Yat-pang was easily accepted to other schools, Sik-kee Au decided to protest his rejection at Berkeley, in part to discover what was going on in the admissions office.

The Berkeley admissions office, however, refused Yat-pang's appeal, on the grounds that Yat-pang did not deserve acceptance: he was "good, but not good enough." This was manifestly untrue, since Yat-pang's academic performance rated considerably higher than the Berkeley median; in other words, he scored better than at least 50 percent of Berkeley freshmen.[2] Sik-kee Au decided to raise a public furor. "I fight this not because it's my son, but for Asian people as a whole," Au told the *Orange County Register*.[3]

Local Asian American civil rights groups, which had received a number of similar complaints, backed the Au family. As Berkeley released admissions data in response to public claims by Asian groups, the Aus discovered that Berkeley regarded Yat-pang as insufficiently prepared *for an Asian*. If Yat-pang were white or black or Hispanic, his admission to Berkeley would apparently have been assured. In other words, Yat-pang's rejection at Berkeley did not seem accidental; rather, it appeared to result from a conscious plan, by the university, to treat applicants differently, based on their ethnic group.

Here was an extraordinary state of affairs. While professing its commitment to "equal opportunity," Berkeley seemed to operate separate racial tracks in its admissions process, resulting in the university "putting a lid on the number of Asians," in the words of Henry Der, executive director of Chinese for Affirmative Action (CAA), a San Francisco-based civil rights group. As word of this spread rapidly through the Asian American community, Berkeley found itself at the center of an intense and acrimonious controversy with national implications.

* * *

Yat-pang Au was indeed refused admission to Berkeley on the grounds of his race. University officials admit this denial is regrettable, but argue that the Au family should understand that Berkeley is attempting a grand project to secure racial justice and multicultural diversity in America. As Berkeley chancellor Ira Michael Heyman put it, "Berkeley must provide effective leadership in an increasingly multiethnic society. . . . We must prepare a diverse student body to govern a state which will increasingly demand a diverse group of leaders."[4]

Diversity is a central principle of the Berkeley admissions process.[5] Prodded by the state legislature,[6] the university seeks to achieve this goal by shaping its student body to roughly approximate the proportions of blacks, Hispanics, whites, Asian Americans, and other groups in the general population.[7] The university regards "proportional representation" as a just distribution of educational opportunities in a democratic society, where each group is entitled to its share of seats in the freshman class.[8] In the absence of such allocation, Berkeley officials fear that the university will become an elite enclave, populated by students of similar background; student interactions will reflect homogenous or monolithic perspectives, and both the university and society will be deprived of the richness and growth that come from a variety of races and experiences.

The problem at Berkeley, as at any selective university, is that admissions policies have in the past been based on principles of merit or achievement. Universities generally attach primary importance to such indices of academic preparation as grade point averages and test scores, although most also weigh extracurricular activities such as sports, arts and music, work experience, and community service. Berkeley discovered, however, that under these conventional measurements, racial groups fared very differently, with Asians typically scoring the highest, whites in the middle, and blacks and Hispanics markedly lower.[9]

In short, Berkeley found the principle of merit admissions in sharp conflict with that of proportional representation or diversity. Chancellor Heyman argued that the reason for this discrepancy was racial discrimination against underrepresented groups. "Higher education at all levels simply cannot wait until social processes in our society allow all groups to start life with the same advantages and to achieve at the same rate."[10] Absent discrimination, Heyman believed, not only would all groups enjoy equal opportunity, they would also perform at an equal pace. Berkeley therefore undertook to alter the ethnic ratios of the campus—what Heyman called "a little social engineering to reach deeply felt needs."[11]

Under Heyman's leadership, Berkeley began to depreciate the importance of merit criteria in admissions, in the belief that such criteria simply reflected, and reproduced, the effects of discrimination. In an effort to equalize racial representation on campus, Berkeley would continue to use merit criteria, but only to measure differences in academic preparation *within* groups. Thus Berkeley would accept stronger Asian applicants over weaker ones, or stronger black applicants over weaker ones, but across racial lines the principle would be modified: Berkeley might well accept academically weaker black students over better-qualified Asians.

The result was an aggressive minority preferential treatment program at Berkeley. But not all minorities would benefit: some would be more equal than others. Minorities such as Chinese Americans and Japanese Americans were considered overrepresented because there were proportionately more of them at Berkeley than in the population. Blacks and Hispanics were considered underrepresented by the same criteria. Berkeley announced its determination to eradicate these mathematical imbalances.[12]

Berkeley officials were irked by the complaints of discrimination from Yat-pang Au and other Asian Americans because they do not believe they are prejudiced against such students: there are just too many of them. In a 1986 interview with the *San Diego Union*, David Gardner, president of the nine-college UC-system, worried that over-representation of Asian Americans hampered his efforts to multiply black and Latino enrollment.[13] An internal Berkeley memo, prepared in 1984, expressed concern that Asian Americans were exceeding their allocated representation, and at this rate white and other minority enrollment would suffer.[14]

Why are there so many Asian Americans at Berkeley? One of the reasons is the rapid influx of Chinese, Japanese, and most recently Vietnamese and Cambodians, who have come to California.[15] Since 1980 the Asian population has grown by 70 percent, and now approaches 10 percent of the state total.[16] For many of these families, Berkeley is a symbol of "making it," a gateway to the American dream. A second reason for their presence at Berkeley is that Asian students perform extremely well academically, the consequence of such factors as a strong work ethic and family encouragement. More than white, black, and Hispanic high school graduates, Asian American applicants have proved equal to Berkeley's competitive standards: the number of Asian students at Berkeley climbed from 5.2 percent in 1966 to 26.2 percent in 1988.[17] Although Asian Americans might view this as an occasion for pride, for Berkeley's admissions office it proved an embarrassment, because Asians were taking seats they had intended for other groups. This situation has given rise to the stereotype of "Oriental overachievers" who are considered an obstacle to the university's vision for diversity.

Berkeley first tried to refashion its ethnic ratios through an "affirmative action" campaign aimed at largely black and Hispanic schools in California. By increasing the applicant pools of these certified minorities, the admissions office hoped to correct the ethnic imbalance in the student body. But Berkeley could not seem to find sufficient numbers of black and Latino applicants who could meet the university's stringent admissions standards. As a result, Berkeley officials say, Chancellor Heyman insisted that admissions standards be revised for minority students to increase their enrollment.

A former law clerk for Earl Warren, Heyman apparently shares the former chief justice's progressive beliefs. "He is a deep and sincere believer in equality of results," remarks Aaron Wildavsky, a former dean of Berkeley's Graduate School of Public Policy who has taught there for more than 25 years. In any event, Berkeley's program of affirmative action went from one of recruiting qualified black and Hispanic applicants to lowering admissions standards in order to raise their representation in each freshmen class. Since Berkeley's faculty could be expected to protest the dilution of the intellectual quality of the student body, Heyman called for rapid implementation of preferential treatment so that, by the time the faculty committees took up the issue, he would have achieved proportional representation or something close to it. "The chancellor knew that he had to move fast because he would be checked by the Senate in time," remarks Berkeley political science professor William Muir, a member of the Senate, which has administrative authority over university decisions affecting the composition of the faculty, the student body, and the curriculum.[18]

Together with high Asian American enrollment, Berkeley's preferential treatment program brought about the desired transformation of a student population that was, as late as the 1960s, 90 percent white. Thus while Berkeley admitted 285 students on affirmative action in 1975, the number of affirmative action acceptances rose to 728 in 1986.[19] In 1987–88, Berkeley announced that it had achieved multiracial "parity": black and Hispanic students were now equal to their share in the general population. This much-desired goal of proportional representation, however, required qualification, for white students themselves were now underrepresented.[20] This underrepresentation continued the next year so that, in the fall of 1989, the number of white students admitted to Berkeley dropped sharply to just one-third of the freshmen class.[21] Whites were now a bona fide minority at Berkeley. The university had exceeded the demands of the proportionalists, boasted Vice-Chancellor Roderic Park. As a force for social change, he added, "Berkeley has a bellwether role."[22]

\* \* \*

Since Asian Americans had been considered overrepresented, university officials said they expected the community to be pleased with multiracial progress on the campus. Thus it was with consternation that Heyman and senior administration officials reacted to an outburst of charges that Berkeley was discriminating against Yat-pang Au and others like him, and indeed seemed to have a ceiling or quota keeping qualified Asians out. Asians strongly suspected, as Chinese activist Henry Der charged, that these students had to demonstrate much higher academic standards than any other racial group to gain acceptance. "As soon as the percentages of Asian students began reaching double digits," remarked Ling-Chi Wang, professor of ethnic studies at Berkeley, "suddenly a red light went on. Since then, Asian American admission rates have either stabilized or declined."[23]

What many Asians saw, in short, was an unjust irony: affirmative action quotas established to increase the number of blacks and Hispanics at Berkeley now seemed to be restricting the number of Asian Americans. A preferential treatment program instituted to help minorities appeared to be hurting a minority group which could scarcely be blamed for the past injuries and deprivations inflicted on indigenous American minorities, such as blacks. Quotas which were intended as instruments of *inclusion* now seemed to function as instruments of *exclusion*.

These charges have been echoed at Harvard and the University of California at Los Angeles, both recently investigated by the Department of Education for practicing illegal discrimination against Asian Americans.[24] Stanford, Brown, and other selective colleges which attract Asians have also faced criticism for imposing upper-limit quotas.[25]

At Berkeley, when the number of Asian Americans declined by 272 from 1983 to 1984, a 20 percent drop in one year, Asian community leaders established a task force, headed by two local judges, Lillian Sing and Ken Kawaichi, to make inquiries. After gathering statistical

information, the task force alleged that Berkeley had instituted a minimum SAT verbal score, a policy with a detrimental impact on Asian
students whose first language often is not English. Local media rallied
to the cause of the Asian community, demanding that Berkeley account
for its admissions practices.

At first Chancellor Heyman denied that any admissions cutoff score
existed;[26] but under pressure, he conceded that it had been in effect
for some time in 1984, but was subsequently discontinued.[27]

Although Berkeley officials accused them of paranoia, Asian activists emphasized the high stakes that the Asian community places on
educational opportunity. For many Asian families, admission to Berkeley
represents a just reward for the hard work of their sons and daughters,
who hope to seize the educational opportunities at Berkeley to vastly
improve their circumstances in life. Thus Asians reacted with frustration,
bordering on desperation, when they saw indications that the admissions
rules seemed to be rigged against them.

Suspicious of Heyman, whom one activist called a "genteel bigot,"
Asian groups at Berkeley next approached the state auditor general
to investigate the university's admissions practices. He found that from
1981 to 1987 whites gained admission to Berkeley at a consistently
higher rate than Asians, even though Asian applicants had overall higher
academic scores.[28] Confirmed in their fears, Asian American leaders
insisted that Berkeley stop what they saw as illegal discrimination against
their children. Local politicians supported these demands, and State
Senator Art Torres commenced hearings on evidence that Berkeley
had quota ceilings for Asian applicants.[29]

Once again, Chancellor Heyman initially denied allegations about
quotas, but as the uproar in the Bay Area mounted, he finally admitted
engaging in discriminatory practices. "It is clear that decisions made
in the admissions process indisputably had a disproportionate impact
on Asians," Heyman said at a press conference in April 1989. "That
outcome was the product of insensitivity. I regret that it occurred."[30]

Although Heyman promised that Berkeley would not discriminate
any further against Asian Americans, his apologia sounded a bewildering
note. Heyman did not argue that Berkeley would return to merit admissions, or abandon its goal of seeking proportional representation. How,
then, could he seek ethnic symmetry for racial groups and simultaneously
assess "overrepresented" Asians in terms of merit? On this crucial
point, at the press conference, Heyman said nothing. He implied that
Berkeley's failure was one of administrative "insensitivity" instead of
being the fruit of deliberate policy. While seeking to allay controversy,

and disperse the restive Asian protesters, Heyman sought nevertheless to proceed with his preferential policies, which are still in effect.

The resurrection of the issue of quota ceilings has given an entirely new complexion to the debate over minority preferential treatment. "It's something that everyone is going to face sooner or later," remarks Berkeley vice-chancellor Park.[31]

Advocates of affirmative action realize that, in practice, it means giving some preference to minorities, especially blacks, in admissions and job hiring, at the expense of equally qualified or better-qualified whites. Although problematic in the sense that the specific minority beneficiaries need never establish any injury inflicted on them by the specific white victims, preferential treatment is justified by its advocates on the grounds that whites, as a group, have imposed grave and painful burdens on blacks over a period of two hundred years. Consequently, they argue, some sacrifices by whites to insure greater black participation in the universities and work force should be willingly endured by anyone who acknowledges the crimes of the past.

But now, for the first time in the United States, preferential treatment appears to be an intramural issue among minorities. At Berkeley, crucible of interracial mixing, whites are themselves a minority, and further, they fall generally in the academic middle. Two minority groups—Jewish students and Asian Americans—fare consistently above the average; their ratio at Berkeley is in excess of their proportion in the population; they are "overrepresented." Two minority groups—blacks and Hispanics—fare consistently below the average; their ratio at Berkeley is said to be lower than in the population; they are "underrepresented."

Given Berkeley's definition of diversity as proportional representation, the university's mandate seems clear: more blacks and Hispanics, fewer Jews and Asians. It is mathematically impossible to achieve ethnic proportionality without decreasing "overrepresented" groups. In the zero-sum game of admissions to highly competitive colleges like Berkeley, affirmative action gains by some minorities seem to require affirmative action losses for others. "The risk was there from the outset," observes Berkeley law professor Stephen Barnett, who has served on university admissions committees. "Proportional representation leads inexorably to quotas, both of inclusion and exclusion. And the term quota, of course, suggests both a minimum and a maximum, a floor as well as a ceiling."

This problem has been compounded by the fact that the pool of applicants to America's better universities, such as Berkeley, has become very large,[32] and the rate of increase in applications far exceeds the rate of increase in Berkeley's freshmen class size. Similarly, at the nation's most selective schools, including those of the Ivy League, admissions slots are both scarce and highly coveted, because applicant totals are several times larger than the available number of seats. Given what a Berkeley admissions study calls "the obdurate reality of large scale differences in patterns of academic performance among California's various racial and ethnic groups,"[33] the university faces the challenge of justifying preferential treatment policies which deny admission, on racial grounds, to the best-qualified students who apply.

The situation is getting more, not less, complicated. According to a study by the California Institute of Technology, around the year 2000 the state will be less than 50 percent white, with the other 50 percent divided roughly equally between blacks, Hispanics, and Asians.[34] With four sizable ethnic groups, each with very different backgrounds and histories of persecution and progress, how is Berkeley going to arbitrate among the claims from all sides? In what way can these disparate groups be fairly treated in the admissions process, so that Berkeley can establish an academic community based on equality and justice? Perhaps for the first time, many at Berkeley are asking whether preferential treatment is a means or an obstacle to this goal.

* * *

Once the platform for the Free Speech Movement, Berkeley's famous Sproul Plaza is now a veritable ethnic smorgasbord, with many students speaking to each other in Spanish, Vietnamese, Swahili, and Tagalog. It is apparent to visitors that the 1960s have not really left Berkeley. There is a thriving street trade in tie-dyed shirts. On the plaza, a man with flashing eyes was reading poetry he said he wrote in San Quentin; admiring students applauded everytime he managed a rhyme or obscenity. A group of middle-aged veterans was selling buttons and T-shirts protesting the Vietnam War almost two decades after it ended. In a health food restaurant, a man was jerking ketchup onto his cottage cheese and discoursing on Aphra Behn. Genius, eccentricity, and clinical insanity seem to merge at Berkeley, giving the place a wistful charm.

Berkeley's Asian American students contribute to this visual diversity. Yet in another sense they stand in sharp contrast to the mood of languorous abandon. Most of them are impeccably groomed, conservative in dress, moderate in manner. They were not to be seen among the group cheering the man from San Quentin. In a subtle yet unmistakable way, the Asian American demeanor is a challenge to the ethos of the 1960s. Asians do not satisfy an understanding of diversity that requires unconventional attire, involvement in assorted causes, and a general identification with the counterculture. In this sense, they remain outsiders at Berkeley.

It is not easy to find an Asian student willing to talk at Berkeley. I passed up two or three who would talk only on condition of anonymity. I approached one student waiting for the library to open, but he was too eager not to miss a minute of reading time. Eventually I found Thuy Nguyen, a cheerful woman who turned out to be a student at UC-Davis. She knew all about Berkeley, though; she was visiting her friend Cynthia Dong, an undergraduate there. They had gone to the same high school in California. Nguyen wishes she had been admitted to Berkeley. She doesn't know why they kept her out, because "other people with a lot lower grades in my class got in." Nguyen expressed an evidently common opinion that Berkeley "doesn't want any more Asians" because "they are trying to keep the quotas even."

Nguyen revealed that her high school GPA was 3.8 (out of a possible 4.0) and her SAT score was 1,000 (out of a possible 1,600). She had a decent list of extracurriculars. Although her grades were excellent, her relatively mediocre SAT put Nguyen below the mean at Berkeley; she was not assured of automatic acceptance. Berkeley's average SAT score is around 1,200.

Nguyen, however, has not had the same advantages in life as most other applicants to Berkeley. She came to this country in 1980 as a Vietnamese boat person. Previously she lived in a refugee camp in Thailand. When her family came here they had nothing, Nguyen said, so they had to live with an American host family for a month; even now they hold menial jobs. Nguyen knew only scraps of English which she picked up at the refugee camp ten years ago, though, as we spoke, her vocabulary gave little hint of this background; she seemed just as articulate as any of her peers.

Despite her own difficulties, Nguyen didn't consider herself a victim. "What do I have to complain about?" she said. She is sympathetic to complaints she hears on campus from black groups: "I know they have suffered a lot more than I have." This seems hard to believe: how does she know this? She doesn't, she said, but she infers it from the way campus activists give moving and elaborate accounts of their persecution. "They seem so hurt all the time."

"I have faced some discrimination," Nguyen said, "but I don't worry about it." Her philosophy is simple. "You just have to be persistent

in what you are doing. Don't worry about how much racism there is
in society. The main thing is to focus on what you can do yourself.
The future is more important than the past, and you can change the
future." Nguyen has plans for herself: she is going to be an architect,
"and maybe design recreation parks."

Contrast Nguyen's case with that of Melanie Lewis, a vivacious
black woman wearing a blue polo shirt and denim shorts, whom I
interviewed outside the university library. Lewis revealed that she
had the same SAT score in high school as Nguyen: 1,000 out of 1,600.
Her GPA was slightly lower: 3.6, but still impressive. Lewis said, "I
knew Berkeley was very selective, so I was very surprised when I
got in here."

Lewis is a strong supporter of preferential treatment for blacks.
Racism thrives in America, she said, noting "racial outbursts" at Berkeley in recent years. Nevertheless Lewis could not remember a single
incident in which she was a victim of prejudice. She said, however,
"You still have that family history. I may be the richest black person
in the world, I may be the son or daughter of Michael Jackson, but
Michael Jackson's ancestors were still stripped of their name and their
person."

At this point Lewis became passionate. "I am oppressed, I will
always be oppressed. Yes, I came from a good family and an economically
stable background. But my race was still deprived, and that will always
live with me. I have the Ku Klux Klan to remind me. Every time
they burn down a house, that reminds me that I live in a country of
racism."

Lewis said that her father is a retired engineer who spent most
of his life in the military; her mother works as a government supervisor.
In view of the fact that she is middle-class, and has not suffered socioeconomic disadvantage, why does Lewis think she should benefit from
preferential treatment? "You know, at places where you have such a
majority of white people, you start getting prejudices everywhere.
That's no good. How can you study with that going on? Systems flow
more easily if you have a better racial mix."

But this seems to result in groups such as Asians being denied
admissions despite their academic eligibility; does Lewis favor quotas—
or perhaps goals—to decrease the percentage of Asians? Lewis didn't
answer directly. She mentioned the case of an Asian student with a
straight-A average who was rejected at Berkeley but threatened to
sue the university, so he was admitted. "If I were him, I wouldn't
want to come here," Lewis said. "I wouldn't fight so hard to go somewhere that didn't want me."

I raised the example of James Meredith, the first black to enroll at the University of Mississippi, who wasn't wanted there either; on his first day of class, President Kennedy had to send federal marshals to ensure his safety. Didn't Lewis think it was right for Meredith to fight for his academic right to be there? The Meredith example inspired her. "Blacks," she said, "have fought, fought, fought to get a chance. I don't see why we shouldn't get that chance." Preferential treatment, for this reason, must continue.

At Lewis' high school, she said, 15 percent of the students are black and 15 percent are Asian. Of her senior class, four black and two white students were accepted to Berkeley, and no Asians. "Everyone said that I got into Berkeley just because I was black," Lewis said bitterly.

Just as it was easy to admire Thuy Nguyen's modesty and courage, it was easy to sympathize with Melanie Lewis, an intelligent young woman placed in a position where she did not get credit for her accomplishments; even if Lewis received no benefit from affirmative action, she would still remain under suspicion of being unfairly advanced by Berkeley. Anyone can be excused for being jittery under those circumstances.

The examples of these two women, one of them Asian, the other black, reveal how affirmative action has largely abandoned its original objective of giving a break to disadvantaged students to enable them to enjoy the same opportunities as their more fortunate peers. If the objective of affirmative action is to favor a promising young person who did not start out on the same line as everyone else, then it is hard to find a better candidate than Thuy Nguyen. Melanie Lewis' argument that despite her socioeconomic advantages she will always be oppressed because she is black seems to be an unwitting argument *against* affirmative action, because it raises the question of how preferential treatment can possibly help such a person. It can raise her standard of living by giving her a Berkeley credential, perhaps, but by her own assertion, even if she gets the best of jobs, and becomes a millionaire, she will still be oppressed. Thus, Lewis' victim status seems secure, and affirmative action only rectifies the situation if it can make her no longer black.

\* \* \*

If the case of Yat-pang Au is unusual, Berkeley officials freely admit that cases such as those of Nguyen and Lewis are typical. Preferential treatment so infuses admissions policy that until 1990 only 40 percent of the Berkeley freshmen class were accepted based on academic merit. In the fall of 1991, that number has been raised to 50 percent—the other 50 percent are accepted under the broad rubric of diversity. "Merit," remarks a Berkeley official, "is no longer the predominant factor in admissions."

The university's affirmative action is carried out through two programs, called Educational Opportunity Program and Special Action. Ernest Koenigsburg, a Berkeley professor of business who has served on admissions committees, explains how the programs work. The University of California system of colleges has established minimum standards to do the work at any of its schools. If a black applicant meets these, with a grade point average of 3.3 (B+) or higher, he or she is virtually certain to be admitted to Berkeley. Such a student would almost certainly get in even with a 2.78–3.29 (between B− and B) grade score, as long as the SAT scores were good, according to Koenigsburg. Whatever the grade average, Koenigsburg said that an SAT score of 1,100 or above would in practice guarantee a black student admission.

Koenigsburg and other Berkeley administrators admit: no white or Asian students can get in with these numbers. White and Asian students need grade averages of at least 3.7 (A−) and they are not assured of admission even with a 4.0 or perfect average. In 1989, Berkeley turned down more than 2,500 white and Asian applicants with straight-A averages.[35]

While whites are disadvantaged by this, Asian students seem to suffer even more. Nearly 30 percent of high school graduating Asians qualify academically for Berkeley, compared with about 15 percent of whites, 6 percent of Hispanics, and 4 percent of blacks.[36] In 1986, on Berkeley's academic index—calculated by a formula that takes into account grade and SAT scores, with special weight for honors achievement—blacks were consistently admitted with scores of 4,800 (out of a possible 8,000), white students needed at least 7,000 to get in, while Asians with scores of 7,000 had only a 50 percent chance of admission.[37]

In short, the data suggest that Berkeley may have set up different ethnic tracks for admission, in which students only compete against their peers of the same skin color. "We basically have a three-track system now," comments former dean Wildavsky. His charge seemed to be confirmed in early 1989 when an applicant to the Berkeley Law School received notification that he could not be offered admission. "However," the admissions office wrote, "We can tell you that you are in the bottom half of the ____ waiting list." In the blank was typed the word "Asian."[38]

Although Berkeley continues to deny that Asian students are disadvantaged compared to white students, university officials freely admit that Asians, like whites, are disadvantaged relative to other minorities. These officials argue that such discrimination is both necessary and justifiable. "We've got to have affirmative action. Otherwise, the whole freshman class will be composed of Caucasians and Asians," said Bud Travers, a dapper, middle-aged senior official at Berkeley, and one of the main architects of its admissions policies over the past decade. The former assistant vice-chancellor for undergraduate affairs, Travers now works in the Berkeley development office. Berkeley considers him the university's point man on the labyrinthine issues of minority admissions and preferential treatment.

Travers was not joking about what affirmative action contributes to Berkeley's race ratios; according to a study by Berkeley's Office of Budget and Planning, merit admissions would result in less than 4 percent of black, Hispanic, and American Indian (sometimes called "native American") students combined.[39] Travers maintained that there is no way to admit more blacks and Hispanics without slackening academic requirements. He argued that certain minorities are entitled to preferential treatment because "Berkeley is a state school, and must serve the various constituencies in the state." Democracy dictates that "all groups should be represented." Nor is that unjust, because "the reason we have academic discrepancies is on account of past and present discrimination." Further, the presence of proportionate numbers of blacks and Hispanics will show those groups that "it is possible to succeed in higher education" and that "they belong here." Such diverse representation, Travers added, will "allow different groups to interact with each other and learn to get along better."

These arguments are reinforced by a seminal article by Professor Randall Kennedy of Harvard Law School in the *Harvard Law Review*. Kennedy argues that preferential treatment reduces racism because it "teaches whites that blacks, too, are capable of handling responsibility, dispensing knowledge and applying valued skills." Because of the contribution of affirmative action to racial harmony, "considering a black's race as part of the bundle of traits that constitute merit is entirely appropriate." Those who are affected adversely should learn to live with the "injustice" of affirmative action because their disadvantages are "simply an incidental consequence of addressing a compelling social need." Even if the program generates resentment, that too is acceptable because "intense white resentment has accompanied every effort to undo racial subordination."[40]

Bud Travers denied the existence of "intense white resentment," but acknowledged that a certain amount of racial tension and grievance was generated by giving some minority groups preference over others. Many white and Asian students at Berkeley "feel that it's unfair that their friends didn't get admitted because they know black and Hispanic students with weaker records who got in," Travers said. He sympathized with these students. "But that's the price we have to pay for diversity." Qualified students who are denied admission to Berkeley can be accommodated at other schools within the University of California, such as UC-Davis or UC-Irvine, he pointed out. "The only way to deal with [the frustration] is to talk about it," Travers said. Asked about particular victims of the program, such as Thuy Nguyen, Travers' message was, "You can't solve every injustice that prevails in an individual life."

Travers' views are fairly typical of admissions officers at selective universities. A pragmatist and realist, he starts from the premise that Berkeley must admit fairly even ratios of whites, blacks, Hispanics, and Asians. He knows that academic criteria won't produce the desired color distribution. Thus he feels compelled to manipulate admissions requirements to change the result. He is no enemy of academic standards, but believes he must subordinate them to considerations of ethnic diversity. He is uncomfortable about denying opportunity to deserving white and Asian applicants, but he supports preferential treatment on the grounds that social justice must prevail over individual rights. Apparently, for Travers, individual rights are not an essential basis for a just and harmonious academic community.

*  *  *

There is no disputing the well-meaning ideals of affirmative action, as outlined by Travers and Kennedy. But it remains an open question whether these ideals are achieved by preferential treatment policies such as the one at Berkeley. The problem is that affirmative action does not stop at the admissions gate. The consequences of university officials applying varied admissions criteria to different racial groups continue to haunt the administration from the time the freshman class comes together.

The root of the problem lies in the manifest differences of academic preparation among students from different ethnic groups.[41] It is not very surprising that student grades reflect this academic mismatch. Bud Travers regretfully conceded that Asians consistently end up at the top of the class, blacks at the bottom. He said this was the case even though Asian students are disproportionately enrolled in engineering and the other hard sciences, which tend to be more difficult.[42]

More seriously, the academic difficulties encountered by affirmative action students who find it impossible to compete effectively with other, better-prepared students, are reflected in Berkeley's extremely high dropout rate for Hispanic and black undergraduates. Whites and Asians graduate from Berkeley at about the same rate: 65–75 percent. That is to say that 25–35 percent drop out before graduation. Hispanics graduate at under 50 percent. More than half drop out. Blacks graduate at under 40 percent. More than 60 percent drop out.[43] According to the Berkeley admissions office, fewer than 50 percent of blacks finish *in five years*, and the figure is less than 40 percent for "special admit" categories.[44]

Berkeley does not release the number of blacks and Hispanics admitted on affirmative action who drop out, but these data are contained in a confidential internal report which tracks freshmen enrolled in 1982. By 1987, five years later, only 18 percent of blacks admitted on affirmative action had graduated from Berkeley; blacks admitted in the regular program graduated at a 42 percent rate. Similarly, only 22 percent of affirmative action Hispanics finished in five years, compared with 55 percent for other Hispanics.[45] The most recent figures suggest that approximately 30 percent of black and Hispanic students drop out before the end of their freshman year; in the words of the report, they seem to stay "only long enough to enhance the admissions statistics."[46]

John Bunzel, former president of San Jose State University, estimates that, at current rates, the large number of blacks who will drop out of Berkeley in the next three years will exceed the total number who earned degrees from Berkeley in the last decade.[47]

What is one to make of these statistics? Berkeley officials seem to respond with a collective but very private sigh. Former admissions officer Travers said that the black dropout rate at Berkeley shows that "the admissions process is not perfect." Berkeley admissions director Robert Bailey says, "Our retention problem shows that we still have a long ways to go." But to critics like Bunzel it seems that the university is doing a disservice to blacks who are admitted with substantially lower qualifications, and thus have a much higher risk of failure.

Travers maintained, "There's no way of predicting who's going to make it and who's not." But a comparison of qualification and success data, showing a strong correlation between the high school "academic index" and grades at Berkeley, suggests that one can guess, with reasonable accuracy, what the chances are that a student or a group of students will graduate. Yes, Travers said, but "Why do we expect that the black graduation rate is going to immediately be the same as the white and Asian rate?" Travers correctly points out that whites enjoy considerable socioeconomic advantages, and that Asians benefit from strong family structure and a history of valuing educational achievement. Blacks and Hispanics are part of a very recent experiment at Berkeley and elsewhere; as Travers put it, "A baby has been born, and its chances of survival will increase as it matures."

Perhaps it would be permissible to risk such high dropout rates if there were no alternative available to these minority students. Better, after all, to have a 25 percent chance of making it at Berkeley than a permanent consignment to the underclass. But is this really the choice? Berkeley admits some of California's best black and Hispanic students, and many of them fail, in large part because of the pressures of a highly competitive environment. Would not these students be much better off at UC-Irvine or UC-Davis, where they might settle in more easily, compete against evenly matched peers, and graduate in vastly greater numbers and proportions?[48]

Travers denied that the lives of dropouts are ruined. "You can argue about whether it's good for someone to go to college at all." A sizable number of minority dropouts, Travers said, do eventually end up with some college degree. They may "bum around for a few years" and then finish up at a community or other UC college, Travers said. What's wrong with that? "Maybe it's *good* for them to go off and have their midlife crisis at 18 or 19. Maybe it's *good* for them to find out that they don't have the skills, go develop them, and then come back." But, as Bunzel pointed out, the argument assumes a high level of self-confidence on the part of the students; otherwise, it is easy to see insecurity leading to greater frustration, even despair.

The issue, of course, is not in the hands of individual administrators like Travers; it lies in the vision and the program under which they operate. In its original conception, affirmative action involved identifying capable but disadvantaged minority students and giving them a break on formal admissions requirements. But there is a desperate shortage of black students who, by any measure of academic promise, can meet the demanding work requirements and competition of the nation's best universities.

Not only is the high school graduation rate of black 18- and 19-year-olds relatively low,[49] but on average, those who do graduate demonstrate levels of literacy comparable to white eighth-grade students.[50] Although enrollment in college continues to rise quickly for most minority groups, black enrollment has decreased, stagnated, or grown very slowly.[51] Among blacks who do seek a college education, many have not taken basic college prep courses in mathematics, science, and social science, the Education Department reports.[52]

Selective colleges which use the SAT standardized test as a measure of academic competence and seek to recruit blacks face a dismal landscape. Despite a slight improvement in black scores in recent years, the overall white-black differential is enormous: 198 points in the aggregate. The Asian-black differential is equally large: 192 points.[53] In 1988, nearly 100,000 blacks took the test. Only 116 scored over 699 (out of 800) on the verbal section of the test; only 342 scored as high on the math section.[54] Fewer than three thousand blacks nationwide scored over 599 on either the verbal or math SAT.[55]

What this means is that the nation's most selective universities have a tiny pool of qualified applicants from which to recruit.[56] Alvin Hinkson, counselor at Prep for Prep, a New York organization that places minority students at prestige colleges, remarked that "everybody wants a piece of these students. The competition for them has become very keen."[57] Many universities offer attractive perks and benefits to induce black students to consider attending, such as free airplane tickets for campus visits, combined with the prospect of generous financial aid packages.[58]

But the small group of extremely well-prepared black students could not fill the 8–10 percent affirmative action goals of the eight Ivy League colleges. Berkeley alone accepted 831 black students in the 1989 freshmen class. Yet there are scores of universities courting these first-rate black students. Once they are accounted for, where do selective colleges find the rest of the black freshmen recruited each year? At the most competitive schools, where the demand for black enrollment is most acute, admissions requirements are drastically abridged or waived. A study by Robert Klitgaard of Harvard showed that "in general, the more selective the college, the *greater* the preferential treatment for minorities."[59] Even when a university manages to get the best-prepared minority students, they still tend to find themselves mismatched on the campus. Thus entering black freshmen at Massachusetts Institute of Technology have SAT scores in the 90th percentile of all students taking the test, but they are in the bottom 10th percentile of the outstanding students in MIT's entering class.[60]

The practical result of affirmative action is well illustrated by a typical case cited by Donald Werner, the headmaster of Westminster Prep School in New Haven, Connecticut. "The University of California at Berkeley made decisions on two of our students, both Californians. Student A was ranked in the top third of his class, student B in the bottom third. Student A had college board scores totaling 1,290; student B's scores totaled 890. Student A had a record of good citizenship; student B was expelled this winter for breaking a series of major school rules. Student A was white; student B was black. Berkeley refused student A and accepted student B."[61]

The consequence is an admissions policy in which, at every level of higher education, certified minority students are placed in "high-risk" intellectual environments where they compete against vastly better-prepared students, and where their probability of graduation is known to be low.

Naturally this artificial misplacement adversely affects the morale of minority students. A study by sociologist Walter Allen of UCLA found that while nearly half of all blacks report grade point averages of 3.5 or better in high school (often predominantly black public schools), nearly two-thirds score 2.9 or below in college. "The observed declines in academic performance from high school to college must be judged as nothing short of spectacular," Allen concludes.[62] Jacqueline Fleming of Barnard College argues in *Blacks in College* that feelings of inferiority further weaken academic performance.[63]

A majority of black students seem unwilling to endure these humiliations; they drop out of college altogether. Dropout rates are particularly high at colleges with ambitious preferential treatment plans.[64] For black college athletes at many schools who benefit from a kind of double affirmative action—preferential treatment on grounds of race, and of athletic participation—only very few make it to graduation.[65] And since affirmative action rearranges black and Hispanic students throughout higher education, nationwide pass rates for those groups are dismal.[66]

Preferential treatment is not the only factor responsible for these figures, of course. Dropout rates are influenced by the home study environment, by individual motivation, by future aspirations, and by financial considerations. But it is reasonable to expect that preferential treatment, by ratcheting up black students at every level in academia into environments where they are not competitive, multiplies the likelihood of failure, and thus compounds the dropout rate.

While university leaders are genuinely concerned about dropouts, and conduct conferences on a regular basis to examine and analyze the "retention" problem,[67] their explanations for the data virtually never consider the effect of affirmative action. The reason for this, some critics argue, is that they are so eager to register impressive black and Hispanic admissions statistics that they become blind to what happens to these students once they enroll. Retention becomes an entirely separate issue, to be addressed by the kind of remedial education efforts which are now commonplace on the American campus. Yet these efforts have not succeeded for the obvious reason that it is a bit late to be teaching students basic reading, writing, and mathematical skills when they are in the high-pressure environs of Berkeley and Princeton, where other students have read Shakespeare and taken advanced calculus.

Thus, it seems that American universities are quite willing to sacrifice the future happiness of many young blacks and Hispanics to achieve diversity, proportional representation, and what they consider multicultural progress.

* * *

When we hear talk about increasing the number of "qualified" minority students and being careful not to "lower our standards," we must recognize these as the catch phrases of the politics of exclusion.[68]

— *Barbara Ransby*
Student activist
United Coalition Against
Racism

Frustrated by the small pool of black and Hispanic students, and troubled by the high dropout and failure rates, many in the education establishment have concluded that disparate scores prove not that many minority students are inadequately prepared, but that the tests themselves are biased. Charges of racism and sexism are commonplace, and the College Board has come under increasing pressure to revise the tests so that black and Hispanic students perform better.

"Standardized tests are used from the cradle to the grave to select, reject, stratify, classify and sort people," remarks Gerda Steel of the National Association for the Advancement of Colored People (NAACP), "and they are used in ways that keep certain segments of the population from realizing their aspirations. Most of all they limit the access of blacks and other minorities to higher education."[69] Educators James Crouse and Dale Trusheim, in *The Case Against the SAT*, maintain that the abandonment of the test would have the desirable effect of increasing black admissions. "The test has an adverse impact on blacks and lower-income kids," Crouse told the *Chronicle of Higher Education*.[70] With the support of minority organizations, similar arguments are advanced by the National Commission on Testing and Public Policy and by the National Center for Fair and Open Testing, sometimes called FairTest.[71]

Ironically, when the SAT was introduced in 1926, the main argument for it was that colleges were admitting students based on highly arbitrary and variable criteria. Jews, Catholics, blacks, and others complained of discrimination and disparate treatment. Richly endowed prep schools such as Deerfield Academy and Choate had historically cultivated relationships with elite universities, so that students from these privileged schools tended to benefit at the expense of equally or better-qualified students from other places. The SAT was aimed at eliminating this arbitrariness, and thus reducing the risks of prejudice.

A number of studies show that the SAT is a fairly reliable indicator of college preparation.[72] Robert Klitgaard of Harvard concludes that "standardized tests usually do quite well, usually better than any other criteria, at predicting academic success at selective universities."[73] Indeed there is evidence that the SAT predicts college performance better than high school grades, and predicts female and minority performance as well if not better than white male performance.[74] The main evidence against the SAT is that some of its questions include words like "sonata," "Alps," and "travelogue." Critics maintain that classical music, skiing, and foreign vacations are all activities that whites predominantly engage in; blacks (and, it is sometimes added, women) cannot be expected to be familiar with these terms, and this introduces "cultural bias."

But College Board President Donald Stewart, who is black, says "it's reverse racism that holds certain assumptions about what a race or a gender should know."[75] The test, he argues, is preparation for words and terms and ideas that students are likely to encounter in college, whatever their cultural background.

James Loewen of Catholic University, who alleges cultural bias in testing, gives an example of an alternate SAT question that would be more comprehensible to blacks.

Saturday Ajax got an LD:

(a) He had smoked too much grass
(b) He tripped out on drugs
(c) He brought her to his apartment
(d) He showed it off to his fox
(e) He became wised up[76]

Loewen's example seems to confirm Stewart's claim that this line of criticism stereotypes blacks. His model presumes that blacks are most at home in the world of slang, womanizing, and drugs. Why a familiarity with this vocabulary is a good preparation for college, Loewen does not say.

This is not to imply that there is no legitimate debate over how effectively the SAT measures college performance.[77] Such a debate, however, must focus on what intellectual criteria the test seeks to measure, and then examine how well it achieves this goal. It seems no more an argument against the SAT that average group scores don't turn out equal, than it is an indictment of the 100-yard dash to point out that whites "disproportionately" hit the finishing tape last. Inequality of results does not by itself prove that the measurement is biased or inadequate.

Asian Americans seem to have no problem with the SAT. Chia-Wei Woo, former president of San Francisco State University, says that Asians succeed in part because they don't waste time complaining about discrimination but rather work extra hard in case outside forces are holding them back. "There is no time to lament," Woo told the *Chronicle of Higher Education*. "We've got work to do."[78] Stanford sociologist S. M. Dornbush, puzzled by the success of poor Asian Americans in the San Francisco Bay Area, conducted a study and discovered a simple answer: Asian Americans "work a heck of a lot harder" to raise their scores.[79]

Nevertheless, a federal judge in New York has ruled that it is an unconstitutional violation of Title IX of the Education Amendments of 1972 for the state of New York to use the SAT as the criterion for its Regents and Empire State scholarships because men, on average, perform significantly better than women.[80] Also, while most schools still use the SAT, an increasing number are downplaying it and one, Bates College, has eliminated the requirement from the admissions process.[81] By restoring subjective criteria, and ignoring the discrepancies in test scores between groups, universities hope that they can more conveniently regulate the composition of their freshmen classes along politically acceptable lines.

Yet this approach has been tried before, with deplorable results. When Harvard and other selective colleges sought to impose ceilings on Jewish student admissions in the 1920s,[82] they did so by reducing their emphasis on measurable criteria of scholarship, on the grounds that these standards were often unreliable, and that what counted was "character." In reality, of course, Ivy League schools worried that they were admitting too many Jews.

In a famous protest against this approach, Justice Learned Hand wrote that concealing or disregarding the evidence of academic disparities does not make those disparities go away. "If there are better ways of testing scholarship, let us by all means have them, but whatever they are, success in them is the chief aim of a college. . . . If anyone could devise an honest test for character, perhaps it would serve well. But I doubt its feasibility. Short of it, it seems to me that students can only be chosen by tests of scholarship, unsatisfactory as those no doubt are."[83]

* * *

While universities can conceal data about affirmative action from the general public, they cannot conceal the consequences from the students. Whatever their views of the social necessity of such programs, students know that their real-life implementation is the "dirty little secret" of American universities. Universities know that they know, and so do minority activists. Many problems derive from the facts, the desire to camouflage the facts, and the university leadership's attempt to make students believe that affirmative action is something other than it is.

At Berkeley, visitors are immediately struck by a phenomenon that seems unexpected at a university which openly celebrates its multicultural flavor. Surveying the campus, the *New York Times* reported "blacks and whites rooting for the same team but sitting in different sections. Floors in the undergraduate library are, in practice, segregated by race. Rarely does a single white or two comfortably join a dining room table occupied mostly by blacks."[84] There are a larger number of blacks and Hispanics on campus, yet rarely are members of either group seen dating, or even socializing with, white students. Berkeley has seen several ugly racial incidents in the last few years, mostly in the form of demeaning epithets and slogans, anonymously bandied about, but nevertheless exercising a menacing influence on minority students.[85]

Troy Duster, a Berkeley sociologist, has conducted experimental research into student relations at the university. Notwithstanding its progressive policies, Duster was surprised to discover "ethnic enclaves" and "balkanization" among racial groups. Even more odd, Duster reported that students from different backgrounds came to college thinking of themselves as "individuals" or "Americans" but, once at Berkeley, began to think of themselves as "African American, Asian American or whatever." Duster found that this feature of student life retards communication among different groups, "each group accuses other groups of being closed and not receptive," and "each group complains about being stereotyped."[86] Although Berkeley officials argue that preferential treatment leads to cultural interaction and educationally enriching diversity, this claim is belied by the self-segregation of minority groups.[87] Indeed, Berkeley administrators admit that some black and Hispanic students spend most of their undergraduate years in these separatist enclaves.

Berkeley students of all races seem to regard preferential treatment as contributing to racial stereotypes, divisions, and balkanization. Dave Thomas, a black undergraduate, said that "there's definitely a feeling by whites and Asians that [admissions] spots are being taken away from them and given to unqualified people." Alfonso Salazar, head of the Hispanic students' organization, told *Insight* magazine, "It is assumed that people of color couldn't make it on their own and that we don't belong here and should be someplace else."[88] Jim Twu, an Asian American who edits the conservative *Berkeley Review*, says it is a standing joke among white and Asian students that you have to have black or Hispanic blood to have a fair chance of getting into Berkeley.[89] A black student at the university complains that he feels defensive every time he walks into a class and sees white faces because "I know they're all racists—they think blacks are stupid."[90] Reacting to criticism of preferential treatment, a Berkeley campus magazine called *African Perspectives* printed a poem with the warning, "Your time is running out, white boy."[91]

Other schools that practice aggressive affirmative action policies also seem to witness both widespread separatism and racial tension. At Oberlin College in Ohio, the administration has set up special interest dorms for minority groups, such as Africa Heritage House and Third World House. Nevertheless, college officials admit that racial hostility persists on one of America's most liberal campuses.[92] A University of Michigan undergraduate wrote in the *New York Times,* "In most of my classes, the few black students sit together, just as they do in the cafeteria. Black students have a kind of unwritten code. When we see each other, even if we don't know each other, we offer a silent greeting in support."[93] Although black students number only 250 at Central Michigan University, an activist group wants college rules to permit them to pick black roommates in campus dormitories.[94] A CMU black student told the *Chronicle of Higher Education,* "If I listen to a rock concert, people will say I'm listening to 'white' music.

They will say that I'm trying to act 'white.' Certain activities are labelled 'white' and 'black.' If you don't just participate in black activities, you are shunned."[95]

Perplexed about how to respond, universities typically accede to minority demands for self-segregation, and publicly argue that these are healthy developments which reveal "pluralism" at work. Thus at Ohio State University, Director of Residence Rebecca Parker says that separatist institutions "need to be seen as a celebration of our differences."[96] Stanford president Donald Kennedy says that one of his educational objectives is to "support and strengthen ethnic theme houses."[97] University of Pennsylvania officials have agreed to fund a separate black yearbook, "Positively Black," even though only 6 percent of Penn students are black, and all other groups are represented in one yearbook.[98]

Embarrassed by the relatively poor preparation of minority students admitted on affirmative action, many administrators approach their academic performance with delicacy, and treat even mediocre performance as an occasion for enthusiasm. A College Entrance Examination board manual on affirmative action recruiting advises university officials to treat black and Hispanic candidates differently from other students:

> Talk in simple, down-to-earth language. . . . Spend some time talking about how people got where they are, and use personal examples. . . . I am not able to connect as well with minority students in a racially mixed setting, because it doesn't permit me to use the occasional language elaboration and other cues that will help students identify with me. . . . For instance, to help students move from fantasy to reality, I often reveal at the proper time that I was a high school dropout.[99]

The University of North Carolina at Chapel Hill sponsors "3.0 Minority Recognition Ceremonies" each year, in which black and Hispanic students who score a B average are honored, along with their parents. No such celebrations are considered necessary for white and Asian students.[100]

In a pamphlet on effective teaching strategies for blacks, Bowdoin English professor Gayle Pemberton argues that while rephrasing a student's question is usually a good pedagogical technique, minority students' questions should not be rephrased for fear of discouraging them. "Minority students, who routinely have been discouraged about their abilities, who are capable of noting, through a professor's words, gestures and style, intimations of their own fears of academic failure, consistently point to what might appear to be trivial to others, as reasons for despair."[101]

While intended benignly, such measures suggest a strong element of condescension toward affirmative action students; consequently, they do little to enhance their morale. The reasons for poor self-esteem among these groups are complex,[102] but preferential patronage seems to exacerbate the problem. Black students interviewed by the *Indianapolis Star* for a series of articles on college life said that professors have such low expectations that they "express amazement" when blacks do well in class.[103] Dwayne Warren, a black political science major at the University of Massachusetts at Amherst, told the *Washington Post,* "Some whites don't expect you to excel, and when you do, it's a shock to them."[104] In order to build black confidence, three students at Iowa State University have produced a video documentary, "Black By Popular Demand," which begins by warning black students what many whites think of them: "A lot of times they assume that just because you're black, you can't read, you can't write, you can't speak."[105] Dayna Matthew, the first black student to gain admission to the *Virginia Law Review* on academic merit, told columnist William Raspberry that by calling into question the achievements of minorities, the University of Virginia's new preferential treatment plan for the law journal "hurts us more than helps us."[106] Even black administrators suffer from these suspicions: when J. Leon Washington was appointed admissions director at Oberlin College in Ohio, his first comment to the *Chronicle of Higher Education* was, "This was not done because I'm black."[107]

Ordinarily, white students may be expected to show some sympathy and understanding for the difficulties endured by black and Hispanic students, but since they consider that affirmative action benefits are awarded at their expense, many respond with callousness and derision to struggling minority peers. As we will discover in a later chapter, white hostility to preferential treatment and minority separatism is a major force behind many of the ugly racial incidents that have scarred the American campus. At least two colleges—Temple and Florida State—now have White Student Unions set up to oppose perceived racial double standards in admissions and campus life.[108] Fred Sheehen of the South Carolina Commission on Higher Education remarks that if universities continue to permit all-black fraternities, pretty soon whites may set up segregated fraternities on the grounds that "white males need a support group too."[109]

These divisions and hostilities are new, and they cannot be attributed to coincidence. There are little reliable data suggesting causal relationships between preferential treatment, racial tension, and minority separatism on campus.[110] Sociologist William Beer of Brooklyn College believes the reason is that university leaders suspect a correlation, and seek "resolute ignorance" on the topic.[111] When there is evidence, university leaders generally ignore or misinterpret it.[112] Yet, as many students will acknowledge, preferential treatment, if it does not cause divisions and hostilities, certainly complicates and intensifies ones that already exist.

* * *

The reason for balkanization is that, to fill the limited number of places in the freshman class, preferential treatment has created, in effect, two sets of admissions standards: one for certified minority groups, and another for everyone else. The basic question of "who belongs" at the university now has two answers; which one you get depends on the color of your skin. Consequently there is no uniform standard of justice which, as Aristotle observed, is the only lasting basis for community. From the moment students arrive on campus, they know that the rules have somehow been politically rigged, and their fate as individuals depends on whether they belong to the favored group or the unfavored group. This is no formula for racial harmony.

Students are naturally a bit insecure when they first arrive at college. They are in a transitional phase of life, they are learning to be adults, many are living on their own for the first time, and they have to confront new ideas and assumptions. For many, their self-assurance is based on the knowledge that they belong at the university, they deserve to be there, someone thought them worthy of admission, and thus they must be good enough for the challenges ahead.[113] Not so with minority students, many of whom know that standards may have been relaxed to let them in. Even if they think that this is necessary, minority students cannot really take pride in such affirmative action; indeed, it makes them feel they have been patronized. It has this effect on both qualified and unqualified minority students, since it is often impossible to know who got preferential treatment and who didn't.

Although their pride cannot allow them to admit that standards were lowered to let them in, affirmative action beneficiaries are well aware of the academic disparities between themselves and other students. Rather than interact with whites and Asians, in an atmosphere where these disparities may be exposed, many minority students avoid such potentially distressing situations altogether. Separatist black and Hispanic groups become a haven from the anxieties that spring from sharp differences in academic preparation among various racial groups. Indeed separatism can serve as a form of group therapy, in which affirmative action beneficiaries persuade themselves that their difficulties on campus are predominantly, if not exclusively, the consequence of rampant bigotry. They view these bigots through lenses of heightened racial awareness, with suspicion bordering on hostility.

Many white and Asian students reciprocate in kind, because they are offended by what they see as university-sponsored discrimination against them. Thus they too begin to view themselves as victims of racism. Since they do not believe there is much they can do about admissions rules which operate upon them even before they arrive on campus, some respond with barely suppressed exasperation whenever they see black and Hispanic students make the slightest mistake, or congregate together on any occasion.

Racial division is the natural consequence of principles that exalt group equality above individual justice. Berkeley officials repeatedly tell students to endure the unfairness of preferential treatment because individual aspirations must be sacrificed to promote equal representation. Paradoxically, a program that began as a campaign to *eliminate* race as a factor in decision making has come to *enforce* race as a factor in decision making. Admissions policies that once sought to extend equal opportunity to all individuals regardless of their background now exalt group membership above individual achievement in allocating scarce seats in the freshman class. The predictable result is a jealous and often bellicose group consciousness among students who do enroll. They think of themselves as ethnic platoons engaged in a silent struggle in which the gains of one necessarily entail the losses of the other. As Professor Duster's research suggests, the group sensibility that is embodied in the admissions process seems to reproduce itself on every level of campus life. This is not exactly the ideal multiracial community envisioned by Chancellor Heyman.

* * *

Even if documented after careful study, the proposition that affirmative action programs do not really help minorities does not eliminate the rationale for the policy, whose advocates offer multiple and sometimes shifting justification for it. One of the preferred arguments for a preferential treatment system such as the one at Berkeley is that the program does not exist for the purpose of equal opportunity, compensation for past discrimination, or even for helping minority students at all. It exists for the purpose of helping universities. This may seem peculiar—how can a university such as Berkeley, which has built its reputation on the highest standards, possibly stand to gain by admitting less well-prepared, poorer-quality students?

The law school at Berkeley has an affirmative action program that reserves 23 percent of the seats in each entering class for blacks, Hispanics, and other certified minorities. Asian Americans and Caucasians cannot compete for these seats. At the request of several congressmen, the Department of Justice is now investigating whether the law school has a quota system in violation of Title IV of the Civil Rights Act of 1964.[114]

Jesse Choper, dean of Boalt Hall, the Berkeley law school, and a noted constitutional scholar, is unruffled. What Berkeley gains from such affirmative action, he said, is something called diversity. "Diversity means that students have different points of view, and that's what the Socratic method seeks, not just a cold, logical lecture, but broader backgrounds brought to the discussion." Choper sees a good legal education as one where "a student gets exposed to different approaches to problems. That seems totally noncontroversial to me." Choper's point is reinforced by a recent official admissions report, which maintains that, in addition to promoting social justice through minority compensation for past discrimination, "there is also an educational logic to Berkeley's commitment. This logic resides in the conviction that a more diverse student body with a broad variety of backgrounds and viewpoints is likely to produce a more dynamic intellectual environment and a richer undergraduate experience."[115]

Choper recognizes that diversity doesn't come for free. "Can it be achieved at no cost? Very few things can." But the price is worth paying, he maintains, for "the raised level of the discussion which results." Moreover, Choper added, the whole notion of merit is elusive anyway. "What is excellence?" he asked. "There is no litmus paper test for it. Excellence is often like beauty, in the mind of the beholder." There is nothing wrong with making prudential selections based on criteria other than grades, when there are so many outstanding students to choose from. "Look. We get 5,000 applicants with 3.5 GPAs and above, who are in the 90th percentile of the LSAT. How do we choose 570 students from among them? We take into account various factors." Choper recalled that not just minorities, but also athletes and "students who play the violin" get some consideration for these nonacademic achievements.

It is certainly true that excellence can be defined more broadly than just by grades or test scores—work experience can inculcate wisdom and skills; extracurricular activities reflect achievement and talent. Hence it makes sense to take into account musical and athletic abilities: competence in music reflects hard work and cultivated taste; even throwing a football suggests qualities of agility, discipline, coordination, and teamwork. But is the color of one's skin a talent, like playing the violin?

Choper winced at this formulation. "That's a gross way of putting it," he said. Then he proceeded to explain why this is so. "Blacks bring a different and special perspective to the classroom." Does he mean that blacks possess, by virtue of being black, a certain vision of the world or, to put it differently, do all blacks think alike? "No, no," Choper quickly responded. "We are simply hoping for diverse points of view."

Why not ask students, in law school applications, to state their philosophical, literary, and religious views on a wide range of questions, and then admit students keeping in mind that the classroom benefits from intellectual diversity? Certainly this seems a more efficient way to achieve the stated goal. "It is possible," Choper said, that "black lawyers can relate to black clients in a way that whites cannot do." He did not have any evidence for this, "but if it is true, there is something to wanting to turn out a certain number of black lawyers."

"There is a perceived need for lawyers to represent certain segments of the population," Choper observed. He gave the example of a black student who grew up in tenements having a different understanding of landlord-tenant law. Perhaps such a student would be more likely to opt for a career defending the interests of the poor. "This would enrich the public service element of the law," he argued.

Some of the arguments on behalf of affirmative action, such as the need for "role models," are extremely difficult to verify; however, Choper's claims are not. The Berkeley law school placement office keeps statistics on where graduating students go on to work. A review of those figures for three years, 1986–88, shows that minority students are no more likely than white students to go into "public interest law"; in fact, minorities were more likely to opt for the relative lucre of private practice, with an average starting salary exceeding $50,000 a year.[116] Minorities also tend to work for bigger firms, with over one hundred attorneys, than white students; in 1988, 63 percent of minorities went this route, compared with 59 percent for whites. Of the 169 minority students whom Berkeley has tracked since 1986, only nine (or just over 5 percent) entered any one of the following three categories: "public defender," "legal services," or "other public interest law," all with average starting salaries of $25,000 per year.[117]

One explanation is that minority students tend to come from poorer families, accumulate considerable debt in college and graduate school, are eager to escape the hardship of their earlier years, and choose to go where the money is. There is nothing wrong with that, but it does undermine the rationale for affirmative action as a creator of lawyers with "black perspectives," committed to serving the black community.

\* \* \*

Berkeley officials say they are reluctant to find fault with affirmative action because they believe that higher education should be democratic, and this entails equal representation for all groups. There is little question that democratically supported state universities should serve the surrounding community. The question is how egalitarian principles should apply to liberal universities whose structure is essentially, and inevitably, nondemocratic. The very existence of selective colleges suggests that liberal education values academic excellence and, however defined, excellence constitutes a principle of discrimination that elevates some over others. Prior to entrance to university there is only one way to determine excellence, and that is on the grounds of academic preparation. No one at Berkeley will go so far as to allege that the idea of excellence is itself undemocratic. But many officials seem uncomfortable with the way that it seems to be unevenly distributed among racial groups.

This disproportion usually leads to the automatic assumption that bigotry and discrimination are responsible for all group differences, as Chancellor Heyman has maintained. This assumption, however, is questionable in most cases,[118] and seems to be disproved in the academic setting by the single case of Asians. Asian Americans fare disproportionately well academically, even compared to whites, which in Heyman's logic suggests that Asian Americans have been engaged in discrimination against whites. But this conclusion is absurd. Clearly other factors can account for variations in the way that groups perform.

Berkeley's "democratic" admissions formula seems based on the erroneous presumption that racial groups are only served through proportional representation in the student body. But that is a premise alien to American democracy, where there is no general presumption that racial, ethnic, or religious minorities can only be represented by persons of similar hue and background. In democratic elections, whites are free to vote for black representatives, men are free to vote for women, Protestants may choose to be represented by a Catholic; in short, democracy does not entail group representation but rather expects that individuals will serve the shared community which transcends these narrower interests.[119]

The American system is based on the conviction that equality is not inconsistent with excellence; indeed, the philosophical conjunction of the two principles supports the vaunted notion of "equality of opportunity." By applying the same standard to everyone, natural talent and hard work are permitted and expected to distinguish individuals on the plane of achievement. Proportional representation for ethnic groups directly violates the democratic principle of equal opportunity for individuals, and the underlying concept of group justice is hostile both to individual equality and to excellence.

Further, by applying preferences and handicaps to racial groups, this policy opens up the university to the shrill tactics of political expediency. A question of fairness, in the sense of justice, has become a question of fairness, in the sense of skin color. Which groups or races benefit, and by how much, is now determined in large part by who exerts the most pressure. Even if some minorities such as blacks and Hispanics profit from this in the short run, it is questionable whether such policies are to their long-term advantage, since it is in the nature of democratic societies that the majority ultimately prevails in a test of force.

\* \* \*

Berkeley continues to flounder in its search for a preferential program that will assign variable weights to ethnic groups without inspiring controversy. Initially the university attempted to purchase peace by offering admission to students who threatened to sue for discrimination. After a two-year struggle, Yat-pang Au was admitted as a junior in the fall of 1989.[120] "We stuck our necks out, and they were finally forced to give my son justice," says Sik-kee Au. "About other children, I don't know."

As individual cases multiplied, Berkeley realized that tacit and tactful acceptances of potential litigants could hardly solve the university's dilemma. Chancellor Heyman continued to defend preferential admissions, shrewdly navigating his way out of each uproar on the part of parents or aggrieved Asian groups. Meanwhile, Berkeley's racial classification policy became increasingly Byzantine—Hispanics would get preferential treatment but not Spaniards, even though both claimed the same racial descent; Filipinos would get preference but not other Asians.[121] (Other schools suffer the same predicament—for example, City University of New York has extended its preferential treatment policies to benefit Italian Americans.[122]) Finally, the confidence of the Berkeley community in Heyman's ability to justify his principles simply eroded. Caught in the political, philosophical, and ethnic cross fire, Heyman announced his resignation as chancellor, effective July 1990.

It was an inglorious end to an impressive career. Ultimately, Heyman's demise was caused by ambition that refused to ground itself in defensible intellectual or moral principle. A Berkeley professor who asked not to be named said, "Heyman figured that this diversity thing was the wave of the future, and he wanted to be out front, doing more than anyone else. He couldn't see that other values were at stake too." The professor smiled wryly. "Heyman himself ended up as an individual sacrifice on the altar of diversity."

Attempting to preempt future controversy, the Berkeley trustees named Chang-Lin Tien, executive vice-chancellor of the University of California at Irvine, as Heyman's replacement. Tien, however, is an expert in heat-transfer technology whose primary administrative achievement at Irvine seems to have been his backing of ethnic studies requirements; he has so far given no indication of how he can restore confidence in the guiding principles of Berkeley's admissions process.[123] His last name may buy him a little time, by making it harder for Asians to allege racial or ethnic bias, but will not excuse him from the responsibility of establishing a new and just admissions policy.

Asian American groups themselves seem compromised, if not corrupted, by Berkeley's preferential handouts. The leading advocate for the elimination of anti-Asian quotas is a San Francisco group called Chinese for Affirmative Action; as the name suggests, and executive director Henry Der explains, the organization *supports* affirmative action for underrepresented minorities, and only favors open competition "between Asian Americans and whites," in Der's words. Melinda Yee, executive director of the Washington, D.C.–based Organization of Chinese Americans, maintains, "We support affirmative action. The issue is not a black and Hispanic issue. It's a white–Asian issue. We believe affirmative action should continue, and recently arrived Asian immigrants should fall under it. They are the ones most victimized. When affirmative action is in place, and you have all the minorities laid out, we're saying each student should be judged on merit."[124] Essentially, Yee is saying that she wants it both ways. First, give us our share of preferential treatment handouts. Once we have got our ration of protected seats, then open up the rest to open competition between whites and Asians. That way, Asians come out ahead in both categories.

But this pragmatic approach ignores the inexorable logic of proportional representation, and admissions officers at Berkeley and other colleges know it. They are just not courageous enough to stretch proportional rationing to its conclusion, and openly defend quota limits on overrepresented groups such as Asians and perhaps Jews. Their public qualms, however, do not seem to prevent them from acting on these beliefs in private admissions decisions, and Asian advocates who defend preferential treatment seem to have little ground, apart from institutional self-interest, for principled objection. Indeed the Asian community at large might question whether it is being well represented by Der, Yee, and other defenders of criteria inimical to merit and achievement, and thus to long-range Asian interests.[125]

Berkeley's abandonment of an effort to apply a neutral standard of academic excellence[126] has cut the university off from the moorings of just principle; now it is buffeted about by the tides of racial pressure groups. Berkeley comparative literature professor Robert Alter remarks that "the numerical quotas have institutionalized racism here." Afro-American studies professor William Banks terms the university's admissions criteria "an algebraic formula with human casualties. We are being hoodwinked by a kind of confused liberalism." Adds John Bunzel, "what people at Berkeley didn't realize is that merit admissions is an *egalitarian* principle, because it means that no matter what your background, if you are among the best qualified students, Berkeley lets you in." When merit gives way to ethnic allocation, Aaron Wildavsky maintains, "there's no stopping point. Each time the university lunges at a problem, it creates ten new ones. I think Berkeley may increasingly depend on our graduate programs to sustain the university's reputation." With all the racial classifications, one Berkeley English professor said, "I feel like we're back to the Nuremberg laws. How long are people going to stand for it?"

A Berkeley admissions committee recently admitted that "there has been an undeniable erosion of public trust and confidence in the basic fairness of Berkeley's admissions process" which "poses a serious long-term threat to the relationship between the university and the larger community which it serves."[127] To make things worse, the Department of Education announced in January 1990 that it would investigate Berkeley's race preference policies based on allegations of illegal discrimination against both whites and Asians.[128] Yet Berkeley's catalog continues to maintain, with almost comic incongruity, that "the university does not discriminate on the basis of race, color, national origin, sex, handicap or age in any of its policies."[129]

It seems that Berkeley's vaunted admissions policy of proportional representation, aimed at producing diversity, is not the best policy model for the American academy. Attractive at first glance, such a policy in reality creates artificial failure for its supposed beneficiaries, and contributes to separatism and strain among racial groups on campus. Under its new chancellor, Berkeley clearly needs a fundamental reexamination of the basic foundations of its admissions policy. So do the majority of colleges and universities that follow in Berkeley's path.

# 3

# Travels with Rigoberta
## Multiculturalism at Stanford

What do you think of Western civilization? "I think it would be a good idea."

— *Mahatma Gandhi*

We have demographics on our side. We have history on our side.[1]

— *William King*
President, Black Student Union
Stanford University

"Hey, hey, ho, ho, Western culture's got to go," the angry students chanted on the lawn at Stanford University.[2] They wore blue jeans, Los Angeles Lakers T-shirts, Reeboks, Oxford button downs, Vuarnet sun glasses, baseball caps, Timex and Rolex watches. No tribal garb, Middle Eastern veils, or Japanese samurai swords were in sight. Observers could not recall a sari, kimono, or sarapa. None of the women had their feet bound or bandaged. Clearly the rejection of the ways of the West was a partial one. Nevertheless it was expressed with great passion and vehemence, and commanded respect for its very intensity.

What were these eager and intelligent students protesting about in early 1988? The weather was beautiful in California, the campus pristine, many of the students hailed from middle-class and privileged families. Yet precisely this comfortable environment seemed to contribute to a vague sense of disquiet. The students appeared to share a

59

powerful conviction that Western culture is implacably hostile to the claims of blacks, other minorities, women, and homosexuals. When they thought about the West, what entered the protesters' minds were slavery, colonialism, the domestication of women, and the persecution of "deviant lifestyles."

The Stanford administration was faced with a bewildering dispute over the content of the undergraduate curriculum being conducted in a manner scarcely different from a political march or a workers' strike. The real targets of the protest—Aristotle, Aquinas, Locke, and other "white males"—had all been dead for hundreds of years. The students resented the fact that the ideas of these men still dominated Stanford's "core curriculum." They shouted slogans and carried placards demanding that the Stanford faculty and administration make major changes in the course offerings.

Viewing the Stanford controversy as indicative of a trend, the print and broadcast media descended on the campus, converting the protest into a national spectacle. One immediate advantage was the kindling of serious discussion, in the pages of newspapers such as the *Washington Post* and the *Wall Street Journal*, over what aspects of the Western heritage should be transmitted to young people through education. At the same time, however, the public spotlight brought the powerful pressure of the media to bear on the question of what books a private university should assign to students. Suddenly the curriculum seemed not an academic issue to be resolved by the faculty, or even the university community, but a political question to be publicly adjudicated in the press.

Protest against alleged Western exclusiveness in the classroom is no longer restricted to Stanford, but is commonplace, and spreading, on the American campus. Now that American society, and American education, have opened themselves to full membership and legal equality for previously oppressed groups, the new activists argue that it is time that the *content* of both the culture and the curriculum reflect the aspirations, literature, history, and distinctive point of view of these groups. Like Berkeley in its affirmative action policies, Stanford is prepared to lead the way in applying principles of diversity to what is taught in universities.

\* \* \*

The reasons for the animus against the Western civilization course are best seen from the perspective of an articulate spokesman from the Stanford faculty. Clayborne Carson is a professor of history and

Afro-American Studies at Stanford, editor of the Martin Luther King papers, and one of the pioneers of Stanford's drive to transform the "great books" curriculum into a new sequence of required courses on "Cultures, Ideas and Values" (CIV), first implemented in the fall of 1989. Previously Stanford steered all incoming students through a core curriculum—an examination of the philosophy, literature, and history of the West, focusing on such thinkers and writers as Plato, Dante, Machiavelli, Voltaire, Marx, and Freud; and on such events as the ascent of Greece, the fall of Rome, medieval Christian civilization, the Renaissance and Reformation, the French and Scottish Enlightenment, and the founding of modern states. The new CIV sequence would substitute a multiple-track system, each examining an issue or field, such as Technology and Values, through a cross-cultural survey of ideas and mores. Such an approach would include Western perspectives, but also African, Japanese, Indian, and Middle Eastern ones. Since the number of texts that can be assigned and discussed in a semester is limited, the relative importance of Western thinkers would be correspondingly reduced. Some of them, such as Homer, Virgil, and Aquinas, would have to make way for new, non-Western voices. A special effort was promised not to imply any superiority of Western ideas or Western culture—all cultures would be sustained on a plane of equality.

Professor Carson is a mild-mannered man, slightly stooped, with a lilting voice. He sat on the patio of the Stanford library, the repository of the Martin Luther King papers. Although the civil rights movement began by simply trying to end legal discrimination, Carson said that now "there is a growing understanding that bringing different groups into society, without changing society in any way, is not only wrong but not very feasible." In the past, "the rules of the game were set by white males." Now they must be negotiated between different groups, all considered legitimate partners in the new debate, all advancing claims of justice as well as power.

The problem with the idea of a canon—a set of required great books—was that "the curriculum is always changing," Carson said. "What was deemed important to know constantly changes, and that is a politicized decision." Now that minority students and 1960s generation professors were more fully represented on campus, "we are pressing a different agenda." Senior faculty, whether liberal or conservative, were "the strongest resistance to change on this campus," Carson said. Thus prominent liberals such as historian Carl Degler and Ronald Rebholz of the English department opposed the new curriculum, not on political but on academic grounds, insisting that it would compromise intellectual seriousness, which was not in anyone's interest. Rebholz, who termed himself a Roosevelt Democrat, said the Western core curriculum should be retained because "if a socialist society is ever going to work, it will need educated citizens. You don't acquire a good education without discipline."[3]

Younger faculty, Carson said, tend to reject the idea of a canon. "What's one generation's standard canonical text is the next generation's pulp," Carson said. "How many people read the poetry of Virgil, or the orations of Cicero?" He permitted himself a chuckle. When he assigned Alice Walker's *The Color Purple* in his Western culture class, Carson said some people raised eyebrows. "Ten years down the road you might say it didn't stand the test of time," he conceded. But such criticism "assumes that the point of teaching a course like this is to introduce students only to those works that have timeless value. If you make that assumption, you are limiting what you can convey to students."

Ridiculing the idea of a preordained set of great books, Carson said, "There is something inherently anti-intellectual about the notion of an educational institution establishing a canon." If scholars in a field agree that a work is important, they are likely to teach it on their own. To establish a canon is to "convey a message about the importance of a work even before students have seen for themselves the content of a work." Canons are by nature inclusive and exclusive: they keep some people in, and leave other people out; this, Carson said, "is just not an important game to play."

Yet if so, how did Carson explain his failure to insist that Stanford completely jettison the idea of a required curriculum, rather than simply replacing the Western cultural emphasis with a multicultural requirement? Was this not simply an exchange of one canon for another? Ideally a multicultural sequence would not be required, Carson said; the reason it must be for the present is that the Stanford faculty and student body are not fully representative of minorities in the culture. If they were, "then a lot of the discussion about Western culture wouldn't have taken place, because the teaching would be quite different from what it is." In other words, multicultural education would occur naturally; it would not require political agitation or coercion. In the interim, the only option was to require new courses—a new canon—and saddle the university with the burden of finding faculty competent to teach the new agenda.

At Stanford, Carson said, younger faculty have established a new alliance with minority students and feminists, and powerful elements in the university administration. The battle of the 1960s, Carson said, was "a battle to get recognized. But now that we are here, we want to know why our courses are peripheral and those of Mr. Senior Faculty are central. We are working to change that."

From the comments of this earnest faculty activist, several themes emerge which are central to the debate over what is taught in the American academy. Reflecting a 1960s' ethos of non-exclusivity, Carson seems opposed to the very idea of a canon or a principle of selection that determines which books undergraduates should read. Such principles seem to produce what may be termed "disparate impact" on ethnic groups; in other words, white males tend to be overrepresented on the reading list. Carson would rather see a political solution to the "problem of knowledge," in which the curriculum is refashioned to reflect and represent a diversity of ethnic cultures and values. This, he believes, is the only just approach to education in a truly pluralistic and democratic society.

Carson is one of the leading CIV proponents at Stanford. His arguments have dominated the debate since the spring of 1987, when a newly formed Rainbow Coalition of minority groups demanded a substantial revision of the three-course Western culture requirement. The requirement, established in 1980, examined fifteen great Western thinkers from a variety of perspectives or "tracks." The courses were popular with undergraduates; a 1985 poll found that more than 75 percent considered them a "positive academic experience."[4]

The Stanford administration, however, soon came under pressure from the campus Rainbow Coalition, which included black, Hispanic, Asian, and American Indian groups. "Western culture does not try to understand the diversity of experiences of different people," charged Alejandro Sweet-Cordero, a member of the Movimiento Estudiantil Chicano de Aztlan, the Hispanic student group on campus.[5] "If you think American culture is centered on the Constitution and the Founding Fathers, then you're going to exclude a major part of what this country is," remarked Stanford student activist William King, calling for non-Western alternatives to provide students with "a different picture."[6] King added, "It was painful to come to Stanford and find that no member of your race was in the required curriculum."[7] Stacey Leyton, a student member of Students United for Democracy in Education, a pro-CIV group, remarked, "It's a strong statement you're making when the only required readings are by whites and males. You're saying that what's been written by women and people of color isn't worthy of consideration."[8] Freshman Joseph Green wrote in the *Stanford Daily*,

"I get tired of reading the thoughts of white men who would probably spit on me if they were alive to face me today. . . . Stanford is sending many students into the world with no knowledge of the challenges facing people of color."[9] And Black Student Union activist Amanda Kemp protested that the implicit message of Western culture is "Nigger go home."[10]

Younger faculty had their own reasons for disliking the Western core curriculum, as Clayborne Carson suggested. The Stanford lineup from Homer to the present, complained history professor Paul Robinson, was a "roadblock" and "arbitrary hazard" for "men and women under 40" who felt "alienated" from this canon of texts.[11] Philosophy professor John Perry said the classics were an "albatross" around the neck of the new generation of professors.[12] These professors emphasized that they sought a more relevant agenda than a fixed list of old books.

Somewhat at a loss about how to respond, President Donald Kennedy did what embattled executives often do in these situations: he established a task force.[13] Ordinarily task forces purchase a good deal of time in order to cope with the new demands—at best, enthusiasm soon dissolves, and everybody forgets about the issue; at worst, the administration gains a postponement or the problem is put off to an unspecified future date. But Stanford's day of reckoning came soon, as the task force speedily put together the outlines of a new set of courses. On January 17, 1987, Martin Luther King Day, Jesse Jackson spoke at Stanford's Black Student Union march and rally, denouncing the Western culture requirement.[14] A few months later, in the spring of 1987, minority students from the Rainbow Coalition forcibly occupied President Donald Kennedy's office for five hours, issuing ten demands including the adoption of the new curriculum.[15]

The following fall, Stanford's 72-member Faculty Senate, which has jurisdiction over curricular matters, met to consider the proposal for the first time. These deliberations took place against the backdrop of chants by students demonstrating outside the building in which the debate occurred.[16]

Mild resistance developed to the new curriculum. English professor William Chace (now president of Wesleyan University in Connecticut) offered a counterproposal, signed by twenty-five faculty members, advocating the retention of the Western core curriculum, but expanded to include more women and minorities. Chace's proposal was voted down.[17] A Stanford undergraduate, Lora Headrick, argued that agitation for change came from a small militant segment of faculty and students; it did not reflect broad sentiment on campus. Headrick founded a group called "Save the Core" to collect petition signatures in favor of the "Western civ" course.[18]

The core curriculum debate came to a head during the first three months of 1988, when the Stanford faculty discussed whether to finally embrace the CIV proposal. From the outset, however, it was clear that the momentum was with opponents of the existing Western culture requirement.

Comparative literature professor Herbert Lindenberger supported the proposed change. "The image of Greece as a civilizing force in the West meant one thing to the Romans who absorbed Greek culture, but it meant still something else to the Renaissance humanists who revived the Greeks to suit their own historical needs, and it meant still something different to the 19th century German scholars who created an idealized Greece to serve as a civilizing ancestor to the newly emerging German nation."[19]

Historian Carl Degler agreed, but said these nuances could be accommodated within the existing Western civilization course; they were not best discovered by studying other cultures. Further, Degler said, "Few historians believe that the culture of this country has been seriously influenced by ideas from Africa, China, Japan or indigenous North America. . . . We are a part of the West not because this country received Italians, Scots, Germans, Greeks, Irish, Poles and Scandinavians within its borders, but because the language, religions, institutions, laws, customs, literature and yes, the prejudices, of this country were drawn overwhelmingly from Europe."[20]

Sounding a sharper tone, classics professor Anthony Raubitschek said that CIV advocates could teach twentieth-century pluralism and multiculturalism if they wished, but that they should retain the earlier segments of the Western culture course, which emphasized ancient and classic texts. "I do believe in affirmative action," Raubitschek said, "but I do not think it should be applied to books and educational programs."[21]

His colleague from the classics department, Gregson Davis, shot back with a call for "structural, not just cosmetic, change." Davis remarked that "Eurocentrism" was "a deeply pernicious distortion of history that is endemic among Western intellectuals." He added, "To say the Zulus created no great works is deplorably racist. Haitian voodoo helps us to grasp some famous scenes from Euripides' *Bacchae*, but it also encourages us to understand the unique experience of the Haitian people—a people whose lives have vitally intersected with our own."[22]

French professor Raymond Giraud offered a therapeutic rationale for CIV. A Western culture program shows "insensitivity to the feelings of those who are led to perceive themselves as outsiders to be assimilated into the dominant culture, and who resent this, or are psychologically harmed by the implication of cultural inferiority."[23]

In an attempt at mediation and appeasement, English professor Martin Evans, who supported the Chace proposal, appealed to the orthodoxies of the CIV crowd. "How can we begin to understand European colonialism without paying due attention to the growth and decline of its prototype and model, the Roman empire? How can we account for the development of sexism if we have never read the writings of Saint Augustine and Saint Paul?"[24]

One of the highlights of the debate was an impassioned speech by undergraduate William King, president of the Black Students' Union. King complained that, under the existing Western culture requirement,

> I was never taught the fact that the Khemetic or Egyptian Book of the Dead contained many of the dialectic principles attributed to Greece, but was written 3,000 years earlier; or the fact that Socrates, Herodotus, Pythagoras and Solon studied in Egypt and acknowledged that much of their knowledge of astronomy, geometry, medicine, and building came from the African civilizations in and around Egypt; or that the Hippocratic Oath acknowledges the Greeks' father of medicine Imhotep, a black Egyptian pharaoh whom they called Aesculapius.
>
> I was never told that algebra came from the Moslem Arabs, or numbers from India. I was never informed when it was found that the so-called dark and wooly haired Moors in Spain preserved, expanded and reintroduced the classical knowledge that the Greeks had collected, which led to the Renaissance, and that they had indoor plumbing and air conditioning. Or that European scholars flocked to the Dar El Hikma or house of wisdom in Cairo to regain the lost knowledge of the classical period and reinvigorate the dying civilization in Europe during the Middle Ages. I read the Bible without knowing St Augustine looked black like me, that the 10 Commandments were almost direct copies from the 147 Negative Confessions of Egyptian initiates, or that many of the words of Solomon came from the black pharaoh Amen-En-Eope. I didn't learn that Toussaint L'Ouverture's defeat of Napoleon in Haiti directly influenced the French Revolution, or that the Iroquis Indians in America had a representative democracy which served as a model for the American system.[25]

Perhaps the reason King wasn't told many of these things is that they are of dubious validity,[26] but Stanford professors were moved by his central point: "I'm here because I believe in the process of equal representation which my ancestors and yours created."[27] Here was a resurrection of the notion of democratic representation, this time applied not to admissions criteria, as at Berkeley, but to the curriculum.

On March 31, 1988, at a sparsely attended meeting, the Stanford Faculty Senate voted 39–4 to change the Western culture course to a new three-course sequence called "Cultures, Ideas and Values."[28] The fifteen-book requirement was abandoned. Six common texts were chosen; professors could choose others they wanted to assign. Annually the six required texts would be reexamined, and changes made if necessary. The new requirement insisted that all courses study at least one non-European culture. Professors must give "substantial attention" to issues of race and gender. The reading list must include works by women and minorities.[29]

Thus the term *Western* was eliminated, to remove any taint or preference for European and American thought. The term *cultures* signaled a new pluralism—not one culture but many. *Values* suggested a certain relativism, in which various systems of thought would be considered on a roughly equal plane. Certainly any hierarchy of cultural values would be alien to the spirit, if not the letter, of the new requirement. Both physically and culturally, "other voices" would find themselves included and indeed emphasized.

In a soothing message to the parents of Stanford undergraduates, deans Thomas Wasow and Charles Junkerman explained that the great books requirement had become a "pedagogic handicap" because it "was conveying the message that works by women and minorities are inferior to those by men of European descent."[30] "Race, gender and class now shape both the domestic and international worlds in which we and our children must live," remarked James Rosse, vice president and provost of Stanford.[31] A Rainbow Coalition cliché had gone from a protest existence on the street to official policy at Stanford University.

The change at Stanford reverberated across the country, reflecting powerful and well-organized movements for curricular reform and a new agenda for what should be taught—the basic raw material of a liberal education. America, the victorious Stanford activists said, had risen above provincialism and ethnocentrism. The country was moving toward a consensus on the "new knowledge" that would reflect the new political society.

As media coverage of the controversy suggested, Stanford is at the forefront of a national movement. "Core curricula" at such places as Columbia University and the University of Chicago are now under fierce attack in the aftermath of the Stanford transformation. At Mount Holyoke College, students are currently required to take a course in Third World culture although there is no Western culture requirement. At the University of Wisconsin, students must enroll in ethnic studies although they need not study Western civilization or even American history. At Berkeley, the faculty recently adopted an ethnic course requirement, making it the only undergraduate course that all students must take. Dartmouth College has a non-Western but no Western prerequisite for graduation. The University of Cincinnati has a new "American Diversity and World Cultures" requirement. Penn State mandates a course relating to "Ethnic Diversity," effective in fall 1991. Some colleges, such as Ohio State University, are going beyond a single requirement: they are overhauling the entire curriculum to reflect what they call "issues of race, ethnicity and gender."[32]

Most colleges still retain a mixture of Western classics and newly introduced texts reflecting the new minority agenda, but the late arrivals are displacing their predecessors as the crusade for curricular diversity gains momentum. Lynne Cheney, chairman of the National Endowment for the Humanities, maintains that it is now extremely rare to find students exposed to a core curriculum in Western civilization, even at major state universities and the elite colleges of the Ivy League.[33] Perhaps Christopher Clausen, chairman of the English department at Penn State University, reflected the emerging consensus when he remarked, "I would bet that Alice Walker's *The Color Purple* is taught in more English departments today than all of Shakespeare's plays combined."[34]

* * *

Changes at Stanford, however, did not come without strident outside opposition. When the Stanford debate erupted, then Education Secretary William Bennett showed up on campus to criticize the CIV legislation. Ironically, a few years earlier, as chairman of the National Endowment for the Humanities, Bennett had awarded a grant to Stanford to explore better ways to teach multiculturalism.[35] But CIV wasn't what he had in mind, Bennett said, denouncing the new curriculum as a "political, not an educational decision."[36] A great university has been "brought low by the forces of ignorance, irrationality and intimidation," Bennett thundered.[37]

Bennett was right to emphasize the political aspect of Stanford's revision; during the controversy, Stanford classics major Isaac Barchas remarked, "The proposal quickly became a litmus test like South Africa to determine if you had the right views on things."[38] Nor was Bennett alone in observing that it was not easy to conduct a reasoned debate in an auditorium with demonstrators outside hurling epithets, reporters taking notes, and cameras flashing.

Nevertheless, many Stanford students and faculty were not impressed by Bennett's critique. If he opposed, on principle, the presence of politics in an academic environment, they wanted to know what Bennett—a political appointee in the Reagan administration—was doing himself at Stanford. Further, both advocates and opponents of CIV said that while pressure was exerted, it did not determine the outcome of the university's decision. William Chace, who proposed the CIV alternative, was convinced that the debate, although heated, was fair-minded, and he criticized Bennett for exaggerating the strong-arm tactics of the activists.[39]

Further, non-Western advocates rejected Bennett's accusations of force allied with ignorance. Yes, Clayborne Carson conceded, there was an animus against Western thinkers, especially the ancient Greeks, but that was the regrettable exception rather than the rule. The new courses, Carson said, were an antidote to Western narrowness and imperialist aggression; they would have an intellectually broadening effect, and by improving understanding of other cultures, they would diminish hostilities among peoples, thus contributing to peace.

Critics of the CIV proposal, such as those who subscribed to Professor Chace's alternative, were sensitive to the charge that, in defending the legacy of Western civilization, they were allying themselves with some of its deplorable and barbaric practices. Chace himself emphatically denied that he was championing what one non-Western advocate termed the "antebellum esthetic position, when men were men, and men were white, when scholar-critics were white men and when women and people of color were voiceless, faceless servants and laborers, pouring tea and filling brandy snifters in the boardrooms of old boys' clubs."[40] Chace emphasized the philosophical diversity of the Western tradition, and in particular, its doctrines of equality and human rights which stand in opposition to practices such as slavery and colonialism and played an indispensable historical role in fighting these evils. Further, Chace conceded that great books have been produced in non-Western cultures, and there is no reason that they should not be taught as well.[41]

The real questions turned on which of the classics should be displaced, what arguments could be given for their substitution, which non-Western texts should be assigned, and how they should be taught;

in short, the debate was not so much over whether to study other cultures, but how and in what proportion. To get an idea of how Stanford manages the new mixture, consider the university's outline for the CIV track on "Europe and the Americas," listing the kind of works that dominate the current curriculum.

*Poets:*      Joes Maria Arguedas, Pablo Neruda, Ernesto Cardenal, Audre Lorde, Aime Cesaire

*Drama:*      Shakespeare, Euripides

*Fiction:*    García Márquez, Naipaul, Melville, Hurston, Findley, Rulfo, Ferre

*Philosophy:* Aristotle, Rousseau, Weber, Freud, Marx, Fanon, Retamar, Benedict

*History:*    James, Guaman Poma

*Diaries:*    Columbus, Cabeza de Vaca, Equiano, Lady Nugent, Dyuk, Augustine, Menchu, Barrios de Chungara

*Culture:*    Films on popular religion and healing in Peru ("Eduardo the Healer") and the U.S. ("The Holy Ghost People")

*Music:*      Reggae lyrics, Rastafarian poetry, Andean music[42]

This is not a mandated list; Stanford professors are given flexibility as long as they ensure "substantial representation" for Third World, minority, and women's works. If the suggested outline seems lacking in both chronological and thematic order, Stanford provides ideological coherence to the multicultural curriculum by urging that texts be uniformly subjected to a "race and gender" analysis, viewed from the perspective of oppressed women and persons of color. Here is how the outline recommends that Shakespeare be taught:

> Works of imaginative literature that establish paradigms of the relationship between Europeans and "others" will be analyzed, e.g. Euripides' *Medea*, whose main character is both "barbarian" and female; the medieval *Song of Roland*, which polarizes Christian and pagan (Muslim) stereotypes; Shakespeare's *Tempest*, whose figure of Caliban draws on contemporary reports of natives in the recently discovered "new world"; Cesaire's *Une Tempête*, an adaptation of the Shakespeare play that uses the Caliban-Prospero encounter as a model, in part, for colonizer-colonized relations.[43]

If it seems unfair to reduce Shakespeare to a mere function of colonial, racial, and gender-related forces, non-Western texts suffer the same indignity. The outline maintains, for example, that "Race, gender and class are all thematized in Chungara de Barrio's autobiography and Anzaldua's poetic essays. Gender is a central issue in Jamaica Kincaid's novel *Annie John*, a mother-daughter story. Roumain's *Masters of the Dew* plays out a class drama around the conflict between traditionalist peasant culture and modern proletarian consciousness."[44]

Perhaps the text which best reveals the premises underlying the new Stanford curriculum is *I, Rigoberta Menchu*, subtitled *An Indian Woman in Guatemala*.[45] In an initial description of its CIV track called "Europe and the Americas," Stanford presented this book as an epitome of the sort of new thinking that was essential in a multicultural curriculum,[46] and it is now regularly assigned to students enrolled in this track. Anthropology professor Renato Rosaldo told the *Christian Science Monitor* that teaching books such as *I, Rigoberta Menchu* as part of a multicultural curriculum generated "the most exciting teaching I've done in 19 years."[47]

Published in 1983, the book is the story of a young woman named Rigoberta Menchu growing up in Guatemala. As a representative of an oral tradition, Rigoberta does not write: rather, her views are transcribed and translated by the French feminist writer Elisabeth Burgos-Debray. Much of the book simply details the mundane: "Rigoberta's Tenth Birthday," "Rigoberta Decides to Learn Spanish," and "Rigoberta Talks about Her Father" are typical chapter titles. It is not always easy to follow this narrative because it is lavishly sprinkled with Latino and Indian phrases; for example, "At times, we managed to scrape a living in the *Altiplano* and didn't go down to the *fincas*."[48]

But integrated into the story, and impossible to miss, is the development of Rigoberta's political consciousness—her parents are killed for unspecified reasons in a bloody massacre, reportedly carried out by the Guatemalan army, and Rigoberta vows to fight back. She begins to see her cause as intertwined with the struggle for self-determination of South American Indians. She rebels against Europeanized Latino culture in all its manifestations, including domestic machismo and political indifference to Indian cultures. She becomes first a feminist, then a socialist, then a Marxist. By the end of the book Rigoberta is attending Popular Front conferences in Paris, discoursing on "bourgeois youths" and "Molotov cocktails"; there is even a chapter titled "Rigoberta Renounces Marriage and Motherhood."[49]

Strangely, in the introduction to *I, Rigoberta Menchu* we learn from Burgos-Debray that Rigoberta "speaks for all the Indians of the American continent." This is no simple autobiography; "her life story is an account of contemporary history." Further, she represents oppressed people everywhere: "The voice of Rigoberta Menchu allows the defeated to speak."[50] Yet Burgos-Debray met Rigoberta in Paris, where presumably very few of the Third World's poor travel.[51] Nor does Rigoberta's socialist and Marxist vocabulary sound typical of a Guatemalan peasant.[52]

If Rigoberta Menchu does not represent the actual peasants of Latin America, whom *does* she represent? The answer is that she embodies a projection of Marxist and feminist views onto South American Indian culture. As Burgos-Debray suggests in the introduction, Rigoberta's peasant radicalism provides independent Third World corroboration of Western progressive ideologies. Thus she is really a mouthpiece for a sophisticated left-wing critique of Western society, all the more devastating because it issues not from a French scholar-activist but from a seemingly authentic Third World source. Her usefulness to Professor Rosaldo is that Rigoberta provides a model with whom American minority and female students can identify: they too are oppressed after all.

But Rigoberta is no ordinary victim. As Burgos-Debray argues, she has suffered from multiple vectors of simultaneous oppression. Rigoberta is a "person of color," and thus a victim of racism. She is a woman, and thus a victim of sexism. She lives in South America, which is a victim of European and North American colonialism. If this were not bad enough, she is an Indian, victimized by latino culture within Latin America.[53]

Rigoberta's claim to eminence is that, as a consummate victim, she is completely identified with the main currents of history. Undergraduates do not read about Rigoberta because she has written a great and immortal book, or performed a great deed, or invented something useful. She simply happened to be in the right place at the right time. She supports the historicist pedagogy of CIV advocates who believe, with Hegel and Marx, that being is historical and that history progresses toward a designated end, in this case the final emancipation of the proletariat.

Rigoberta's victim status may be unfortunate for her personal happiness, but is indispensable for her academic reputation. Rigoberta is a modern Saint Sebastian, pierced by the arrows of North American white male cruelty; thus her life story becomes an explicit indictment of the historical role of the West and Western institutions. Her very appearance and tribal garb are a rebuke to European culture; for Rigoberta to style her hair, or wear a suit, would corrupt her with Western bric-a-brac. As it stands, she is an ecological saint, made famous by her very obscurity, elevated by her place in history as a representative voice of oppression. Now it is her turn to be canonized—quite literally, for her to enter the Stanford canon.

\* \* \*

Non-Western societies have, of course, created works of literature and art of the highest order. China, India, and Egypt are very old civilizations whose ancient philosophers and painters make Western cultures of the time appear quaint and primitive. Nor is an appreciation of those achievements inaccessible to the Western student. Many scholars have devoted their entire lives to investigating and comprehending other cultures on their own terms, in their own languages, with a minimum of distortion and condescension.

No one at Stanford or other campuses has denied that students would benefit from exposure to the great works of non-Western cultures, such as the *Ramayana*—the *Iliad* of Indian folklore. Originally composed in Sanskrit by the poet Valmiki, the *Ramayana* tells of the amorous courtship of Prince Rama, the abduction of his wife Sita by the monster Ravana, Rama's mystical pursuit of the demon across a continent of dieties, spells, and strange beasts, culminating in a final battle between the avenging prince and his concupiscent adversary.

Another valuable addition to a great books curriculum would be the *Gitanjali*, written in the early part of this century by the Bengali poet Rabindranath Tagore. In many high schools in India, one of its poems is offered as a daily prayer.[54] W. B. Yeats, who wrote the introduction to the English translation of the *Gitanjali*, said he discovered in Tagore a world that he had always dreamed about, but never encountered, either in reality or in imagination, in the West: "These verses will not lie in little well-printed books upon ladies' tables, who turn the pages with indolent hands that they may sigh over a life without meaning . . . but, as the generations pass, travellers will hum them on the highway and men rowing upon rivers. Lovers, while they await one another, shall find this love of God a magic gulf wherein their own more bitter passion may bathe and renew its youth." Somehow Tagore managed to capture "a whole people, a whole civilization," and he did so grandly, nobly, without polemic.[55] Yeats would certainly be of the view that any curriculum in literature would be enriched by Tagore's spiritual poetry.

An examination of the greatest achievements of non-Western cultures would surely include the *Analects* of Confucius, the Confucian exegesis of Mencius, the *Tao Te Ching* of Lao Tzu, the *Tale of Genji*, the Upanishads and Vedas and Bhagavad Gita, Averroes and Ibn Sinha, the Koran and the Islamic commentaries, as well as select contemporary works from Asia, Africa, and Latin America.

But such an approach is not at all what the Stanford non-Western advocates had in mind. During the CIV debate, the university's history department chairman said that while his faculty may be genuinely interested in other cultures, they possessed little or no training in those areas, and could hardly be expected to master new fields. Even with recruitment, he added, "It's not exactly easy to find experts on the Mongol empire."[56] Ultimately Stanford decided that it would not hire a new group of professors with knowledge of Third World cultures; rather, current faculty with expertise in Western classics would now familiarize themselves with, and then teach, CIV courses. The decision to retain existing faculty influenced the content of the CIV curriculum. While it would be unrealistic to expect someone who knows little about Indian culture to teach the Upanishads, the Stanford faculty was generally quite happy to teach *I, Rigoberta Menchu*, since the latter represents not the zenith of Third World achievement but rather caters to the ideological proclivities of American activists.

Similarly, Stanford student activists insisted upon the *I, Rigoberta Menchu* approach because they were generally not animated by the desire to learn about the greatest achievements of distant cultures. "The protesters weren't interested in building up the anthropology department here, or immersing themselves in foreign languages," remarked Walter Lammi, a Stanford philosophy professor. "There are obvious ways in which our curriculum could be enhanced," added humanities professor emeritus Ronald Hilton, "but they are not followed because there is no pressure group pushing the administration that way."[57] "We're not saying we need to study Tibetan philosophy," observed Chicano activist Alejandro Sweet-Cordero in the *Chronicle of Higher Education*. "We're arguing that we need to understand what made our society what it is."[58] Another Stanford activist told me, "Forget Confucius. We are trying to prepare ourselves for the multicultural challenge we will face in the future."

If future practical advantage is the significant academic criterion, perhaps the two great non-Western developments that students should study in close detail are the rise of capitalism in Japan, which increasingly threatens American dominance of world markets, and Islamic fundamentalism, apparently the only serious ideological opponent of Western liberal democracy. When I mentioned these global developments the Stanford student grimaced. "Who gives a damn about those things? I want to study myself." Although raised in the United States, his brown skin points him toward his own "non-Western" heritage. Thus does the multicultural project reveal its own paradoxical provincialism.

Outside Stanford, we see the same narrow and somewhat procrustean approach to the Third world. Recently Graywolf Press in Saint Paul, Minnesota, published *Multicultural Literacy*, which has quickly become an influential and widely used textbook for young Americans about "global culture." The book ignores the philosophical, religious, and literary classics of Asia and the Middle East. Even the best of contemporary non-Western writing is ignored: there is nothing from V. S. Naipaul or Shiva Naipaul, nothing from Jorge Luis Borges, nothing from Naguib Mahfouz, nothing from Wole Soyinka, nothing from Octavio Paz, nothing from Mario Vargas Llosa, nothing from Gabriel García Márquez. Instead the book consists of thirteen essays of protest, including Michele Wallace's autobiographical "Invisibility Blues" and Paula Gunn Allen's "Who Is Your Mother? The Red Roots of White Feminism."

In addition, the book contains an E. D. Hirsch–style compilation of alleged Third World vocabulary, clearly chosen by Western ideological criteria—thus we encounter such terms as Abdul-Jabbar, Allende, ancestor worship, Arafat, ashram, barrio, beatnik, Biko, Bogota, Cajun, Cardenal, child abuse, condom, covert operations, dadaism, de Beauvoir, domestic violence, Dr J, economic violence, Farsi, Friedan, genitals, Gilgamesh, Greenpeace, Harlem, Hopi, Hurston, indigenous, internment camps, juju music, karma, kundalini yoga, Kurosawa, liberation theology, Little Red Book, Mandela, McCarthy, migrant worker, misogyny, mutual assured destruction, neo-Nazi, New Right, nuclear freeze, Ohibwa tribe, Plath, premenstrual syndrome, prophylactic, Quetzalcoatl, rap music, safe sex, samba, sexism, socialized medicine, Soweto, Tutu, wars of liberation, Wollstonecraft, Zimbabwe.[59]

\* \* \*

The effects on students of a Stanford-style multicultural curriculum can be seen in the example of Megan Maxwell, a recent graduate of Stanford. Although she was not active in the Rainbow Coalition, she supported the new CIV curriculum, and agreed with Jesse Jackson's call for American blacks to be described henceforth as African Americans. Instead of reading Joseph Conrad's *Heart of Darkness,* a European view critical of imperialism, why not read African writers who speak more directly to the suffering imposed on them, she argued. In a Western culture curriculum dominated by white male figures, she said, "I would have real problems identifying with America."

Her clean-cut appearance, Yale T-shirt, and preppie watch and jewelry warned me not to expect too much radicalism. Maxwell wasn't against the Western culture texts; "I just want the history of blacks and women to be studied, so they aren't lost in the shuffle," Maxwell said. She argued, "I don't have contempt for Western ideals. But perhaps they need to be changed or broadened. There were also ideas put out by non-whites that are as valid." In her own major, American history, Maxwell pointed out that she benefited from reading about the voices of slaves and oppressed people in this country, and she emphasized the importance of blacks tracing their cultural heritage to Africa.

But while Maxwell was appropriately severe on Western culture, which enslaved blacks, why did she seem so upbeat about African culture, which sold Maxwell's ancestors into lifelong slavery? In Basil Davidson's *The African Slave Trade,* the author remarks, "Pressured by the need for European goods, the lords of Africa sold their folk to the mariners who came from Europe." He adds, "As elsewhere in the world, those who dealt in slaves could make their fortunes: what was more, they could not make their fortunes in any other way. If 'everyone in Liverpool' was investing in the trades that derived from slave labor, so was 'everyone in the Congo.' " Finally, Davidson observed:

> It is wrong to consider this African experience as one that was ordered and imposed from outside, with the African part of it a purely negative and involuntary one. This view . . . mirrors a familiar notion of African incapacity, and it has no place in the historical record. Those Africans who were involved in the trade were seldom the helpless victims of a commerce they did not understand: on the contrary, they understood it as well as their European partners. They responded to its challenge. They exploited its opportunities.[60]

Confronted with this account, Maxwell became very quiet and did not say anything for several seconds. She now seemed aware of the implications of the term *slave trade*. Trade implies a buyer and a seller. We unequivocally condemn the buyer of slaves, the white man, but isn't an equal share of guilt borne by the black seller of slaves, the tribal chieftains?

After a moment, Maxwell pointed out that "In every culture people are selling their own into slavery. The Romans had slaves—didn't they?" This was so. "I wonder if it is possible to study history without attaching moral judgments to it," Maxwell said, adding, "I don't know if I can blame anyone for slavery." Moral judgments, she speculated, were "not always productive." But she agreed that this was not at all the approach of CIV at Stanford. The new curriculum sprang out of the passions of the civil rights and feminist movements, which were hardly value-neutral. Notions of historical and even contemporary guilt and blame, inherent in terms like imperialism, colonialism, slavery, oppression, bourgeois and proletariat, oppressor and oppressed classes, carried heavy moral freight. Maxwell reluctantly conceded that if blame was to be assigned, it must be distributed fairly.

A short while after our discussion of African complicity in the slave trade, Maxwell modified her earlier statements about the importance of American blacks tracing their roots there. And she expressed new reservations about "African American" as a term of self-description. "I very strongly identify myself as an American," she said. "I prefer to call myself a black American."

*  *  *

If her lack of objectivity about African slavery was surprising for one so intelligent, Megan Maxwell had only Stanford to blame. The texts that her professors assigned seem to have given an unbalanced view of certain factors that are central to an accurate picture of her identity as an American black. A list of "alternative required readings" prepared for Stanford by Professor Clayborne Carson included Walter Rodney's *How Europe Underdeveloped Africa*, a Marxist analysis which downplays and even distorts African involvement in the slave trade. Rodney maintains that African chieftains were "bamboozled by European goods." The Europeans cunningly "exploited the political differences between African nations." Rodney even speaks of "grave doubts" about slavery on the part of African rulers. For the chiefs of the Congo and Benin, he asserts, "it took a great deal of persuasion and pressure from Europeans to get them to sell male African prisoners of war."[61] There is a voluminous literature on slavery for Rodney to draw on, but he does not substantiate these condescending claims—he merely states them. Davidson and others provide empirical reasons to think these claims are false. Yet nowhere does Rodney confront these contrary arguments; indeed he does not even mention them, even though they were published only two years earlier, while he was writing his own book. The point is not that Rodney is a Marxist and a radical; Davidson too was both. Nor is it a question of whether Rodney is right or wrong; rather, the point is that Stanford students deserve exposure to both sides of the debate, but receive only a single narrow point of view.

It does not seem fair to blame a student like Maxwell who took her textbooks as factually reliable for espousing their conclusions. But it could reasonably be asked whether such eclectic and one-sided accounts as Rodney's are a proper basis on which to build ethnic pride and understanding. Stanford seems to be inadvertently denying its idealistic minority students an intellectual foundation for their convictions.

Recently John Stanfield, professor of sociology and Afro-American studies at William and Mary College, edited for re-release the book *Bitter Canaan*, written by one of the century's most prominent black scholars, Charles S. Johnson. *Bitter Canaan* was bitingly critical of contemporary claims that the African state of Liberia was a land of freedom and opportunity for blacks, including American blacks who emigrated there in the nineteenth century. "Successive generations have developed corrupt leaders, the machinery of government has been clogged with incompetence and vice, education has been neglected," Johnson writes.[62] Further, Johnson describes how former American slaves established an aristocracy and repressed the native blacks. *Bitter Canaan*, although a recognized *tour de force* at the time of its publication in 1930, has been out of print for almost half a century. But Stanfield maintains that it is a mistake for blacks to ignore self-criticism. "*Bitter Canaan*, with all its realism, would have demystified the black establishment's heaven," he wrote in the introduction.[63] Nevertheless, it is virtually impossible to find a non-Western studies course in which this book is assigned today.

Much more typical is Frantz Fanon's *The Wretched of the Earth*, which is on the Stanford list. A psychiatrist from a middle-class family who studied in Europe, Fanon nevertheless presented himself as a spokesman for the poorest and most deprived victims of colonialism. Much of his book is a crude rationalization for violence: the revolutionary, Fanon says, "is ready for violence at all times," awaits a "murderous and decisive struggle" with his adversary, and rejoices in "searing bullets and bloodstained knives."[64] In a breathless introduction, Jean-Paul Sartre argues that both colonizer and colonized are caught in a historical trap which can only be broken by assassination. "You must kill," Sartre advises. "To shoot down a European is to kill two birds with one stone, to destroy an oppressor and the man he oppresses at the same time: there remain a dead man, and a free man."[65] Although ostensibly directed at African readers, both Sartre's and Fanon's comments cater to a guilty Western audience. The book enjoyed an enormous vogue during the 1960s, when the Marxist dream of the "new man" that Fanon exalts still captured the imagination of many. With the collapse of Marxist orthodoxy even in the Soviet Union and the Eastern bloc, these ideas seem naive and, outside the university, Fanon has lost much of his cultural authority.

* * *

It is easy to sympathize with the feeling of inadequacy that many minority students experience when they encounter a curriculum that seems overwhelmingly dominated by whites. The claim by Stanford activists that other cultures count for something too is more in the nature of a psychological plea than a political demand. Even though the concerns of the students are legitimate, Stanford and other colleges have not had an easy time in coping with them. One important reason for this is the existence of some very inconvenient facts about the Third World.

To understand why an authentic non-Western curriculum might cause problems, we should recognize that the movement for curricular expansion arose in the aftermath of the civil rights, feminist and homosexual rights struggles of the 1960s and 1970s. For its advocates, the purpose of studying other cultures is to affirm them as alternatives to Western mores, to celebrate the new pluralism and diversity. Stanford classics professor Marshall McCall put it bluntly: "The pressure is on here to affirm those who have been 'out,' and to spare those cultures and traditions any criticism."

The basic difficulty is that, by and large, non-Western cultures have no developed tradition of racial equality. Not only do they violate equality in practice, but the very principle is alien to them, regarded by many with suspicion and contempt.[66]

Moreover, many of these cultures have deeply ingrained ideas of male superiority. The Koran stipulates that "men have authority over women because Allah has made the one superior to the other." The renowned Islamic scholar Ibn Taymiyya advises, "When a husband beats his wife for misbehavior, he should not exceed ten lashes."[67] Many Chinese continue to abide by an old saying from the *Ts'ai-fei lu,* "If you care for your son, you don't go easy on his studies. If you care for your daughter, you don't go easy on her foot-binding." In addition to non-Western practices such as dowry, purdah, and wife-burning, in countries such as Kenya, Somalia, Indonesia, and the Sudan women are routinely circumcised in a manner which deprives them of sexual pleasure for life; in most cases, the clitoris is cut off with a knife and the sides of the vulva are stitched together, almost always without the use of anesthetic.[68] Feminism is simply not indigenous to non-Western cultures.

It is perhaps pointless even to bring up the issue of non-Western attitudes toward homosexuality or other "alternative lifestyles," which in various societies are enough to warrant segregation, imprisonment, even capital punishment. In Cuba homosexuals are often thrown in jail and in China, they are sometimes subjected to shock treatment which is credited with a high "cure rate."[69] Basil Davidson, in his book *The African Genius,* observes that African tribes such as the Nyakyusa, although very tolerant in matters of sex, regard homosexuality as a sin and a sickness "occasioned by witchcraft."[70]

Since the racial and feminist agenda of the new advocates of diversity finds little support in other cultures, it seems reasonable to expect that these cultures be roundly denounced as even more backward and retrograde than the West. But, for political reasons, this is totally unacceptable, since the Third World is viewed by American minority activists as suffering the same kind of oppression that blacks, Hispanics, American Indians, women, and homosexuals suffer in this country. It is crucial for the activists to maintain victim solidarity. As a result, instead of being subjected to charges of misogyny and prejudice, these cultures are ransacked for "representative" figures who are congenial to the Western progressive agenda—then, like Rigoberta Menchu, they are triumphantly presented as the "repressed voices" of diversity, fit for the solemn admiration of American undergraduates.

Unfortunately, such treatment seems no less uncritical than the academic distortions of non-Western cultures in the past. For generations, accounts of faraway cultures by European researchers were taken to be factual and objective, until they were found to contain unexamined prejudices, often hostile to the societies they were studying. Whatever their motivations, such scholarship is now rightly regarded as suspect. In Edward Said's *Orientalism,* for example, he justly chastized Western scholars for making up an Orient that wasn't actually there.

> The Orient was almost a European invention, and had been since antiquity a place of romance, exotic beings, haunting memories and landscapes, remarkable experiences. . . . Orientalism is a Western style for dominating, restructuring, and having authority over the Orient. . . . European

culture gained in strength and identity by setting itself off against a sort of surrogate and even underground self. . . . There emerged a complex Orient suitable for study in the academy, for display in the museum, for reconstruction in the colonial office, for theoretical illustration in anthropological, biological, linguistic, racial and historical theses about mankind and the universe.[71]

Today's multicultural curriculum manipulates and amputates the Third World in precisely the same way. It subordinates the understanding of Asia, Africa, and Latin America to Western ideological prejudices. And it reflects a new cultural imperialism no less narrow and bigoted than that of the colonialist researchers in safari outfits and pith helmets.

* * *

A second major problem faced by those, at Stanford and elsewhere, who demand equal curricular "representation" for ethnic groups, is the extreme shortage of non-Western, black, and female figures of real eminence in a large number of fields. Asked if he could list great women and persons of color in his field, Kenneth Arrow, a Nobel laureate and Stanford economics professor, said that all the truly outstanding economists in the world have been white men. Could he name a single black and female economist of note? He rubbed his chin, finally offering a name in each category: W. Arthur Lewis, and Joan Robinson. Any others? He could not think of any. He hastened to add that there were, of course, "some promising young people who can't be picked out yet." But if Stanford demanded that his department teach the work of female and black thinkers, Arrow admitted that he and his colleagues would face a serious problem.

Eckhart Forster, a Stanford philosophy professor, supported the new CIV curriculum. How was his department adapting to the new demand for diversity? Well, he said, Stanford had a chair in Chinese philosophy. This was, he uncomfortably admitted, "the only other area where traditionally philosophy has been done." Could he name any African philosophers? "Not to my knowledge."

Forster maintained that it was a "very complex" question as to what kind of society produced philosophers. "If a society is suppressed, there may not be the opportunity to philosophize." He said that political systems and even climate may contribute to the conditions that encourage or discourage a philosophical temperament. He pointed out that even in the West, philosophers seemed to issue out of very particular environments, at particular moments in history. It was not easy to explain, for instance, the concentration of philosophical and literary talent that Greece produced around the fifth century before Christ.

Forster was unable to name a great female philosopher in the past. He named some promising contemporaries: Ruth Marcus, Margaret Wilson. But for a long time, he said, women were not thought fit for universities. "The philosophers of the Middle Ages were priests," he said, "and women were not in the priesthood." But to ensure gender representation, he said, "we could broaden the definition of philosophy." For instance, "you could try and find a poet like Sappho and treat her philosophically."

Impressive as Sappho's verse may be, it stretches the definition of philosophy to study her in this department. The risk of attempting curricular accommodation based on race and gender is that it can result in lesser works being taught simply because of the skin color or gender of their authors. In *A Room of One's Own*, Virginia Woolf poses a difficult and important question: why has there never been a female Shakespeare? Woolf speculates that if Shakespeare had had an equally gifted sister, she could never have made it onto the London stage, and probably would have died anonymously. "A woman must have money and a room of her own if she is to write fiction," Woolf argues.

Woolf's brilliant analysis is justly celebrated by feminists, but it leaves many of them deeply uncomfortable, and it is not hard to see why. In debating why there is no female Shakespeare, Woolf concedes that there is no female Shakespeare. Woolf provides a plausible explanation for the absence of female accomplishment in literature—by extension, in other cultural fields as well—but what can such explanation bring but a tinge of regret? Many contemporary feminists argue that women have accomplished just as much as men, but that their achievements have been ignored and minimized by patriarchal culture; consequently, there is an academic industry to uncover and publicize previously ignored female works. Woolf punctures their enthusiasm by coolly announcing that it is "unthinkable" that any woman in Shakespeare's day could produce what he did—there simply wasn't the intellectual and social background available to women to treat such diverse raw material so richly.

For the new advocates of diversity to content themselves with providing reasons for cultural underrepresentation might be more faithful to the historical record, but would greatly limit their ambitions. They might blame imperialism, or racism, or sexism for the lesser accomplishment of minorities and women, but the fact of lesser accomplishment would remain.

\* \* \*

How do Stanford faculty, by and large, cope with teaching other cultures that they don't know much about, and which seem to continually produce information that is contrary to the ideological preferences of diversity advocates?

Stanford English professor Linda Paulson was both enthusiastic and apprehensive about the new CIV curriculum. "It's no longer legitimate to take a look at white man's philosophy and white man's literature and assume that it is always the proper mouthpiece for culture," she said. "There are a lot of other voices that need to be found and heard." Yet she acknowledged difficulties in finding enough of them to teach. Universities have a strong bias toward the written word "and I don't see any way to get around that." Paulson said it was easier to study African art or migration patterns at the same time as Greek civilization in the fifth century B.C., but since African culture was oral, there just wasn't any literature to read. "That may be ultimately racist and prejudicial—it probably is—but I'm not an anthropologist," Paulson said.

Paulson seemed oddly distrustful and hesitant; she constantly criticized her own remarks as possibly racist, and emphasized her own inescapably biased white female perspective. Mentioning the existence of oral cultures, Paulson said that as far as her classes on literature were concerned, "I'm not willing to give up on the written word." Her defensiveness suggested that she was conscious of making an outrageous claim.

What made Paulson most uncomfortable was being asked to teach cultures that she knew little or nothing about. Like a number of the Stanford professors who voted for the new curriculum, Paulson was beginning to realize that CIV was making her own credentials less relevant. In fact, even if she knew a great deal about non-Western cultures, as a white person she still felt technically disabled from providing a "non-Western perspective." The logical implication was that Paulson should make way for Rigoberta Menchu, or someone of like authenticity.

Paulson did attempt to compensate, as best she could, for her deficiency. She confessed to a guilty love of Milton, but denounced him in the same breath as "an ass . . . a sexist pig." Paulson suggested a way that she could continue to teach effectively despite her latent prejudices. "Maybe what we should be doing is teaching suspicion, a kind of irreverence toward the canon." In such an approach Western writers such as Dante and Milton would be read, but then exposed as unprogressive. By condemning the West, the norms and values of other cultures would be implicitly elevated, although it would not be so important to study them.

Paulson is a typical example of a serious scholar whose commitment to the intellectual life has come into conflict with her political sympathies. On purely intellectual grounds, she said, Stanford students "need to have a sense of history, of philosophy as it develops, of what Christianity means as a historical force." Thus some exposure to the classics was essential. Yet for ideological reasons, it was important to assign minority and non-Western contemporary works, and here Paulson was confident that she would come up with enough names to satisfy members of the Rainbow Coalition which had always, she said nervously, found her "pretty reasonable." There was a note of anxiety in Paulson's voice which she did not seem to acknowledge, but it appeared every now and then in her remarks, as when she insisted that it was dangerous not to study other cultures: "It is *unsafe* to be provincial."

Like Paulson, Stanford classics professor Marshall McCall is an honest scholar who expressed reservations about CIV, supported the final CIV requirement, and now recognizes the risks in the way it is taught. McCall admitted that it would be very difficult to confront embarrassing facts about Third World norms and attitudes in a politically charged environment. As an example of such sensitivities, some young blacks who have converted from Christianity to Islam may be unaware that the prophet Mohammed owned slaves. Young black women of a feminist bent may be further distressed to discover that he was a polygamist. Although McCall said it was essential for Stanford to resist political pressure to manipulate evidence to suit student sensitivities, "I'm not sure that I would get up in the Faculty Senate or a Stanford dorm and say any of this," he acknowledged.

There are on the Stanford faculty a considerable number of progressive-minded teachers who do not wish to compromise their scholarship for the sake of ideology, but who find themselves pressured and intimidated in this direction. This group is the "swing vote" in faculty committees and in the Faculty Senate, and only by winning their continued acquiescence can Stanford CIV activists maintain their current momentum. The question is for how long the activists can subdue and overcome intellectual and moral qualms about their agenda—on this depends the future of the victim's revolution in the classroom.

\* \* \*

While queasy but cooperative liberals such as McCall and Paulson struggle with practical difficulties attached to teaching other cultures, non-Western advocates also face two serious problems of principle. Anyone who wishes to offer convincing intellectual justification for Third World and minority representation must meet objections which, to date, go without a response.

The first concerns the rational justification for an approach that assigns books and course material based on ethnic and gender categories. The arguments for group representation in the curriculum are identical in substance, and very nearly in form, to arguments employed by fundamentalists who are pressuring the public schools to teach "creation science" alongside evolution. The creationists maintain that evolution does not constitute truth or knowledge; it is merely a theory. They have an alternate theory, which represents the conviction of a distinct social group. Yet their view has been neglected, indeed forced out of the schools; they are victims of discrimination. Their theory deserves representation in the curriculum, so that students may be exposed to all points of view.

Implicit in this argument is a denial of the ability of scholarship to make any meaningful distinctions between valid and invalid claims. The fact that evolution is a theory does not mean that all theories are equally plausible. Similarly, it seems possible to make distinctions on intellectual and esthetic grounds between, say, *Othello* and *The Color Purple*. It does not appear the function of the academy to hold group referenda on which books are worth reading, or which authors represent racial constituencies—this would transform the intellectual agenda of universities into a political one. Certainly arguments can be made to include or exclude a theory or a book in a science or literature course, but such arguments must be made in terms of scholarly merit, which is the only currency in which the academy is qualified to trade.

The second problem is that it is not clear in what sense it is meaningful to classify Homer the Greek and Augustine the North African and Faulkner the American Southerner in the same group as white males, thus necessitating the inclusion of black and female perspectives for balance. If the classics reflect a shared white male perspective, why has nobody precisely identified it? Would Homer be vindicated if he were a Mongolian, Aquinas if he could demonstrate Peruvian heritage, Faulkner if he could unveil a black ancestor? It seems unlikely that being white and male are the reasons for anyone's greatness of thought; rather, those are features, historically accidental, that happened to coincide with great minds who were working at particular times in particular environments. If whiteness and maleness are the cause of great civilization, then nonwhites and females are truly deprived in an incurable sense. Personally, I believe this gives too much credit to white males, a considerable number of whom are markedly lacking in Homeric qualities. Fortunately, the great thinkers of the white male perspective did not think of themselves in this way. Thus, as Stanford student Isaac Barchas argues, instead of denouncing the classics, minorities and women might do a lot better to challenge the *proprietorship* of books which are not white male property but the common heritage of civilization.[72]

\* \* \*

The central irony of the argument that seeks to favorably contrast non-Western cultures with the West is that the very principles admired by the activists have been most fully developed in Western countries, and are only now being realized in other countries. Consequently, a "Western culture must go" program threatens to undermine basic principles of equality, democracy, and economic development on which countless Third World natives are pinning their hopes for the future.

Bernard Lewis of Princeton University argues that to abolish Western culture is simply to restore the institution of chattel slavery. Conventional wisdom holds the West responsible for slavery. But in fact slavery has existed in virtually all societies known to human history. Asia and Africa and America before Columbus all practiced slavery. What is peculiarly Western, Lewis maintains, is the *abolition* of slavery, and it was not the force of slave armies, but the conscience of the slave-owning countries, which toppled the institution. As Emerson said of the emancipation of slaves in England and America, "Other revolutions have been the insurrection of the oppressed. This was the repentance of the tyrant."[73]

The same is true of women: Western ideas have helped to bring about basic rights for women that were, until very recently, regarded as preposterous in many countries of the world. A repudiation of the West in those countries, as has happened in Iran and some of the Arab world, could briskly lead to the restitution of the harem, the veil, polygamy, and even more brutal customs of wife-burning and female child abortion.[74] Even now there are apologists for female clitoridectomy and wife abuse in the Third World who take comfort from Western exaltation of "indigenous customs."[75]

Right now the developing world is experiencing, often for the first time, the exhilaration of freedom. In Asia, for example, the open market is emancipating the lives of millions of people who were previously dependent on the government for the most basic livelihood. Free enterprise has brought such prosperity to Hong Kong and Thailand and South Korea and Japan that even Communist countries are promiscuously opening their doors to capitalism. Similarly, democracy has spread powerfully through much of Latin America, a continent habituated to dictatorship. Today most of Latin America is democratic, largely due to human rights policies begun by President Carter and continued by Presidents Reagan and Bush. The example of this continent, where the voting rate is much higher than that in America or in most other industrialized democracies, proves that the poor are not too hungry to vote; they do not consider the ballot box to be an irrelevancy or cruel hoax.

Given these developments, it seems sensible to affirm the democratic and economic systems which are so desperately sought by these peoples and which hold out so much promise for their future. Jacob Neusner, professor of Judaic studies at Brown University, recently asked, "Why did capitalism not begin in India? Why is there no science in Africa? Why does everybody want what we have: science and technology, prosperity and democracy—that is, our philosophy, our economics, our politics?"[76] These are good questions, but instead of dealing seriously with them, a large number of Western scholars who have never spoken to a native of El Salvador or Haiti or India or the Philippines spend their time denigrating Western white male culture and vaunting every exotic Third World custom they encounter.

Many Third World people are grateful for at least one aspect of Western power—the way in which Western norms forced the suspension of brutal indigenous traditions that would otherwise have continued. In India, for instance, the British stopped the practice of *sati*, whereby a widowed woman would prove the worthlessness of life without a husband by flinging herself onto the dead man's burning pyre; if she refused, she was often tossed into the flames. In some instances, all female members of the family immolated themselves. Was it an unwarranted "imposition of Western values," or of a "white male perspective," for the British to act in this way?[77] If so, does anyone now quarrel with the outcome?

It does no credit to developing countries to assert that their oppression is in itself evidence of cultural merit. To celebrate the works of the oppressed, apart from the standard of merit by which other art and literature and history is judged, is to romanticize their suffering, to pretend that it is naturally creative, and to give it an esthetic status that is not shared or appreciated by those who actually endure the oppression.

\* \* \*

As one embarks upon the study of other cultures, one realizes another strange fact: curiosity about other cultures appears to be a distinctively Western trait. Professor McCall said it was "absolute rubbish" for members of Stanford's Rainbow Coalition to assert that Western culture was "an idealized, self-congratulatory, white-male-dominated version of itself." On the contrary, he said, it was "irresistibly curious about others," a trait which went all the way back to the ancient Greeks. In fact today's Western societies are as hungry for news about other places as they were in the time of Herodotus.

Further, McCall added, Western culture was distinctive in the fact that it is so introspective. "Part of the greatness of our tradition is the fact that it is so critical of, or contentious with, the status quo." A tradition that includes Plato, Aristotle, Aurelius, Augustine, Aquinas, Luther, Hobbes, Locke, Rousseau, Marx, Jefferson, and Nietzsche can hardly be termed monolithic or uncritical. It encompasses the advocacy of totalitarianism and freedom, of monarchy and oligarchy and democracy, of Christianity and paganism and agnosticism, of the cause of the rich and the poor, of patriarchy and feminism, of free will and predestination—in short, of widely divergent views of humanity. Nor were these thinkers uncritically attached to the idea of the West, or even their native countries; even an ardent traditionalist such as Edmund Burke believed that patriotism demanded a criterion of judgment apart from naturalization. "To love our country," he said, "our country must be lovely."

Stanford professor Kenneth Arrow remarked that while "there is a tendency to dismiss all of Western culture as racist, sexist, and oppressive, the fact is, everybody at this university is a part of it: black, white, women, men. To some degree, they have all assimilated." Arrow pointed out that "the libertarian or democratic features that were essential to the debate over the curriculum were precisely out of the culture that they were protesting. The respect for diversity, for argument, that they showed comes directly out of this culture, not from anywhere else." Even what Arrow conceded was an element of "moral brow-beating" and "playing on guilt feelings" was distinctly Western. It is the white man, more than anyone else, who can be "played" with the tactic of the "guilt trip." Only the white man can be intimidated by a catalog of his forefathers' errors and crimes.

This points to the ultimate irony of Third World and minority oppression theory—it is entirely Western in its conception and formulation. Few have carefully considered to what degree it resembles the authentic convictions and aspirations of the peoples of Asia and Africa, even if it is exploitatively used by elites in those countries to justify their policies. The premier ideologist of oppression, Karl Marx, was not exactly a Guatemalan. Here is one overrepresented white male in the Stanford curriculum. Yet no one at Stanford or elsewhere has suggested that Marx presents a Eurocentric viewpoint which can be safely discounted if not dismissed or pilloried.

A further paradox is that Marx and Engels, the most acceptable white males in the new curriculum for diversity, were not themselves averse to bigotry. When he learned that Marx's son-in-law Paul Lafargue, who had a small amount of Negro blood, was running as a socialist in a district which also contained the Paris zoo, Engels observed: "Being in his quality as a nigger a degree nearer to the rest of the animal kingdom than the rest of us, he is undoubtedly the most appropriate representative of that district."[78] Marx himself praised the discoveries of French ethnologist Pierre Trémaux, who argued that the human race was the product of evolution, but that Negroes resulted from social degeneration. "The backward negro is not an evolved ape, but a degenerate man," Trémaux observed. Marx hailed Trémaux's work as marking "a very significant advance over Darwin,"[79] and termed a Creole man who married his niece a "gorilla offspring."[80] Marx also approved of European imperialism in Asia because he considered Asian culture so inferior that it was incapable of entering historic development without a European push. Marx frequently referred to the "semi-barbarian, semi-civilized communities" of China and India, noting that they had "no history at all, at least no known history. What we shall call their history is but the history of successive invaders who founded their empires on the passive basis of the unresisting and unchanging society."[81] This facet of Marx and Engels was totally unfamiliar to all the Stanford activists with whom I spoke.

\* \* \*

Whatever the source of its merits, Western culture has undoubtedly produced works that are worthy of the examination of any curious and thoughtful person. Far from affirming the status quo, these works, carefully read, deeply question established intellectual and political powers, which is why so many tyrants have persecuted men of ideas. In the earlier part of this century, Walter Lippmann observed that "the religious and classical heritage creates issues that are too deep and too contentious to be faced with equanimity." The reason we are tempted to abolish the classic tradition, Lippmann said, is that "We are afraid of it, afraid to face any longer in a modern democratic society the severe discipline and the deep, disconcerting issues of the nature of the universe, and of man's place in it and of his destiny."[82]

Although Stanford CIV advocates frequently accused the Western civilization course of harboring a political agenda, no one has ever offered convincing evidence that courses in the classics tend to produce conservatives, and indeed several serious students emerged from such core curricula as confident radicals. When Gary Kates, now a history professor at Trinity College, was a student some years ago, he took a class with Allan Bloom, author of *The Closing of the American Mind*. Expecting to encounter a raging and inflexible conservative, Kates said, "his interpretations of Rousseau's *Émile* were brilliant, and his teaching style was so engaging that it seemed as if Socrates himself were leading the class." Kates added, however, "The students returned not more conservative, but more radical. They found Rousseau's attack upon vanity, inequality and social hierarchies inspiring . . . they identified too many similarities between 18th century France and 20th century America for them to feel very comfortable with conservatism."[83] In a similar vein, 1960s' activist Tom Hayden has endorsed the idea of a great books core curriculum on the grounds that "classical philosophy is the highest level of inquiry and knowledge" which is essential for a rational and effective radicalism.[84]

As these activists have observed, the Western tradition offers powerful and moving treatment of the issues of slavery and equality. Partly this is because Western thinkers have been forced to confront difference much more than thinkers in other, more culturally homogenous, less cosmopolitan, traditions. In *The Merchant of Venice*, Shakespeare puts into the mouth of Shylock the Jew one of the most moving indictments of prejudice known to literature.[85] His eloquent protest against anti-Semitism challenges the ethnocentric principle by replacing it with a principle of justice based on equality. Such passages, which abound in the classics, should dispel the notion that Shakespeare and others were oblivious to issues of racial and ethnic difference, or incapable of addressing with considerable subtlety questions of equality that concern us today.

Indeed, the Shylock passage is not, contrary to first impression, a simple sermon on egalitarianism. Perceptive critics have observed that Shakespeare only concedes Shylock the lowest common denominator of humanity; in fact, all the characteristics Shylock invokes in common with the Christians involve sensations of feeling or passion; they are animal instincts. Shylock says nothing about the ability to appreciate art or music, or about love and sacrifice. Yet only in the crudest and most philistine analysis does this make Shakespeare a racist. In fact, he articulates through Shylock the very basis of modern liberal society. A careful understanding of questions of ethnocentricity and difference, gained from passages like this, can be a powerful weapon against racism, provincialism, and ignorance.

It is the teaching of the classics that the cosmopolitan society is only possible when human beings acknowledge their differences and take them seriously. That is the first step toward genuine cultural exchange, toward authentic relations with the "other." Such differences do not disappear when academic pundits issue paeans to cultural diversity and tolerance; rather, they demand an intellectually and morally serious exploration of the kind of life to which various cultures call their citizens, and the highest values embodied in those cultures. The diversity project, at Stanford and elsewhere, does not seem courageous or open-minded enough to embark on this perilous, but thrilling and ultimately rewarding, intellectual enterprise.

* * *

Throughout the Stanford debate, the administration showed little actual concern with the education of students. President Donald Kennedy appeared indifferent to the outcome of the argument, hoping merely to divert the attention of university alumni. "His special focus was alumni donors," remarked a Stanford official. "He was scared to death that the donations would slow down."

Shortly after the CIV controversy, Stanford's news service director Bob Beyers resigned; in all his 28 years of service, he said, he never experienced such intense efforts by the Stanford administration to "adopt a corporate public relations model," to apply "internal pressure for bureaucratic image enhancement," and to "mandate publication of bowdlerized reports" and "suggest that editors stonewall legitimate news inquiries."[86] In short, Stanford was eager that full information not get out to the general public, especially to parents and alumni donors.

"Why do you think they thought of the name CIV?" asked Stanford history professor Lewis Spitz. "Don't you get it? All the old boys fondly remember their Western Civ courses. By calling the new program CIV, you give them the impression that nothing has changed around here. Of course that's a big lie, but that's what our administration is saying, and they have a good number of people fooled."

Perhaps the worst abdication in the Stanford case came from

the university faculty, who have placed ideological prejudice at the center of their curriculum, so that students are not only deprived of full exposure to the Western tradition, but they do not even get a genuine and comprehensive understanding of non-Western cultures. Their curricular diet now consists of little more than crude Western political slogans masquerading as the vanguard of Third World thought. Not only does the new multiculturalism deprive students of an opportunity for learning about themselves and others, but it distorts other cultures and peoples and makes future global understanding more difficult.

History professor Spitz said, "Even at Stanford, our incoming students are really quite philistine. The Western civilization requirement was, in a sense, remedial. It transmitted the very basics of our culture—nothing too esoteric, you know, did the Greeks come before the Romans, that sort of thing. But now we are opting for deliberate ignorance of ourselves, and an ideological approach to the study of other countries."

These influences are expanding beyond the reach of the CIV curriculum, into other courses and into the fabric of campus life. In late 1990, the university adopted a new required course for all entering freshmen, on American diversity, focusing on the works of blacks, hispanics, feminists, and homosexuals. In addition, Stanford sponsors residential education sessions intended to raise consciousness on race and gender issues, which former Stanford instructor Walter Lammi termed "an indoctrination program, which one of my students described as 'unrelenting water torture.'" It is not easy to go through Stanford without feeling these pressures, and ultimately they affect students' ability to learn.

In a recent editorial in the *Real News,* identified as "The African-American Journal at Stanford," editor Toni Long seemed to reflect the new sensibility cultivated by multicultural education as a preparation for American graduates to enter society. "It's about time black people stop being so forgiving. It's about time that we remember that 400 years hasn't been so long. It's about time that we stop apologizing for being hostile, emotional, and militant. It's about time we take sweeping actions to send a message to the racist oppressors that we are tired of your shit."[87]

No wonder that Stanford's new political indoctrination is generating qualms among serious observers who know what goes on in the classroom. In a moment of introspection, even Donald Kennedy speculated that recent events at Stanford "may have rekindled doubts among our friends as to whether we are a community dedicated to rational process and deserving of their respect."[88]

Many American universities are eagerly committed to a multicultural curriculum, but the case of Stanford is typical of the problems caused by the diversity activists' ideologically motivated interest in other cultures. Colleges would promote better understanding among students, and future respect among cultures, if they taught both Western and non-Western philosophy, history, and literature in a more balanced and truthful manner.

# 4

# In Search of Black Pharaohs
## The Roots of Protest at Howard

> An unjust law is a code that is out of harmony
> with the moral law. One has a moral
> responsibility to disobey unjust laws.
> — *Martin Luther King, Jr.*

Many Americans were surprised when in 1989 students at Howard University conducted a series of nonviolent protests culminating in the resignation of Republican party chairman Lee Atwater from the Howard board of trustees. The event, which captured the imagination of black students across the country, and received enormous press attention, is a landmark of contemporary black protest. Thus it provides a revealing comparison and contrast with the civil rights struggle of the 1960s, as well as an unusual look at the secret anguish and longing in the hearts of young blacks today. These concealed emotions are a crucial facet of the victim's revolution on the American campus.

Ostensibly concerned with the Atwater appointment, the Howard protest actually reveals much deeper concerns that students on a traditionally black campus have about the cultural status of blacks, especially black males, in America today. Despite the benefits of desegregation and legal equality, many young blacks feel socially delegitimized. Their life in the present is made difficult by the sense that they have no past from which to draw self-respect and dignity, and no future in which past and current inadequacies can be salvaged.

Thus young blacks are engaged in a search for cultural identity—

a geography and history and literature of which they can feel proud. Rail though they may against the "white male" perspective of the classics, black students require more than the relish of exposing Aristotle and Aquinas as racists. For all its alleged bigotry, Western civilization is a towering human accomplishment; those who reject it feel a powerful need to place themselves in another, equally resplendent, cultural lineage. In a brief but bold stroke in early 1989, Howard students attempted to break the pattern of hopelessness, to defeat the forces of injustice and repression, to discover a flourishing black culture in an unlikely venue, and to emerge from struggle with new prospects and possibilities.

* * *

On January 15, 1989, Lee Atwater, the chairman of the Republican National Committee, delivered an impassioned speech at the Ebenezer Baptist Church in Atlanta, Georgia. Speaking on the sixtieth anniversary of Martin Luther King's birthday, Atwater praised King as "a political meteor, who streaked across the night sky, and for far too short a time, lit up the horizon with a startling brilliance and intensity." Cheering Coretta Scott King, wife of the slain civil rights leader, Atwater said, "The real legacy of your husband's work is the action that it spawned— the action of nonviolence." Atwater celebrated Mrs. King's effort to recruit a one hundred thousand-member "army of nonviolent soldiers who will battle the evils of poverty, violence and racism." The King holiday was no mere national holiday, Atwater concluded, it was an "anniversary of action."[1] Little did Atwater realize that he was cheerleading for direct action that would soon cause him profound embarrassment.

Shortly after his appointment as GOP chairman, Atwater declared the party's goal for the next several years: "a redoubled political effort to reach out to those Americans who have not historically been part of our coalition."[2] Clearly, Atwater's program made political sense. Without minority votes, especially black votes, Republicans would have difficulty becoming a majority party and staying there, Atwater understood. Without black votes, the GOP would find it hard to recapture the Senate and virtually impossible to break the Democratic stranglehold on the House of Representatives.

It might seem odd for the GOP to entrust the project of minority recruitment to a political strategist habituated to using divisive and confrontational tactics to mobilize the slumbering "silent majority" in the South. Atwater, after all, was a South Carolina boy who first learned his strategy working for Dixiecrat segregationist, now Republican senator, Strom Thurmond. During the 1988 election Atwater helped to destroy Democratic candidate Michael Dukakis' electoral base in the South by exposing the Massachusetts governor's furlough program, exemplified by black convict Willie Horton, who used a weekend release to assault and rape a white woman in Maryland. Democratic leaders from vice presidential candidate Lloyd Bentsen to Jesse Jackson denounced the Horton ad campaign as racist.

But there is another side to Atwater—the chuckling, raunchy Southerner who has grown out of the stiffness of his plantation tradition; who once toured the South playing backup guitar for rhythm and blues groups such as the Coasters, the Drifters, and Percy Sledge; who visited singer James Brown in prison. The *New York Times Magazine* called Atwater "a political synthesis of Huck Finn and Machiavelli."[3] President Bush and GOP leaders hoped that Atwater's flamboyance would help to broaden the appeal of a party which has the image of being stuffy and restrictive.

During the 1988 campaign, Atwater implemented the Horton strategy so widely and effectively that, after the result, Washingtonians joked that the only national mandate that President-elect Bush now had was to reform the Massachusetts prison system. Once the election was over, however, the Republicans quickly forgot about Horton. Their adversaries did not. In an election postmortem, Dukakis campaign manager Susan Estrich, a professor at Harvard Law School, argued that "all other things being equal, there is nothing racist about being tough on crime, and there's no reason that calling one's opponent soft on crime should have racial overtones." But in fact "all other things are not equal in America." Willie Horton was "a black murderer who raped a white woman. There is no more powerful metaphor for racial hatred in this country than that." Thus, Estrich concluded, Atwater and Bush won the election through transparent appeals to racism.[4]

This is perhaps a self-serving conclusion. Whatever the historical symbolism, it is unfortunately the case that blacks are convicted of a disproportionate amount of violent crime in this country. The disparate causes do not alter the fact. Estrich conceded that blacks constitute approximately 12 percent of the American population, but nearly 50 percent of the prison population.[5] Willie Horton was not a mere metaphor; he was a real-life convict who brutalized an innocent family. If the Republicans wanted a good example of rehabilitation management gone awry, and of the human cost of social experimentation with criminal release, Horton was a pretty good choice. Estrich is right that to present the image of a black male assaulting a white woman is to engage visceral fears among whites, but this does not seem to be an argument for exonerating the criminal, or repressing criticism of the policy securing his release. While Estrich made much of the racial overtone of the criticism of Horton, no one raised the question of whether Horton's attack was racially motivated. Further, none of the GOP's commercials actually showed a picture of Horton; it was the media and the independent political action groups which stressed his skin color.

One might expect Atwater, in the face of all this, to strongly protest Estrich's line of reasoning. But apparently Republicans are better at winning political battles on the ground than at shaping the way the battle is viewed retrospectively. Atwater virtually apologized for the Horton episode. "I am sorry he was black," Atwater remarked. "Looking back, we should have used a white guy."[6] His critics have accused him of cynical accommodation—they say Atwater is content to make history, and surrender the history books; in practice the wily fellow knew exactly what he was doing. Whatever Atwater's motivation, he greatly underestimated the power of the postgame analysis to shape current and future events. He was to get a sharp lesson from students at Howard University.

* * *

It is not all that surprising that the appointment of a conservative Republican would cause a bit of political indigestion at Howard. As the university's first black president, Mordecai Wyatt Johnson, once put it, Howard is a "place with a mission."[7] Howard was founded in 1866 for the education of newly emancipated slaves; from its beginnings, it has stressed education as an instrument for the economic and social advancement of blacks. James Cheek, president of Howard from 1969 to 1989, called it "a battleground for blacks to confront ignorance, where truth grapples hand-to-hand with falsehood, where understanding comes face-to-face with confusion."[8]

The *Encyclopedia of Black America* credits Howard with producing a larger percentage of the nation's black professionals than any other college in the country.[9] As America's premier black university, its contemporary character has been decisively shaped by the civil rights movement, in which several Howard alumni served with distinction: Supreme Court Justice Thurgood Marshall, who argued the *Brown v. Board of Education* desegregation case; Vernon Jordan, past president of the National Urban League; Atlanta mayor Andrew Young; New York mayor David Dinkins; Virginia governor Douglas Wilder; Congressman Mike Espy; and Christopher Edley, director of the United Negro

College Fund. "Our image," boasts Howard associate dean Joseph Rier, "is one of a liberal, progressive institution, working to break down barriers for our people."

Howard students harbored many grievances in late February 1989, the time that university president James Cheek announced Lee Atwater's appointment to the board of trustees, but Atwater was "the straw that broke the camel's back," according to Alonza Robertson, managing editor of Howard's student newspaper, *The Hilltop*, for 1988–89. Ron Howard, a political science professor at the university, explained some of the incredulity he felt at learning of the appointment. "This is the guy who was responsible for the racism of the campaign, for the Willie Horton issue. It didn't seem appropriate to turn around and reward the guy who kicked us in the pants."[10] Richard Wright of the communications department found Atwater's nomination "divisive" and "insulting." Howard's campus newspaper reported that it was tragic to appoint a trustee who "supports apartheid,"[11] an apparent allusion to Atwater's opposition to divestment of U.S. funds from South Africa. Politics professor Joe McCormick argued that Cheek's desire to maintain Howard's ties with both political parties revealed his "Booker T. Washington syndrome"; he was an "accommodationist." This charge, in the black community, carries a suggestion of racial apostasy: collaboration with the "white establishment" may purchase short-term gains, but is achieved at the price of political solidarity.

With the assistance of junior faculty such as Ron Howard and Joe McCormick, student groups met to plan a protest. Four groups were involved: the Howard University Student Association (HUSA), the Progressive Student Movement, the campus NAACP, and a group called the Black Nia Force; *Nia*, members explain, is Swahili for "purpose," and theirs is a black consciousness group.

On Friday, March 3, 1989, the plans were in place. More than a hundred Howard students charged the stage during the university's convocation ceremonies. The protesters expected newly named trustee Atwater to be there, but he wasn't. The scheduled commencement speaker, entertainer Bill Cosby, was prevented from speaking by boisterous chants of "Just Say No to Atwater" and "How Far Will Howard Go for a Buck?" Far from being chagrined, Cosby told local media that he supported the students.[12]

Ironically Cosby was being honored by Howard for the same reason as Atwater. Neither is a Howard alumnus, but Cosby had recently directed a substantial portion of his Hollywood fortune to black university education, including a 1988 gift of $20 million to Spelman College.[13]

No doubt Howard hoped that he would include the nation's premier black institution in his future philanthropic plans. Like Atwater, in other words, Cosby was expected to help Howard secure its financial foundations.

Although Cosby himself presents the national image of an "accommodationist," portraying bourgeois virtues on his television show, this was not held against him at Howard. University administrators pointed out that Cosby is a role model; an entertainer who made it big, he commands the same respect as Michael Jackson or Diana Ross. "We are not here to protest Bill Cosby," shouted protest organizer April Silver of the Black Nia Force into the microphone, "but we have to make sure that you understand we are taking control of this."[14] Taking control was an important part of what this protest was about.

The motives behind the Howard protest are illustrated by the role played by a young undergraduate, Ras Baraka, who is the son of black activist and poet Amiri Baraka. Amiri Baraka (formerly LeRoi Jones) was militant in the heady antiwar and civil rights demonstrations of the sixties, but faded from public view shortly after. To some extent, Amiri Baraka joined the establishment he sought to destroy; in the early 1980s, for example, he received $12,500 in grants to write poetry from the National Endowment for the Arts.[15]

Young Ras has started out on a similar activist path, outlining his philosophy of black consciousness for the Howard campus paper.

> Historically the black man has been put in a position where he has been denied, suppressed, oppressed, and downright treated with no respect. He has first been enslaved. His religion taken and altered. His mathematics, science, etc. stolen and poisoned. The mother of civilization, he has been repudiated, disrespected, stepped on, and raped. The black man has been Jim Crowed, denied justice, and reduced to three-fifths of a man, the level of an animal. The world now under the white man's rule is decaying and on the way to death. The water is no good, the ozone layer is being destroyed, there are all kinds of diseases and wars. Sex has become outrageously misinterpreted, religion has been infiltrated, the mind has been infiltrated, and unless someone acts fast, the world is on the brink of destruction.

Ras Baraka saw the need for unified resistance. "Whether you are a separatist, integrationist, communist, socialist, Christian, Muslim or other, you must realize your potential and join together on the basis of dissatisfaction and take control."[16] The Atwater protest energized

Baraka's hopes. Ascending to the stage, he yelled, "We are here to oppose Lee Atwaterism."[17] There was thunderous applause from the crowd.

* * *

Young Baraka's alienation may resemble that of his father in the 1960s, but it was immediately apparent that the Howard protest was markedly different from the civil rights agitation of previous decades. While the students were controlling the stage, for instance, Howard officials were praising their idealism to the *Washington Post*. "I thought the revolution among our black youngsters was dead, but hallelujah," proclaimed Alyce Gullatee, director of Howard's drug abuse center.[18] Associate Dean Joseph Harris said, "The outpouring was fantastic. I think this is what the university is about."[19] Political science professor Lorenzo Morris said, "Here most of the faculty share the perspective of the students."[20] The oddity of the situation was that the students were using force to arouse not a recalcitrant but a supportive establishment. Far from being shocked and outraged, the faculty and administration, with the exception of the hapless President Cheek, sided with the rebels. What kind of confrontation was this?

The artificiality of the demonstration was largely lost on all involved, including the media. Atwater himself refused to criticize the protesters, noting simply that "it's incidents like this that strengthen my resolve to work hard to show my sincerity."[21] Taken seriously, this was an encouragement to protest—the more students take over the stage and denounce Atwater, the harder he works to realize their agenda.

Meanwhile, emotions on the convocation stage were infectious. "Our people will never be defeated," the students chanted, egged on by several professors and deans.[22] The *Washington Post* reported that "students drew down the American flag in the main courtyard and raised a red, black and green flag of African liberation."[23]

The convocation protest was only the beginning. On the following Monday, March 6, leaders of Howard student groups met to discuss follow-up strategy. They set up four committees to handle Security, Negotiation, Food, and Media. This was preparation for a takeover of the main administration building, a daring grab that took President Cheek by surprise. Cheek is a moderate Republican, with a history of civil rights activism. Probably the last thing he expected was to see his erstwhile tactics turned to his own disadvantage. Surrounded by excited students carrying overnight kits, backpacks, and duffel bags, Cheek and other administrators quietly left the building.

The protest lasted three days. The students submitted their "List of Demands" which included:

- An Afrocentric curriculum for Howard
- Academic credit for community service
- Elimination of a proposed 15 percent tuition increase
- More efficiency in financial aid processing
- Better security for dormitories
- Removal of Atwater from the board[24]

The administration promised to negotiate over most of the demands, but President Cheek said Atwater's appointment was not negotiable. Cheek did emphasize, however, that he was not to blame for Atwater. "Contrary to several reports, I did not nominate Atwater for election to the board."[25] Cheek pointed out that no one on the existing board of trustees had voted against Atwater, although there were three abstentions.[26] Throughout Cheek displayed a strange combination of vacillation and pugnacity; while disavowing responsibility for the Atwater appointment, he obtained a court order to evacuate the students.

The press also played a crucial role. Alonza Robertson, one of the protesters, remarked that "we were able to manipulate the media. We could literally dictate what the articles said the next day." Robertson pointed out that reporters, themselves often a product of the era of the 1960s, seemed just as excited as the Howard students over what was going on. Robertson reported that protest organizers were careful to stage scenes for media consumption. They allowed themselves to be photographed inside the occupied building, reading from the Bible and Koran. Some were actually seen studying, while the cameras flashed. Kindly donors and local businessmen supplied food, providing "human interest" sidebars for the press.[27]

Since the students presented themselves as an oppressed proletariat, they inspired solidarity from the Howard staff: food workers, janitors, campus policemen. Just when they were most needed, a number of Howard security officers took the opportunity to call in sick.[28] This so-called "sick out" occurred partly in sympathy with the students, partly because the officers decided that this was an opportune time to put in their own demands for a pay increase.

Not only were the students insistent on their demands, but as individual demands were met by the administration, the protesters kept adding new ones. This was consistent with Jerry Rubin's famous

instructions to activists in the 1960s: make demands that cannot be
fulfilled, refuse to yield, whenever a demand is addressed immediately
substitute another, equally impossible, demand in its place.[29] This ad-
vice, it appears, was followed by the Howard activists. Their new
demands included:

- No disciplinary action against the protesters
- No liability for students for destruction of property
- Students should review all new members of the board of trustees
  for their approval
- Howard must establish a graduate Afro-American studies
  department
- Howard must establish a separate department for "community
  service"
- The administration must renovate the dorms, on a schedule to
  be announced and published in the student newspaper
- Class withdrawal date should be extended to allow students to
  take the term off without penalty[30]

With the escalation of press coverage, President Cheek was becoming a national spectacle. Beginning his retreat, Cheek issued a
one-page statement on Wednesday, the third day of the occupation,
saying he would not punish any students if they evacuated the building
the next day. He followed this concession with a threat: "Any student
or other individual who persists in occupying any university building
or otherwise disrupts university operations will be arrested and/or
expelled."[31] Most students ignored this bureaucratic proclamation as
empty posturing. Instead of complying with Cheek's terms, they increased the temperature of their denunciations. They sensed that Cheek
was the one who was vulnerable. It was his job that was on the line.

National black leaders saw the evening news and decided to become
involved. The Congressional Black Caucus arranged a meeting with
the students. Marion Barry, then mayor of Washington, D.C., showed
up to announce to reporters, "I used to do this myself. If I were
them, I'd probably feel that way too."[32] Amiri Baraka surfaced, a virtual
ghost from the past. "I'm proud of my son and Howard should be
too. He's practicing all the things they were supposed to be teaching,
like self-respect and self-determination."[33] Jesse Jackson descended
on the protest, in a single breath denouncing Atwater and appointing
himself mediator and umpire of the standoff. Jackson praised April
Silver, one of the young organizers of the protest, as someone "in

the tradition of Rosa Parks,"[34] a reference to the intrepid woman whose refusal to move to the back of the bus in December 1955 propelled the Montgomery boycotts and ushered in the civil rights movement.

Atwater did have some support from the board, but it was rather feeble. Republican lawyer William Brown of Philadelphia said Atwater could bring benefits for Howard, and therefore student protest against him was "shortsighted. Kids tend to look at things in black and white and are sometimes impractical."[35] One student argued that his peers should not "discriminate" against Atwater because he was white.

These struggles, if viewed in Clausewitzian terms, represent a matching of strength and willpower on the two sides. Contrast the will of Lee Atwater with that of the students. "I'm not bitter," Atwater told the *New York Times*. "As long as I'm chairman, I'm going to continue to be involved in minority concerns.[36] One can sympathize with Atwater's plight; thinking, as he does, in terms of political strategy, this appeared to be a no-win situation. How could he engage the debate in a way that would improve his position at this point? The only possible response appeared to be a dignified retreat.

Meanwhile, the students pressed on. "Everybody, hands in your pockets and don't move no matter what they do," one student shouted. "We've got to remember Martin Luther King," yelled Deric Angeletti. "He's looking down on us right now."[37] Ras Baraka told the press the students would remain in the building "as long as it takes."[38] Michael Lewis, another student, announced that "we are prepared to hold the building as long as possible, physically and mentally, until our demands are met."[39]

\* \* \*

At the worst moment, when all the political ground had slipped out from under him, President Cheek decided to make a show of force. This action, however, derived from weakness, not strength. Already Cheek had agreed to most of the students' demands. Not once during the controversy did he state his principles or say why the students were not entitled to indulge in acts of civil disobedience, or why the force he now summoned was a reinforcement, not a substitution, for the cause of justice.

Hordes of police surrounded the administration building and prepared for a forcible entry. "When I saw the officers with the masks," recounted April Silver, "that's when I felt the intensity."[40] The police, far from stirring respect for law or even mundane fear, actually solidified the students' perception that they were part of a cause larger than themselves. Finally the establishment was revealing its evil colors. The appearance of the law was the ultimate legitimation of the principle of lawlessness.

Policemen were interrogated about what *they* did for the civil rights movement. The riot gear of the police and the hum of an airborne helicopter only added to the delirium. "The tears wouldn't come down," April Silver remembered. "It was like a fear I couldn't realize."[41]

The students, it turned out, had little to fear, because the foremost issue on the minds of Howard administrators, black politicians, and Atwater himself, was avoiding a forced evacuation. Mayor Barry said Atwater should resign "for the sake of peace."[42] President Cheek himself told police it was "too risky" to enter the building. "We could not risk anyone getting hurt."[43] Jesse Jackson called Atwater on the telephone, when Atwater had already lost his nerve, having watched yelling students confronting armed policemen on television. According to an Atwater aide, it was Jackson's call which settled the issue.

Atwater resigned from the Howard board, writing a lengthy "I am not a racist" apologia for the *Washington Post* a few days later.[44] No doubt Atwater's retreat was based on a commendable desire to avoid police occupation, and students getting hurt, but it was difficult to avoid the suspicion that he was conceding in principle to the protesters. Jubilant, the students declared that now that they had finished off Atwater, it was time to destroy what Ras Baraka called "Atwaterism."[45]

The students held a victory celebration. "You have to concede the power of the students," April Silver declared.[46] But if anyone suspected that the protesters would leave now, they were mistaken. New demands were added: an increased budget for financial aid, appointment of a student delegation to help pick trustees, Bill Cosby (a hero for siding with the protesters) for the board. Protesters prepared new signs and banners. "Atwater is finished, but the struggle is not. It's not over. Please boycott classes. We have not achieved all our goals yet."[47]

Many professors obligingly cancelled classes; some even postponed exams.

Howard's School of Social Work got into practical training, substituting strategy lessons for classes. By this time students from other black colleges were being bused into Howard, either to add to the protest fervor or simply to watch in admiration.[48] Jesse Jackson pressured President Cheek to sign a "covenant" with the students conceding virtually all their demands, then congratulated the protesters. "Howard, you won. Those around the country who act like Atwater will get the Atwater treatment. You have inspired the entire nation."[49]

Some students were still not fully satisfied. "It's not over yet," Felicia James said. "I want to see follow-through action."[50] Another student told the *Washington Post,* "Where the hell's my Pell Grant and my student loans?"[51] But Howard student council president Garfield Swaby said, "We left the table with everything we wanted."[52] April Silver condescended to President Cheek, reaching out to touch his hand as he silently left the final negotiation. "We thank you for your cooperation," Silver said. "We're glad things worked out the way they did."[53]

In fairly typical style, Cheek attempted to hide his humiliation and take credit for the outcome. In a letter to Howard alumni, he said, "What has occurred on Howard's campus is refreshing. We have demonstrated to the world that challenges can and will be accepted and met in a fashion that will continue to catapult our university into the 21st century." Further, "I am particularly proud of the academic and spiritual climate that pervades our campus. I say this because, in an era characterized by individual and collective self-aggrandizement, our students, staff and faculty have demonstrated admirable integrity and willingness to sacrifice for the common good."[54]

If evidence was needed of the futility, even fatuity, of this message, Cheek himself supplied it a few days later, when he resigned the presidency of Howard after twenty years of service.

\* \* \*

The Howard University protest is an important synecdoche for black protest in the contemporary era. It is surprising, therefore, to see what superficial analysis attended the event. Typical was columnist Carol Randolph of the *Washington Times,* who observed that "I had begun to think young people were becoming less idealistic," and was "pleasantly surprised to see Howard students passionately display concern over something other than money."[55]

But Howard students did not confine their protest to the idealistic issue of Lee Atwater's appointment. Their demands included calls for dormitory renovation, tuition reduction, postponement of academic deadlines, and financial aid processing. The Howard protesters repeatedly stressed the importance of these issues. "I had a flooding problem in my dorm," remarked Alonza Robertson. Lee Willis said, "There hasn't been heat in my room all winter." Football player Todd Meiklejohn complained of leaky pipes. Garry Willingham said when he turned on the shower "suddenly you get this burst of scalding water." Danielle Miller mentioned roaches.[56] Warren Nelson said he had waited in a registration line for thirteen hours. Karen Diamond said financial aid personnel were often rude and unhelpful.[57]

While Howard students seemed entirely justified in their complaints about living facilities, financial aid processing, and security, it is not obvious why Lee Atwater should have become the target for protest on these grounds. It would seem more sensible to protest against the existing board of trustees, rather than a person who had not yet taken office. But Howard students were uniformly outraged at the idea of attacking such distinguished civil rights leaders as trustee John Jacob, president of the National Urban League. Although they disliked President Cheek, they were clearly reluctant to organize demonstrations prior to Atwater's appointment. "It just didn't occur to us," Alonza Robertson said. Part of the reason, he acknowledged, was the problem of using strategies developed during the civil rights movement for a black-on-black protest. "That wouldn't work," said Robertson. The protesters seemed to have a clear sense of the moral ambiguity of such a protest.

Not only was Atwater innocent of these day-to-day problems at Howard, but he also promised to help address them. Presumably some of the money he would help attract to Howard could be applied to dorm renovation, and to alleviate the financial aid crunch. The main complaint about Atwater, in the words of senior Isaiah Turner, was that "he was telling us that black men are dangerous." Did Turner, then, identify with Willie Horton? Not at all, he said, "I wouldn't let the guy out of jail." On the other hand, "The worst thing you can say to the South is: this black man is going to rape your daughter." Atwater used Horton to foment precisely these Southern fears, Turner charged.

Atwater's initial claim that Horton's race was totally irrelevant is perhaps a bit much. The students' point that, even if anchored in the crime statistics, Atwater used Horton to play on fears of black crime is probably valid. The irony, however, is that one of the biggest complaints at Howard—if the campus newspaper's reports are any indication—is the crime rate in Washington, D.C., that is hurting Howard students. *The Hilltop* echoes this in issue after issue. The April 7, 1989, edition, for instance, coming right after the Atwater controversy, reported as its lead story: "Donald Hatch, the AIDS rapist who terrorized the Howard community in the fall of 1987, was sentenced last week."[58] It turns out that Hatch "raped and orally sodomized a Howard student after threatening her with a hypodermic needle which he claimed was contaminated with the AIDS virus." Hatch was black, but got no sympathy; rather, Howard students proclaimed the sentence "marvelous."[59] Alonza Robertson said that burglaries are common at Howard, especially during breaks when students go home, and the campus does not provide adequate security. "A couple of girls were raped here recently," Robertson said matter-of-factly.

In the Horton case, however, both the convict and his crimes were far from home base. Howard students tended to think of Horton as an *issue*, not as a dangerous con who sadistically attacked an innocent couple. The entire moral equation would be changed if Horton attacked a black family. Yet Howard protesters did not find it at all inconsistent that they would protest Atwater's political use of Horton while insisting that the administration bolster campus security to avoid further local burglary and rape.

There seems little question that Atwater was the wrong man in the wrong place. Howard students admit this: they often describe the Atwater appointment as the "last straw," implying that many grievances predated him. Even after Atwater resigned, the students continued to press demands, suggesting that he was only part of their agenda. Atwater's main problem was simply that he was a white man who came along just when black students were ready for an ambush. Atwater provided a plausible and convenient point of fixation for a whole host of complaints that had little or nothing to do with him. He also contributed a black-and-white backdrop to the protest, thus generating melodrama, and providing the media with a journalistic paradigm to give the protest moral meaning—it was no isolated phenomenon, but rather, the latest installment in the narrative of the civil rights revolution. The contemporary civil rights debate abounds with moral ambiguities and frustrations; Atwater helped Howard students and their media allies to repair to an earlier time, when things really were black and white. I asked several Howard students whether they would have protested in the same way had a black man, even a conservative, been named to the board. Uniformly, they said no.

\* \* \*

Howard trustee and trade consultant Thaddeus Garrett attempted to allay student fears during the protest by arguing that "this university needs money. The primary responsibility of a trustee is to raise money, and Atwater will do that."[60] Both Cheek and Atwater stressed the issue of his fund-raising prowess. But conversations with protesters show that this was precisely the wrong way to diffuse the tension—indeed it was a sure way to exacerbate it.

The reason is not obvious. Although technically a private university, Howard is largely dependent on the federal government. In fact, the university was officially incorporated in 1867 through an act of Congress. Of Howard's $254 million budget for fiscal year 1989, more than $175 million was appropriated by Congress.[61] In 1987–88, Howard tuition was $4,500, considerably below many area colleges, yet more than 60 percent of Howard students are on some form of financial aid.[62] How, then, could students refuse to embrace Lee Atwater? Why would they, instead, proclaim with Ras Baraka, "This is not a brothel. The president of our school does not have to stoop to get government money like this."[63] Other Howard students spoke in similar terms. "We're not going to be made whores." "How does Cheek think he can prostitute the mission of Howard?"

A little probing reveals much deeper concerns, on the part of Howard students, about the university's relationship with the federal government. These concerns are not easily articulated, because students realize their dependence on Congress. But with this dependence comes not gratitude but insecurity and resentment. "We're like children who depend on parents," said Alonza Robertson. "If you take your parents' money, you are going to have to listen to their orders."

Robertson said he would like to see Howard reduce its reliance on federal funds. "Personally, I think we need to tap alumni and corporate giants for funding." Booker T. Washington III, a Howard student involved in the protest, preferred to replace federal aid with reparation payments by whites. "Blacks built the foundations of this country. But where's our 40 acres and a mule?" Washington advocated measures for large-scale financial transfers from whites to black families descended from slavery. This, he said, was delayed reimbursement for wages historically denied.

When President Cheek boasted that he had raised federal appropriations to Howard by 400 percent, many Howard students were not pleased, instead they were embarrassed. When Atwater spoke about all he could do for Howard, "that's the wrong thing the guy said," in the words of Isaiah Turner, a graduating senior. "Howard's not for sale. We don't want your money." Turner rejected Atwater's role as a "great white knight." The great strategic blunder, then, was to make an explicit point of Atwater's ability to secure Howard's place at the federal trough.

Young blacks today want independence, moral as well as financial. They realize they might have to live with federal reliance, but they would rather it be kept quiet and out of sight. The enthusiasm of Atwater's defenders threatened to explode the illusion of some Howard students who want to remain on the federal take, yet at the same time serve as the independent conscience of the nation.

* * *

Some of the powerful psychological forces behind the Howard protest can be seen in the person a youthful and soft-spoken man whom several of the protesters cited as a role model. Political science professor Alvin Thornton conceded that the protest he helped organize was only tangentially concerned with Willie Horton. He expressed far greater alarm over Atwater's goal of recruiting blacks to the Republican party, especially blacks who tend to be better off economically—taxpayers instead of welfare recipients. "The last thing we need as a people is to have our most fortunate separated from our least fortunate," he said.

Thornton understands society largely in terms of class conflict; therefore he sees a problem of preventing blacks who join the bourgeoisie from adopting the class consciousness of landowners. Constant social pressure is needed to keep middle-class blacks thinking in proletarian terms, Thornton suggested. He does not seem hopeful about the task, but he sees it made more difficult by someone like Atwater trying to hasten black defection to the Republican party. For Thornton the GOP is simply the party of racism, whether the overt racism of old or what he calls the "sophisticated racism" of Lee Atwater and George Bush.

The real challenge facing the black community, Thornton candidly stated, is the lost identity of the black male. "For the forseeable future," Thornton said, "he will not have cars, money, or the material goods that give significance to his existence." As a consequence, his self-image is low. "We have to convince the black man that he is significant." Only then will he exercise social responsibility, Thornton added. Unfortunately, today's black male places responsibility on everyone except himself: "on cops, on social workers, on the woman in the household." Social programs that only emphasize women and children will fail, Thornton predicted.

Thornton believes in families—he spoke fondly of his own—but he is convinced that "a black nuclear family is doomed to fail in the inner city." Nuclear families may be the ideal, Thornton said, but they are a reality only in the black middle class. "In the ghetto the kids are all mixed up." Thornton speculated that we may have to turn to African traditions, based on polygamy, where people take care of children as children, not worrying about whose they really are. The children exist, they need love and care, therefore adults assume the responsibility.

But Thornton admitted that this vision is extremely difficult to sustain in practice, requiring, it seems, an even greater sense of social responsibility than the nuclear family, where our fundamental obligations are only to our own. Can the natural bonds between parent and children be artificially generated through a social ethos based on communal necessity? At this point, Thornton's eyes filled with tears.

Thornton, it turns out, was motivated to protest less by an aversion to Lee Atwater's unscrupulous campaign tactics, and more by serious concern over the dissolution of black identity, particularly that of the black male. Keeping Lee Atwater off the board, it need hardly be said, provides no remedy for that.

* * *

Articles in Howard student publications verify student fears about a separation of values between the black middle class and the ghetto. Yvonne Bonner, a senior liberal arts major, angrily denied that, as a middle-class black, she was abandoning the brothers and sisters in the slums.[64] Bonner asked: why weren't any of the candidates for the Howard student elections saying, "Guess what folks, I want to start a revolution"? She concluded: "We as direct products of middle-class African Americans can't stand the word 'revolution.' It's the ugly word that we can't relate to for fear of being called radical."

A second factor behind the protest is Howard's peculiar status as a "historically black" school. Barnard scholar Jacqueline Fleming, in a recent study of black colleges, raises the question of whether Howard, Fisk, Spelman, and the rest are "anachronisms in contemporary society," relics of segregation which have "outlived their usefulness."[65] Consequently there is pressure on students of black colleges like Howard to establish their relevance: perhaps one way to do this is through spectacular protest, just as in the halcyon days of the 1960s. This way students at the old segregated schools confirm that they have not lost their idealistic fervor or sense of mission.

Protest also has its psychological rewards. It returns blacks, even middle-class blacks, to a sense of collective identity. Elias Canetti speculated in *Crowds and Power* that all crowds long for "the moment when all who belong to the crowd get rid of their differences and feel equal."[66] All distinctions of family, property, and class are immediately abolished— in fact, crowds tend to revel in *destruction* of property because it is a reminder of those distinctions. The problem with the feeling of equality, however, is that it is only a feeling. When the crowd disperses, the old divisions and hierarchies return, this time with greater force, because after the delirious victory it is heartbreaking to go back to the old settled order.

Alonza Robertson recalled, "Students were amazed by the power they had when they came together. It's like someone who suddenly has a gun, and realizes what he can do with it." While the protest was going on, "It made us all feel like we were part of history." Undergraduate Booker Washington III said, "It gave me a sense that with unity we can get things done." Individually, Washington added, "I couldn't do a damn thing."

When the protest ended, the students confessed to a sense of disappointment and loss. "Students would really like to see this happen again," Robertson said. "We are ready and willing." It seems that, for these students, protest is a way of dissolving class and cultural differences and finding a common identity. Perhaps this is a good thing. An occasional big protest may be therapeutic, but it is impossible to avoid the confusion and anomie that seem to follow, when all the demands are met but none of the underlying problems are really addressed.

* * *

Anyone who spends time at Howard will soon discover that the dominant political and academic enterprise of the students and faculty is aimed at discovering a cultural past that blacks can be proud of. This impulse is extremely strong in America's black community, and was reflected by Jesse Jackson when he announced that he was changing the designation of blacks to "African Americans." To many this must have seemed an arbitrary change in the racial nomenclature—"onomastic restlessness," one Washington, D.C., pundit called it—but Jackson's name change was a response to the new search for cultural affirmation among black Americans. This drive is particularly intense on the part of the young, and it is the rage at Howard, at other black colleges, and among Afro-American societies and black groups on virtually every campus in the country.

Ever since slavery, blacks have attached a great deal of significance to how they are named. "After the coming of freedom, there were two points upon which all the people were agreed, and I find this was generally true throughout the South: that they must change their names, and that they must leave the old plantations for at least a few days or weeks in order that they might really feel sure they were free," wrote Booker T. Washington in his classic, *Up from Slavery*.[67] In her *Narrative and Book of Life,* Sojourner Truth remarked that "afterward I told the Lord I wanted another name, other than Sojourner, cause everyone else had two names."[68] The black scholar W. E. B. Du Bois argued in *The Seventh Son* that the letter *n* in Negro was always capitalized until slave owners started using the lowercase, in "recognition of our status as property"; later, Du Bois maintained, capitalization of Negro became a symbol of ethnic pride, and failure to use the uppercase was viewed as an insult.[69] In the 1960s, the term Negro lost its appeal and was replaced by the term "black."

Today the two names that appeal to many black Americans are "African American" and "people of color." The first evokes a link to a home continent as descriptions of European immigrants (Italian Americans, Polish Americans, Greek Americans) do. The second, from the Haitian *gens de couleur,* expresses the solidarity of American blacks with other oppressed people around the world. In the past few years, articles have surfaced in the mainstream press, noting the new mood of black Americans. The *Los Angeles Times* found a renaissance of interest among young blacks in African fashions: leather pendants of "Mother Africa," Kinte cloth caps and scarves, and natural hairstyles.[70] The *Washington Times* and the *New York Times* both noticed that black students today seem to have forgotten about Martin Luther King, extolling Malcolm X instead as the "voice of a new generation."[71] Black music, especially rap, appears obsessed with the fighting spirit and message of self-reliance that Malcolm X promoted in the 1960s.[72] By contrast with Martin Luther King, a homegrown American who formulated his rhetoric in classic American terms, invoking Jefferson and Lincoln, Malcolm X was a native of the Caribbean who rejected the Western tradition altogether, appealing to an African identity that was distinct.[73]

The academic outlet for the new black odyssey into the past is the Afrocentric curriculum. This was one of the central demands of the Howard protesters. Perhaps elsewhere it makes more sense, but not at Howard, whose catalog not only contains an Afrocentric curriculum, but basically is an Afrocentric curriculum. This emphasis is appropriate, since Howard is expected to produce some of the nation's most serious and comprehensive scholarship about Africa and black history.

Howard's Department of African Studies and Research lists sixty-five courses including: Algerian Arabic I and II, Zulu I and II, Amharic I and II, Zezeru/Shona, Kabyle, Hausa, Fula, Mende, Bassa, Yoruba, Ibo I and II, Wolof I and II, Lingala I and II, Swahili I and II, Tswana I and II, Xhosa I and II, and African language structure, plus seminars in semantics and linguistics. It is certainly possible for roots-minded blacks to study the major languages of Africa.

The same department has courses in Africa and the world economy, revolution and change in Africa, foreign policy making in African states, Islamic culture and philosophy, political organization of the African village, African social history, Islam and Christianity in African literature and film, educational systems in Africa, African political thought, and so on.

The African studies and research department should not be confused with the Afro-American Studies program, which lists twenty-five more courses, including black experience in education; black philosophy, religion and ritual; politics of black autobiography; black experience in the Caribbean; black women in America; the Harlem Renaissance; comparative black literature; pan-African thought and politics; black aesthetics; and contemporary black poetry.

Even the French department has a strong Afrocentric slant: there are courses on Franco-Caribbean civilization and literature; Franco-African civilization and literature; Caribbean literature in French; Haitian literature: novel; African literature in French: novel; African literature in French: poetry; Afro-French theater; women in African literature in French; Afro-French folklore; and Pan-Caribbean Literature.[74]

Frank Snowden, professor of classics at Howard, is puzzled by the fervent call for Afrocentric emphasis at Howard. "I don't know what it means," he confessed. "It's a fad." Snowden counted approximately one hundred courses that bear directly on the topic. He said, "It's hard to graduate from here without a strong exposure to the Afro-American experience."

But while some fads are frivolous, others reflect important changes in the culture. At Howard, the new passion for Afro-awareness is more than a passing fancy. Alonza Robertson, a lanky youth with a *Hilltop* T-shirt dropped over him like a tent, confirmed its deep significance for students. All over campus, Robertson noted, there are signs which say "African *in* America." They suggest the "emergence of racial pride" on campus, Robertson maintained. His newspaper often publishes articles on African dialect; a recent one erupted into Yoruba: "O rele kok dele, O roko ko do ko, O tun wa, toko, Oroko doko Orokota" with the explanation in parenthesis ("inability to attain a definite goal").[75]

"Everyone here is interested in Egyptology," Robertson said, "You know, how language and mathematics and medicine got started, and how the Greeks stole it. Everybody assumes the Greeks just thought of this, but someone had to teach them. Blacks did it. Blacks had the first university in Timbuktu, blacks built the pyramids, blacks invented the obelisk which Alexander the Great stole. The founding fathers of this country stole a lot of their ideas and symbols from the mystery schools of Egypt. Amazing, isn't it? The Washington monument is actually based on an African concept. And *Newsweek* recently came out with something on how Adam and Eve were really dark skinned. Blacks can really get into that."

Robertson expressed a widely held sentiment at Howard when he said, "We feel that Africans did great things in the past. It's a contrast with what this society says about blacks. History teaches us that we can be great again." He paused. "We're not just ignorant savages in the jungle, which is the idea you get. We have culture too."

The same theme resounded at the Howard Student Association. "If you don't know where you come from, how can you get anywhere?" Booker Washington III asked. He is very dark, and holds that as a badge of honor; even his T-shirt advertises himself as a "Black Beauty." Washington's notion that the past provides the foundation for identity in the present, and progress in the future, is profoundly conservative. But despite his name, Washington refuses to locate his past in this country; to him, it cannot be a Western past. "Western civilization leaves us out," he said. "When they founded American society, they didn't have us in mind. We were property. It's *their* independence, *their* Declaration. We're not three-fifths of human beings."

But the Howard protest itself seemed distinctively Western, anchored in principles of civil disobedience that Martin Luther King appealed to, but that went further back, via Thoreau, to Thomistic and Aristotelian treatises on just and unjust law.

This suggestion particularly irritated Robert Turner, vice president of the Howard student association. "Oh no," Turner said. "Our protest was a pragmatic thing." It was simply a mechanism for achieving the desired result. "If we knew the method that traditional Africans used, we'd go that way."

"The African tradition is very spiritual, less oriented toward conquest," Turner said. Booker Washington added, "African thought is not individualistic." Perhaps here was a clue to his reasons for believing that individual achievement outside the group was impossible; collective solutions were the only feasible and legitimate ones. "Our biggest problem as Africans is losing our identity," Washington said. "It's very hard to get that back."

The other Turner, Isaiah, broke in. "You know," he said, "people are always calling blacks angry. They say, look at what blacks have, nice cars, nice clothes, so why are they so angry? Our culture does not come from the racist Greeks. Our ancestors were Africans. Yet we were brought here in chains, against our will. If someone takes you away from paradise, you can never get back."

* * *

Howard classics professor Frank Snowden pointed out that there was a tendency to label the ancient Greeks and Romans as racists because they are considered the founders of Western civilization, and the West practiced racism. But this is what Snowden, in his book *Blacks and Antiquity,* calls "the error of attributing to the past racial attitudes and concepts which derive from certain modern views regarding the Negro."[76] Snowden's study, combining archeological, historical, and literary evidence, shows the extent of African (primarily Ethiopian) influence on classical civilization, from Homer to the early Christians. This influence was real, Snowden argues, and yet quite limited. Egyptian influence was considerable, but Egypt is a Middle Eastern, not an African, culture. Snowden also demonstrates, contrary to popular prejudice, that Greco-Roman culture did not practice racial discrimination and had no concept of it.

The opinions expressed by ancient writers bear this out. The first blacks to appear in Greek literature, Snowden wrote, were "Homer's blameless Ethiopians." They were portrayed as "dear to the gods and renowned for their piety and justice." Seneca praised the independence of the African spirit. When Cambyses threatened to conquer and enslave the Ethiopians, Seneca wrote, "instead of embracing servitude with outstretched arms, they sent envoys and made reply in the independent words which kings call insults."[77] Although the Greeks took slaves and drew sharp distinctions between Greek and barbarian, Isocrates pointed out that this differentiation was not racial, it was cultural.[78] Snowden quoted an impressive array of authorities to show that "color antipathy, considered by itself, formed no bar to social intercourse in antiquity," that "the ancients were quite free from the antipathy of the color bar," that they "showed no trace of color prejudice," that Greek society "had no color line," that they "did not fall into the error of biological racism," that "men were classified not as black or white but as free or servile," and that racial prejudice is in fact a "modern curse."[79]

Unlike many moderns, the ancients had no racially based doctrine of beauty, in which fair skin was intrinsically preferable to dark skin.

Sextus Empiricus noted that although men agree on the existence of beauty, they disagree on what constitutes beauty—Persians prefer white skin, Ethiopians dark skin, and most other people (including Sextus) some intermediate shade. Herodotus was emphatic in his belief that Ethiopians were the most handsome people on earth. Martial said that although he was being pursued by a woman whiter than a swan, he preferred a girl blacker than a jackdaw. Although satirists frequently made jokes about interracial marriage, especially concerning offspring, Snowden argued that ancient Greece and Rome were "societies which had no prohibition against miscegenation."[80]

Snowden advocated further research into the question of African influence on ancient Greece. But he said he could not understand the current undiscriminating hostility toward the origins of Western civilization. "We can't get around the fact that the Western tradition is central to human development," he said. He claimed that blacks should appreciate how hospitable the ancient Greeks and Romans were to principles of universalism, to differentiation based not on accidental features but on intellectual and moral criteria, what Martin Luther King would later call "the content of their character."

All over the country, there is a new black scholarship, which seeks to establish the greatness of Africa based on an appropriation of the achievements of Egyptian civilization which is held to have taught the ancient Greeks and Romans most of what they knew.[81] This amazingly popular notion is promoted by speakers on the lecture circuit, on talk shows, and in books and pamphlets circulated among black organizations; it is now virtually part of the conventional wisdom among blacks on the American campus. "Black students are flocking to these ideas. What can we do about it?" Professor Snowden said.

The most prominent work of the genre is Cornell professor Martin Bernal's *Black Athena: The Afroasiatic Roots of Classical Civilization.* "The political purpose of *Black Athena*," the author announces at the outset, "is to lessen European cultural arrogance." Bernal goes on to argue that Egyptian civilization was "fundamentally African. . . . I am convinced that many of the most powerful Egyptian dynasties . . . were made up of pharaohs whom one can usefully call black."[82]

Although scholars are agreed that there is little reliable evidence for many of Bernal's claims,[83] which rest a good deal on ancient Greek and Egyptian myths, Bernal attacks "the argument from silence" whereby "if something has not been found, it cannot have existed in significant quantities,"[84] and he goes on to suggest, again on the basis of myths and stories, that therefore it *did* happen. Possibilities metamorphose into probabilities, and probabilities into certainties.

Reviewing *Black Athena* in the *New York Review of Books,* Oxford classicist Jasper Griffin tried to be positive, but could barely conceal his chagrin. What does it mean to say that cultures can be "usefully called black," Griffin wondered. "Bernal is anxious that his Egyptians shall be, as far as possible, not just in Africa but actually black Africans."[85] Bernal claims that Athens and Athena derive from the Egyptian goddess Nt or Neit; he makes many such word connections between Middle Eastern and Greek concepts. Griffin warned that "Etymologies are not simply a matter of finding a resemblance between one word and another." Nevertheless, aware of Bernal's mounting popularity and the moral significance ascribed to his project, Griffin described Bernal's book as sympathetically as possible.

Bernal is, in fact, no classicist but an expert on modern Chinese politics who has made an amateur foray into new territory. It is easy to dismiss his scholarship as shoddy, but his importance lies in the attention and wide distribution being given his work which, as Griffin hinted, seems to be a response not to academic but to political consider-ations. For instance, at a recent conference to discuss African and Afro-American scholarship, Joseph Baldwin, who teaches psychology at Florida A. & M. University, expressed anger about reports that fault the black family for illegitimacy. If black families were judged by white standards, he argued, they may be found deficient. But because "black people had families before they came to America," black families were more appropriately analyzed by comparison with African families, which would show them in a much better light.[86] Molefi Kete Asante, head of Afro-American Studies at Temple University and a major propo-nent of Afrocentricity, argued that "the problem is that we have been divorced from the African continent psychologically and culturally and, in a real sense, our souls have been stolen."[87] The objective of Afrocen-tric study, in this analysis, appears to be a recovery of soul, supported by a special view of history.

Professor Snowden of Howard mentioned another popular text, *Black Women in Antiquity,* which claims that Cleopatra was a black woman, in fact an "African queen."[88] The author of one essay in this book, John Clark, maintains that Cleopatra was always considered a Negro "until the emergence of white supremacy." Among the items of proof: in Shakespeare, Cleopatra is described as "tawny." Clark also cites Ripley's *Believe It Or Not.* Clark locates Cleopatra in the *Book of Acts,* although Snowden said that he had the reference wrong. Finally Clark cites a picture of Cleopatra drawn by a modern black artist, Earl Sweeney. Snowden shook his head in disbelief. Cleopatra was not a black woman, he said. "In fact, she was not even an Egyptian."

Cleopatra was descended from Ptolemy of Macedon, a region north of Greece. Snowden said that other recent literature he has come across maintains that Hannibal was a Negro. Not so, Snowden said, he was from the Mediterranean; there is no evidence that Hannibal had an African lineage. Historians are agreed on this point.

What seems particularly odd about the black choice of Egypt as a founding civilization is that the Egyptians themselves were avid practitioners of the slave trade. In Egypt, "Negro slaves were far more numerous than in the Roman Empire," David Brion Davis writes in his Pulitzer prize-winning study, *The Problem of Slavery in Western Culture*. The political attempt to credit Greco-Roman ideas to the Egyptians is thus decidedly bizarre. Davis argues, "Moslems not only accepted the legitimacy of Negro enslavement, but were inclined to think of black Africans as a docile race who were born to be slaves. The Arabic word for slaves, *abid*, was increasingly confined to the negro." In 1498, Davis reports, a virtual race riot broke out in Cairo because of an interracial marriage involving one of the chiefs of the sultan.[89]

According to historian Murray Gordon, in a recently published study on slavery in the Arab world, the Arab countries began their importation of slaves into what is now the Middle East approximately 1,000 years before the European slave trade began. Moreover, slavery persisted in the Arab countries much longer; Saudi Arabia, for instance, only formally abolished it in the early 1960s, and reports of the practice still occur in some of the nomadic Arab tribes, where boys are said to sell for $240, girls for $160. Of the eleven million blacks sold into Arab slavery, Gordon notes, "little has been written about this human tragedy."[90]

Snowden said that the purpose of all the ersatz scholarship "is to develop black pride." Black pride, he conceded, needs a boost. "But how can you build black pride on lies and distortions? Black people have suffered enough lies. What we need is truth."

\* \* \*

Recently the *Washington Post* reported on an exhibit of the Pharaoh Ramses II, sponsored by the Egyptian government on the Texas State Fairgrounds.[91] Infected with the new African scholarship, which has spread outside the academy into black culture, a black group in Dallas announced a boycott of the exhibit unless it was acknowledged that Ramses II was, in fact, a Negro. "We are tired of people using our culture and our history to make money off us," remarked Dallas Jackson, one of the protest organizers.

Abdel-Latif Aboul-Ela, Egypt's cultural emissary to the United States, was clearly embarrassed. "I wish people would not involve us in this kind of mess which we have nothing to do with," he said. "They should not use us, involve us in this racial problem. . . . We are not in any way related to the original black Africans of the Deep South." Aboul-Ela noted that there is an enormous difference between saying that Egypt is geographically located in the continent of Africa, and saying that Egypt had a Negro civilization. "Ours is an Egyptian heritage and Egyptian civilization 100 percent. We cannot say by any means that we are black or white. We are Egyptian, with our culture and traditions and religions."

Historians generally agree with Aboul-Ela that Egypt, although geographically located on the African continent, developed a distinctly Egyptian civilization. This civilization was influenced by immigration patterns from the European north and from southern Africa, although there is no question that most of the philosophical and scientific cross-fertilization occurred with the northern countries. Nevertheless, argues Frank Yurco, an Egyptologist at the University of Chicago,

> Whenever a non-Egyptian group moved into Egypt, they were accepted. New groups became Egyptianized. When you talk about Egypt, it's just not right to talk about black or white. That's all just American terminology and it serves American purposes. I can understand and sympathize with the desires of Afro-Americans to affiliate themselves with Egypt. But to take the terminology here in the United States and graft it onto Africa is anthropologically inaccurate.[92]

More than seven hundred thousand visitors attended the Dallas exhibit, organized by the Museum of Natural History Association, but no one raised these well-accepted facts, or criticized the substantive claims of the protesters. Apparently in some quarters black protest is regarded as therapeutic. When the vapors subside everybody can get back to business. This reaction seems not a little condescending toward black grievance; in fact, it merely glosses over real problems that will not go away, but keep surfacing again and again, each time with greater intensity.

Perhaps it is important to address the longing of American blacks for a lineage of which they can be proud, even if this means subscribing to historical distortions. Marcus Garvey himself proposed this strategy. "There is good ground to say that civilization started in Africa. . . . Search the Bible and find facts that will support this argument but hold to it with a grip that will never loosen. Things that may not be true can be made true if you repeat them long and often enough. Therefore always repeat statements that will give your race status and advantage."[93]

There are many valid arguments against subscribing to the salutary "noble lie," but one is decisive. Even if it were deemed necessary for blacks to adopt a mythic view of their past, elaborating such a myth should not be the task of the university. It is rather politicians and theologians who may be expected to comfort and inspire the people in this way. The university cannot engage in such an undertaking without repudiating its fundamental purpose: the disinterested pursuit of truth. The university is not responsible for the preservation of political and psychic order. Often its mission is to disturb the peace, or arouse the conscience. No one who supports the university can live with noble lies, however benignly intended.

Nor should black Americans who care about the problems of African development knowingly promulgate lies and inventions about the continent, its history, and its culture. However detached they may be from modern Africa, they maintain ancestral ties with it, and should not collaborate in a campaign which is destructive to African interests. Africa has its own identity, which is crying out for understanding. Development in Africa is contingent upon knowledge of Africa as she really is.

Blacks in the university seem to have undertaken a kind of intellectual "Back to Africa" effort, as a replacement for previous efforts in this area which did not succeed. Practical experiments of the "Back to Africa" movement, popularized by Marcus Garvey and his United Negro Improvement Association, were largely failures—some blacks did return to Africa, only to discover that there was little there to sustain them; for better or worse, they belonged in America.[94] Contemporary Back-to-Africa proposals, such as the one advocated by Louis Farrakhan, seem no less quixotic.[95] As a substitute for any real return to Africa, which involves unpleasant confrontations with African reality, we seem to be witnessing an effort to establish "Africa in America," or more precisely a fictionalized Africa catering to the domestic concerns of American blacks.

Contrary to the claim of Howard student Isaiah Turner, African culture was never "paradise," and probably never will be. Paradise is not exactly a place; the title of Thomas More's *Utopia*, which means "nowhere," implies that the utopian is intrinsically opposed to the practical or realizable. Paradise has been variously located at the beginning of time and at the end of history. Turner's remark is not surprising; the search for paradise has motivated much of our striving for perfection and progress, and on a spiritual level such ideals may be useful and invigorating. But it makes little sense to raid the Library of Congress to discover an African paradise that actually existed. On the surface Africa may suggest idyllic primitivism—itself an old Western myth[96]— but authentic African virtues such as spiritual depth and freedom from materialism must be balanced against human sacrifice, tribal warfare, executions, female circumcision, infanticide, and primitive medicine.

James Baldwin wrote in *The Fire Next Time*, "The Negro has been formed by this nation, for better or worse, and does not belong to any other—not to Africa, and certainly not to Islam."[97] It is in their American identity, Baldwin suggests, that blacks must discover a legitimate basis for ethnic pride. Richard Wright, a Howard communications professor who opposed the Atwater appointment, agreed. "Ultimately we must teach our young people to find their identity in the American experiment. I cannot support this enterprise of looking elsewhere for political reasons—elsewhere turns out to be nowhere. We cannot create this psychic reality and go live in it. I understand it: it's an attempt to take a break from the ugliness of the present. But we've got to learn to face today's realities. It's less important to say: once we were something. It's more important to say: what are our current needs? What our youngsters need is not so much pride in the past, as hope in the present."

As Wright suggests, a scholarly attempt to rediscover Africa, or relocate Egyptian civilization, is of little importance in achieving the contemporary goals that black Americans seek. The civil rights movement wants better access for blacks into the corporate boardroom; wants government contracts in defense and technology increasingly awarded to minority firms; wants more blacks elected and appointed to administer the complex workings of modern American society. Can this agenda possibly be squared with a separatist cultural movement that calls for a "return to African roots," even if it is only an intellectual and not an actual return? Gaining a stronger position in a technologically sophisticated market, as well as political control in a complex society, inevitably means coming to terms with capitalism and democracy, two distinctively Western institutions.

\* \* \*

The dust has now settled at Howard University. What should we make of the protest, in retrospect? While it was certainly a victory, in fact it did little or nothing to address what people at the nation's leading black institution are really concerned about. The university administration showed little leadership in confronting the real questions. Not even the issue of civil disobedience was debated at Howard; it was taken for granted. As Dean John Rier said, "It was a legitimate protest. Our constitution guarantees the right to civil disobedience, doesn't it? It's got to be in there somewhere." There was no mention of Abraham Lincoln's Springfield Lyceum speech—"There is no grievance that is a fit object of redress by mob law"—and no mention of Thoreau. At the very least, an opportunity for learning was lost.

Martin Luther King, Jr., argued that civil disobedience is not an end in itself, but a "means to awaken a sense of moral shame in the opponent. The end is redemption and reconciliation. The aftermath of civil disobedience is the creation of the beloved community."[98] The Howard protest had no such effect; indeed, judged against King's exacting standard, it takes on a hint of parody. The Howard activists converted nobody, since there was no one to convert. After the takeovers ended, the black community remained as troubled and fragmented as ever. Divisions may have been camouflaged, but they were not healed.

Since the administration sympathized with most of the student demands, the obvious question is why they didn't go directly to the deans. Conversation ought to be the preferred mode of raising serious issues and getting them addressed. The usual answer is that the administration, though basically supportive, can be "insensitive." If so, the Howard protest can be understood not as a confrontation with a fundamentally hostile regime, but as a kind of collective tantrum aimed at getting attention. A child is aware of the natural affinity of his parents for his needs, but every now and then he feels the urge to hurl a book through a window, or smash a plate. That is what the Howard students did, and understood themselves as doing, and that is what the faculty and administration understood them to have done. The protest cannot be equated with the heroic and difficult struggle for basic civil rights in the 1950s and 1960s.

One ironic footnote to the Howard controversy is that, if the protesters are right in their claims about the Greeks stealing their ideas from the Africans, their argument provides a strong justification for all students studying the Greek classics on the grounds that Plato and Aristotle do not reflect an exclusive white male perspective but rather ideas which originated in Africa or, to put it even more fashionably, the Third World. On this premise, Stanford and other colleges can now, in a single course on Greek philosophy or literature, satisfy both a Western and a non-Western requirement.

Howard now has a new president, Franklyn Jenifer, who has pledged to make fund-raising his top priority.[99] For the foreseeable future, however, like other historically black colleges, Howard will continue despite its financial crunch to attract intelligent and idealistic students such as Isaiah and Robert Turner, Booker Washington, and Alonza Robertson. These students are searching for principles of truth and justice on which to base their lives. Their quest for self-understanding, both individually and as a people, is a legitimate one. What they need from the university is not coddling and illusion, but intellectual and moral leadership to prepare them for the challenges they must face as adults. The best such leadership is by precept integrated with example, and it is here that the Howard administration has failed its students.

# 5
# The New Censorship
## Racial Incidents at Michigan

Arguments are extremely vulgar, for
everybody in good society holds exactly the
same opinions.

— *Oscar Wilde*

On February 4, 1987, undergraduate Ted Sevransky, hosting his talk show on the University of Michigan radio station WCBN, asked listeners to call up with their favorite racial jokes. Several did. Black students at Michigan were stunned by this open and callous display of racial insensitivity. They protested bitterly to the administration and to the radio station. Sevransky immediately retracted his comments and apologized. "The station should not take the responsibility for what I alone did," he said. He acknowledged "bad judgment and poor taste." He said if he had contributed to racism on campus, he would do everything he could "to fight racism with all the means at [his] disposal."[1]

But the matter did not end there. Black activists pointed out that this was no isolated incident. In January of that year a flier declaring "open hunting season" on "porch monkeys" was slipped into a lounge at the university where black women were meeting.[2] This, together with the radio station incident, tapped into a deep wellspring of isolation and frustration that was now unleashed. "I know that I'm not wanted here," undergraduate Heather Robinson told the *Chicago Tribune*.[3] Student Jason Dotson said, "You can feel the intensity in the classroom. You can see it in the teacher's eyes. You see it in the students' faces. You're always under scrutiny. People who basically hold your future in their hands don't want you here."[4] Junior Kourtney Thompson remarked that white students are "shocked when I say something intelligent or meaningful. It's as if they're saying: what are you doing knowing that?"[5] Walter Allen, then a sociology professor at Michigan, told the *New York Times*, "There is a consistent pattern of students feeling alienated and unwelcome. The experiences range from unkind words to physical assaults."[6]

Although administrators threatened firm penalties, the incidents continued. In early 1988, Michael Wilson, an undergraduate at Michigan, walked into his French class and found a poster on the blackboard which said: "Support the K.K.K. College Fund. A mind is a terrible thing to waste—especially on a nigger."[7] That March, a university official received a flier containing a poem written in black dialect, titled "If Duh Dean Don't 'Pologize." A copy was sent to the campus affirmative action office.[8] In early April 1989 posters announcing "White Pride Week" were tacked up on various kiosks around campus, and on doors of the Center for Afro-American and African Studies. They called for a celebration of "yachts, sailboats, navy blazers, cool white presidents, all the kids we know are our own, polo stuff, L. L. Bean, Land's End and plantations."[9]

Since the mid-1980s, many other campuses have experienced similar incidents.[10] The National Institute Against Prejudice and Violence, based in Baltimore, Maryland, has tabulated more than 250 such incidents at more than two hundred colleges over the past five years. The Center for Democratic Renewal, a monitoring group in Atlanta, Georgia, reported that such incidents have increased fourfold since 1985.[11] This research is not systematic, yet there is enough of a record for alarm, and more evidence seems to pile up every month. After reporting on case after case of racial intolerance, the *Washington Post* editorialized, "The college campus, which a quarter of a century ago became the spawning ground of civil rights activism, now seems to be breeding a new and especially distasteful racism."[12]

* * *

American campuses have seen an apparent explosion of bigotry in the past few years, to the consternation of university officials and the national media. Just when the nation appeared to be reconciled to the changes of the civil rights movement, these incidents erupted in quick succession. Perhaps most disheartening, they seemed to indicate a repudiation by the younger generation of a massive social project that the nation has undertaken for more than two decades.

The conventional explanation for these racial outbursts has hardly been satisfactory. "Many white students are part of a generation that has no personal memory of the bloodiest struggles of the civil rights movement," the *New York Times* suggested.[13] Reginald Wilson of the minority concerns office of the American Council on Education argued that young people have not learned from their parents and teachers the progressive lessons of the 1960s. "We can place a great deal of fault with educational institutions for not educating students about the history of the country up to the time they were born," Wilson stated. "That would have given them some sensitivity to what preceded them. They could see the difficulties of overcoming racial barriers and the need for programs to rectify the problems of the past."[14] A *Washington Post* editorial asserted that this ignorance and prejudice was encouraged by a Republican president. "Ronald Reagan may not be to blame for these specific incidents, but he cannot escape responsibility for the climate he has done so much to create."[15]

Many commentators, both on and off the campus, seem to feel that racism is a sort of cultural constant with white people. Either it manifests itself openly and unashamedly, Bull Connor style, or it burrows beneath the surface, revealing itself in more subtle ways. Only through rigorous consciousness-raising and programmatic remedies such as preferential treatment for minorities can society overcome its natural instincts and fight bigotry; even then, racism remains latent, ever ready to spring to the surface. Any resurgence of racism, therefore, must reflect a relaxation of the strict moral and societal curbs that alone inhibit the visceral bigotry of white Americans.

If this analysis were correct, it would follow that racial incidents would erupt most frequently in the Deep South, where racism had its ancestral home, and expressed itself most openly and brutally. The forced integration of the University of Mississippi and other Southern schools is not so far in the past, and it would not be surprising if many young Southerners rankled at having to study and eat and live with blacks.

The anomaly of racial incidents on the campus, however, is that they occur predominantly and even overwhelmingly at Northern universities.[16] The majority of such incidents have taken place in the Northeast,[17] not exactly Reagan country. The state with the largest number of incidents is Massachusetts.[18] According to Professor Walter Massey of the University of Chicago, "It is ironic, to say the least, that institutions at which racial attitudes are most liberal, according to survey results, are the very places where racial conflict is increasing."[19] Joseph Duffey, chancellor of the University of Massachusetts at Amherst, reacted to one incident by saying, "People here pride themselves on being liberals. They think things like this only happen in Forsyth, Georgia."[20] Responding to racial incidents at the University of Michigan, freshman Brian Sterling told the *New York Times,* "I think of these things happening in the South, not in Ann Arbor. But if they're doing it here, it has to be worse at other places."[21]

Not so. While some Southern schools, notably the South Carolina military academy, The Citadel, have experienced racial tension, the pattern is far less pronounced than on the liberal East Coast. Out of one hundred racial incidents classified by region, only seven occurred in the South.[22] After initially resisting integration, Southern colleges appear to have absorbed minority students relatively well. Forrest Woods, who teaches philosophy at Southern Mississippi University in Hattiesburg, explained that "the South has always had closer personal relationships between whites and blacks. With the institutional changes that came after the civil rights movement, the South has made adjustments. There's a feeling that the issue has been fought and is now behind us."

Whatever the cause, blacks are the heroes on the sports teams and leaders in many student organizations at the University of Alabama; Mississippi State University, which did not start admitting blacks until 1965, elected the school's first black student body president and black vice president in March 1989.[23] The University of Mississippi's Interfraternity Council raised $20,000 to renovate a new residence for the black fraternity on campus whose house was vandalized.[24] At Wake Forest University in North Carolina, Kappa Alpha fraternity volunteered to stop using the Confederate flag as a house symbol.[25] The current hypothesis about race relations on campus offers no good explanation for these striking displays of open-mindedness on southern campuses.

Nor does it explain why, as student attitudes on race have grown more progressive, upsurges of racial hostility appear to be increasing in frequency.[26] In the 1940s, for instance, Gallup data show that a majority of Americans supported segregation, considered whites superior to blacks, and even held that whites should have the first chance at good jobs.[27] By 1980, 88 percent of whites supported full integration of schools, 80 percent considered whites and blacks equal in intellectual and other faculties, and nearly 100 percent believed in equal opportunity in the job market.[28] Even on issues affecting their personal and private lives, such as living in the same neighborhood with blacks, having blacks over to dinner, or intermarriage, white attitudes have liberalized enormously over the past few decades.[29] These views have become *more* liberal since 1980; despite the supposed decay of progressive values in Reagan's America, the retrenchment or backlash feared by many civil rights activists has not materialized.[30] Further, young people consistently hold more tolerant views than their elders on these issues, and this is true of the 1980s as well as earlier decades.[31]

These data, whose reliability is accepted by all sides of the debate, have befuddled many polemicists, who have not found it easy to explain why, if racism were to blame for most or all minority problems, these problems endure and even worsen as white bigotry abates. "Many silly reasons are given, as is usual in cases when a single good one is not to be found," as Abraham Lincoln once said in an 1843 campaign speech. The real causes of racial tension and racial incidents on campus are not hard to discover, for those who are willing to look. Even the universities have searched everywhere except at the root of the problem. Many undergraduates, however, know exactly what is going on; this is one area where the administration would do well to listen to, and learn from, its students.

* * *

At the University of Michigan Student Union, senior and anthropology major David Makled was sipping coffee and reading the local newspaper. He did not mind being interrupted, however, and agreed to discuss his views about race, a subject he said he had been thinking about a good deal recently. Makled described his politics as "moderate," somewhat conservative on economic questions, rather liberal on social questions.

Blacks, Makled said, are the most talked about subject at the university. People talk about "minorities," Makled said, but "everybody knows that the term minorities means blacks." Raised in a household habituated to talking about discrimination—Makled's father is Palestinian—"racism goes against a very basic and religious sense that we have," he said. But most white students like himself don't think about blacks as victims of ongoing racism. "To many people, the racial incidents seem like hype, you know, crybaby stuff."

"We didn't grow up in a situation where blacks were legally persecuted," Makled said. In fact, "a lot of people take great pains to show they are not racist." All around him, Makled remarked, blacks are treated with almost excessive deference. "In admissions, blacks are anything but disadvantaged. They are advantaged." Makled is not impressed by reports that tests of aptitude and intellectual competence are racially biased. Most whites assent to such reports, he said, "because they don't want to be racist. You always have to defend yourself.

The worst thing to be today is a racist. I always find myself saying: I am not a racist, but . . ."

While not opposed in principle to affirmative action, Makled maintained that "in its most blatant form, it is a form of racism." He said it was a product of the Black Power movement, which he contrasted with Martin Luther King's movement for equal rights and integration. "King is a hero as far as I am concerned," Makled said. "Most people in their hearts believe that everyone should have an equal chance." King's crusade was "an even-handed and very moral approach." Yet Makled said it was striking that, during the university celebration of Martin Luther King Day, "a lot of people carried pictures of Malcolm X." Malcolm X appeared to have displaced King as the hero of young blacks, Makled said.

"Black Power says you don't need to do well in university," Makled observed. "You don't need to improve your SAT scores. You are special as you are." He said there was a clear conflict between student activists who wanted to promote integration and higher standards for minorities, and those who wanted to promote separatism and Black Power. "Are they trying to end racism, or are they trying to promote a Black Power agenda?" Whatever the goal, Makled said, "whites are now Public Enemy Number One."

Makled has observed the prevalence of racial jokes at Michigan, some of which found their way onto the airwaves. Commenting on the student disc jockey who told racial jokes, Makled said, "Definitely the person was being insensitive. You usually save jokes like that for your friends, or at least an audience you're aware of." Makled appeared to suggest that racial humor must be kept underground, out of public view. But while supporting punishment for offenders like the insensitive disc jockey, Makled commented that black protesters on campus were not interested in justice so much as in converting the unfortunate event into political capital. "It's a power grab," he said. "They've found out that it's easy to get a bunch of people together and get the president jumping."

Makled was joined at this point by Andrew Milot, a senior from Boston majoring in history. Milot identified himself as a political liberal, from a "progressive" family. "For me, affirmative action is a lamentable but necessary thing," he said. "It is a shame that the pros and cons of it cannot really be discussed here." Was this because of a recent Michigan gag rule prohibiting racially stigmatizing speech against minorities? "No, no," Milot said. "There is a censorship going on that's not written. There's a lot of public intimidation."

Makled broke in here. "Who's going to submit an article attacking affirmative action to the student newspaper? You are sure to be called a racist. Who needs that?" Both students laughed. "These questions are legitimate," Milot said. "They need to be discussed intelligently. But whites cannot really bring them up." This, he said, was true for issues of sex as well, though to a slightly lesser degree. "Racism is the big fish and sexism is the little fish that latches on to the big fish," he said.

Nevertheless, Milot frequently found himself questioning his own motives. "The first question I ask is: am I a racist and to what degree?" He asks because "racism is presented as a wall of white male sentiment that the liberators are trying to scale or break down." Milot asked: What about "dynamic" or "reciprocal" racism? At Michigan, he said, "It seems that racism and sexism refer to white males. Whites are really scared of being branded." Black women, by contrast, enjoy "immunity."

Milot suggested that a number of whites joined minority protesters in their periodic demonstrations for the sole purpose of proving, to themselves and others, that they were not racists. "When battle lines are drawn and you stand on the right side, you feel secure. You're wearing a button and taking over a building. All of a sudden you feel: hey, I am not a racist. Look, I'm *fighting* racism."

As a child, Milot said, "I gained the image of myself as oppressor, of the black as oppressed." At college, however, "I found that there was an element of truth to the stereotypes. I found myself questioning things all over again. I grew up learning to stomp on prejudice. Now I am discovering that prejudices are not based on absolute error."

Milot condemned George Bush's employment of Willie Horton commercials during the 1988 campaign as "sleazy." On the other hand, Milot said, there was nothing wrong with using skin color to make judgments about people when full information was unavailable. If he saw black youths sauntering down the street late in the evening, Milot said, he would definitely cross the street. "It's not just skin color," he emphasized. "It's clothes, it's style of walk, it's language. Everybody adds these things up. Black skin tells me that someone is probably from the inner city. If I saw a black man in a three-piece suit, I wouldn't cross the street. If I saw a hundred blacks at a convention at the Hyatt Regency, I wouldn't run." Milot conceded that generalizations about groups may not apply to particular individuals. But people have a right to look out for their safety, he said.

Both students returned to the issue of frank discussion of the racial and gender taboos on campus. "Usually," Milot said, "you confront a prejudice by saying: is this true? What is the evidence for it, and against it? I really believe that people today respond to the truth." But, Milot said, "Now there are truths that are not socially safe. There is a fear that the truth will have its revenge." The campaign against racial and sexual stereotypes, both students said, was based on claims that were not borne out in their personal experience. "I'm tired of being lied to," Milot said. "They're fighting racism with lies."

The paradoxical consequence seems to be a sort of liberation for both students. "There has been a lingering guilt with me for a long time," Milot said. He felt partly responsible for the historical crimes of slavery, segregation, and subjugation. "But now I feel like *I'm* the one under attack. To some extent, I have lost my old guilt." He cracked a smile. Both students resumed sipping their coffee.

What is most significant about the comments of these two students is that they seem to reflect hidden sentiments that are often concealed from public view. In conversations about race and gender, but especially race, people tend to mask their opinions, revealing only what they think they ought to think. Yet Milot and Makled's views about preferential treatment imposing obstacles on whites, especially white males, are hardly peculiar or marginal; according to a 1986 survey by Michigan's Institute for Social Research, 75 percent of whites said it was "very likely" or "somewhat likely" that they would be denied a position in favor of an equally or less qualified black.[32] Nevertheless, when asked whether blacks come from a "less able race," only 3.5 percent of white respondents "strongly agreed," 10.6 percent "agreed somewhat," and more than half strongly disagreed.[33]

These two students responded fairly typically for white students confronted with perceived unfair advantages enjoyed by blacks. In a 1980 study by Stephen Johnson of Ball State University, white students participated in an experiment where a black student was rewarded after a test, even when it was clear that she had not scored as high as white competitors. White students responded to this with a sharp increase in racial hostility and derision toward the black student, and toward blacks in general.[34] This behavioral response was entirely independent of individual opinions about the desirability of affirmative action.

What is one to make of Northern liberals like Makled and Milot who react with such pique to the plaintive cries of campus minorities? Precisely because of their backgrounds, they don't feel part of the old-style racism identified with the Deep South, they are wounded and outraged at being on the racism suspect list, and consequently they denounce the entire process as inquisitorial and opportunistic. It is striking to see how dulled their identification with black suffering has become, perhaps because they have transferred their sympathies to themselves, in the belief that an old victim class has turned upon its former oppressors and their children with a vengeance—whites are the real victims now.

Both Milot and Makled agree that their grievance is not with minority fellow students, but rather with the programs of the university which encourage inequality, distrust, and excess. Is it possible that the policies of the University of Michigan, although calculated to promote racial tolerance and harmony, are actually generating and strengthening hostility?

* * *

In order to discover the meaning of the apparent proliferation of bigotry on campus, it is important to examine the tone and context of the incidents. At Yale University in 1988, someone painted a swastika and the words "White Power" on the school's Afro-American Center.[35] The letters "KKK" and other racist graffiti were found scrawled in the halls of Aurora College, west of Chicago.[36] At the University of Wisconsin at Madison, members of the Zeta Beta Tau fraternity held a mock slave auction in which pledges painted their faces black and wore Afro-wigs.[37] At Pennsylvania State University, someone distributed job applications for minorities with multiple choice categories— source of income: (a) theft, (b) relief, (c) welfare, and (d) unemployment; place of birth: (a) charity ward, (b) cotton field, (c) back alley, (d) free clinic, and (e) zoo.[38] At Northern Illinois University, white students in a pickup truck yelled slurs at blacks attending a speech by Jesse Jackson, and campus buses were tagged with fliers which said "Niggers Get Out" and "Get Your Black Asses Back to Africa."[39] At Purdue in early 1987, a wooden cross was found doused with fuel that remained unlighted because the perpetrators fled to avoid discovery—they were planning a burning in front of the Black Cultural Center.[40]

These reports, reminiscent of the bigotry of the pre–civil rights era, involve actions that are clearly calculated to inflame the black community. They are not random expressions of anger. The racist symbols are almost inevitably directed at black individuals, affirmative action offices, or Afro-American centers and departments.

When racial incidents of this nature occur, they are severely punished. At Michigan, the student disc jockey who broadcast racial jokes was immediately removed from his position, and despite his prompt apology and assumption of full responsibility, the radio station was also shut down temporarily. Two white students who verbally taunted a black Denison undergraduate were suspended for a semester, and university trustee Clifford Tyree said immediate suspension would be the penalty for racial harassment.[41] At the University of Wisconsin, the fraternity holding a mock slave auction was suspended by the Inter-fraternity Council for five years.

Sometimes disputes of an ambiguous nature are interpreted as racist. Perhaps in fact they are racist incidents, but in these cases there is not enough proof of motivation to know for sure. At the University of Massachusetts in mid-1987, a fight broke out between a white student and a black student. According to the *New York Times,* the white student "shoved the black student, causing the student's glasses to fall and break." The student got a $115 fine and a year's probation. This matter was treated as a racial incident.[42] At Berkeley, students took the bicycle of a black female undergraduate and hung it up in the shower; they also smeared ice cream on her door. This prompted a sit-in by the African Student Association, demanding that the offenders be expelled; local newspaper comment focused on an "upsurge of big-otry." Later it turned out that a Hispanic and an East Indian student were responsible for what they considered a campus prank that seemed to have nothing to do with race.[43] A University of Pennsylvania fraternity staged a raucous party at which two black strippers performed; the administration condemned not the pornographic show but the "racism" of the choice of strippers, and shut down the house for a year and a half.[44] At Georgetown, a native of India complained of racial discrimina-tion, and received publicity in the campus newspaper, because during one scene the director of a school play asked him to take off his shirt as the script demanded; this the student found to be an offense against his cultural heritage.[45]

Stanford University was in turmoil for weeks in 1988 when some-one painted black features on a Beethoven poster, and President Donald Kennedy ordered a full investigation into the "racial incident." The resulting ten thousand-word report reveals the complex anatomy of the episode. Apparently a white and a black student, coresidents in the black theme house *Ujamaa,* were arguing about whether Western music had an African heritage. The black student maintained that Beetho-ven was black, a claim which his opponent found ridiculous. Later that evening, intending a joke, the white student painted an Afro hairstyle and exaggerated the lips on a Beethoven poster and hung the result outside the black student's door. Other black residents of the dormitory found the poster offensive, and called for the white student to be expelled from his housing. The Stanford administration complied.[46] Significantly, this "racial incident" is repeatedly cited in university literature justifying Stanford's expansive antiracism programs.

According to a spokesman for the Department of Education, the number of ambiguous or unsubstantiated racial incidents may inflate the numbers and give the false impression of a national epidemic of campus bigotry; in fact, he said, documented incidents of campus racism have not increased since 1980. Nevertheless there is no question of an increased *perception* of racial hostility on campus, which may explain why ambiguous events are sometimes seized upon as racist. Recently the *Washington Post* analyzed racism on campus, featuring University of Massachusetts undergraduate Myriam Santiago. As a Puerto Rican, Santiago found herself the victim of pervasive racism, but she did not cite a single clear-cut instance. Rather, she said, "I make an effort to talk to people, but you can tell by someone's body language when they don't want to talk to you."[47]

White students sometimes complain that if a black student is victimized, even in a nonracial context, the incident is immediately advertised as proof of racism; by contrast, when black students victimize whites, even in a manifestly racial atmosphere, the incident is often dismissed as insignificant. In the Stanford poster incident, the university ignored the actions of residents of *Ujamaa* who punched holes in the white faces of posters on campus, and who put up signs that said, "Avenge *Ujamaa*. Smash the honkie oppressors."[48] At Michigan in 1982, a black student murdered two white undergraduates, for which he is now serving a life sentence; yet no one raised the issue of race or racism. In the fall of 1987, a dozen black youths crashed a Theta Delta Chi fraternity party at Berkeley, pulling knives, yelling racial epithets, and injuring two white students who ended up in the hospital. "There were 11 cop cars and two ambulances, and *we* were the ones worried about a lawsuit," fraternity member Jon Orbik told the *Christian Science Monitor*. "Can you imagine the media if it had been the other way?"[49] When a rash of black-on-white muggings took place at Brown University in 1989, the university refused to characterize the incidents as racial, and would not release any information to the student body or the press.[50]

There are even indications of the faked racial incident. At Tufts University, white student Ian Kremer showed up at the campus police with bruises. He said he was a victim of assailants who hit him with a blunt instrument and yelled "Pinko," "Jew boy," and "nigger lover."

Kremer said the reason for the attack was his progressive politics on racial issues. Previously little known on campus, Kremer became an instant celebrity. "Hate is alive and well at Tufts," he opined in the campus newspaper.[51] Immediately the Afro-American Society organized a march, at which more than one hundred students showed up. Everyone sang and said prayers. University president Jean Mayer called a "Day of Reflection," issued an open letter to the community denouncing racism, and called for classes to discuss prejudice and violence. Undergraduate Valerie Bolling told the *Boston Herald* that the incident was a "spark" that would "awaken the community to what's going on."[52] University chaplain Scotty McLennan told the *Boston Globe,* "From Forsyth County to Howard Beach to U.Mass-Amherst, there is a resurgence of racism in this country. For better or worse, Tufts is not unique."[53]

The only problem with this orgy of consciousness-raising was that, during its emotional height, the police discovered that Kremer's story didn't hold up. Students approached the police, saying they were 10 feet from the spot where Kremer claimed to be assaulted. They saw and heard nothing. Campus police visited the scene of the alleged crime and found no disturbances in the snow. It turned out that there were custodians who were cleaning up adjoining Eaton Hall; they heard nothing. University police detective John Flaherty said that Kremer's injuries did not square with his description of how he was hit.[54] Ultimately, Kremer was discredited. None of this diminished the enthusiasm of the protesters, for whom the alleged assault seemed more of a pretext than a cause for mobilizing the campus.

Nor was this a unique incident. At Smith College a few years ago, a black student defaced her own door with racial slurs, in order, she later admitted, to draw attention to racism. At Amherst a Ku Klux Klan-style cross-burning turned out to be perpetrated not by white racists but by black activists, also for the purpose of highlighting racial injustice on campus.[55] Emory University erupted in the summer of 1990 when a black student, Sabrina Collins, checked into the hospital claiming to be struck mute as a result of emotional trauma caused by racial slurs and abuse. After an investigation, both the school and local prosecutors concluded that the alleged incidents were a hoax, probably perpetrated by Collins herself.[56] At the State University of New York at Binghamton, a Jewish activist was recently charged with painting anti-Semitic slurs near a Jewish sanctuary, then organizing a rally of three hundred students to protest racism, sexism, and anti-Semitism;

he was quoted in the student newspaper saying, "Does it take an incident like this before Jews and everybody else get together to do something?"[57]

* * *

Many of these incidents are clearly bizarre, and the motives of the students are often far from clear. When these unfortunate episodes occur, university officials are responsible for dealing with them in a mature and sensible manner. Their objective should be to discover the facts, establish guilt, and mete out appropriate punishment. How, in practice, do university leaders respond?

• At the University of Massachusetts at Amherst in 1988, after five whites were accused of beating two blacks, approximately one hundred students, most of them black, occupied New Africa House on campus. The university disciplined the white offenders, but the protesters called for tougher penalties. They were obliged: the reprimands of the white students were converted into suspensions. Meanwhile, Chancellor Joseph Duffey brought baskets of food to the students while they were occupying his building. He also agreed to renovate New Africa House, to increase minority enrollment by 50 percent, and to add ethnic foods to the university cafeteria menu. He thanked the protesters "for reminding us of obligations we share as members of a community of learning."[58] Duffey also called upon the students to assist him in lobbying the state legislature for more funds for minority initiatives, although he later added, "I am not suggesting they occupy the governor's office."[59]

• After racist fliers appeared at the University of Wisconsin in 1987 and 1988, without demands from student protesters Chancellor Donna Shalala announced plans to double the number of freshmen minority students, to hire seventy new minority faculty members, to draw up plans for mandatory cultural orientation for all incoming students, and to revise the university curriculum to increase representation for black and Hispanic courses.[60]

• When students at Eastern Michigan University complained in 1988 of racial intolerance on campus, citing no specific incidents but merely an atmosphere of "subtle racism," the administration set up a 24-hour "minority concerns hotline" for prompt reporting of racist abuse. Several months passed, however, and the hotline received few calls.[61]

• Provoked by what they considered a prevalent atmosphere of insensitivity to minorities, 89 protesters at Pennsylvania State University seized the chancellor's office and staged a 15-hour sit-in, issuing demands for minority faculty hiring and more African studies courses. Chancellor Bryce Jordan agreed not to press criminal charges and to grant amnesty from university rules; moreover, he praised the action, observing that the protesters were "motivated by a genuine belief that immediate action was required to address the concerns of Penn State's black community."[62] The administration also invited a team of social scientists "to study the university's racial climate."[63]

• Forty minority activists took over part of a dormitory at Hampshire College in Massachusetts, holding it for nine days. The administration subscribed to a sixteen-point agreement, including provisions for a new dean of multicultural affairs, increased funding for minority projects, and a special adviser for the students who had staged the occupation.[64]

• Rutgers chancellor T. Edward Hollander was not displeased that members of the Union of African Student Organizations prevented him from speaking by seizing his platform during a university conference. "I've waited for 10 years for students to show that kind of unrest," he told the *New York Times*. "They asked for five minutes to speak, and I turned them down. But I knew if they wanted to say something, they would. If this were 20 years ago the conference would have been taken over totally by the students and no one would have had a chance to speak." Hollander/said he was "delighted" with the disruption.[65]

These examples could easily be multiplied. What they illustrate is that very small provocations often suffice to mobilize takeovers, sit-ins, and other campus disruptions. It should not be assumed that these are acts of great courage on the part of the protesters, because virtually never are they exposed to punishment; indeed, they are typically praised for their display of passionate commitment. Being "motivated by genuine belief," to quote the president of Penn State, may be admirable in many cases. But it is equally important to examine the content of that belief; if mere depth of conviction is sufficient to establish one's moral credentials, then who will condemn the most excessive fanatic?

University officials seem moved by the fact that sizable numbers of minority students are agitated. It is the fact of their distress, rather than the plausibility of their grievances, that brings the greatest responsiveness. It is surely appropriate to take into account the demands of an aroused conscience. Yet it is equally essential to probe the causes of disquiet, if one hopes to address what is really bothering the students. The obliging way in which administrations succumb to the protesters sometimes suggests a lack of genuine interest in their needs, an effort to humor and appease the demonstrators so they will pack up and go home, and a refusal to deal with more enduring concerns.

* * *

At the University of Michigan, the radio station incident energized black students to form a United Coalition Against Racism (UCAR), which the administration agreed to fund. Shortly after that, the same students established the Ella Baker-Nelson Mandela Center for Anti-Racism, which was given college facilities.[66] The student activists, however, were not satisfied. They maintained that "institutional racism" could not be effectively countered without a strong minority presence on the faculty. Therefore, UCAR demanded that all black professors be given tenure right away.[67]

They also insisted that money be appropriated for an all-black student union.[68] If this seems antithetical to the goal of integration that minorities purportedly seek, then consider the analysis of a group called Concerned Faculty at Michigan, published in the student newspaper:

> Behavior which constitutes racist oppression when engaged in by whites does not have this character when undertaken by people of color. For example, a white person may not proclaim a lounge or a campus organization only for whites. Yet there is an important place on this campus for Black Student Lounges, the Black Student Union, etc. Such associations do not oppress whites, because people of color are not in a position to deprive whites of the powers, opportunities, and recognition they need to advance their interests.[69]

President Harold Shapiro of Michigan (now president of Princeton University) said that he could not agree to give all black professors tenure, but proceeded to appropriate $27 million to increase the presence of minority students and faculty on campus.[70] Pressured by Jesse Jackson, who gave a rousing speech at the university, Shapiro also consented to give the newly formed Black Student Union a $35,000 annual budget. When Charles Moody, vice provost for minority affairs, proposed "sensitivity training programs" for students, using "outside human behavior experts," Shapiro agreed to that too.[71] The university announced a program to recruit minority students from inner-city schools. Moody was placed in charge of a drive to entice black faculty to Michigan, a program that would begin by tracking black students working to finish their PhDs. "We're looking at changing the culture of this institution," Moody declared. "People may not like the message, but they know what the message is."[72] President Shapiro thanked Jackson for his "assistance," and (sounding a familiar note) declared, "It is the aspiration of this university to achieve representation of blacks among faculty, staff and students proportionate to their numbers in the population."[73]

These measures brought results. "Nineteen New Black Faculty Welcomed to Campus," reported the *University Record* a few months later.[74] Most of them were in fields such as education, physical education, and sociology, the fields in which the most blacks get PhDs.[75] In the fall of 1988, Michigan boasted a large increase in minority enrollment for the freshman class: 21 percent, up from 16.9 percent the previous year.[76] The administration announced that there were 352 black students in the freshman class, up from 294 the previous year. Hispanic and Asian enrollments were up too.

There were also setbacks. No sooner did the "sensitivity training" programs go into effect than some black students denounced them for promoting racial stereotypes.[77] When Dean Peter Steiner met with black students to announce new initiatives aimed at increasing minority faculty, UCAR branded him a racist for his remarks in a campus newsletter where Steiner wrote, "Solving the problem of under-representation of blacks on university faculties will require many things, including a revolution in blacks' attitudes toward higher education comparable to that among white women in the last two decades." UCAR concluded that Steiner's remark, which implied that blacks were not sufficiently oriented toward higher education, showed "a regrettable lack of sensitivity to racial equality." UCAR steering committee member Kimberly Smith told the campus newspaper, "It makes you angry because you like to believe that such blatantly racist attitudes don't exist anymore."[78] Steiner offered no public defense against this criticism.

After President Shapiro left for Princeton, Interim President Robben Fleming established a grievance procedure to target racist actions in the student body. But Student President Ken Weine called Fleming "racially insensitive" on the grounds that "Fleming has repeatedly failed to combat institutional racism. Visible examples of this failure include his refusal to cancel classes in honor of Martin Luther King day, his effectively mute behavior in the face of Dean Peter Steiner's racist comments, and his lack of leadership on the implementation of a mandatory course on diversity."[79]

Shapiro's permanent successor turned out to be a former engineering professor at the University of Michigan, James Duderstadt, a tall, strawberry-blond man who has a reputation for an adept and nonconfrontational management style. By this time, more than one hundred programs were in effect at the university to combat racism.[80] Duderstadt plastered the campus with posters calling on students and others to be alert to endemic racism, and to report it when they saw it. It was almost as though the campus had endured a succession of violent rapes, with the criminal still at large. Duderstadt declared Michigan "a model of how a diverse and pluralistic community can work for society."[81]

Yet, even as the University of Michigan redoubled its antiracism agenda, administration officials noticed that the appetite of minority groups never seemed to be sated, while hostility among whites—the intended beneficiaries of all the consciousness-raising—continued to increase. "I found it very disturbing," Duderstadt said in an interview. "It was not what we had predicted. But it is to be expected that, in a new project like this, there would be tensions and surprises."

In late 1988, Michigan student and faculty activists came up with a new proposal. Since racial tension on campus seemed to continue unabated, why not institute a comprehensive policy to define and enforce racial etiquette, assigning penalties for speech that violated it? Actually this idea had been around since 1987, when interim president Fleming, a lawyer, raised it with the faculty. But now, with the university rapidly conceding to activist demands, the proposal gained new force and momentum, and student groups saw opportunities to broaden its impact. Campus feminists weighed in, observing that sexism was no less a social evil than racism, and urging that the proposed policy take into account sexually stigmatizing and degrading speech as well. Meanwhile, homosexual groups on campus insisted that derogatory remarks against "alternative lifestyles" be included under the rubric of "sexist language."

Concerned Faculty of Michigan, comprising approximately twenty media-savvy younger faculty mainly from the humanities and social science departments, pressured President Duderstadt to accept the antiracist gag rule; after some hesitation he agreed. "We have very capable student activists, just like in the sixties, when Tom Hayden was here," Duderstadt said. "They know how to create media events better than we do. When we don't listen to them, the press treats the university as a hotbed of racism. It can put us into a response mode."

Duderstadt's reference to the 1960s was ironic, in this context, because one of the central concerns of the protesters, epitomized by the Free Speech Movement at Berkeley, Michigan, and elsewhere in the 1960s, was freedom of speech. But now, at the behest of the new generation of protesters, everyone seemed to agree that some curbs were necessary, and the only debate was over precisely what restrictions ought to be imposed. Vice President for Academic Affairs Mary Ann Swain wanted the sanctions to apply not just to students but also to professors. "Harassment in classrooms is based on theories held by teachers, and that environment has prevented minorities from having the same advantages afforded others."[82] Not just racial epithets but also "theories" that promoted "institutional racism" should be outlawed, she urged.

By and large Michigan faculty seemed willing to go along with some censorship of student speech, but they protested any curbs on what they themselves could say. English professor James Winn drew a distinction between "directed, irresponsible and ugly discriminatory speech as opposed to what people may take offense to in a teaching situation."[83] Vice President Swain countered that an exemption for faculty classroom conduct would not address the real problem—where, after all, did the students with the epithets pick up their ideas if not from the classroom?—but she agreed that faculty should not be repeatedly investigated for the same complaint, even if it were lodged year after year. She proposed a one-time racial motive clearance system.[84]

The activist Concerned Faculty of Michigan now made a further demand. A policy to prosecute insensitive speech was not enough—it must be adjudicated by minority students themselves. How could it be administered by deans such as Steiner whose racial views were under suspicion? The implication was that people like Steiner should be the object of inquiries, not conducting them. "Concerned Faculty has documented many times how the administration has failed to recognize its own racist practices. To insist that administrators may define what counts as a racist act, overriding the perspectives of oppressed people of color, is itself a racist policy. Such a determination can only be made by a body representative of the entire campus, including a preponderance of people of color."[85]

Since blacks comprised less than 10 percent of the Michigan student body, it was hard to see how a judiciary committee could be both "representative" and at the same time include a "preponderance" of minorities. Nevertheless, Concerned Faculty got a respectful hearing. There was no audible dissent from other professors at Michigan, nor any efforts to organize faculty resistance to the mounting campaign against free speech. The mood, among most students and professors, was essentially one of acquiescence.

* * *

Universities often pride themselves on being "ahead" of the society of which they are a part. Because they are immersed in the solvent of ideas, members of a university community consider themselves less prone to social prejudice, less the slaves of conventional opinion, more willing to stand up for unpopular beliefs, more dedicated to norms of liberty—especially that liberty of mind which defines the university. Today we tend to condemn German professors who were intimidated into silence over the dismissal of Jewish scholars, while at the same time we admire the courage of historian Marc Bloch who supported the French resistance and was shot for it. Paradoxically, about the same time that the U.S. Supreme Court was teaching the nation a lesson in tolerance, striking down laws that restricted burning the flag, Michigan and other colleges were legislating freely against unpopular forms of expression.[86] While the arts community, in the name of esthetic freedom, called for tolerance and even public subsidy of painting and sculpture painfully offensive to basic standards of civility and decency, Michigan was leading the university movement to ban speech that a minority deemed offensive. Is it possible that the nation as a whole is more progressive on the issue of free speech than the administrators, faculty, and students of the most enlightened enclaves of our society?

President Duderstadt said he was well aware of the dangers to free speech posed by the new policy. "Racial harassment gets into issues of expression—no question about that," he said. Nevertheless, he viewed the issue as one of balancing different social goods. "We're weighing speech against the hurt feelings of minorities. It's a narrow and difficult line to walk." Duderstadt wasn't so concerned with anti-feminist remarks, but he said that "when it comes to race, you really have to throw out the rulebook."

After different campus groups prepared their own drafts, the Board of Regents, by a vote of five to two, approved a final version of the policy on "Discrimination and Discriminatory Harassment."[87] The new policy defined as punishable "any behavior, verbal or physical, that stigmatizes or victimizes an individual on the basis of race, ethnicity, religion, sex, sexual orientation, creed, national origin, ancestry, age, marital status, handicap, or Vietnam-era veteran status." A policy that started out by identifying racially offensive speech as a distinctive evil worthy of the harshest condemnation, even prevailing against the right of free expression, was now expanded to regulate theological controversy (attacks on a person's religion), moral criticism of "sexual orientation," and stigmatization of "Vietnam-era veterans," a special class of soldier whose protection might be taken to imply that U.S. veterans of other wars are less worthy of admiration.

The policy offered examples of discriminatory harassment:

"A male student makes remarks in class like, 'Women just aren't as good in this field as men,' thus creating a hostile learning atmosphere for female classmates."

"Students in a residence hall have a floor party and invite everyone on their floor except one person because they think she might be a lesbian."

In an explanatory section, the policy guidelines answered a series of hypothetical questions:

*What about freedom of speech?* "The university recognizes and respects the fundamental right to free speech. But freedom of speech does not include the right to harass or injure others."

*What will happen if I make a complaint but I don't have any witnesses to support it?* "Experience at the university has been that people almost never make false complaints about discrimination."

*What about classroom discussion?* "The university encourages open and vigorous intellectual discussion in the classroom. To reach this goal students must be free to participate in class discussion without feeling harassed or intimidated by others' comments."

The policy went on to outline reporting procedures. Hearings would be held to adjudicate complaints. Penalties could range from "reprimand" and "removal from university housing" to "suspension from specific courses" and "expulsion."

Shortly after the policy went into effect, the American Civil Liberties Union filed a lawsuit in federal court on behalf of an anonymous psychology graduate instructor who claimed to be restricted in freely airing his ideas for fear of punishment. The ACLU's stance was a surprise to some, because the organization is a strong supporter of civil rights as well as the First Amendment, and it was not clear which way the ACLU would go in the event of a conflict. But standing on principle and resisting pressure not to get involved for fear of polarizing supporters, ACLU executive director Ira Glasser made his group the only national organization to challenge the new campus orthodoxy.

Contrary to the expectations of some of the students who suffered penalties, the Bush administration did not speak out against censorship on campus; Education Secretary Lauro Cavazos was silent on the issue. The ACLU applied enough legal pressure, however, that Michigan modified its policy. The new guidelines still restricted speech, but they were narrower in their parameters of enforcement. In the fall of 1989 the entire Michigan policy was struck down as unconstitutional by U.S. District Judge Avern Cohn.[88]

With reference to the anonymous instructor who sued, Judge Cohn observed that it was perfectly proper, in that field, to consider the biological and psychological evidence for sex differences between men and women as a possible explanation for why the two fared differently in spatial and verbal tests, or why they entered particular fields— say engineering as opposed to publishing. Yet, Cohn agreed, such consideration may be considered "sexist," and it was entirely possible that it would be prosecuted under the Michigan "interpretive guidelines." Cohn concluded that "it is firmly settled in our constitution that the public expression of ideas may not be prohibited merely because the ideas are themselves offensive to some of their hearers."[89]

Distressed but hardly discouraged, several Michigan students, faculty, and administrators continue to attempt to devise new policies that would survive First Amendment challenge while still restricting offensive expression. It seems that a university that was once dedicated to maximum freedom of mind and conscience now finds itself struggling to guarantee the *minimum* freedom insisted on by the law.

* * *

Such hostility to free expression in the name of race and gender sensitivities is now the norm, not the exception, on the American campus. Harvard law professor Alan Dershowitz wrote, in reference to the situation at universities, "although the far right in America has been the traditional enemy of the First Amendment, some of the greatest dangers to freedom of speech today are being posed by elements of the left."[90]

On May 16, 1989, Washington reporters beheld the somewhat unusual spectacle of a joint press conference by former attorney general Edwin Meese and Morton Halperin of the ACLU to denounce free speech abuses by university officials and campus activists. "There is a double standard," Halperin charged. "There is a trend at universities to discipline students who write or speak out in ways deemed insensitive to minorities. But there are not cases where universities discipline students for views or opinions on the left, or for racist comments against non-minorities."[91]

The Meese-Halperin press conference was called to announce a settlement won by the ACLU on behalf of James Taranto, a student columnist at the *Daily Sundial* at California State University at Northridge. The campus paper at UCLA had printed a cartoon ridiculing

affirmative action in early 1987, and when controversy broke out the
school suspended the editor who allowed the drawing to appear. Taranto
wrote an article criticizing university officials at UCLA for censorship,
at which point his own paper's adviser, Cynthia Rawitch, an assistant
professor of journalism at CSU-Northridge, suspended Taranto from
his editorial position for publishing controversial material "without per-
mission." Oddly, other editors at the *Daily Sundial* approved the censorship, editorializing that a student journalist had learned "a valuable
lesson in common sense."[92] Thanks to the ACLU, Taranto got his
suspension reversed.[93]

In the fall of 1989, Nina Wu, a junior at the University of Connecticut, put up what she considered to be a humorous poster on her
dormitory door. Among the categories of people who were "unwelcome"
in her room, the poster allegedly listed "bimbos," "preppies," "racists,"
and "homos." She was brought up on charges by the administration
and found guilty of using the word "homos" in violation of a policy
which prohibits "making slurs or epithets based on race, sex, ethnic
origin, religion or sexual orientation." She was expelled from her dormitory and the dining hall, and restored her privileges only when she
filed suit in federal district court in Hartford.[94]

The Student Press Law Center, a division of the Reporters' Com-
mittee for a Free Press, is a nonpartisan group based in Washington,
D.C., which promotes free speech on the campus. In July 1988 Mark
Goodman, executive director of the center, issued a statement noting,

> We are extremely concerned about incidents . . . which we believe
> reflect a growing wave of campus censorship inflicted under the guise
> of fighting racism. Faced with a real concern about an important issue,
> universities appear to be accepting the misguided notion that viewpoint
> suppression is an appropriate means to their end. We note with some
> irony that this same means was used a generation ago against students
> who were advocating equality and desegregation.[95]

The center gave several examples.

At Evergreen State College in Washington, the student editor
was suspended from the campus newspaper by the school communications board for "lack of coverage" of ethnic and minority issues. At
the University of Kansas, the student host of a radio news show was
prohibited from airing an interview with a local Ku Klux Klan leader.
At the University of South Carolina, the student newspaper was threatened with a funding review by administrators when it published a stu-

dent's poem satirizing presidential candidate Jesse Jackson.[96] In December 1989 a Duke University administrative board suspended the student editor of a campus humor magazine for a satirical article that made fun of the work habits of dining-hall workers, several of whom are black.[97]

Obviously free speech restrictions are not limited to minority and women's concerns.[98] Offenses against the sensitivities of blacks, feminists, and homosexuals, however, appear to offer the most frequent occasion for suppression of speech. Because of the preferential treatment universities afford these groups, their outrage is immediately magnified across campus, and demands for immediate action ensue. According to the *Chronicle of Higher Education*, censorship against racial and sexual speech offenders on campus is now practiced by Emory, Middlebury, Brown, Penn State, Tufts, and the universities of California, Connecticut, North Carolina at Chapel Hill, Pennsylvania, and Wisconsin; many of these schools are patterning their codes of sanction on the Michigan model.[99] Institutions considering censorship include: Arizona State University, Eastern Michigan University, and the University of Texas at Austin.[100]

At the University of Pennsylvania, "ethnic harassment" is defined as "any behavior, verbal or physical, that stigmatizes or victimizes individuals," for example, "a person is told that he or she will not succeed in a particular field because they speak with an accent," or "a supervisor, co-worker, peer or instructor is inconsistent with his or her treatment of persons of different ethnic ancestry."[101] Shortly after this rule was passed with his support, President Sheldon Hackney, with no apparent sense of contradiction, wrote a passionate defense of the government-funded artwork of Robert Mapplethorpe and Andres Serrano and denounced congressional efforts to restrict such subsidy.[102]

At Tufts, the administration proclaimed three separate "zones" on campus—public areas, where speech could not be regulated; classrooms, dining halls, and libraries, where "derogatory and demeaning" speech could be punished; and dormitories, where offensive remarks would be held to violate students' "right to privacy." Protesting Tufts students dubbed the university a "concentration campus," and used tape and chalk to demarcate the three zones which they marked, "Free Speech Zone," "Limited Speech Zone" and "Twilight Zone."[103]

It seems to be only in the realm of racial and gender issues that professors and students provide overt justification for repression of speech. James Laney, president of Emory University, has argued that censorship of bigoted statements is warranted.[104] Law professors Richard Delgado and Mari Matsuda would impose tort and criminal liability on white students for "racial insults."[105] At the New School for Social Research, a faculty instructor found a painting of blacks at an art show offensive, and proceeded to deface it. He was not charged with vandalism; indeed other faculty came to his defense. John Jeffries, associate dean of the Graduate School of Management at the New School, remarked that "freedom of expression is no more sacred than freedom from intolerance or bigotry."[106]

When Stanford proposed a rule to punish racist and sexist speech, undergraduate Canetta Ivy of the Council of Student Presidents told the *New York Times,* "We don't put as many restrictions on freedom of speech as we should."[107] "Muzzle the Stanford bigots," wrote English major Sharon Gwyn, a campus activist who graduated in 1990.[108] And Stanford professor Robert Rabin, chairman of the Student Conduct Legislative Council, argued that free speech rights extend only to victimized minorities, since the white majority does not need such protections.[109] When Wisconsin passed a censorship rule, Student Association president Steve Marmel remarked in *USA Today,* "It's okay to call a person any of the millions of derogatory terms man has for fellow man—just not the racial, ethnic or sexist ones. Those who are so narrow and insensitive as to fail a major social exam deserve to be kicked out with the rest of the F-students."[110]

During a 1989 Stanford Law School debate over free speech curbs, two law professors urged censorship. Thomas Grey told the Law School Forum that students should be punished for "obscenities, epithets, and other forms of expression that by accepted community standards degrade, victimize, stigmatize or pejoratively characterize people on the basis of personal, cultural or intellectual diversity." Charles Lawrence maintained that "traditional ways of thinking about free speech do not take into account important values that are expressed elsewhere in the Constitution." The First Amendment, he added, "presupposes a world characterized by equal opportunity and the absence of societally created and culturally ingrained and internalized racism, sexism and homophobia."[111] Stanford constitutional scholar Gerald Gunther protested, "Let us be wary, very wary indeed, of all temptations to fight bigotry by resort to the force of the law,"[112] but the majority of the audience, both students and professors, clearly sided with Grey and Lawrence, and Stanford's censorship rule was adopted in August 1990.[113]

* * *

Both Michigan's gag rule as well as the climate of antagonism to free speech that it has created have resulted in the harassment and punishment of students and faculty whose views fall outside the range of acceptable orthodoxy. In 1988, while the censorship provisions were being debated, a student who made fun in class of homosexual acts was sentenced by the Michigan administration to write a public apology, titled "Learned My Lesson," to be printed in the *Michigan Daily*, and to attend Gay Rap sessions.[114] In Michigan's Department of Social Work, a student who argued that homosexuals could be "cured" was cleared of a charge of gender-based harassment, but his comments were found worthy of "review by the appropriate social work professionals in considering his suitability as a professional social worker."[115]

Michigan's informal settlement of other complaints also illustrates how an atmosphere of censorship and prosecution can exercise a "chilling effect." A campus fraternity which used an American Indian name agreed to "relinquish all reference to Native American culture" following protests and threats by the university vice president for social services. In another case, a white dental student who expressed his opinion that "minorities have a difficult time in the course," after meetings with his professor and the dean, recanted in a three-page letter of apology to those whom he had offended. A male undergraduate who sent a computerized message to a female student observing that some allegations of "date rape" were false received prompt threats of prosecution from an administrator, who went on to warn that such discussion "reflects an insensitive and dangerous attitude toward date rape. . . . The reality of rape in our culture is that women rarely make false accusations. . . . The effect of your message on the reader is offensive, hostile, and demeaning. University policy prohibits such acts of discriminatory harassment."[116]

Faculty debate is technically immune from prosecution under Michigan's gag rule, but it, too, can be vulnerable in the new atmosphere of selective tolerance. An early casualty was Michigan sociology professor Reynolds Farley, acknowledged as America's leading demographer in the field of race relations. His books *Blacks and Whites: Narrowing the Gap* and *The Color Line and the Quality of Life* are widely assigned textbooks.[117] Farley is also a popular teacher who has served on the faculty at Michigan for over twenty years. A self-proclaimed liberal Democrat, he has challenged the Republican position on public policy issues in his field over the past several years.

In the fall of 1988, however, Farley found himself roundly denounced in the *Michigan Daily* for remarks he made during his Sociology 303 class on racial and cultural contacts. Some black students took offense, and contacted UCAR and other minority organizations on campus, which moved in concert to bring Farley before a public tribunal. UCAR charged in the campus newspaper that Farley showed "insensitivity" to Malcolm X and Marcus Garvey, who are both associated with the black consciousness movement. One student alleged that Farley had called Malcolm X a "red-haired pimp."

Farley told the *Michigan Daily* that he had discussed Malcolm X's importance but also pointed out that "he had a checkered career."[118] Malcolm X had, in fact, served as a pimp, a career he himself discusses at some length in his *Autobiography*. "To this day, I don't know what color hair Malcolm X had," a frustrated Farley added. He also stated that he had quoted some "prejudicial statements" in class "to help describe the history of race relations."[119]

At my request, Farley prepared an itemized explanation of his alleged classroom errors.

> The quotes were in every case things which I either did not say, said while quoting or rephrasing someone else's words, or said in a context which gave them a different meaning than when the words appear by themselves. One quote, for example, reads: "Marcus Garvey was a fraud who thought he was a king because he wore feather plumes in his hat." The protesters do not tell how I first discussed the importance of Garvey as a black nationalist leader at great length, then noted that established black leaders often described him as a pompous man who may have raised funds for his own purposes. The words I used were meant to convey their opinion of Garvey, not my own.
>
> Another quote reads: "Mexicans are lazy because of poor nutrition." Although I never used those words, this issue came up when I quoted a speech from a Texas congressman who asserted that Mexicans were unclean, illiterate, and peonized. My purpose in quoting him was to exemplify the use of Social Darwinism to justify immigration quotas in the 1920s.
>
> Yes, I have used the word "nigger" in class. I used it when I quoted from an essay by W. E. B. Du Bois describing his bitter experiences in Nashville and I assigned books by Langston Hughes and Richard Wright which used the term with some frequency. I did not use nor would I ever use such pejorative terms to designate an individual or group myself.

These explanations, which Farley offered orally at the time, were ignored, he said. Certainly his detractors were not mollified. Michigan senior Starry Hodge, a student in his class, said that "Farley is insensitive to issues of racism and sexism." The class, she added, "perpetuates a racism that's in the university as a whole." She called for "someone who's sensitive—preferably a person of color" to teach the course in the future. Sociology department chairman James House might have been expected to dismiss these complaints as absurd, but instead he said he would convene a faculty executive committee to meet with students and discuss their grievances about Farley.

At this meeting, one of Farley's colleagues, sociology professor Mary Jackman, came to his defense. "I've always found him to be quite sensitive," she said. This resulted in Jackman herself being denounced for insensitivity. "Mary Jackman's testimony regarding her personal relationship with Farley is quite irrelevant to the issue at hand," wrote UCAR activists Tracye Matthews and Kimberly Smith in the campus daily.[120]

Eventually, Farley said, the whole business subsided without any action being taken. He maintained, however, that his reputation has been "gravely damaged" by irresponsible charges which were never substantiated. The university, he said, "would not stand up for academic freedom and open expression"—an inconceivable situation were the professor, say, criticized by students for attacking the Constitution or praising Karl Marx—and Farley has decided to suspend his course on race relations indefinitely.

"Issues of civil rights have become more, not less, complex," Farley argued. "Yet such questions as racial differentials on test scores and racial differentials in black and white family structure are now surrounded by intimidation. The discourse at the university has been narrowed." When Michigan recently debated a mandatory course on race relations for all undergraduates, Farley said, "the activists promoting the course weren't interested in an intellectually or historically balanced survey. They wanted a polemical course. They don't want students to be familiar with all aspects."

Affirmative action, Farley said, "has good arguments in favor of it, on grounds of justice. Personally, I think it's quite consistent with our historical commitment to racial equality." On the other hand, he said, "a case can be made that preferential programs cast aspersions on the achievements of blacks." The problem, Farley said, "is that we cannot have this argument here without the risk of being attacked and stigmatized."

"Everybody in the 1960s expected the civil rights movement to narrow the gap between the races," Farley said. "The fact that it didn't happen has generated enormous bitterness, which now needs an outlet and sometimes a target. When I was teaching my class, I could sense this. Students would ask questions that were clearly aimed at generating incidents, fodder for activism."

Thus the minority victim's revolution has alienated one of its strongest potential supporters, while the administration's effort to promote understanding has, curiously, brought about intellectual closure and intimidation at Michigan.

\* \* \*

The reason Michigan's minority activists have had such success with their claims for preferential treatment and censorship is "silent backing from the faculty," in the words of Reginald Wilson of the American Council on Education, who supported the students while he was Martin Luther King Visiting Professor at Michigan. "It was very different from the sixties," Wilson said. "The faculty didn't join the picket lines. They worked behind the scenes and through the system to give the students what they wanted."

A typical example is Michigan law professor Alexander Aleinikoff, a former antiwar activist who now exercises a strong influence both on student activists and administrators. A youthful, dark-haired man with a mustache, he sat forward in his office chair, surrounded by books on history and law. Aleinikoff volunteered to justify the recent events at Michigan.

Aleinikoff observed that stringent measures were desirable because antiblack and antifeminist sentiments have risen over the years. In fact, such sentiments were fashionable today, he asserted, while "it used to be uncool to express those views." Aleinikoff argued that preferential treatment for blacks is essential because "we live in a racist society" and "if you apply neutral standards to an unjust system, you simply replicate the existing inequality." Further, he maintained that all standards have been established by white males; therefore he is not convinced they can be applied to blacks and women.

Asked whether this was true of scientific standards as well, Aleinikoff said yes; even a question such as "how a cockpit should be constructed" has been settled by white norms. If minorities or women were in control, Aleinikoff said, perhaps cockpits would be built differently. The laws of gravity, he conceded, would stay the same.

Aleinikoff had reservations about affirmative action, but asked, "What's the alternative? How do you get more black doctors without affirmative action? There will be no black students in the top law schools—maybe two or three. You are going to have to change standards." Given these inevitabilities, Aleinikoff saw no alternative but to expand affirmative action, and fight ensuing white resistance. Arguments about treating races and sexes equally did not impress Aleinikoff, who said that Martin Luther King's ideas were obsolete. "This is a fight between Martin and Malcolm," he said. "Martin was right—at the time. But color-blind is a norm that has now come to haunt us. Now we have new problems, so we need new norms."

Aleinikoff had reservations about Michigan's gag rule. "I could be violating it as we speak," he admitted. On the other hand, he said, "There is some speech that contributes nothing to the dialogue. To me, racial epithets are not speech. They are bullets. They can be outlawed in the same way that bank robbery can be outlawed." Aleinikoff dismissed references to the First Amendment. "What white students are very good at doing is moving the discussion to abstract principles."

In his famous essay on "Repressive Tolerance," Herbert Marcuse condoned "withdrawal of toleration of speech and assembly from groups and movements which promote aggressive policies, armament, chauvinism, discrimination on grounds of race and religion, or which oppose the extension of public services, social security and medical care."[121] Aleinikoff said he used to agree with Marcuse in the 1960s, when he was a student activist, but now as a professor he had to qualify Marcuse's theory. Prohibiting speech so broadly was a "top-down solution" that could breed "defensive intransigence" among enough people to get the policy overturned. Aleinikoff favored social pressure and social control; he brought up "sensitivity training" programs as a worthy supplement to the Michigan gag rule.

Aleinikoff agreed with Concerned Faculty that epithets directed at whites were not bullets, and should not be punished. Asked about the word "honky," Aleinikoff said, "I don't think any white is hurt by the word honky. I think we all deserve to be called honky." In fact, Aleinikoff suggested, the term was a compliment of sorts. "It's a badge of white superiority."

The conversation with Aleinikoff was briefly interrupted by a phone call from a Democratic congressional office in Washington, D.C. Aleinikoff discussed strategy for putting pressure on the university to acquiesce in his antidiscrimination agenda. "These are internal issues," he explained with a smile, "but a little outside pressure can't hurt."

* * *

Considerably more vociferous than faculty members such as Aleini-koff are the student champions of the Michigan gag rule. Kimberly Smith and Tracye Matthews, both natives of Detroit, graduate students and leaders of UCAR, have been most often quoted in the media and featured on talk shows; they are humorously but respectfully described on campus as the "Hayden and Hoffman of the 1990s." They are proto-typical college activists with access to printing facilities, local media, and a network of student workers. Over lunch at the Bicycle Club in Ann Arbor, we discussed the obviously bitter racial atmosphere at Michigan.

Kimberly Smith voiced a common critique of established standards; she said the real problem for minorities today was the idea of merit. "Basically what scores measure is privilege." The whole notion of differ-ence, she added, "perpetuates class differences. It doesn't do anything to close the gap between the haves and the have-nots." For Smith and Matthews, diversity programs were less a means to assure that students from less fortunate backgrounds found a means to raise their academic and cultural level in a demanding university environment; rather, they were a means for leveling the notion of merit altogether. These students made no distinction between deserved and undeserved academic reward; all difference was a social construction based on suspect categories of gender, class, and race.

But in that case, why should colleges like Michigan have affirmative action programs in which promising minority and female students seek to promote diversity within an intellectually challenging framework? Perhaps universities should abandon standards altogether—instituting admissions lottery programs or eliminating grades on the grounds that merit criteria are either loaded or irrelevant. These suggestions struck Smith and Matthews as eminently sensible, and both warmed to me, convinced that I saw the good sense of their arguments.

The gag rule, Matthews said, was "not a free speech issue. I don't think racist speech is protected by the Constitution." Asked about John Stuart Mill's argument, in *On Liberty*, that even offensive speech served the purpose of illustrating error, both students looked blank. Were they not familiar with *On Liberty?* Neither had read it. What about Mill—had they heard of him? No, both students said, the name didn't ring a bell.

Both Smith and Matthews linked race issues with gender issues—they described themselves as "double victims." Smith said, with unin-tended irony, "It's hard to decide if you're more oppressed by racism or sexism." But what about differences of scale: would it be more offensive for a white woman to call them "nigger" than for a black man to call them "baby"? Not really, Smith said. "It's not just 'Hey baby.' It's driving down the street, looking out of the car, the tone of voice, the whole thing. Women deserve to be protected from that kind of thing." The gag rule, however, claimed to target "fighting words" that could be a prelude to physical confrontation. Historically, Smith said, remarks aimed at women often led to sexual assault. The two women agreed that prosecutions were warranted.

Smith and Matthews expressed strong support for affirmative action, but criticized Michigan's remedial program for affirmative action students. "Blacks are counseled away from engineering and computers," Smith said. "They are counseled into physical education and education." In effect, she said, white students were placed on a fast track and blacks on a slow track. While whites advanced intellectually, blacks were "left behind to play with their toys."

Because of the academic imbalances created by preferential treatment, virtually all colleges now offer remedial programs which include basic English composition, writing skills, and elementary math. While it is understandable that minority students find these programs insulting, it was odd to hear Smith and Matthews' complaint, given that they had earlier maintained that all these standards and differentiations were irrelevant and meaningless anyway. Yes, Smith admitted, distinctions were irrelevant in fact, but physical education and education degrees carried a "stigma" and thus they brought less reward in jobs later on. In fact remedial programs themselves, Smith said, have "racist connotations. Students here are told not to take hard courses, and to plan to stay around for five or six years."

\* \* \*

For all their hyperbole, the two Michigan women seemed shrewd in picking up the artificiality and condescension of the university's culture of preferential treatment. They also recognized it as broader than a mere admissions program, since once minority students got to campus, there were whole bureaucratic regiments ready to escort them through the often rough academic terrain. While all this attention was well intentioned—surely counselors are concerned about minority dropout rates when they urge students in the direction of the "soft" curriculum—Smith and Matthews were right to sense that they are being patronized.

It seems important that university leaders learn to treat minority students like other students. While they may come from economically deprived families, and while many have struggles ahead of them, these are not reasons to treat them like inferiors. The Michigan administration, however, continues to coddle and pamper minority students, and is then surprised when they respond with hostility rather than gratitude. But undergraduates think of themselves as adults or near-adults and do not like to be handled with the delicacy reserved for children.

Few people are interested in actually defending racial or sexual epithets. There is no legal prohibition against restricting "fighting words." The problem arises from the desire of minorities to enjoy their new political power while insulating themselves from criticism, and from the willingness of the universities to fashion free speech curbs to back this up. Yet it must be acknowledged that policies like affirmative action raise valid philosophical and practical questions, where differences of opinion cannot be automatically attributed to racism, as some social scientists allege.[122] Yet the venerable university tradition of disputation seems to have yielded to the contemporary practice of indoctrination.

One popular argument on the campus, echoed by Aleinikoff, Smith, and Matthews, is that tolerance for different, even disagreeable, points of view is a good idea, but this does not extend to tolerance of intolerance. On these grounds, it is considered acceptable to censor sentiments regarded as racist, sexist, and homophobic. The problem with this argument is that it provides an equally compelling justification for censoring Plato, the Bible, the Koran, Hobbes, Marx, Nietzsche, Dostoyevsky, and many others who were "intolerant" of self-determined and unregulated lifestyles.

While the Michigan leadership makes ritual pronouncements about its allegiance to free speech, at no point has President Duderstadt offered arguments as to why free expression and open debate are worth protecting despite excesses and abuses that will inevitably occur. During the controversy, the administration's approach has been to steer within constitutional boundaries while imposing maximum permissible restraints on what students can say. Nor has Michigan offered reasons for legal restraint as the most effective means of reducing campus bigotry. Even if a policy is just, it does not follow that its prosecution is effective in achieving its goal. Coercion is not a useful instrument of persuasion; it breeds resentment and rebellion and only increases the distance between the law and the citizen who is expected to obey it. President Duderstadt seems surprised at how much resistance his antidiscrimination policies have provoked. Yet it is not hard to predict that when you accuse whites and males of habitual bigotry, they are not eager to join the chorus. Abraham Lincoln made this point in criticizing the prohibitionists of his day.[123]

Everyone knows that discrimination is a touchy subject. But sensitivity can be heightened to the point where no one knows what may or may not give offense, where white and male students feel they must tiptoe around blacks and women. At Michigan, architecture professor James Chaffers delivered a lecture in which he called the term minority "insulting . . . minority is the late 20th century term for nigger."[124] This fact surely would come as news to most students and faculty at Michigan. No one seems able to keep track of the changing vocabulary, and a white student who used the term *minority* would hardly be giving proof of racist sentiment, conscious or otherwise.

The efforts of the administration at Michigan and other schools to regulate and enforce a social etiquette have created an enormous artificiality of discourse among peers, and thus have become an obstacle to that true openness that seems to be the only sure footing for equality. For when sentiments are outlawed, they tend to go beneath the surface, where they fester and emerge in the form of rebellious humor and other sometimes ugly gestures which can lead to "racial incidents." The consequence of such policies, therefore, is to promote rebellion in the name of harmony, to exacerbate bigotry while claiming to fight it, and ultimately to undermine the norms of fairness and exchange which are central both to the university and to minority hopes for racial understanding and social justice.

# 6

# The Last Shall Be First

## *Subverting Academic Standards at Duke*

> Of course he wrote it for me; that is a condition of the black woman. Nobody else understands it, but I *know* that William Shakespeare was a black woman.[1]
>
> — *Maya Angelou*

In an effort to place itself at the nation's academic forefront, Duke University made two controversial decisions in the mid- to late 1980s. First, starting in 1984, the prestigious North Carolina school decided to recruit a new group of scholars to make Duke a frontier for a "new scholarship" in the humanities. These fashionable scholars go by esoteric names—deconstructionists, postmodernists, structuralists, poststructuralists, reader-response theorists—but they are embarked on a shared enterprise: exposing what they say is the facade of objectivity and critical detachment in such fields as law, history, and literature. "There is no knowledge, no standard, no choice that is objective," remarks Barbara Herrnstein-Smith, former president of the Modern Language Association, now a Duke English professor. "Even Homer is a product of a specific culture, and it is possible to imagine cultures in which Homer would not be very interesting."

Because the old notion of neutral standards corresponded with a white male faculty regime at American universities, minority and feminist scholars have grown increasingly attached to the *au courant* scholarship, which promises to dismantle and subvert these old authoritative structures. They view it as a mechanism to change the structure and content of what is taught in the classroom, as well as a source of academic

157

rewards, in terms of jobs and promotions. Not coincidentally, the new scholarship also offers a comprehensive critique of those institutions and procedures of liberal society—democracy, free markets, due process—that seem to hinder social progress, understood as an expanded egalitarian franchise.

Duke's second major policy decision was to alter its preferential recruitment program for black faculty. In 1988, the university announced a new affirmative action policy of *requiring* every department and program to hire at least one new black by 1993 or face administrative penalties. Faculty and administrators at Duke argued that the usual inducements had not materially changed the ethnic composition of the faculty, which remained overwhelmingly white; consequently, something close to a quota program was needed.

These two ambitious hiring programs seem unrelated, but in fact there is an underlying unity: both offer a powerful challenge to the notion of standards of merit, on the level of both faculty eligibility and course content. The questions of who is qualified to teach, and what is worthy of being taught, would no longer be taken for granted at Duke. Although critics would charge that Duke was abandoning standards altogether, this was hardly the case: Duke was merely instituting a new set of criteria by which both competence to teach, and teaching method, would be judged.

A number of universities are seeking to follow Duke in both recruitment areas. The University of Wisconsin has announced plans to hire seventy minority professors over the next three years.[2] Williams College has said it will fill 20 percent quotas for minority faculty by the early 1990s.[3] Purdue University has promised that the first five departments which find and hire a black will receive funds for an additional faculty position.[4] Northern Illinois University has stipulated that departments hiring minority professors will receive a bonus equal to two-thirds their salaries.[5] By design, half of the appointments at Hampshire College in Massachusetts over the past three years have gone to minorities.[6] Virtually all universities are in intense and open competition to lure black, Hispanic, and American Indian professors to campus.

As far as the new scholarship is concerned, Carnegie Mellon announced, shortly after Duke, that it intends to establish "one of the nation's first poststructuralist undergraduate curricula."[7] Brown University has inaugurated an undergraduate semiotics program, while Indiana University now has a Semiotics Center for graduate study. Princeton, the State University of New York at Buffalo, the University of California at Irvine, and Johns Hopkins University are all striving for recognition in *au courant* fields.

These critical assumptions have now found their way into general textbooks and the guiding presuppositions of literary organizations. In the prospectus for a standard textbook on literary history, Harvard professor Sacvan Bercovitch explains his relativist methodology: "Individualism, self-reliance and liberal democracy are no more or less absolute, nor more or less true to the laws of nature and the mind, than the once-eternal truths of providence, hierarchy and the divine right of kings."[8] The American Council on Learned Societies, in a recent document, *Speaking for the Humanities*, maintains that democracy cannot be justified as a system of government inherently superior to totalitarianism; it is simply an "ideological commitment" that the West has chosen.[9] At the Modern Language Association meeting in December 1989, the *au courant* agenda was everywhere evident, including at sessions on "Is There a Brechtian Semiology?" "Feminist Intertextuality: Rewriting as Resistance," "Literary and Critical Theory from Lesbian Perspectives," and (Duke's own contribution) "The Muse of Masturbation."[10]

Duke is trying to establish itself as the leader of the new thinking. "We are hot and everyone knows that," remarked English professor Frank Lentricchia of Duke. "I don't think anyone else in the country can boast of the line-up of home run hitters that we've now got here."[11] "We are the mainstream—what we are doing here is what most of the best colleges do, or aspire to do," boasted Herrnstein-Smith.

Can this momentum be sustained, at Duke and elsewhere? More importantly, what impact will it have on what students learn? The Duke experiment is being eagerly watched across the country. Since it has been in effect for some years now, it is not too early to make a preliminary assessment of the university's sustained effort to set new standards for hiring, scholarship, and teaching on the American campus.

*  *  *

Big changes on campus sometimes come about accidentally, without conscious planning. In 1984–85 Duke president Terry Sanford resigned in order to pursue political ambitions; he is now a senator from North Carolina. Duke's provost and dean of the college also retired around the same time. "The university administration basically turned over," remarked Stanley Fish, currently chairman of Duke's English department. "And then, that same year, the conservatives hired Frank Lentricchia." Fish speculated that it was Lentricchia's master's and PhD degrees from Duke that got him hired from Rice University. "I don't think those old fellows realized that Frank's interests had changed so dramatically in the intervening years. It was all very serendipitous."

Administrators at Duke were happy to court Lentricchia, who had developed something of a flamboyant reputation in literary circles. The *Village Voice* identified him as a champion of postmodernist criticism, and called him "the Dirty Harry of contemporary literary theory."[12] Lentricchia builds his scholarship on his own ethnic identity. "Being an Italian makes me different," he said. "You cannot escape your name. I grew up knowing that I was not like somebody else. . . . I knew I was not an American."[13] Yet Lentricchia found that he could not develop unqualified enthusiasm about his ethnicity.

> I saw in the early sixties the civil rights movement down here. I witnessed marches, I heard the ugliest things said to other human beings that I had ever heard, and that made me suspect my Italian background. When I saw racism, it also made me see that cultural unity is purchased sometimes on the basis of exclusion and destruction and domination of other human beings. That made me not want to be a great rooter for Italian-American ethnicity.[14]

"Nothing passes through a mind that doesn't have its origin in sexual, economic and racial differentiae,"[15] Lentricchia maintains. "I come to a text with specific hangups, obsessions, worries, and I remake the text, in a sense, for me, for my times."[16] Lentricchia argues, "The text is a dead entity up until the point that a human mind interacts with it. If the human mind does not interact with it, Shakespeare is dead and gone forever. The moment you have started talking about a text, you have injected an interpretation. The text is not speaking; you are speaking for the text. You activate the text."[17] Lentricchia publicized these ideas in books such as *Criticism and Social Change* and *Ariel and the Police*.

At Duke, Lentricchia assumed the position of editor of the *South Atlantic Quarterly*, published by Duke University Press. One of the oldest literary quarterlies in America, the magazine was founded by John Spencer Bassett, who wrote powerful and controversial essays attacking racial intolerance.[18] Lentricchia announced that he intended to restore this emphasis on racial questions, broadened to include works on Third World literary criticism, homosexuality, feminism, and Japanese culture.[19]

During the search and interview process, Lentricchia made valuable contacts with senior university administrators and gradually sold them on his plan to transform the humanities at the school. Drawing on a $200 million university endowment campaign, Duke made offers, in some cases in excess of $100,000, to Lentricchia's designated "academic superstars." In 1985 Stanley Fish was recruited from Johns Hopkins and appointed chairman of the English department. He brought with him his wife, Jane Tompkins, a feminist scholar who was also offered a position. Fish hired Frederic Jameson, a leading Marxist scholar, and his wife, as well as Lee and Annabel Patterson, who teach great books "from below," which is to say, from the perspective of blacks, feminists, and the proletariat. Most recently, Duke hired feminist theoretician Barbara Herrnstein-Smith, former head of the Modern Language Association. In academic circles, Duke's humanities departments are known as the "Fish tank."

"Ten years ago the idea of hiring a couple would have been thought of as morally and intellectually wrong," Stanley Fish said.[20] He said he recruited literary stars in the same way the National Basketball Association did players. "It's analogous to what's happening in the NBA. You no longer have the firm assumption that a star will play his whole career with one team."[21] Thus Fish converted fashionable academics into free agents.

Gradually Duke's humanities departments were being transformed. Oddly, the administration had little idea of the nature of its acquisitions. "The guys who brought us here knew little about us personally," Fish said. The dean of arts and sciences, Richard White, was a botanist by speciality. "His field of expertise is ferns," Fish chuckled. "He had to be told what Third World Studies is, what feminism is. But he's learned. Now he teaches seminars on 'feminism and botany.' Did you know that? He really does." Similarly, Provost Phillip Griffiths, a mathematician, "had no position whatsoever on literary criticism," Fish said. "Now he's one of our major backers."

Administrators confirmed Fish's account. "Look, what we wanted was academic excitement, and these fellows sure knew how to generate that. They are cutting-edge. Whatever they're doing, they get attention. That's our objective," commented Malcolm Gillis, currently vice provost for academic affairs at Duke. Gillis suggested that, in the academic marketplace, the new scholarship was raising Duke's stock value. What else Duke students, undergraduate and graduate, were getting in the classroom was apparently not a question carefully considered by anyone besides the *au courant* scholars themselves.

But as a consequence of these decisions, the Duke classroom is a changed place, where students are exposed to theories that, only a short while ago, would have been considered extravagant, bizarre, even ridiculous. A Duke catalog from 1960–61, for instance, emphasizes courses on English composition, thinking and writing clearly, persuasive speaking and argumentation, along with courses on Chaucer, Shakespeare, Milton, the English novel, modern European drama, and American literature from 1800 to 1920.[22]

But now, at Duke, Professor Lentricchia teaches an English course titled "Paranoia, Politics and Other Pleasures" which surveys such material as Don DeLillo's *White Noise*, Mario Puzo's *The Godfather*, and Francis Ford Coppola's *Godfather* movies. Lentricchia's purpose is to demonstrate that organized crime is "a metaphor for American business as usual."[23]

Jane Tompkins offers courses on the writers and movie makers of the American West. "I'm trying to ask about the novels of Louis L'Amour the same questions that Shakespeare scholars ask of Shakespeare," she said. Recently she assigned novels by L'Amour, Zane Gray, and movies such as *Stagecoach*, *The Wild Bunch*, and *The Searchers*. Tompkins finished the course with a comparison to science fiction movies such as *E.T.* and *Close Encounters of the Third Kind*.[24]

Annabel Patterson uses Shakespeare's plays as "a vehicle to illuminate the way 17th century society mistreated women, the working class and minorities."[25] Janice Radway's courses are aimed at changing "the distribution of power in certain cultural practices. We ought to insist repeatedly on the status of cultural studies as explicitly interventionist."[26] In Radway's book *Reading the Romance: Women, Patriarchy and Popular Literature* she applies literary and anthropological techniques "from a consciously feminist perspective" to study the reasons why women read romance novels. Somewhat severely, she faults Harlequin books because they "refuse to ask whether female values might be used to feminize the public realm," because they "leave unchallenged the male right to the public spheres of work, politics and power," and because they "avoid questioning the institutionalized basis of patriarchal control."[27]

Barbara Herrnstein-Smith observed, "Minorities and women perceive and experience the world differently. These perspectives now collide with those of white males. My teaching emphasizes these perspectives, which are a necessary solution to our invisible procedures of discrimination."

\* \* \*

Duke's decision to establish minority faculty hiring quotas came about, not as a result of the cajoling of a Frank Lentricchia, but partially in response to orchestrated protest by student and faculty activists in early 1988. The Duke administration was concerned with the low numbers of minority professors—only 31 for the entire university, out of a faculty comprising 1,399, with 35 out of 56 "hiring units" at Duke composed wholly of whites.[28] Nevertheless, the 2.2 percent presence of minorities should be placed in its historical context: Duke only started admitting black students in the early 1960s; the first black faculty member, Sam Du Bois Cook, came to the government department in 1966–67. Like other universities, Duke had an affirmative action program to seek out and attract minority faculty.

Nevertheless, a group called the Committee on Black Faculty, established by Duke president Keith Brodie, was thoroughly dissatisfied with progress to date. "It became clear to us that something needed to be done," Erdman Palmore, sociology professor and chairman of the committee, told the *Greensboro News and Record*.[29] Education professor Joseph Di Bona went further, maintaining that without more black faculty, existing minorities at Duke would lead "disembodied lives."[30] He added, "Structurally this institution is racist. The way to overcome it is to make a determined effort to understand this, and then do something about it."[31]

Minority students were mobilized by a series of rousing speakers who visited the campus in connection with Black History Month and Student Activism Week. Black feminist Maya Angelou denounced the slow pace of affirmative action, which reflected "society's implied statement that we can only use a certain number of blacks at a time."[32] Civil rights activist Julian Bond and former student leader Abbie Hoffman also spoke, chastizing students for their apathy, and urging them to adopt the old protest fervor of the previous two decades.

In consultation with student groups, members of the Committee on Black Faculty developed a resolution that would require all departments at Duke to hire at least one minority professor by 1993. "We wanted to come up with a resolution that no one could easily evade," said Palmore. "We basically copied the contents of a court order handed down to the University of North Carolina at Chapel Hill." What Chapel Hill was being forced to do, Duke would voluntarily impose on itself. Nevertheless, support for the new policy was not expected to be universal. "We knew that this sort of program would carry a stigma in some people's eyes," admitted Palmore. "We tried fooling around with the name. We used to call it the add-on policy, but that didn't sound so good. Now we call it the opportunity appointments."

On March 17, 1988, Duke's Academic Council, a representative faculty group which decides hiring and curricular matters subject to the administration's approval, debated the resolution. Chairman Philip

Stewart, professor of romance languages, agreed to an amendment that softened its language, requiring departments to establish not quotas but "incentives" for minority recruitment, an amendment which Stewart told the campus daily enjoyed the support of the "overwhelming majority" of council members.[33]

Although Palmore said he was satisfied by the "good faith" reflected in the amended resolution, members of the Committee on Black Faculty decided to stage an *en masse* resignation to generate media attention and thereby reopen the issue. Palmore said he was reluctant to join in, because the tactic seemed to subvert legitimate procedure. But finally he agreed. "I told the other members that if it would help their cause, I too would resign." On April 8, 1988, all seven members of the committee resigned, sparking a media flurry and igniting a new activism among campus minority groups.[34] "It was really kind of a spontaneous sort of thing: we heard about the resignations, and it spurred us on," commented Tim Tyson of the Student Action Cooperative.[35]

President Brodie, a psychiatrist by profession who is sympathetic to minority activism, defended the modified resolution of the Academic Council, on the ground that it did not make sense to establish requirements that could not always be met. Under threat of sanctions, he said, a department may be pressured to hire unqualified applicants who "may not be motivated to carry out the research activity that would be required for a tenure appointment." Thus, Brodie said, "At the end of the day, we would have benefitted from their presence and then run into the awkward situation of not granting them tenure." By encouraging cynicism, a compulsory hiring program could be self-defeating.[36] "We do no one any favors by lowering our standards," he concluded.[37]

These statements led religion professor Melvin Peters, a member of the Committee on Black Faculty, to denounce Brodie as a racist. "That's just insulting," he said. "It's visceral and unwitting racism."[38] Student groups professed outrage, and Mark Lasser, a junior, threatened to organize a protest that would invite national media to witness the dressing up of the statue of James Duke in the center of campus in a Ku Klux Klan outfit.[39] Duke students began to collect petition signatures demanding a reconsideration of the compulsory hiring proposal by the Academic Council; some two thousand five hundred students signed; other signatories included William Griffith, Duke vice president for student affairs, and the mayor of the town of Durham.[40]

Under considerable pressure, Academic Council chair Stewart

agreed to bring the matter up again. Robert's *Rules of Order* made no provision for doing so, but "even Robert's has something called suspension of the rules," Stewart said.[41]

Not everyone was supportive of this new turn of events. Several white students complained that Duke was succumbing to pressure politics from minority groups. Speeches organized by the Student Action Cooperative were occasionally booed.[42] More articulate resistance came from black undergraduate Ben Rogers, who said quotas would be demoralizing to the minority faculty hired under such a program. Rogers also remarked that there were some departments where black faculty could not plausibly be said to enrich learning. He said he would feel better if a professor teaching him Chinese had a Chinese background. "Having a black professor in that class would not give me added confidence."[43]

Law professor Thomas Rowe argued, as he had during the first Academic Council debate, that compulsory hiring was undesirable because "making promises you don't have good reason to think you can keep is a bad way to show commitment to anything."[44] Environmental studies professor Kenneth Knoerr protested, "You are asking us to do something we can't do."[45] In a setback for the protesters, two black faculty opposed the compulsory element of the proposal. Bert Fraser-Reid, professor of chemistry, said the real problem was the shortage of black PhDs, especially in the sciences.[46] And Jacqueline Johnson Jackson, a psychiatry professor and the second black faculty member hired by Duke, said compulsory hiring would make minority recruits appear less competent.[47]

Philosophy professor Rick Roderick, a member of the Committee on Black Faculty, responded that the proposed requirement "cannot be equated with quotas. Quotas have consequences if you fail. The only consequence here is that you have to show why you have failed. Some obviously don't want to do that."[48] Pharmacology professor Theodore Slotkin said, "Whether we achieve the goal is a separate issue. Without the goal of being required to do so, we will fall short."[49]

Right before the Academic Council's second debate on the issue, minority groups at Duke organized a rally of about three hundred students on the Main Quad. "We want more black faculty," philosophy professor Roderick declared amidst applause. "We are not asking for it. We are demanding it."[50] Student activist Karim Deane said, "The only time a lot of students here have contact with a black person is when they go get something to eat or in class maybe once a year. In the United States, a black is forced to live in the white culture to survive, but a white does not have to learn ours. Black faculty can change that."[51] Appearing at the rally, President Brodie found himself facing angry minority students. He apologized for his earlier remarks about the risk of lower standards. "They sound foolish, which they were," he said.[52]

Reversing himself, Brodie agreed to sign the petition calling for compulsory minority hiring. "Initially he wasn't enthusiastic," remarks Palmore, "but when he saw where things were going, he jumped aboard."

By all accounts, Brodie's signature on the petition broke down the resistance of the Academic Council. To ensure victory and provide a moral backdrop for their position, activists staged a candlelight march and vigil in front of the Duke chapel the day before the council vote. The next day, one by one Duke professors switched their votes from those of the earlier debate. The final tally was 35–19 in favor of mandatory minority hiring. The faculty also approved new funding for fellowships to enable minorities to attend Duke's graduate schools.[53] President Brodie said, "The time had come for us to take a stand. I support this resolution because it sends the right signal." In other words, neither Duke nor Brodie could now be accused of racism.

* * *

"There is no compromising of academic standards here," said Malcolm Gillis, the stocky, cheerful vice provost at Duke, adjusting his wide tie. "I wouldn't stand for it." An economist by profession, Gillis maintained that it was possible to encourage the new diversity without a loss of quality.

Gillis said he didn't understand why Stanley Fish, Frank Lentricchia, and the new team in the humanities departments generated so much controversy. "As I understand it, what they are saying is that objectivity is impossible, that knowledge is relative to historical and cultural conditions." Gillis permitted himself a wink. "Hey, I thought everybody knew that. But seriously, what I do know is that these fellows generate a lot of sparks. Do you know that applications for our graduate program are up 340 percent in the last five years? These students are so good that, hey, before these guys came here we would have been happy to take the bottom quintile of these applicants. The bottom quintile."

With nearly 40 percent of doctorates from American universities now going to foreign students, Gillis asked, "Where are we going to get faculty in this country over the next 20 years? We simply have to tap into pools previously unused. That means minorities. That means women."

Offering an economist's rationale, Gillis said that Duke's motivation for minority hiring quotas was self-interest. "That guilt stuff don't work on me. It's been tried, but they've given up. It don't work." Gillis observed that Duke was looking out for itself in its attempt to diversify. He was not apologetic about wooing black faculty from other colleges, nor about raiding black schools. "Let the other universities worry about themselves," he said. "We're unorthodox, because we're concerned with results."

Gillis pointed out that Duke had a responsibility to North Carolina, and its 25–30 percent black population. "We cannot ignore our constituencies," he said. Yet he criticized other colleges which attempt to appease minority activists by suppressing free discussion. "As long as I'm here, there will be no fetters on the free exchange of ideas. What the hell is a university all about if not open debate? That's just a given. It should be expected, even invited."

Gillis also said that minorities hired at Duke would have to meet the university's current academic requirements for promotion and tenure. "Some colleges are exempting minority faculty from the promotion and tenure review process. You won't see us doing that here." While he acknowledged that departments may feel pressured to hire substandard faculty under the new rules, Gillis said he was confident that Duke could resist such temptations. "It's tough, but we're determined to succeed. Our reputation depends on it."

* * *

The project to hire more black faculty at Duke and other colleges faces a serious obstacle: an extremely small number of PhD degrees is awarded to blacks each year, and the rate at which blacks go into postgraduate education is not rising, according to statistics published annually by the U.S. Department of Education. Although blacks constitute 11–12 percent of the U.S. population, they receive just over 2 percent of PhD degrees. Moreover, approximately half the total number of doctorates awarded to blacks in recent years are in a single field: education.[54] Openings in academic departments generally call for faculty who have specific areas of expertise: thus an English department may require a Shakespearean scholar, or a physics department a nuclear theorist. Young black scholars must be matched with the particular vacancies in American universities, even under affirmative action programs. In many major fields, however, there is a dearth of blacks with doctorates. In 1987, new black PhDs included: one in computer science; three in chemical engineering; fourteen in economics; three in political science; nine in anthropology; two in philosophy; four in religion; and eleven in American literature.[55] Recently published data for 1988 show that there were no new black PhDs in the United States in the fields of astronomy, astrophysics, botany, oceanography, ecology, immunology, demography, geography, European history, classics, comparative literature, German, Italian, Russian, Chinese, Japanese, or Arabic literature.[56]

In a feature article, the *Chronicle of Higher Education* tracked the four blacks who received mathematics PhDs in 1988. Three were male, one was female—American University's Elaine Smith, and her degree was in mathematics education, which doesn't usually count under the math category. Strictly speaking, there were no black women who earned math PhDs in 1988. And Elaine Smith planned to take a job at an experimental public school in Washington. "I want to have more influence at an early age," she said. Emery Brown, who got his PhD from Harvard, has begun medical residency in Boston; he plans a career in medical research and statistics, which may or may not include teaching. Dennis Davenport, who received his doctorate from Howard, has joined Miami University. And number four, George Edmonds, has at the age of sixty-one taken a job at Elizabeth City State University.[57] In short, only two of the four black math PhDs in 1988 took university jobs.

Approximately forty American blacks have earned mathematics PhDs over the past five years, according to a survey by statistician Donald Hill of Florida A. & M. University. "It's really pathetic to read all the letters from universities that are desperately trying to recruit blacks for math," he said.[58]

It comes as no surprise, given the number of black PhDs, that the American Council on Education has reported a continuing drop in the number of full-time black faculty, corresponding with a continuing rise in the number of full-time white faculty.[59] Further, a large percentage of black faculty are concentrated in historically black institutions such as Howard and Spelman.[60]

Why do so few blacks seem to go on to graduate school and embark on an academic career? The simple answer is that it usually makes little economic sense for them to do so. With so many companies eager to pay competitive salaries to bright young black graduates, few have an incentive to postpone earnings further to go on to graduate school. The few who do gain advanced degrees in such fields as computers or engineering find lucrative positions waiting for them in the private sector. In the first five years after earning a PhD, blacks who joined college faculties earned an average of $30,000, compared with $37,000 for blacks who chose other career tracks.[61]

The frustration of those who seek to expand minority faculty hiring in universities is heightened by the knowledge that more than one-third of American professors will retire by the year 2000.[62] College officials predict shortages in the humanities and social sciences.[63] Thus, college departments will see a large number of vacancies which would be open to minority scholars. Unless the downward trend in black PhDs is reversed, however, it will be difficult for black faculty to fill even the positions vacated by retiring minorities.

Surveying the arid landscape, several college officials sounded a desperate note to the *Chronicle of Higher Education.* "The pipeline is drying up," said James Werntz, vice-chancellor of the University of North Carolina at Charlotte. "There just aren't many minority professors out there," said Jay Strauss, affirmative action officer for the University of Arizona. "We'll be lucky to break even. We're just bidding against each other. It's a kind of academic musical chairs," noted Varro Tyler, executive vice president at Purdue University.[64] Williams College spokesman James Kolesar told the *Christian Science Monitor* that "only about 2 percent of the black PhDs granted each year are in subjects we teach. Even if they are all high quality, that leaves less than one in 10 to choose from—and *everyone* is clamoring for them. Our problem is, how do you hang onto these people?"[65]

As a consequence, affirmative action in faculty hiring has led to frenzied competition for the tiny group of new black PhDs, combined with a great deal of financially motivated hopping of black faculty from one place to another—this practice allows colleges to count the same minority professor several times. The result of this so-called "black market," which Duke encountered as soon as its quota program went into effect, is an array of university programs that have understandably raised controversy.

First, more colleges are buying off minorities from predominantly black schools, offering them money and benefits that Howard and Fisk and Tougaloo cannot possibly match. "We're experiencing difficulty in hiring qualified Afro-American faculty," Wendy Winters, dean of liberal arts at Howard told the *New York Times.* "We're faced with being raided. Some schools are extremely aggressive in pursuing our Afro-American scholars."[66]

Second, universities are looking to foreign academics of the right hue. This practice has drawn fire from Reginald Wilson of the American Council on Education, who said that hiring West Indians and Caribbeans should not count toward hiring blacks because "Africans who may be educated in England cannot understand the experiences of black Americans."[67]

When Williams College tried to get away with filling its Hispanic slots with Spaniards, minority activists put a stop to the practice with the allegation that "what the college considers 'Hispanic' are really white Europeans who don't have a clue what it's like to be Chicano or Puerto Rican."[68]

Third, universities have started unusual practices such as paying blacks to pursue a PhD, stopping hiring searches as soon as a black applicant turns up, and accepting minority faculty even when there are no particular vacancies and when their fields of specialty don't correspond with department needs. Bucknell University recently funded positions for five new black faculty, to be hired in whatever fields they could be found.[69] The University of Iowa hired seven black professors even though none of them filled specific openings in departments.[70] Miami University increased its black faculty from seven to thirty-two under a recruitment program which ends the department search as soon as a minority candidate is found.[71] Colleges such as Duke have also run into the problem of bidding up the salaries of minorities so that, even with fewer academic credentials, they are often paid considerably more than their white counterparts in the same departments.[72]

In 1984, the provost at San Francisco State University approved two new positions for the English department "but with the stipulation that the candidates recommended be non-white. Let me underscore that the stipulation is an absolute condition."[73] Ohio Wesleyan University places ads seeking "blacks for a tenure-track position."[74] In September 1989, the director of a Wayne State faculty search committee wrote a memorandum to colleagues insisting that the new positions "must be filled by a minority person."[75] Explicit exclusion of whites may violate Title VII of the Civil Rights Act, so many colleges "invite nominations and applications from minority and female candidates," but quietly exclude nonminority candidates from serious consideration.[76]

* * *

Of the handful of minority professors that Duke can already tabulate for its black hiring program,[77] undoubtedly the best-known is Henry Louis Gates, a prodigious scholar who was wooed away from Cornell University, partly by Duke's willingness to offer a job to Gates' wife, who is a potter.[78] Gates, who did undergraduate work at Yale and graduate study at Cambridge, was approached by Duke as early as 1986, "before the black faculty hiring initiative," he carefully pointed out. Nevertheless, Gates conceded that he too would be counted toward the minority quota, since his appointment came through in 1989.

"It doesn't really bother me," Gates said. "In fact, it made the idea of coming to Duke more attractive. I felt I wouldn't be alone. There was a time, you see, when black scholars wanted to be the only one on the block, what Du Bois used to call the Talented Tenth. But today most black scholars want company. Partly it's just social. We want our children to be socialized not just as upper middle class, but also as black."

Gates maintained that the notion of America as a "melting pot" only applied to European immigrants, never to others. "White ethnic groups came here and they all became white. Previously they didn't think of themselves that way—they were Latvians or Czechs or Germans. But here they were all just white folk. Of course that option was never open to blacks and Hispanics and other Third World immigrants." Consequently, people of color seek not a melting but an *affirmation* of difference, Gates said. "That's why most black scholars study something black—we have to study ourselves, to find out what makes us different, and what is most valuable about that experience." Gates' scholarship concentrates on attempts to define a distinctive black "voice" in African and American literature.

Breaking out in a grin, Gates said, "We black scholars are enjoying our new marketability. Don't tell me about Cornell's loss and Duke's gain. I'm not going from Master Cornell to Master Duke, you know. I am free to make my own choices." Gates said that, paradoxically, the intense bidding war for black faculty among American universities was the "only way for society to become aware of the problem—to find out how few of us there really are."

The reason for the shortage of black PhDs, Gates said, is that "we don't have a long tradition of academic families." Yet, at the same time, "I don't think white people are trained to see black intelligence. The only way I've seen it happen is through affirmative action." If preferential treatment resulted in substandard appointments on occasion, Gates wasn't concerned. "We have the right to have mediocre scholars, you know. Just like white people. It's racist to say that all blacks have to qualify for the Nobel prize to be hired by universities." Standards will rise over time, Gates predicted, as clusters of black academics, recruited by the most aggressive American universities, cultivate and train a new generation of black scholars.

Gates rejected, however, the contention that all academic standards are a veneer for white male privilege, which is what some of his colleagues in the Duke English department believe. "I don't question the idea of standards," Gates said. "I only question how standards have been produced and applied." Gates differs from some of the more radical critics of the standard curriculum in that he does not want to throw out the idea of a canon; rather, Gates said it was important to develop an alternative minority canon of works that could be taught alongside the classics of European culture. Toward this end, Gates has edited the *Norton Anthology of Afro-American Literature,* which is intended as a standard textbook on black writers. "I'm a restorationist," Gates said. "When I was in grad school in the 1960s everything black that could be found was reproduced. But some of it was terrible. We've got to make discriminations within the corpus of black literature, and keep that which is worth keeping. We have to allow ourselves to be coopted, and to coopt. Sure, this means joining the establishment, but what's wrong with that? We are needed to keep those guys honest."

"I'm much more conservative than my colleagues," Gates admitted. "I do believe that some works are better than others. Some texts, black or white, use language that is more complex, more compelling, richer. I'm not in favor of Chinese lantern literature: you know, paper thin and full of hot air. I believe we can find works by blacks that are complex and reflect layers of experience otherwise scarce, otherwise ignored." He sighed. "My friends on the left think I'm hopeless." Fortunately, he said, they dare not attack him very fiercely. "You can't criticize black people too much or you'll be called a racist."

In order to develop an alternative canon, Gates said it was essential for black scholars to work together with feminists. "We're allies. They need us. We need them." He credited Women's Studies with "paving the way for Black Studies." Further, white feminists had elevated black authors such as Zora Neale Hurston and "created a new market for our work. We need a bigger market than just blacks. That market is white women." Gates identified what he called "a rainbow coalition of blacks, leftists, feminists, deconstructionists, and Marxists" who had now infiltrated academia and were "ready to take control." It would not be much longer, he predicted. "As the old guard retires, we will be in charge. Then, of course, the universities will become more liberal politically."

There is a new breed of scholar-advocate in the American academy, vaunted by faculty and students alike as being in the vanguard of both scholarship and social change. Prominent among these activist professors are Edward Said at Columbia, who is an English professor and a radical Palestinian; Derrick Bell at Harvard, who teaches law and agitates for civil rights issues; Noam Chomsky at MIT, a linguist who has adopted a series of disarmament and Third World revolutionary causes; Catherine MacKinnon at Yale, who is both a professor and a radical feminist; and Henry Louis Gates. Unlike some of his fellow scholar-advocates, Gates' politics may be outside the mainstream (for instance, he has been an outspoken defender of the rap group, 2 Live Crew, as an authentic expression of African American culture) but he respects the basic ideals of liberal education. The question, however, is whether "moderates" like Gates can continue to consolidate their gains without losing control of the forces they have helped to unleash.

* * *

All preferences are principled.[79]
 — *Stanley Fish*
   Chairman of English department
   Duke University

The flashiest colors in the rainbow coalition are sported by Stanley Fish, chairman of the Duke English department. During our interview Fish wore a bold shirt and gold chain, although he seemed equally proud of his deep tan and casually brushed back silver hair. In a newspaper photograph from several years ago, Fish looked pale and pinstriped, the consummate Northeastern academic. Clearly he enjoyed his new intellectual and social status. Fish's office is at the Duke Law School, where he has a double appointment from the university. Where did he get his law degree? "I am not a lawyer, but I am a law professor," he explained.

Throughout his remarks Fish referred to the "in crew," the "path breakers," the "superstars." He was contemptuous toward Lynne Cheney, head of the National Endowment for the Humanities, for asserting what he called "the error of objectivism." Objectivists, Fish said, believe in enduring intellectual, cultural, and moral standards, without realizing that "history is the crucible in which standards emerge and become sociologically and politically established." Fish acknowledged that it was possible to believe in objective truths, and yet apply them differently in different situations. But, he said, the "traditional view" misses the crucial point that there are no distinctions between standard and application, between observer and subject matter. "The norms and standards to which our behavior conforms *are* us," Fish said. "They aren't a set of rules we consult."

Thus philosophers think they are discussing the "real world,"

Fish said, "but all they are addressing are questions related to philosophy. Outside the field, they have nothing to say to anyone." Similarly, Fish said, his own relativism was a literary position; it had no implications for his views on politics, or the way he lived his life. "People like Cheney raise the specter that we don't have any standards," he said.

> They worry that there will be young people walking around acting in a random, nihilistic way, or perpetually perplexed about life. But that doesn't follow from my position at all. I'm just saying that our standards are acquired through socialization. My critics assume a world in which persons are not socialized. Actually, it is impossible to live without standards. The only question is, where do standards come from, how are they realized, whose standards prevail?

Fish was in a metaphysical frame of mind. "Belief and knowledge are considered to be two different things. But they are not," he said. Since all knowledge is historically and socially conditioned,

> the best we can hope to do is convert someone from their set of beliefs to ours. This is persuasion. It has nothing to do with truth or knowledge. It is an art, as the old rhetoricians knew. Fortunately our belief structures contain, within themselves, the possibility of alteration, of adopting a new opinion. From what I am saying, it obviously follows that persuasion is contingent, probabilistic; it cannot hope for certainty.

In a specifically literary context, Fish established his reputation with the invention of "reader response criticism," which emphasized the predominance of the audience's critical reaction to the text over the intention of the author, or a presumption of inherent meaning.

In their influential 1949 essay "The Affective Fallacy," W. K. Wimsatt and Monroe Beardsley argued that poems possess coherent meanings which do not vary depending on the reaction of the reader. A poem should not be confused with its psychological effects, they said. Otherwise all sorts of absurd interpretations would peacefully coexist with sensible ones, without a criterion of critical differentiation; the result would be "impressionism and relativism."[80] Wimsatt and Beardsley were affiliated with the so-called New Critics, who dominated the field of literature in the earlier part of the century. Led by such figures as T. S. Eliot, Robert Penn Warren, John Crowe Ransom, and Cleanth Brooks, they upheld a standard of literary judgment based upon the text itself, independent of external influences.

Fish pooh-poohed this approach. Through an ingenious reading of a line from Milton, he showed in *Surprised by Sin,* the book that made his critical reputation, how the circuitous prose, use of double negative, and the punctuation all conspired repeatedly to alter the reader's natural critical response in the process of reading.[81] The final meaning of the sentence was subordinate to this technique and method of reading, according to Fish. Indeed, Milton may even have wanted readers to misconstrue his elaborate phrases in *Paradise Lost,* Fish boldly suggested, so that in stumbling from line to line, forming premature opinions and then having to revise them, we would be constantly reminded of our fallen state.

However implausible this may sound,[82] it amazed many young literary critics with its cleverness and audacity. A few academic fogies raised the specter of nihilism, but Fish struck back with a revision of his earlier critical testament, this time proclaiming the sovereignty of "interpretive communities" to establish a broad agreement over what texts meant, and thus insure against utter interpretive chaos and idiocy.[83] Of course what these communities agreed upon would have no claim to truth or objectivity, being itself determined by historical circumstance.

This approach, no less than Fish's earlier theory, raises the prospect of interpretive nihilism, but Fish maintains that this risk is more than overcome by its benefits of exhilarating freedom—the freedom that comes from the unaccountable exercise of power. "Does might make right?" Fish asks in his latest book, *Doing What Comes Naturally.* "In a sense, the answer I must give is yes, since in the absence of a perspective independent of interpretation, some interpretive perspective will always rule by virtue of having won out over its competitors."[84]

It is little wonder that another group, besides youthful iconoclasts, was drawn to Fish's ideas. "The political left loved it," Fish said. "They began to say: once you realize that standards emerge historically, then you can see through and discard all the norms to which we have been falsely enslaved." In other words, Fish seemed to recognize, relativism paves the way for a toppling of the old rules, and the establishment of new ones based on political strength. Fish's role in subverting these hierarchies of the *ancien régime* are an important clue to his role in the minority victim's revolution on campus.

Duke would "in all likelihood" fail to meet its minority hiring numbers, Fish said, but "probably it was the right thing to do." Fish added, "Our *modus operandi* is not independent of the minority, affirmative action consciousness." He said the Duke black hiring plan was entirely congruent with its hiring of scholars such as Lentricchia, Tompkins,

Herrnstein-Smith, and himself. Both decisions, he argued, help to realize "our historicist, postmodernist, poststructuralist moment."

Fish went on to criticize those who, during Duke's faculty affirmative action debate, spoke up for basic qualifications. "They want a definition of quality that excludes considerations of race, sex and so on," he said. "But once you have subtracted from the accidents of class, race, gender, and political circumstance, what is it that you have left?"[85] Merit is "a political viewpoint claiming for itself the mantle of objectivity," Fish told me. "All educational decisions are political by their very nature."

If this were so, why should even private universities be allowed independence or academic freedom? Why not turn over the schools to the rough-and-tumble of democratic politics, and let legislators make decisions about admissions, faculty, and curriculum? Fish grinned. "Sure, I might be in favor of that. *It depends.* That's what I'm always going to say. If universities do things that are horrible, such as conduct McCarthyite witch hunts, then I can envision situations where I'd like to see government intervention." In Fish's situational ethic, not even university autonomy is sacrosanct; it is an arbitrary value, with no claim to special reverence. Much more important are political exigencies such as the agenda of minority activists on campus.

* * *

No doubt some of the terminology of Fish and the Duke critics will strike those outside the circles of literary theory as somewhat arcane. To understand what is going on, it is necessary to recognize new developments in humanities scholarship which have changed the intellectual landscape.

Traditional literary criticism is perhaps best embodied by Samuel Johnson, who brought a commonsensical intelligence to bear upon his interpretation of a novel, play, or poem.[86] Johnson believed that, by and large, there was a collective literary judgment that worked, over time, to confirm the greatness of particular works. If a piece of literature survived the scrutiny of serious minds over generations, it survived Johnson's test of the true classic; its reputation was protected from the charge of provinciality or fashion. Thus its prestige acquired a timeless quality. In his *Preface to Shakespeare*, Johnson argued that the Elizabethan playwright had survived precisely such a critical test.

This view of literature informed the work of most of the great critics, from Samuel Coleridge, William Hazlitt, and Matthew Arnold to T. S. Eliot and Lionel Trilling. These critics were hardly narrow in their interpretive approach; they did not restrict themselves to either a literal reading, or to the stated intentions of the authors. They admitted the utility of external disciplines—history, sociology, psychology, philosophy—as means of enriching the meaning of the text. Thus multiple meanings could often enhance the experience of reading. But this certainly did not mean that these critics considered literary value to be totally subjective, or that texts may mean whatever we want them to. They viewed the reader as secondary or subordinate to the text; his function was to illuminate the work, not to supplant it.

Much of modern literary criticism is based on the surprising premise that poems and novels do not mean anything in particular; they do not correspond to any specific "reality," either material or metaphysical. Jacques Lacan, who has greatly influenced *au courant* criticism, wrote that "it is the world of words that creates the world of things."[87] Terry Eagleton, author of a widely used textbook on literary theory, wrote that modern interpretation rejects from the outset "the commonsensical belief that objects exist independently of ourselves in the external world, and that our information about them is generally reliable."[88] The genesis of this approach is probably Austin Warren and René Wellek's influential book *A Theory of Literature* (1949), which maintained that the definition of literature was problematic and posited circumstances under which Shakespeare might be displaced by the Manhattan phone book or by graffiti.[89]

Today there are numerous schools of criticism based on the denial of textual meaning: formalism, hermeneutics, psychoanalytic theory, semiotics, structuralism, Marxism, deconstructionism.[90] Stanley Fish rejects identification with any of these, but only to embrace all of them, which is not hard, because the various systems are symbiotic, drawing on many of the same sources, and operating toward the common end of destroying traditional literary criticism, and perhaps indeed the literary text itself.

Formalism traces itself to prerevolutionary Russia. Led by Roman Jakobson, the Russian formalists argued that literature is a collection of verbal "forms" that do not necessarily correspond to any external feelings, intentions, or reality. Formalists dissected the words of texts, establishing linguistic patterns and oppositions, but all for their own sake, not to make a point of any sort. Sound, imagery, syntax, rhyme, and narrative technique assumed a life of their own; they were not read in relation to what the poem or novel actually said.[91]

Linguistic or hermeneutic criticism assumes that words do not express or reflect realities. Hans-Georg Gadamer argued in *Truth and Method* (1975) that all interpretation is situational: the text does not exist in and of itself, but is utterly a creation of the culturally conditioned reader.[92] Thus Gadamer maintained that literary meanings were not constant but changed dramatically over time. According to this logic, *Hamlet* is not one play but many plays, possibly an infinite number, and to stubbornly maintain that the plot is about a young man seeking revenge for his father's murder is to reveal oneself as very narrow and parochial.

Structuralism and semiotics apply various linguistic models to analyze relationships within a work of literature. A fair example is Tzvetan Todorov's analysis of Boccaccio's *Decameron*, in which Todorov designates all the characters as "nouns" and their actions as "verbs," concluding that the work is nothing more than one long sentence, combining the nouns and verbs in different ways.[93] For making arguments like these, Todorov is regarded as a critic of genuine stature.

Psychoanalytic critics read literature as basically a product of the author's unconscious and subconscious life. In *The Dynamics of Literary Response*, Norman Holland described literature as a largely unconscious attempt by writers to transform their deepest anxieties into socially acceptable meanings through plot, character, dialogue, and other conventional devices.[94]

Marxist criticism trades the intrinsic meaning of what the author says for what it regards as truly important—the historically determined class divisions that reveal the characters as members of the proletariat or bourgeoisie.[95] Marxist readers go on to explain what happened in the plot as a commentary on the historic struggle between these social classes. Readers are not expected to compare these inevitable laws with historical reality; verification of prophecy is a bourgeois notion. A sample of Marxist criticism is the acclaimed study, *Prison Literature in America*, by Rutgers professor H. Bruce Franklin, in which the author argues that "most non-whites recognize that they are in prison not for what they have done as individuals but for what they are collectively," adding that "the prison system [is] largely designed to replace the earlier form of black chattel slavery."[96]

Finally there is deconstructionism. Inspired by Jacques Derrida and Paul de Man, deconstructionists hold that all literature is empty of meaning. Whereas structuralists try to find linguistic parallels and contrasts in texts, deconstructionists labor to discover ingenious, and sometimes bizarre, contradictions which render the work "radically incoherent." Focusing on the distance between word and subject—"signifier" and "signified"—Derrida and de Man demonstrate that literary reality is an illusion, that fact dissolves into fiction, that literal meaning cannot be divorced from metaphorical meaning.[97] Critics have maintained, however, that the spectacular oppositions—between male and female, noun and verb, and so on—that the deconstructionists have identified are more in the heads of the critics than in the texts themselves.

There are disagreements and debates among these various new schools of criticism, but they are united in a general effort to capsize the author and his work in order to shift semantic authority to "imperial readers." Texts are often read in such a way that their manifest meanings recede into invisibility. In his popular textbook *Literary Theory*, Marxist critic Terry Eagleton noted that "this book is less an introduction than an obituary," but the supposed death of literary criticism does not deter him from proposing a new "form of study which would look at all the various sign systems and signifying practices in our society, all the way from *Moby Dick* to the Muppet Show, from Dryden and Jean-Luc Godard to the portrayal of women in advertisements and the rhetorical techniques of government reports."[98]

René Wellek, one of the co-founders of the *au courant* scholarship, has lately expressed alarm over this increasing critical arbitrariness. Among many of our intellectuals, according to Wellek, we are witnessing "an attempt to destroy literary studies from the inside . . . the rejection of the whole ancient enterprise of interpretation as a search for the true meaning of a text." The *au courant* critics, Wellek charged, "deny that there is a correct interpretation and hence encourage sheer caprice, arbitrariness and finally anarchy."[99]

The implications go beyond the field of literature. It is truth itself which the *au courant* critics spurn, or more precisely, by reducing all truth to the level of opinion they spurn the legitimacy of any distinctions between truth and error. Yet what is the goal of liberal education if not the pursuit of truth? If education cannot teach us to separate truth from falsehood, beauty from vulgarity, and right from wrong, then what can it teach us worth knowing? Edward Shils of the University of Chicago points out that for academicians to deny that truth is preferable to falsehood is just as absurd as for the medical profession to deny that health is preferable to sickness.[100] Yet this is the odd situation in which Duke and other *au courant* universities now find themselves.

\* \* \*

As a consequence of such ideas, at Duke and elsewhere, the notion of enduring intellectual standards has been rendered antiquated.

There is no determinate standard against which classroom evaluations, or student papers, can be measured. Thus grading assumes a pointless character; it doesn't reflect what the student produced, only the arbitrary and politically motivated preferences of the teacher, which need no further justification. As for the reading list and classroom discussions, it is no longer necessary to struggle with *Paradise Lost* to try and figure out what the poem means, or what Milton tried to convey. It is instead entirely respectable to read popular novels and watch movies in class. It is not difficult to see the appeal of this pedagogy to students.

Perhaps less evident is the attraction of *au courant* scholarship to professors, especially to the younger generation of faculty. Through the centuries, the plays of Sophocles and Shakespeare have endured far above all the books that critics and scholars have written about them. Critics have to write books about poets, but poets rarely write poems about critics. The Yale deconstructionist Geoffrey Hartman has complained about "the automatic valuing of works of art over works of commentary," and expressed his desire to lift criticism from its "second class status in the world of letters." The *au courant* scholarship has this benefit, as Stanley Fish plainly outlines:

> Perhaps the greatest gain that falls to us . . . is a greatly enhanced sense of the importance of our activities. No longer is the critic the humble servant of texts whose glories exist independently of anything he might do; it is what he does, within the constraints embedded in the literary institution, that brings texts into being and makes them available for analysis and appreciation. The practice of literary criticism is not something one must apologize for; it is absolutely essential not only to the maintenance of, but to the very production of, the objects of its attention.[101]

The *au courant* scholarship also multiplies the academic possibilities for graduate students and professors who are under pressure to "publish or perish." There is only one *Hamlet*, but a thousand brilliant essays on *Hamlet*. Not only does the traditional critic appear a mere expositor, parasitic on the original work, but even this subservient enterprise seems to offer increasingly limited opportunities: most of the analytical possibilities for *Hamlet* appear to be exhausted. What is a late twentieth-century critic, who wishes to take the world by storm, expected to do? Structuralism, reader-response theory, and deconstructionism offer a way out. They suggest a way for the critic to take control. He too can create. For him, criticism is not liberation of the text, but liberation from the text.

Some *au courant* critics even write badly in order, they say, to call language, culture, and learning itself into question and even bring them into disrepute: thus terms such as "focalized," "heterodiegetic," "indexical" "syntagmatic," and "constative" occur frequently. Who can fail to be impressed by a passage like this one, by Geoffrey Hartman of Yale:

> Because of the equivocal echo-nature of language, even identities or homophones sound on: the sound of Sa is knotted with that of ça, as if the text were signalling its intention to bring Hegel, Saussure, and Freud together. Ça corresponds to the Freudian Id ("Es"); and it may be that our only "savoir absolu" is that of a ça structured like the Sa-significant: a bacchic or Lacanian "primal process" where only signifier-signifying signifiers exist.[102]

Some may find its pomposity amusing, but this sort of analysis also helps the literary professionals to claim a specialized field for themselves. Through professionalized jargon, however meaningless, critics assert their claims to special expertise and consequently to special recognition and privilege. And these intellectual gymnastics of the new scholarship have now become very profitable in the academy. The *au courant* critics have invented, within the academic world, a new form of literary consumerism.[103] The author supplies a product—a novel or poem—which the critic or reader fashions to his own use. University departments have generated a sophisticated interpretation industry, which includes product variation, division of labor, diffuse franchises and markets, government and philanthropic subsidy; critical careers rise and fall, academic fortunes are made and lost, depending on the laws of supply and demand in the literary bazaar. Because of their large salaries and lavish lifestyles, the Duke critics have been variously described as "closet capitalists" and "the richest Marxists in the country."

The cynical procedures of the new scholarship are coolly described by the character Morris Zapp in David Lodge's satire, *Small World*. After delivering a paper called "Textuality as Striptease," Zapp is confronted by a colleague who asks, "Then what in God's name is the point of it all?" The point, Zapp replies, "is to uphold the institution of academic literary studies. We maintain our position in society by publicly performing a certain ritual, just like any other group of workers in the realm of discourse—lawyers, politicians, journalists."[104]

* * *

Some commentators have justly lamented the futility of this critical enterprise, and lamented the fate of the humanities if the *au courant* scholars continue to enjoy academic hegemony.[105] But in their apocalyptic warnings about "creeping nihilism," these writers generally overstate the intrinsic importance of the new scholarship. They do not recognize that strange and abstruse literary and philosophical movements have gained the allegiance of large segments of the intelligentsia in the past, and in this respect the current deconstructionist fad is not very different from Cambridge neo-Platonism or late medieval Averroism; indeed *au courant* esotericism bears a clear resemblance to rigorous scholastic disputations about the number of angels who can dance on the head of a pin. It is probably the case that Dante and Shakespeare will continue to be read long after Stanley Fish and Geoffrey Hartman are reduced to literary footnotes.

The real problem is not reader-response theory or deconstructionism *per se;* rather it is the extent to which they serve the ends of a political movement that has propelled them to the forefront of the victim's revolution on campus. In other words, Stanley Fish's politics are less significant than the politics which have created Stanley Fish. It is the ideology which the *au courant* critics serve which explains their popularity across various disciplines. To illuminate this underlying ideology, one simply has to ask who most benefits from, and thus gravitates toward, the new scholarship.

For a younger generation of scholars, with a highly developed sense of activism, the *au courant* thinking offers special political rewards. This fact may not be evident because of the facially neutral appearance of critical approaches such as deconstructionism, which appear uniformly hostile to all texts, whatever their claims to authority. But in fact deconstructionists treat some works with uncharacteristic respect, and their authority is left unchallenged. Marx, for instance, never seems to be deconstructed, neither does Foucault. Lacan seems exempt from the treatment, and so do Derrida and Barthes. Malcolm X and Martin Luther King appear to enjoy immunity. There may be an entire gender exception for women. In fact, the targets of critics at Duke, Yale, and elsewhere fit a distinct cultural pattern. Yet if, as we frequently read, Zora Neale Hurston is just as good as Milton, why not subject her to the same exacting critical undoing?

In a candid moment, the deconstructionist J. Hillis Miller revealed that his critical project sought "to demolish beyond hope of repair the engine of Western metaphysics."[106] Geoffrey Hartman recently observed that, contrary to the general view of the academic world, deconstructionism is not merely destructive; it also has a positive function. It could fairly be described as "restitutive criticism," Hartman wrote. While plundering classical Western texts, Hartman called for a "Philomela Project" defined as "the restoration of voice to mute classes of people." The motive was to "produce a conspicuous increase of guilt-feelings about culture as such." For deconstructionists abroad, "the challenge becomes how to support Third World writing . . . without reinstating once again the contested notion of privilege."[107]

Meanwhile, Frederic Jameson of Duke, a Marxist theorist, has signed up with the Fish brigade because he sees the *au courant* enterprise as consistent with his mission: "to create a Marxist culture in this country, to make Marxism an unavoidable presence in the American social, cultural and intellectual life, in short to form a Marxist intelligentsia for the struggles of the future."[108] In the same vein, Michael Ryan wrote in *Marxism and Deconstruction*, "The deconstructive criticism of absolutist concepts . . . can be said to have a political-institutional corollary, which is the continuous revolutionary displacement of power toward radical egalitarianism."[109]

W. J. T. Mitchell, a literature professor at the University of Chicago and editor of the influential journal *Critical Inquiry*, recently described his own conversion to poststructuralism during a 1968 conference at Johns Hopkins University. "A parade of luminaries arrived from Europe and talked in this new language, and we wondered if the world was changing before our eyes." Mitchell added that the radical experience of the 1960s left him and many others "looking for a way to reconcile professional with political commitment. Along with Marxism and feminism, post-structuralism offered a way of doing that."[110]

Jane Tompkins of Duke showed the nexus between relativism and political activism. "The New Critics had objected to confusing the poem with its results in order to separate literature from other kinds of discourse and to give criticism an objective basis for its procedures," Tompkins wrote. "The later reader-response critics deny that criticism has such an objective basis because they deny the existence of objective texts and indeed the possibility of objectivity altogether. . . . The net result of this epistemological revolution is to repoliticize literature and literary criticism. When discourse is responsible for reality and not merely a reflection of it, then whose discourse prevails makes all the difference."[111]

The critic, in other words, is free not just to create literary mean-

ings, but also to impose his or her political views on the general understanding of culture. The traditional norms of scholarship no longer
rein in the activist instinct. Fish and other theorists have provided a
justification and license for uninhibited ideological proselytization. These
rationales seem precisely catered to an academic generation, weaned
on the protest politics of the 1960s, which seeks to reconcile scholarship
and ideological activism.

Although most poststructuralists, reception theorists, and deconstructionists deny ideological motivation, that some are involved in
activism is irrefutable. Frank Lentricchia, for instance, supports numerous left-wing causes and sports "Go Left" vanity plates on his fashionable
old Dodge.[112] Duncan Kennedy, a similar-minded activist associated
with the Critical Legal Studies movement at Harvard Law School, has
proposed that janitors be paid as much as law professors (although
not that law professors be paid as much as janitors).[113] Jonathan Culler,
author of *On Deconstruction*, was a protest organizer with Students
for a Democratic Society in the late 1960s. Deconstructionist Jacques
Derrida writes, "I have always been well known for my leftist
opinions."[114] It is quite reasonable to suppose that these men would
find any argument for fusing political virtue with scholarship enormously
appealing.

\* \* \*

What is the specific appeal of this critical project to minorities?
It is precisely because *au courant* thinking is seen as advancing the
ideological claims of the minority victim's revolution on campus that it
enjoys its current status. Yet the attraction of minority students and
faculty to the new scholarship is not obvious. As we investigate further,
it becomes clear that minorities derive some short-term benefits from
the *au courant* scholars, but these apparent advantages must be weighed
against the long-term costs to minority interests.

First, by maintaining the arbitrariness of all standards, the Duke
critics make it more respectable, within the university, for minority
students and minority faculty to be recruited without reference to the
"outdated" or "reactionary" notion of academic merit. Once the concept of "academic standards" is shown to be a shibboleth, there is no
reason not to cast it aside and adopt whatever alternative seems expedient.

Second, the *au courant* critics suggest that affirmative action,
whether on the student or faculty level, is not a program of compensating
the disadvantaged for historic discrimination, but rather a means of

enriching the university through the importation of "minority perspectives" that could not possibly be supplied by whites. The reduction of
intelligence to race and gender categories—"white intelligence," "black
intelligence," "female intelligence"—allows some people to establish
their academic credentials on this basis, and feel justified in doing so.

By reducing truth to bias, and knowledge to ideology—in short,
by politicizing scholarship—some minority activists believe they can
win greater rewards than by struggling to pass traditional academic
review criteria, such as publishing requirements for hiring and tenure.
In 1987, for instance, approximately 175 black professors gathered at
Howard University to form the National Congress of Black Faculty.
Ronald Walters, a Howard professor who headed the new group, complained that "black faculty members have difficulty getting published
in mainstream journals."[115] The general assumption was that academic
journals conspired to exclude the research of blacks.

Historically these suspicions may be justified, since until the 1960s
it was not uncommon for scholarly journals to refuse to publish black
scholarship. Now, however, most journals actively seek out minority
authors, and even in the case of journals who do not do this, the
general procedure for accepting articles is a "blind" review in which
editors are unaware of the race and background of writers making
submissions. Nevertheless, no one at the conference raised the possibility that substandard work was to blame for article rejections. Instead
J. Owens Smith, president of the California Black Faculty and Staff
Organization, said, "Why shouldn't we mobilize 18,000 professors?
We should sit down with scholarly journals and ask them why they
haven't published a black scholar in years."[116]

The *au courant* scholarship also offers classroom benefits. Minority
scholars, concerned about the relative scarcity of Third World, black,
and feminist "great works," can now in good conscience assign Alice
Walker instead of Jane Austen and *I, Rigoberta Menchu* instead of
Rousseau's *Confessions*. They can give up the idea that it is necessary,
or even desirable, to study the classics of Western thought in order
to enrich their lives. Moreover, minority scholars may now believe
that, if the Western classics are studied at all, they should be read
from a "minority perspective" which enriches the text. Instead of Plato's
dialogues enlightening them, they now enlighten Plato's dialogues.

Finally, minorities discover in the *au courant* scholarship a justification for the systematic promotion of their grievances against the basic
systems of American society which are now commonly considered "institutionally racist." These systems—such as democracy, the free market,

due process, and so on—are largely procedural, and are intended to establish a neutral framework that allows all citizens to pursue happiness and safeguard their rights. Such institutions, however, can prove to be obstacles to the new social agenda. Minority demands, for example, always run the risk of being thwarted by the majority, which in a democracy can outvote such claims. The *au courant* scholarship counsels minorities that these ostensibly neutral principles and systems are in fact ideologically loaded, and in some cases mere facades for bigotry.

\* \* \*

Minority hopes for harvesting gains from the *au courant* scholarship rely on the concept of meaningful "perspectives" that, as members of racial groups, they bring to the classroom. These perspectives, however, prove elusive when efforts are made to define them.

I asked Erdman Palmore, who teaches a course on race relations at Duke, what constitutes a black perspective. Palmore shook his head. "I have no idea," he said. "I am white. If I knew what a black perspective was, we wouldn't need blacks to provide it." Why then was he, a white man, teaching a course that engaged issues of black history and black consciousness? "It would be better to have a black teach my course," Palmore agreed. Did he think it was possible for a woman to teach Shakespeare? Palmore looked puzzled. "Oh, I see what you're getting at. He was a man. Yes, that is a problem. I don't know the answer, I must confess."

The notion that one has to embody a trait or condition in order to understand it is a strange one. As a Duke professor unsympathetic to *au courant* trends points out, human beings are capable of putting themselves in the place of others, and vicariously participating in their experience. Obviously we cannot "become" someone else, but to the extent that understanding is possible, we can share in the thoughts and experiences of our fellows. It may be hard work if we are trying to comprehend someone of a very different cultural background, but that seems to be what learning is about—bridging those chasms.

The problem with the idea of ethnically determined "perspectives" is that it condemns us to an intellectual and moral universe in which people of different backgrounds can never really hope to understand each other. We are forever resigned to seeing fellow human beings from the outside—empathy becomes difficult, if not impossible. As the *au courant* critics sometimes admit, the only principle for the reconciliation of our differences is Fish's dictum that "all preferences are principled." This atomized view of social life can hardly be expected to promote racial harmony. By contrast, the idea of a universal shared humanity, despite the vagaries of circumstance and the accretions of history, creates a common basis for understanding, friendship, and community.

Because there are natural biological differences between men and women, it perhaps makes sense to speak of a "male" or "female" viewpoint. But unless we are willing to sanction the idea of natural difference between races—seemingly a racist idea—it is pointless and possibly dangerous to sanction the validity of "white" and "black" perspectives, any more than we can approve the old Nazi notion of "Jewish science."[117]

No doubt history and culture have contributed to somewhat different group interests and characteristics, but these seem to be not natural but conventional. It is not human beings who differ intrinsically, but their environments. And despite shared experience, groups show enormous internal differences; as the Commission on the Humanities observed about literature, "Some Greek or Navajo myths are more profound than others. Some black autobiographies are more enlightening than others. Some of Shakespeare's plays are more effective dramatically than others. It is in no way undemocratic to recognize these distinctions, and only confusion and bigotry gain by denying them."[118] One does not need to validate separate ethnic perspectives to study how people respond differently to different circumstances; this intellectual project falls well under the domain of the traditional disciplines.

There is also the risk of minority and gender stereotyping that results from an invocation of ethnically and sexually distinct "perspectives." Since these perspectives have plausibility only within the ideological framework of the *au courant* scholarship, outside those quarters they become an invitation for derision and amusement. Religion professor Melvin Peters of Duke complains that "blacks must not only fight the traditional battles of securing a place in academia, but today they must also fight against the prevailing suspicion about their competence."[119]

In fact, some black professors believe that the faculty handouts and quotas of Duke and other colleges ultimately work to the detriment of minority intellectual advancement in the academy. Kenny Williams, a black female English professor at Duke, remarked that she frequently suffers from assumptions that she was hired and promoted solely on the basis of race and gender. "I want to be accepted on the basis of merit," she said, adding that she dissociated herself from "the race-gender-class group."[120]

Minority graduate students suffer the same problems of group stereotyping. "When you raise a question relating to race in class," observes Phyllis Jackson, the only black to be awarded a doctorate in art history in 1989, "everyone then wants you to be the specialist on race. It's suddenly your issue, rather than an issue everyone should consider."[121]

A strong case can be made that standards of merit, strictly applied, are ultimately in the interest of blacks and other minorities. Without rigorous preparation, promising black scholars can find themselves depressed and frustrated.[122] Without taking tests seriously and attempting to raise scores, minority institutions suffer embarrassment and frustration.[123] "Many blacks consider intellectual competition to be inappropriate," complain black psychologists Jeff Howard and Ray Hammond in the *New Republic*. Yet "competition is an essential spur to development." As a result of their view that the rules are rigged, blacks sometimes do not put in the "time, discipline and intense effort" that is required to raise one's standards, to place oneself in the same league as one's peers, according to Howard and Hammond. This gives rise to what they term "rumors of inferiority."[124]

Is it really a service to young blacks and other minorities to convince them that most measures of social achievement are bogus, that an unjust system is out to get them, that indices of progress are nothing more than white norms, that hard work won't get them very far under the current regime? In the most basic areas of preparation for life, such as learning to think and write clearly, many minority students appear to face sufficiently daunting obstacles, in the form of negative peer pressure and inadequate public school programs. These students seem better off when they are encouraged to improve their performance than when they are induced to believe that measures of performance are rigged against them.

The leadership of historically black institutions seems to understand this better than the champions of minority causes at predominantly white universities. President Joffre Whisenton of Southern University argues, "There are no ethnic standards of academic excellence or administrative efficiency—no white standards, no Chicano standards, no black standards, no Asian-American standards, no Hispanic standards. We must measure up to the standards which operate as dispassionate norms."[125] In a recent study, Jacqueline Fleming of Barnard produced evidence to suggest that, although students at black colleges start out less well prepared than their black counterparts at mainstream institutions, they show more progress and development during their four years.[126]

Standards of merit will always, and should be, debated to discover how well they measure the skills that are sought. This debate, however, has nothing to do with whether groups end up overrepresented or underrepresented, because the standards measure not group but individual performance. One can only raise the statistical average of a group by improving the achievement of the individuals within it.

*  *  *

Students of all races display the effects of Duke's new style of teaching. While the *au courant* critics have developed a strong aversion to great works, it must be said in their favor that the best of them have carefully studied these works, and know them thoroughly. The problem is that they do nothing to foster in students the same broad-based cultivation that is a necessary prelude to any exercise in deconstruction. These critics know Milton and Shakespeare because they were taught not by deconstructionists but by traditionalists who exalted these poets as worthy of a lifetime of study. By contrast, Fish and his colleagues demonstrate open contempt for the notion of a "great book," and this attitude is infectious. One English major I talked to at Duke said that he wouldn't touch Milton because "I know what the guy was up to—he was a sexist through and through."

When undergraduates first encounter *Paradise Lost* in college, they realize, often to their consternation, that Satan is presented with beguiling charm, and God is, by contrast, a bit of a bore. On an issue of the greatest moral seriousness, students must confront the distinction between appearance and reality, style and substance. Instead of permitting students the full force of this confrontation, the *au courant* criticism reduces scholarship to a game, and the most successful students are the ones who learn to play it best. At Duke, the students seemed to indulge in a good deal of fashionable sophistry, such as "Good is for each one of us to determine" or "Beauty is in the eye of the beholder." When confronted with Plato's counterarguments in the *Gorgias,* and pressed to justify the philosophical premises of their own statements, however, they found themselves at a loss, and were surprised at their inability to defend their positions. They could not reply to Plato's argument that statements like these confuse the *appearance* of good or beauty with the *thing itself.* They were ignorant of the issue raised by the most elementary critical response to Milton.

But it is clear that these students would like to grapple with these issues. They show a natural riotousness and iconoclasm, which Plato also detected among the youth of his day, but underneath that swagger, as Plato also knew, many students are searching for enduring principles on which to base their beliefs. When they discover, at places like Duke, that there is no wisdom to be found, their adolescent rebelliousness turns anarchic and nihilistic. However original were some of the papers of graduate students that Duke professors showed me, it seemed an ersatz brilliance, initially enthralling but ephemeral, like a surrealist painting of Mona Lisa with a mustache. John Henry Newman diagnosed this malady a century ago—when the wellsprings of the soul run dry, he wrote, the soil no longer produces fruit or flowers but only "weird, often exhilarating, chemical concentrates of literature and art."

The term *anomie* derives from a Greek word meaning lawless or without norms, standards, and principles. The thoroughgoing assault on standards of academic merit, both among the faculty and in the classroom, at universities such as Duke seems to produce anomie among students—listlessness, boredom, and a dulling of the critical faculties for which even the most fervent political activism cannot compensate.

Their professors, however, do not point out the students' faults but encourage them—indeed these characteristics seem to be the temperamental desiderata of the *au courant* scholar. Consequently students who follow the required intellectual etiquette get good grades, and earn extravagant recommendations for academic jobs.

While this is a tempting route to take in the short run, perhaps students should consider what they ultimately get out of this education. Michel Foucault remarked of Jacques Derrida, "He's the kind of philosopher who gives bullshit a bad name." But a long time earlier, Socrates in the *Euthydemus* characterized the temperament of mind that was equally applicable to the Sophists of his day as to the Duke critics in ours. "Mastery of this sort of stuff would by no means lead to increased knowledge of how things are, but only to the ability to play games with people, tripping them up and flooring them with different senses of words, just like those who derive pleasure and amusement from pulling stools from under people when they are about to sit down, and from seeing someone floundering on his back."

\* \* \*

Although most *au courant* disciples think of themselves as progressive activists, or at least on the progressive side of history, their philosophy releases relativist and nihilist forces that culminate in coercive ideologies. This is the paradox of the relativist authoritarian. Anarchy, whether social or intellectual, has a tendency to lead to tyranny, as Tocqueville observed long ago.

The radical skepticism cultivated at Duke and elsewhere is based on the rejection of the possibility of human beings rising above their circumstances—they are presumed entirely to be products of their race, gender, class, and sexual orientation. All principles are subordinate to political and social pressure and expediency. Consequently, when these forces drive the culture in an undesirable direction, it is impossible, under *au courant* norms, to develop nonarbitrary reasons for resistance. For example, if Germans during the 1920s and 1930s were mere "products of their time," on what grounds of principle could they be expected to oppose the rising tide of fascism? This is not merely a theoretical issue, as the deconstructionist movement found out in recent years, but embroiled in a controversy that is an object lesson about the real-world price of critical indulgence.

Deconstructionists were alarmed when it turned out that the philosopher Martin Heidegger, whom Jacques Derrida called the progenitor of deconstruction, harbored strong Nazi sympathies until (and probably during) World War II. "The Führer, and he alone, is the sole German reality and law, today and in the future," he said in 1933. In a letter requesting endorsements for a speech praising Hitler, Heidegger wrote, "Of course it is clear that no non-Aryans should appear on the signature page." His correspondence is always signed, "Heil Hitler." Heidegger even welcomed the collapse of the independence of the universities, on the grounds that procedural freedoms were meaningless; true liberation would come from the "blood and soil" regime of the Third Reich.[127]

This information was ignored or dismissed as an aberration until it recently surfaced that Paul de Man, a Yale professor known as the godfather of deconstruction, wrote pro-Nazi and anti-Semitic articles for several years during the early 1940s in a Belgian newspaper. Among other things, de Man called for resistance to "Semitic infiltration of all aspects of European life." He called for Jews to be deported to an island colony. He praised French collaboration with Hitler, noting that "the necessity of immediate collaboration should be obvious."[128]

At first de Man's students and protégés—some of them Jewish—heatedly denied or downplayed his anti-Semitism. Later they acknowledged it but put it down to de Man's youthful eros. The most candid of them admitted the damning force of the revelations, but in a rearguard action denied any connection between de Man's political writings and his literary theories.[129] But de Man did not abandon or recant his youthful opinions: instead, throughout his later life he lied about his Nazi record, refusing to express a word of remorse about it.

In a lame apology, deconstructionist J. Hillis Miller observed that de Man "was by no means in these early writings totally fascist, antisemitic and collaborationist,"[130] implying that these qualities are not so bad in moderate amounts. Equally anemic was Geoffrey Hartman's argument that perhaps de Man's difficulty in facing up to his own past explains his later resistance to the charms of language, rhetoric, and propaganda.[131] Meanwhile Derrida employed the techniques of deconstructionist discourse to argue that de Man's wartime writings were contradictory, their meaning opaque, and their intention indeterminate.[132]

For the uninitiated, however, there is nothing uncertain in de Man's writings. *Mein Kampf* itself is riddled with contradictions and might be ultimately meaningless; yet, for its author and for millions of Jews, the message was perfectly clear. Far from suggesting a volte-face, de Man's later writings, contrary to Hartman's suggestion, seem to justify his behavior. "It is always possible to excuse any guilt," de Man wrote in *Allegories of Reading*, "because the experience always exists simultaneously as fictional discourse and as empirical event and it is never possible to decide which one of the two possibilities is the right one. The indecision makes it possible to excuse the bleakest of crimes." Even the left-wing *Nation* asks: "Is it possible to read this now without thinking of de Man's collaboration?"[133] The magazine referred to the case as an "academic Waldheim."[134]

At Duke, reaction to the revelations was pensive, uncomfortable, saturnine. Frank Lentricchia, for one, has not joined de Man's apologists; instead, he spoke out promptly and severely. The issue, however, involves not just personality but also political philosophy. Jane Tompkins did not hesitate, before the revelations, to describe the reader-response criticism that is de rigueur at Duke as a "close relative" of deconstructionism.[135]

In a debate on deconstructionism in the *New York Review of Books,* Charles Griswold of Howard University alleged, and his opponent Denis Donoghue admitted, that "nothing in deconstruction provides an ethical criticism of Nazism."[136] Griswold maintained that "deconstruction dissolves notions of personal accountability and responsibility," indeed it "renders theoretically unintelligible basic moral terms such as good and evil."[137] The Duke critics must confront the question of the opening that relativist theories create for totalitarian ideologies, and the way in which cognitive skepticism can sometimes accompany, and accentuate, malignant political fanaticism. The rejection of authority can sometimes produce a paradoxical embrace of authoritarianism. As Nietzsche once put it, men would rather believe in nothingness than believe in nothing.

* * *

It often surprises outsiders to discover how philosophical movements can become entrenched on campus without the university leadership having much idea of what is going on. Duke is the classic case of
an upwardly mobile Southern school seeking to be worthy of the slogan
printed on many undergraduates' T-shirts, "Harvard of the South."
Courting the latest intellectual fashions, as well as media headlines,
Duke's administrators have adopted strategies which have sorely depre-
ciated traditional academic standards to the detriment of its students'
academic prospects.

The issue is not simply whether there is more than one way to
understand literature, or whether it is desirable to increase the presence
of minorities on the faculty. The real question is whether, as a liberal
arts university, Duke will continue to uphold principles of justice and
excellence, or whether those principles will be casually jettisoned for
the unabashed pursuit of power and expediency. Like other schools
which have climbed aboard the *au courant* bandwagon, Duke must
answer the question of how the arbitrariness of intellectual standards
squares with the university's claim to teach its students about truth
and freedom and justice. After all, it is the fate of a multicultural community which is at stake.

# 7

# Tyranny of the Minority
## *Teaching Race and Gender at Harvard*

Somebody must have been telling lies about
Joseph K., for without having done anything
wrong he was arrested one morning.
— *Franz Kafka*

On February 9, 1988, Stephan Thernstrom, Winthrop Professor of history at Harvard University, opened the campus newspaper to read the headline, "Students Criticize Class as Racially Insensitive."[1] Thernstrom discovered that the class in question was "The Peopling of America," a course on the history of ethnic groups that he jointly taught with another eminent Harvard scholar, Bernard Bailyn. Three of his black students had charged him with "racial insensitivity." Wendi Grantham, a junior and chair of the Black Students Association political action committee, alleged that Thernstrom "said Jim Crow laws were beneficial," and that he "read aloud from white plantation owners' journals" that painted a "benevolent" picture of slavery. The students took their complaints to Harvard's Committee on Race Relations, an administrative committee set up by President Derek Bok to arbitrate such matters. An unnamed source on the committee said the case was being investigated.

"I was absolutely stunned when I read this," Thernstrom recalled. "None of the students had come to me with their complaints. And the comments they attributed to me were a ridiculous distortion of what I said in class. I simply did not know what to make of it."

Many on the Harvard campus were surprised, too, because Thernstrom had a good reputation as a progressive. *Perspective*, a campus journal, characterized Thernstrom as "one of the stars in the liberal firmament."[2] Thernstrom's published works, going back to the early 1960s, are specialized and highly respected in his field.[3] He is identified with the "new social history" that emphasizes the experience of common people, not just the policies of kings and "makers of events." Indeed he viewed his Harvard course as a "people's history" of America, one which would enlighten students about the complexity of civil rights issues and raise their social consciousness.

Stung by what he viewed as a meretricious and baseless attack, Thernstrom wrote a letter to the *Harvard Crimson* observing that, both in class and during office hours, he was "open to any student who wants to speak with me." By attempting to adjudicate their griev-ances through administrative committees and in the media, Thernstrom warned, students were engaging in a "McCarthyism of the left" which could exert a "chilling effect" both on academic freedom and on freedom of expression.[4]

Undergraduate Wendi Grantham responded to Thernstrom in the newspaper.[5] "I do not charge that Thernstrom is a racist," she said. Nevertheless,

> as a black student, I am left to question his sensitivity when affirmative action is incompletely defined as "government enforcement of preferential treatment in hiring promotion and college admissions." . . . I am also left to question his sensitivity when I hear that black men get feelings of inadequacy, beat their wives, and take off. . . . I am also left to question his sensitivity after reading his letter to the editor in *The Crim-son*. . . . I also find it interesting that he never once says in his letter, "I apologize if what I said was misinterpreted." Never does he question himself.

Thernstrom's colleague Bailyn came to his defense, noting that far from being a bigot, Thernstrom "spent a great deal of time disarming racist attitudes."[6] But the episode had already ignited a campuswide debate on what forms of controversial information should be barred from courses. Carolivia Herron, head tutor of the Afro-American Studies department (who has since moved to Mount Holyoke College), told the *Harvard Independent* that "by convention there are certain things that are forbidden to be spoken in the classroom." As an extreme example, Herron cited the case of a biology teacher who maintains theories of white racial superiority, but in all cases, Herron said, profes-sors should be wary of presenting information in a context that would offend minorities.[7]

"I presented factual material in an objective and dispassionate way," Thernstrom protested. He pleaded guilty to the charge of quoting from Southern plantation journals: "It is essential for young people to hear what justifications the slave owners supplied for their actions." Thernstrom maintained that his review of segregation and Jim Crow laws was narrative and analytical, covering the usual arguments from the textbook. "I simply described the effect of these laws, and have to assume that it is the content of the laws that the students found hurtful." Similarly, Thernstrom said he supplied the familiar claims on both sides of the affirmative action question, and it had not even been Thernstrom himself who supplied the controversial definition; it was offered by another author in a book that Thernstrom had merely edited.

Yet, reflecting on the episode, Thernstrom's main concern was not irate students, but the lack of support he received from Harvard.

> I felt like a rape victim, and yet the silence of the administration seemed to give the benefit of the doubt to the students who attacked me. Maybe I was naive, but I expected the university to come to my defense. I mean, that's what academic freedom is about, isn't it? Instead I was left out there by myself, guilty without being proven guilty. I could not even defend myself, because the charge of racism or racial insensitivity is ultimately unanswerable.

On February 18, 1988, a few days after the Thernstrom incident, Dean of the College Fred Jewett issued an open letter to the Harvard community.[8] Without mentioning Thernstrom, Jewett said that "recent events" compelled him to "speak out loudly and forcefully against all kinds of prejudice, harassment and discrimination." The most common incidents, Jewett said, "occur in comments or actions where the students or faculty members involved may be partly or wholly unaware of the import of their words." Jewett added, "While such incidents may not require formal college discipline, they should elicit from appropriate college officials and from the community warnings and clear messages about the inappropriateness and insensitivity of such behavior. Every member of this community must be alert to this most insidious kind of intolerance and be ready to state publicly that it can have no place at Harvard."

In short, far from coming to his defense, Jewett appeared to give full administrative sanction to the charges against Thernstrom.

At the same time, Harvard issued its "Procedures for Dealing with Concerns of Racial Harassment," prepared with the assistance of the affirmative action office and the dean of minority affairs. It defined this offense as consisting of any actions or words "which cause another individual or group to feel demeaned or abused because of their racial or ethnic background."[9] Revealingly, the emphasis seemed to be not on the objective content of the behavior or language, but on the subjective response of the self-proclaimed victim. This statement, too, was widely viewed as an administrative rebuke to Thernstrom.

It was not until a month later, on March 9, 1988, that Dean of the Faculty Michael Spence (now a graduate dean of business at Stanford) clarified that Thernstrom's academic freedom would be protected: no disciplinary action would be taken against him. Spence did, however, praise the course of action of Thernstrom's accusers as "judicious and fair," because they had followed university grievance procedures.[10] A couple of weeks later, Harvard president Bok said Thernstrom had a right to teach as he wished, but professors should be aware of "possible insensitivity" in lecturing. Bok wished the whole matter hadn't got so much press, because "public controversy often leads to rigid positions."[11]

Thernstrom read these statements as equivocal at best: according to Harvard, he had the right to be racist, if he wished; but by defending himself publicly, he was being unreasonable and inflexible; he should try to be more "sensitive" in future. Meanwhile, the integrity of his critics and their charges remained unquestioned. As for Stephan Thernstrom, he has decided, for the foreseeable future, not to offer the course. "It just isn't worth it," he said. "Professors who teach race issues encounter such a culture of hostility, among some students, that some of these questions are simply not teachable any more, at least not in an honest, critical way."

\* \* \*

Thernstrom's experience was not unique, as Ian Macneil, who was Robert Braucher Visiting Professor of law at Harvard in 1989, will testify. Macneil's reputation was placed on the line during the spring semester when Bonnie Savage, the student head of the Harvard Women's Law Association (HWLA), in a widely publicized "open letter" accused him of "repeated instances of sexism in both your contracts textbook and your classroom discussions."[12]

Savage's main charge was that, on page 963 of Macneil's textbook, he illustrates the legal concept of the "battle of the forms" with a line from Byron's *Don Juan:* "A little still she strove, and much repented,/ And whispering, 'I will ne'er consent'—consented." Savage commented that "depicting a woman . . . being dominated has no place in a contracts textbook." Further, Savage suggested that by implying that "women mean yes when they say no," Macneil was "promoting a dangerous misperception" that had been discredited in "rape law."

To this Savage added what she described as several "flippant, disparaging remarks" that Macneil had allegedly made when dealing with language that might be considered sexist. Among them: "Posner was the grandfather—or should I say grandmother?—of this idea." "That would be a strawman—or do we use that word anymore?" "Sauce for the goose, sauce for the gander—I don't know, is that sexist?" Savage concluded, "Sexist language is not a joking matter. By using sexist language, you encourage sexist thought and, in essence, promote hostility against women."

At first, Macneil says, he thought the letter came from a crank, but then he realized that Savage was writing on behalf of the Harvard Women's Law Association, which claims one-third of female law students as members. Further, Savage had sent copies to five senior law school officials for their consideration in the event that he "might be considered for tenure."

Realizing that the situation could become very serious, Macneil prepared a response,[13] accusing the Harvard Women's Law Association of publicizing the grievances of "unnamed informers." In a point-by-point rebuttal, Macneil argued that Byron's *Don Juan* quotation was "a perfect summary of what happens in the Battle of the Forms." When parties attempt to negotiate contracts on their own terms, they believe that they are not dealing on the other person's terms; yet they go ahead with the contract, knowing that both parties' initial terms cannot have been satisfied. In short, "each side consents while whispering he or she will ne'er consent," Macneil explained. The legal point had nothing to do with gender, he added. If the Harvard Women's Law Association would supply him with "an equally concise, apt and literate quotation which makes this point without sex identification," Macneil said, he would use it in future revisions of the casebook.

Macneil recalled making some of the quips that Savage documented but claimed that "the joke is about the difficulties of using the poor old common everyday English language." If he were to stop students or himself every time they used a gender-specific phrase, Macneil said, "the class would come to a grinding halt." Finally Macneil said he believed his humor was in good form and was part of his teaching style.

Again, the local media entered the fracas with such stories as

"Law Prof Denies Sexism Charge."[14] And the HWLA publicized its version of the story in its newsletter distributed around campus. Finding Macneil's response "distressing," the HWLA noted, "A teacher who sought to be fair and effective would want to address the criticism, not by defensive denial, but by listening, trying to understand, and attempting to make the classroom comfortable for all. There is no use for a hidden curriculum which makes women unable to concentrate."[15] The implication was that Macneil's alleged sexism was so offensive that female law students could not study in such an environment. It was a barrier to learning and therefore a form of discrimination.

As before, the administration remained silent throughout the controversy, allowing Macneil to fend for himself against his feminist adversaries. Eventually the publicity subsided, but because of the nature of the charges, their gravity, and their essential unanswerability, Macneil, like Thernstrom, felt that "I could not really clear myself."

A few months after the Macneil controversy, in September 1989, Harvard released new guidelines for sexual harassment by faculty members. A section on "Sexism in the Classroom" warned that "Alienating messages may be subtle and even unintentional, but they nevertheless tend to compromise the learning experience of both sexes." Professors were asked not to "focus attention on sex characteristics in a context in which sex would otherwise be irrelevant. . . . For example, it is condescending to make a point of calling only upon women in a class on topics such as marriage and the family, imposing the assumption that only women have a natural interest in this area."[16]

Macneil had little doubt on whose side the Harvard administration ended up in his dispute with the HWLA.

Macneil has chosen not to seek an extention of his teaching appointment but to move on to Northwestern University School of Law. Bitterly recounting his Harvard experience, Macneil said, "These days conscientious teachers are under constant stress trying to maintain effective student-teacher relations in the face of various forms of near-paranoia. The buzzword is sensitivity, and the intimidation is intense."

While several of his colleagues "made private supportive gestures," Macneil said, "no one at Harvard Law School or Harvard University recognized the dangers to academic freedom." He concluded, "The most common response on American campuses in general, and Harvard University in particular, to those who would destroy academic freedom is, at best, apathy and avoidance, and, at worst, cowering appeasement."[17]

*   *   *

These are not simply two regrettable episodes of professors running into a bout of bad luck with truculent students. There is a reason why Thernstrom and Macneil encountered such bitter resentment, with the result that such instances will continue to occur, and frequently; indeed there is every reason to believe that they are happening now on campuses across the nation. American higher education has succumbed to a new politics of racial and sexual "sensitivity," which now dominates debate on all controversial questions involving race, gender, or sexual orientation.

In her article denouncing Thernstrom, Wendi Grantham observed, "This is not politics. This is personal. . . . Whites control the American power structure, thus they can listen to discussions on apartheid or race relations without feeling threatened. But in similar discussions, blacks cannot divorce their personal lives from racial theory, because racist sentiment attempts to deny their daily lives and questions their validity as human beings."[18] For Grantham, "academic freedom is not truly equal, nor is freedom of speech, when the majority's freedom is greater than that of the minority."[19] In short, Grantham viewed the issue not as a question of freedom, but of power; not as one of accuracy, but of sensitivity.

When professors teach about race and gender, remarked Harvard government professor Martin Kilson, "You're not talking about Ming art or ancient Greek drawings, you're talking about something that's up close for a lot of people."[20] Kilson's point is that minorities, especially blacks, feel a special personal engagement in issues such as slavery and segregation. These institutions may not have directly affected young blacks, but they have left a deep psychological imprint. Black students feel a strong stake in the teaching of what they consider their personal experience.

This was evident during the Thernstrom controversy when Camille Holmes, president of Harvard's Black Students Association, said that affirmative action should not be defined as preferential treatment. "That definition sounds like you're holding a gun to someone's head and saying: hire these incompetent black people."[21] Another black student told a local newspaper that Thernstrom's main failing was that he "refused to acknowledge the way in which we experience his course." Particularly irksome was Thernstrom's failure to apologize. "This was a reaction which illegitimized my feelings, as a black student, about what was said."[22]

These sensitivities seem to cover the entire agenda of civil rights issues. Even on such questions as crime rates, unemployment, illegitimacy, and drugs, Harvard sociologist Nathan Glazer observes, "We have to deal with some very bad news when we talk about blacks, the largest American minority. We have to talk about unpleasant matters, matters that blacks will find upsetting and depressing, and that can only make them unhappy."[23] Consequently the university has a special responsibility to ensure that professors are free to deal with controversial material without intimidation. Universities are not forced to engage these issues, but if they choose to have a curriculum that includes Afro-American Studies and Women's Studies departments, and courses on race and feminism and homosexuality, they cannot legitimately suppress debate on these questions. Yet Glazer, who teaches courses on ethnicity, remarks that "the level of sensitivity is so high, it's hard to figure out what you can and cannot say."[24]

On many campuses, minority and feminist sensitivity translates into academic taboos. Administration officials and faculty committees seldom resist these taboos; typically they enforce them, both through regulations and through ostracism, with a rigor that puts everybody who deals with these questions on constant guard.

## The Case of Murray Dolfman

Nobody in Professor Dolfman's class in legal studies at the University of Pennsylvania could identify where the term "servitude" could be found in the American Constitution, so Dolfman commented that there were "ex-slaves" in the class who should have an idea. "I don't know if I should have used the term," Dolfman recalled, "but it got students to think of the Thirteenth Amendment right away."

Shortly afterwards, a few minority students came up to Dolfman and accused him of racial insensitivity. A second charge against Dolfman was that he had once told a black student to change his pronunciation from "de" to "the." Dolfman said that he met with the students, and apologized if they had taken offense. "I told them that I understood and shared their concerns, that I am Jewish and during *seder* we pray: When we were slaves unto Pharaoh." Dolfman also pointed out that it would be important for students, in courtroom argument in later years, to speak in a clear and comprehensible manner.

"They seemed to understand," Dolfman recalled, and the matter was dropped for a few months. But after that, during Black History Month, it was brought up again and again, Dolfman said, "to illustrate just how bad things are at Penn."

The adrenalin generated by the Black History Month rhetoric

brought about a demonstration of minority students, several dozen of whom occupied Dolfman's class and prevented him from teaching. "They read a document of indictment to my students," Dolfman said. President Sheldon Hackney met with Dolfman and asked him to refrain from public comment, even to abstain from defending himself against accusations. Then Hackney joined the ranks of the accusers, telling the campus newspaper that conduct such as Dolfman's was "absolutely intolerable." Dolfman was pressured to issue what he termed a "forced apology," and to attend "racial awareness" sessions on campus. The university subsequently decided not to renew Dolfman's teaching contract for a year.

Dolfman is now back at Penn, a chastened man. "The message has been driven home very clearly," Dolfman said. "You can't open your mouth on these issues now without fear of being humiliated."[25]

## The Case of Pete Schaub

When Pete Schaub, a business major at the University of Washington at Seattle, enrolled in a Women's Studies class in early 1988, he expected to learn about "the history of women and the contributions they have made." Schaub said his mother was a 1960s' rebel who divorced his father and moved to rural Washington state to live "close to the land."

"Introduction to Women's Studies," taught by Donna Langston and Dana-Michele Brown, was not what Schaub had expected. On the first day of class Brown asserted that "the traditional American family represents a dysfunctional family unit." Students who protested that their families were functional were shouted down by teaching assistants hired by Langston and Brown. "Denial, denial," they yelled in unison. A few days later Langston brought guest speakers to talk about masturbation. "They said you don't need a man," Schaub said. "They proceeded to show how to masturbate with a feather duster, and they had dildos right there."

When Professor Brown claimed that U.S. statistics showed that lesbians could raise children better than married couples, Schaub asked for the source. "I asked after class," Schaub said. "I wasn't challenging her." But the teacher "wouldn't hear of it. She said: 'Why are you challenging me? Get away from me. Just leave me alone.'" A member of Brown's undergraduate circle called Schaub a "chauvinist goddamn bastard." The next day, Schaub was banned from class. The teacher had two campus police officers waiting in the hall to escort him away.

Schaub protested to the administration, but nothing happened for several weeks. Finally he was permitted to go back to class, but advised by Associate Dean James Nason to drop the course.[26]

## The Case of Julius Lester

A few years ago, Julius Lester, a professor of Afro-American Studies who has taught at the University of Massachusetts at Amherst for nearly two decades, published a book about his conversion to Judaism. *Lovesong* included criticism of black novelist James Baldwin, whom Lester charged with making anti-Semitic remarks.

All fifteen of Lester's Afro-American Studies colleagues collaborated on a forty-page report which called for Lester to be expelled from the department. "It was obvious that I was no longer wanted around," Lester said. "Members of the department disparaged my work, refused to speak with me, and there were overtones of anti-Semitism." Lester added that he had been suspect in the department since 1984, when he had criticized Jesse Jackson's claim to be the spokesman for the whole black community.

Lester has since been transferred to the Judaic and Near Eastern Studies department, where he now teaches. In the Afro-American Studies department, "there is a certain ideological perspective," he said, and penalties follow "if one departs too much from it, or is critical of it. I was just exercising a different perspective."[27]

## The Case of Rosalind Rosenberg

When the Equal Employment Opportunity Commission (EEOC) sued the Sears company for failing to hire a sufficient number of women in sales, Sears said it simply could not find women who wanted to take that kind of job, and asked Rosalind Rosenberg, a feminist scholar at Barnard, to testify about historical reasons why women preferred certain jobs over others.

By agreeing to testify, Rosenberg placed herself in opposition to Alice Kessler-Harris of Hofstra University, the main witness for the EEOC. After the trial, Judge John Nordbert of the U.S. District Court of Northern Illinois concluded that Rosenberg was "a well-informed witness who offered reasonable, well-supported opinions." By contrast, he criticized Kessler-Harris for relying on "sweeping generalizations . . . not supported by credible evidence." Sears won the case.

Rosenberg, however, suffered in the feminist community of which she had been, until then, a member in good standing. Academic journals such as *Signs* and *Feminist Studies* denounced her decision to testify, and in an unusual move, members of the Coordinating Committee of Women in the Historical Profession and the Conference Group in Women's History passed a resolution at the American Historical Association annual meeting stating, "We believe as feminist scholars we have a responsibility not to allow our scholarship to be used against the interests of women struggling for equity in our society."[28] Nothing was said about any higher obligation to truth unfettered by ideological predisposition.

\* \* \*

The problems of teaching race and gender, especially in university departments of Afro-American Studies and Women's Studies, go back to the introduction of such programs. Beginning as an experiment initiated at San Diego State University in 1970, Women's Studies has grown to be a separate program or independent department in over five hundred American universities.[29] Similarly, Afro-American Studies has expanded from seventy-eight programs in 1978 to some three-hundred fifty now,[30] and several universities have set up major African and Afro-American research centers, such as the Center for the Study of Black Literature and Culture at the University of Pennsylvania; the W. E. B. Du Bois Institute at Harvard; the Carter G. Woodson Institute at the University of Virginia; the Africana Studies and Research Center at Cornell; and the Frederick Douglass Institute at the University of Rochester.

In many cases, universities agreed to open such departments and programs following protests and takeovers by students in the late 1960s and early 1970s.[31] Although the 1960s' protesters insisted on the fundamental right to dissent, their enthusiasm for it evaporated shortly after they were allowed to enter the establishment. By temperament, these activists were not partisans of robust argument for its own sake; they were fierce exponents of a set of values which they characterized as peaceful and life-affirming, and hostile to alternative views which they called warlike and bigoted. Having gained a measure of power, the protesters wanted to consolidate and use it to fight the social evils they perceived all around them. Thus from the outset minority studies departments reflected the determined ideological focus of their activist founders.

The official incorporation of radical perspectives did not satisfy everyone, however. Some black leaders and intellectuals who had been active in the civil rights movement expressed concern about possible consequences. In 1969, NAACP executive director Roy Wilkins accused college administrators of trying to "buy peace at any price" by setting up "sealed-off Black Studies centers" for "racial breast-beating."[32] Around the same time, Bayard Rustin warned that "black studies should not be used to enable young black students to escape the challenges of the university by setting up a program of 'soul courses' that they can just play with and pass."[33] And educator Kenneth Clark, an authority cited by the Supreme Court to justify its desegregation ruling in *Brown v. Board of Education,* resigned from the board of Antioch University because the college was "silent" while black militants "intimidate, threaten and in some cases physically assault the Negro students who disagree with them"; in fact, Clark said, Antioch was "permitting a group of students to inflict their dogmatism and ideology on other students and on the total college community."[34]

There have been changes since the 1960s: Houston Baker of the University of Pennsylvania charts four phases of the development of Afro-American Studies. The first phase was the establishment of pilot projects as a concession to the clamor of the counterculture; the second brought academics like St Clair Drake and Eileen Southern from historically black schools to supervise the newly installed Afro-American Studies programs; the third phase involved the staffing and expansion of these programs, and the development of "new paradigms"; we are now in the fourth phase, involving a further expansion of special programs as well as penetration into the mainstream disciplines.[35]

Women's Studies has seen, if anything, more proliferation. One reason for this is the widespread availability of qualified female PhDs who enter the academy, as compared with the very small number of black PhDs. In fact, Glenn Loury, formerly of Harvard's Afro-American Studies department and now at the Kennedy School of Government there, complains that "feminists used the civil rights issue to seize power in the universities. They now have the chairs and tenured positions. Although we helped this to come about, yet we blacks have reaped very thin gains."

Both Afro-American Studies and Women's Studies claim credit for a significant corpus of work in the past two decades. It is certainly true that St Clair Drake's *Black Folk Here and There,* Nathan Huggins' *Harlem Renaissance,* and Eugene Genovese's *Roll, Jordan, Roll* have influenced scholarship in the fields of history, sociology, and literature. So have such landmark texts such as Sandra Gilbert and Susan Gubar's *The Madwoman in the Attic,* Elaine Showalter's *The New Feminist Criticism,* and Carol Gilligan's *In a Different Voice.*

Most of these studies, however, were not produced in Afro-American Studies and Women's Studies departments.[36] Two of the classic studies of the black family, W. E. B. Du Bois' *The Negro American Family*, written in 1903, and E. Franklin Frazier's *The Negro Family in the United States*, written in 1939, were produced long before the introduction of Afro-American Studies departments. The question, therefore, is not whether Afro-American Studies and Women's Studies produce important scholarship, but whether such scholarship would not have been produced in the absence of such programs. Major scholars of the black experience, such as St Clair Drake, Allison Davis, Kenneth Clark, Vivian Henderson, and W. Arthur Lewis were all trained in traditional social science fields.[37] Even now, many scholars who teach Afro-American Studies and Women's Studies have joint appointments in other departments.

For universities, one of the main attractions of the so-called "studies" programs is that they are means to increase the representation of female and minority faculty on the campus. Walter Allen, a sociologist at UCLA, argues that Afro-American Studies appointments are irrelevant for the likes of St Clair Drake and Carter Woodson, but essential for younger scholars of color trying to gain a foothold in the academy. "Without these programs, many campuses wouldn't have black professors. The departments have been playing an affirmative action role," Allen says.[38] Because the raison d'être of these departments and programs is less scholarly than political, however, they have developed the academic stigma of being what Harvard's former Afro-American Studies chairman Nathan Huggins called the "poor second cousin," tolerated but never fully accepted by professors in traditional or mainstream fields.

\* \* \*

The main academic justification for Afro-American Studies and Women's Studies is that they provide distinctive black and female "perspectives" that are otherwise ignored in the mainstream departments. Houston Baker of the University of Pennsylvania calls for a "quest to identify a Black Aesthetic, so as to break the interpretive monopoly on Afro-American expressive culture . . . held from time immemorial by a white liberal critical establishment."[39] In a Women's Studies text used at Harvard and other schools, feminist author Bell Hooks claims, "I write from the particular experience of living as a black woman in the United States, a white-supremacist, capitalist, patriarchal society, where small numbers of white men constitute ruling groups."[40]

What exactly are these race and gender viewpoints? Usually these are defined at a high level of generality, but occasionally academics have offered specific examples. One scholar who teaches race relations maintains that white cultural values emphasize logical argument, civility, and sexual restraint whereas black cultural values emphasize emotional argument, and social and sexual spontaneity.[41] An Afro-American Studies professor at Temple University gives an exhaustive listing of "white norms"; even Santa Claus, he maintains, is an example of white "symbol imperialism" which oppresses blacks.[42] Elaine Showalter, who teaches Women's Studies at Princeton University, argues that male researchers typically ignore women's issues; thus a feminist perspective would emphasize much-needed research into female eating disorders such as the "binge-purge syndrome."[43]

The invocation of black and female perspectives is not restricted to speculative fields such as literature, but also to mathematics, law, and science. A feminist advocacy group, the Center for Women Policy Studies, has attacked the SAT standardized test on the grounds that most of the questions tend to be about "science, sports and war" which are masculine interests, while only a few questions are about "relationships, clothing and appearances," which are feminine strengths.[44] Some feminists have argued that science itself is a masculine discipline;[45] Harvard biology professor Ruth Hubbard criticizes the hard sciences for overvaluing systematic knowledge, such as the information obtained in laboratories, and undervaluing "orally transmitted knowledge," such as recipes and other household wisdom.[46]

Two prominent legal scholars maintain that the experience of oppression gives persons of color a unique perspective on law.[47] Leslie Bender of Syracuse University School of Law argues that "the feminine voice can design a tort system that encourages behavior that is caring . . . and responsive to others' needs and hurts," far preferable to the "masculine voice of rights, autonomy and abstraction."[48] In 1988 about fifty black students seized the dean's office at the Harvard Law School, calling for "diversifying the curriculum to reflect the experience of people of color and women and to insure that these issues are properly integrated into the teaching of all first-year courses."[49] In a much-publicized incident, Harvard Law professor Derrick Bell refused to teach his courses, announcing that he would take unpaid leave until Dean Robert Clark gave a tenured appointment to a black woman. Although Bell said it was necessary for Harvard to provide students with a black female perspective, the only black woman on the law faculty, visiting professor Regina Austin, condemned Bell's protest as patronizing and "just another manifestation of patriarchy."[50]

Elizabeth Fox-Genovese, who heads the Women's Studies program at Emory University in Atlanta, acknowledged that "much of this talk about white and black perspectives is pure nonsense. In fact, it degrades us to speak as though rationality and logic were entirely masculine white concepts. And black and female authors deserve better—Zora Neale Hurston, for example, didn't want to be a 'black female.' She wanted to be Shakespeare." Stephen Carter of Yale Law School questioned the widespread belief that slavery and domestic subjugation helped forge a distinctive black and female perspective. "Just because we have a shared experience of oppression as blacks doesn't mean that other people cannot understand it." And Randall Kennedy of Harvard Law School has taken on the "new minority scholarship" in a much-discussed article in the *Harvard Law Review*. "Stated bluntly," Kennedy said, advocates of a black perspective on law "fail to support persuasively their claims of racial exclusion or their claims that legal academic scholars of color produce a racially distinctive brand of valuable scholarship."[51]

Perhaps the worst consequence of dividing scholarship into "black" and "white," or "male and female," argues Michael O'Brien, a history professor at Miami University of Ohio, is to balkanize the academy. "Academe has become a kind of parliament, with each member a self-appointed delegate from a particular constituency. Each one struggles to be heard and seeks allies in an effort to attain power." O'Brien argues that "cultural egocentricity has replaced cosmopolitanism as the ethic."[52] The quest for diversity thus risks its own forms of closure and parochialism.

* * *

The distinctive perspective of the field is typified by Harvard Women's Studies professor Alice Jardine's class on "French Literary Criticism," whose November 22, 1989, session is fairly representative of numerous Women's Studies classes I attended, at Harvard and elsewhere.

The atmosphere in Jardine's course resembled a political rally. The seminar group was almost entirely female: twenty-five women versus three men. Headbands and turquoise jewelry, loose long shirts, and pins advertising various causes filled the room. There were no blacks in the class; a couple of the women were Asian. The mood in Jardine's class, while not exactly festive, was bustling, energetic. A student went to the board and put up a poster of a "Fifty Foot Woman"; everybody smiled at this emblem of female power.

Jardine, a vivacious woman who likes to sit on the front of her desk when she lectures, began with what she called "the usual announcements." First, she advertised a lecture by a Marxist feminist on "Killing Patriarchy" which "should be quite fun to go to." Next, English professor Joseph Boone was giving a paper. "He's one of our few male feminists," Jardine explained. "He was recently denied tenure here on account of his feminism." Jardine said students should "show support" for Boone by attending his lecture. She also announced a rally to protest sexual harassment.

It was time for students to describe their term papers. A male student volunteered to provide "a feminist reading of Ernest Hemingway." Loud chuckles. Jardine offered a friendly jibe at "Ernest." The students weighed in, everybody commenting on "Ernest" and his famous misogyny.

A female student gave a précis of her paper on Bessie Head's novel *Maru,* which is about tribal conflict in South Africa. This brought gasps of admiration. *Maru* was about how different African tribes learned to get along, the student said, symbolized in the end by the marriage between a man and woman from different tribes. But Jardine's student thought she spotted something interesting between the tribal woman and a female friend. She didn't say it was lesbianism, but she did say it was "important." Her only regret was that "heterosexual union comes at the price of female relationships in *Maru.*"

Throughout these descriptions one female student offered ribald one-liners about a man who lost his penis, penises that were cut off, accidents in which every part of the victim was recovered—except the penis. These brought loud and unembarrassed laughter from the professor and other students.

Eventually Jardine got around to the day's text, Marguerite Duras' *The Ravishing of Lol Stein.* "I am reading not for the story," she said. "I am reading for the signifiers." She proceeded to employ post-structuralist analysis, making acronymns from the first letters of sentences, adding up lines, and producing ingenious if implausible mathematical diagrams. "There are a lot of tropes in the novel: vegetable, animal, mineral, and so on," Jardine went on. "The *v* of vegetable," she said, "is perhaps the *V* which is Lol Stein's middle name." One student asked if Duras intended any of this; it seemed so remote from the language of the novel. "Duras must have been a mathematical genius," the student blurted out. "I've met Duras," Jardine said. "I think all of this was massively unconscious. Massively."

Jardine peppered the students with the names of the usual post-structuralist authorities: Foucault, Derrida, Julia Kristeva, Lacan. Her language alternated between French and English; the especially titillating and radical quips were all in French. I was struck by the frequency of her appeals to authority, "Most feminist theorists think . . . ," "It is widely agreed by feminists that . . . ," and so on.

Talking with students after class, I found that they took all of this with extreme seriousness; there was not a hint of irony in anything they said. Comfortable, well-fed, and obviously intelligent, their conspicuous embitterment with and alienation from American society were hard to comprehend. Besides, whatever the malady, it was hard to imagine it being remedied by this sort of intellectual fare, so esoteric and yet so vulgar, so free-wheeling and yet so dogmatic, so full of political energy and yet ultimately so futile.

\* \* \*

The unifying characteristic of race and gender education programs is that they are results-oriented; they have a point of view. It is certainly the case that individual professors in university English or history departments will incline to their own interpretations, or espouse a set of interpretations that could plausibly be termed "ideological." An English professor may identify with the New Criticism; a philosopher may think of himself as a historicist; a sociologist may apply functionalist analysis. More conventionally ideological styles, such as libertarianism or Marxism, may provide a frame of reference for particular scholars in various fields. In no other area, however, is there a shared orthodoxy for the entire department, indeed for the *entire field.* In fact, there is typically a wide range of positions within departments, and universities usually go out of their way to assure that these differences are reflected in the curriculum. But this is not the case in Women's Studies and Afro-American Studies.

Speaking at a conference of Afro-American scholars, Dona Marimba Richards of Hunter College defined the way the topics were approached: "We see ourselves as necessarily activist scholars who are committed to the self-determination of our people."[53] Molefi Asante, chairman of the African Studies department at Temple University, says that being black is an essential, though not sufficient, condition for presenting a truly "Afrocentric" perspective in the classroom. "You cannot call any African-American discourse, merely because it is uttered by a black person, Afro-centric. Much of so-called black discourse is essentially white or Eurocentric discourse by black people."[54] Asante's point is that Afro-American scholarship must be politically radical in order to qualify as truly black. Similarly, Harvard's Derrick Bell denounced his black faculty colleagues as "people who look black and think white."[55] Thomas Kochman, a white professor who teaches courses in race relations at the University of Illinois, maintains that at the outset of his classes he announces his political solidarity with the black cause, otherwise he does not believe he will receive "support and cooperation" from blacks.[56]

These sharply defined notions of pedagogic authenticity also obtain in history, sociology, and American studies courses dealing with race and gender. Jane DeHart, a historian at the University of North Carolina at Chapel Hill, remarked that "many of us gravitated to the new scholarship on race, gender and class as a key to understanding, and changing, power relations in society."[57] Linda Kerber, past president of the American Studies Association, defines the outlook in her field: "Freed from the defensive constraints of cold war ideology, empowered by our new sensitivity to the distinctions of race, class and gender, we are ready to begin to understand difference as a series of power relationships involving domination and subordination, and to use our understanding of power relationships to reconceptualize both our interpretation and our teaching of American culture."[58]

Perhaps nowhere are these pedagogic and ideological premises more strongly and consistently found than in Women's Studies departments and programs. Women's Studies professor Sandra Gilbert of the University of California at Davis compares feminism to a religious conversion, noting that "most feminist critics speak like people who must bear witness, people who must enact and express in their own lives and words the revisionary sense of transformation."[59] Myra Dinnerstein, director of the Southwest Institute for Research on Women at the University of Arizona, observes, "The origin of Women's Studies lies in the women's movement—there wouldn't have been women's studies if there wasn't a consciousness that women were a group that was being discriminated against." Dinnerstein maintains that feminist presuppositions lead to radical conclusions. "Learning about women is itself revolutionary."[60]

Often these political implications are explicitly stated. Janet Lee, a Women's Studies professor at Mankato State University, maintains in a catalog description that in her class

> a central objective is feminist praxis in action. . . . Central is the goal of integrating feminist theory and an understanding of racial inequality into a class analysis so that we may understand the status of all women under capitalist patriarchy. Also included is an analysis of poverty, social welfare, and the consequences of Reaganomics on individual women's

lives. Race is integrated throughout the course. The class is taught from a feminist perspective.

Lee adds, "Also as integration of content and process, theory and action, we have collectively participated in direct collective action for social change. This gives hands-on experience in strategies for social change." She observes that grading is based in part on "participation in the action project."[61]

Many scholars assert that it is simply impossible to oppose feminism and be hired to teach Women's Studies. In fact, the Committee on the Status of Women at the American Association of University Professors (AAUP) maintains that criticism of feminism or Women's Studies is impermissible because it has a "disparate impact on women faculty and chills the intellectual climate for academic women."[62] Within the parameters of feminism, debate may be entertained, but feminism itself is not open to question. "Feminist education has become institutionalized in universities via Women's Studies programs," remarks feminist writer and teacher Bell Hooks.[63]

Women's Studies even has its own distinctive terminology. Professors frequently speak of *(her)story* and *malestream* thought.[64] The term *freshman* is now *first-year student,* one must say *Ms* instead of *Miss, waiters* are *waitpersons* or *waitrons,* committees are headed by *chairpersons* or *chairs.*[65] Some feminist teachers won't spell the term *women* because it includes the word *men;* instead, they prefer *wimmin* or *wombyn.* One professor at Washington University in St. Louis refuses to use the word *seminar* because it smacks of masculinity; instead she prefers the term *ovular;*[66] a faculty women's committee at McGill cannot bring itself to say *seminal.*[67] President James Freedman of Dartmouth, who calls himself a feminist, accuses the *Dartmouth Review* of "ad hominem and ad feminem" attacks.[68] Yale historian Howard Lamar says that his course on "Cowboys and Indians" should now be called "Cowpersons and native Americans."[69] It is now commonplace, in scholarly books and journals throughout the humanities, to find the term "she" used generically, as in "When a scientist makes a discovery, *she* submits it for peer review."

At Harvard in the fall of 1989, an introductory course on the study of women, "Women's Studies 10 A," assigned the following texts: Friedan's *Feminine Mystique,* Hooks' *Feminist Theory: From Margin to Center* and *Talking Back: Thinking Feminist, Thinking Black,* Banks' *Faces of Feminism,* de Beauvoir's *The Second Sex,* Davis' *Women, Race and Class,* and Donovan's *Feminist Theory.* Some of these books are certainly worth reading, but they all reflect a similar, if not identical, understanding of gender difference. None of these books can be described as even mildly critical of feminist ideology.

This one-sided reading list seems to falsely imply that the breadth of views about women's roles in society are reflected in the course. Certainly most women in America do not identify themselves as feminists. In fact, survey data indicate that a majority eschew the feminist label.[70] If women's studies is "political" in the sense that it speaks for women, where are non-feminist or antifeminist women to be found? Where are their arguments to be heard, or are we to assume that they are bereft of arguments?

Ironically, some of the same people who most stridently oppose a great books canon seem most active in devising their own consciously ideological and highly exclusive canon for race and gender education. This project has authoritative sanction in the form of a handbook published by the American Sociological Association for those who teach race and gender called *An Inclusive Curriculum*. It includes model course formulations and reading lists drawn from such courses across the country. In the section on gender, a rough tabulation indicates that approximately 90 percent of the texts are explicitly feminist, and the rest relate to feminist concerns; there is no text that could fairly be described as antifeminist, and there is virtually no material that falls outside the familiar feminist agenda.[71]

At Women's Studies conferences, not only are the ideological goals of the academic program discussed, but also how to camouflage these goals for marketing purposes. At a 1985 conference, for instance, Penny Gold of Knox College recommended that Women's Studies programs should be renamed Gender Studies:

> If the goal is to reach as many people as possible, Gender Studies may be the best name. It is not immediately identifiable with a particular political movement. Related to wider student appeal is also, of course, wider faculty and administrative appeal. It may be easier to get [appropriations for] Gender Studies through faculty committees.[72]

The trend for the future appears to be toward greater radicalism. Allison Jaggar, Women's Studies chair at the University of Cincinnati and head of the Committee on the Status of Women at the American Philosophical Association, recently denounced the nuclear family as a "cornerstone of oppression" and eagerly anticipated scientific advances to eliminate such biological functions as insemination, lactation, and gestation. "One woman could inseminate another . . . men and nonparturitive women could lactate . . . fertilized ova could be transferred into women's or even men's bodies."[73] For the first time, Harvard and Yale have assembled Curriculum Committees to explore course material on "Gay, Lesbian and Bisexual Studies."[74] Washington University in St. Louis now has an academic group, the Organization for Changing Men, which seeks to show students that they "are locked into homophobic constructs" in their daily life.[75] Kenyon and other colleges are beginning programs in Men's Studies, which apply feminist principles in opposition to what one professor calls "the white, male, heterosexual, able-bodied, Christian, middle-class norm."[76]

One reason for this increasing radicalism is that, with the collapse of Marxism and socialism around the world, activist energies previously channelled into the championship of the proletariat are now "coming home," so to speak, and investing in the domestic liberation agenda. A good metaphor of this is that Angela Davis, former vice presidential candidate of the U.S. Communist party, is now professor of the politics of reproduction at San Francisco State University.[77]

* * *

The monolithic ideological focus of the so-called "studies" programs seems to have produced a relentless, even fanatical, conformity of thought in which "diversity" loses its procedural meaning and assumes substantive content. In other words, "diversity" does not refer to a range of views on a disputed question, but rather entails enlisting in a regiment of ideological causes which are identified as being "for diversity." For instance, to be "for diversity" you must believe that homosexuality as a sexual preference is morally neutral, or that women have been victims of domestic incarceration through history; if you resist these notions, then you are "against diversity" and eligible for sanctions and abuse.

The paradox is heightened by the recognition that this campus heckling and ostracism is generated on behalf of minorities. In a democratic society, this comes as a surprise. Indeed, the American founders and later Alexis de Tocqueville feared the political and intellectual "tyranny of the majority." They assumed that in a regime of majority rule, the danger is that the majority will inflict its views on the unwilling minority. The founders considered various strategies to counter this danger.[78]

But hardly anyone predicted the possibility of a tyranny of the minority, or more precisely, tyranny in the name of minority victims.

Marching under the banner of equality, the new race and gender scholarship seems in reality to promote principles of inequality—minority sentiments are placed on a pedestal while majority sentiments are placed on trial. Those who challenge this intellectual framework are accused of collaborating in the historic crimes perpetrated against minorities.

How is this bullying pedagogy carried out, and what effect does it have on students, especially minority students on whose behalf Women's Studies and Afro-American Studies claim to be working?

\* \* \*

Afro-American Studies and Women's Studies are only part of the American university's ideological project in sensitivity training. Columbia, Brown, Dartmouth, Wayne State, Michigan, and many other colleges now have sensitivity education seminars aimed at countering the perceived resurgence of bigotry among students, notably white men. William Damon, the chairman of the education department at Brown University, argues that "racial education programs should emphasize discussions in which trained instructors . . . provide clear justification for any racially or ethnically sensitive admissions or hiring criteria that students may see on campus. . . . It is important to make such programs mandatory, so that they can reach students who otherwise might not be inclined to participate."[79]

Most sensitivity programs take precisely the shape that Damon advocates. At a recent such session at Dartmouth, for example, students were urged to step forward and confess their bigoted impulses; one student broke into tears as he admitted being a homophobe, while other students sighed and clapped, welcoming him into the ranks of the enlightened. Although intended therapeutically, the sensitivity session quickly assumed a different character. Initial calls for "tolerance" of different lifestyles rapidly metamorphosed into demands that "intolerant" students be identified and punished. Students who would not endorse the substantive agenda for "diversity" were termed fascists, Ku Klux Klansmen, and cross-burners. Les Grant, a politically conservative black student who refused to support divestment of Dartmouth investments from companies doing business in South Africa, was hung in effigy in the main administration building.

Harvard's main conduit for sensitivity education outside the classroom is the university's annual AWARE week, whose main organizer is the assistant dean of minority affairs, Hilda Hernandez-Gravelle. AWARE is an acronymn for Actively Working Against Racism and Ethnocentrism. "I don't want to be a racist . . . but I think I might be," the posters emblazoned across AWARE fliers said. In the fall of 1988, political scientist Robert Detlefsen attended AWARE sessions and published an article in the *New Republic* describing an atmosphere rife with excess.[80] These are some of the statements he recorded:

> Professors should have less freedom of expression than writers and artists, because professors are supposed to be creating a better community.

> When delivering a lecture, one should be careful not to introduce any sort of thing that might hurt a group.

> Throwing tampons at the male, sexist dogs of Dartmouth was educational.

> These places [Ivy League colleges] may be the slickest form of genocide going.

This was the tone of the speakers, who were professors from Harvard and nearby colleges. The AWARE week keynote was delivered by Colgate professor John Dovidio, who spoke about "Racism among the Well Intentioned," a group of offenders that he placed at about 85 percent of the population. One professor called for racially or sexually offensive material to be edited out of lectures. Another surveyed the English language to find words like "Snow White" and "black magic" which, to him, indicated the omnipresence of racism. The only dissident voice was Harvard government professor Harvey Mansfield, who said that race and gender hypersensitivity threatened to chill free discussion of issues such as affirmative action that needed to be addressed. Although Mansfield was permitted to speak, his remarks were widely rebuked as evidence of precisely the problem faced by Harvard and other universities seeking to fight bigotry.

Although some of the AWARE rhetoric may have been simply a form of ethnic cheerleading, Detlefsen detected a mean and anti-intellectual tone running throughout the conference. For instance, some of the speakers equated legal rights for blacks in the United States with apartheid in South Africa; others compared the attitude toward minorities at Harvard with that of the Ku Klux Klan in the South. Given the magnitude of these defined evils, drastic remedies were in order. The result of the facile accusations of AWARE speakers, Detlefsen predicted, was that "innocent persons are certain to be the targets of censorship and character assassination at the hands of a zealous squadron of thought police."

Indeed such scapegoating had happened before, and would happen again shortly after the conference. When a group of dining-hall workers at Harvard held a "Back to the Fifties" party, Minority Affairs Dean Hilda Hernandez-Gravelle denounced them for racism on the grounds that their nostalgia for the 1950s probably included segregationist sentiments.[81] When Professor Ron Heifitz of Harvard's Kennedy School of Government assigned the movie *It's a Wonderful Life,* he was forced to cancel the screening because black students protested that the household maid reflected a stereotype. "The portrayal was sociologically accurate, and the woman was presented with dignity," Heifitz told me. "But the students felt that blacks should not be shown doing such jobs." In December 1989 Linda Wilson, the new president of Radcliffe, Harvard's sister school, was denounced by feminists who charged that, by not calling herself a feminist, she was "doing violence to herself."[82]

When I went to see Dean Hilda Hernandez-Gravelle, she was busy with the preparations for the 1989 AWARE week. On the notice board she had pegged the names of "designated race relations tutors," one assigned to each Harvard house. She had handpicked them for their proven opposition to conscious and unconscious bigotry, she explained. Their job was to "monitor the racial atmosphere," report "violations of community," and "raise consciousness" of the students. The presence of local sensitivity monitors had upset some students who compared them to the neighborhood spies in totalitarian countries, but Hernandez-Gravelle dismissed the analogy as absurd.

For her "house workshops" on racism, Hernandez-Gravelle said she had hired a Cambridge-based "facilitator company" called Visions, Inc. In its promotional package Visions defines racism as "the systematic oppression of people of color." Apparently there is no such thing as black racism, or racism directed against whites. Yet Visions defines a bewildering variety of forms of racism: "personal and interpersonal racism," "institutional racism," and "cultural racism"—defined as a preference for "one's cultural heritage and values over that of another." In short, Visions seems to believe that one has to be a cultural and moral relativist in order to avoid being a racist.[83] Another pamphlet in the AWARE packet concerned "conditions which help or hinder racial learning." Students are urged to "accept the onion theory, that they will continue to peel away layers of their own racism for the rest of their lives."[84]

Hernandez-Gravelle is a small, demure woman who nevertheless speaks in a deliberate tone, conveying ideological fervor. A native of Puerto Rico with degrees in education and social psychology, she said her "mandate" at Harvard was "to create programs that address and adjudicate issues of race relations." She reports to the dean of the college, Fred Jewett, who issued the "open letter" against Thernstrom. According to Hernandez-Gravelle, the most typical complaint she deals with is "exclusionary language in the classroom. When material is presented, the contributions of the community of color are downplayed or not treated at all."

When black and Hispanic students come to her with problems, which apparently happens on a regular basis, Hernandez-Gravelle said she "helps them to externalize their experience rather than internalize it. A minority student may fear that he is wrong, or that he deserves to suffer these indignities. I tell them: this is not your fault. You are not weak or hypersensitive." The Thernstrom case, Hernandez-Gravelle said, was "hard and yet typical." She blamed the controversy on "defensive behavior on the part of the professor." She saw her job as "to give support to the students." As for academic freedom, "The professor may invoke academic freedom and get away with it. But what about the right of the students to feel free? What about their right to be treated in a respectful way?" Too many professors, she said, "want to be in safe castles without making the effort to include other perspectives."

Hernandez-Gravelle conceded that her role was a sort of ideological monitor of the faculty, even in fields that she knew nothing about. "Of course this is a political agenda," she said. "What isn't a political agenda? Maintaining the traditional curriculum is a political agenda."

Criticizing the *New Republic* for its report on the previous year's AWARE week, Hernandez-Gravelle said it was "a unique opportunity for students to confront their own hidden prejudices. The writer of that article simply refused to expand his vision." As for the magazine's charge that all the panelists, with the exception of Harvey Mansfield, were stacked in favor of one side, Hernandez-Gravelle retorted, "Mansfield was a crazy extremist on one side. There were no extremists on the other side. Everybody else was very sensible and perceptive on the issues."

\* \* \*

Lawrence Watson's actual title is assistant dean for academic administration in the Graduate School of Design. Because of his activist bent, however, Harvard considers him an authority on issues affecting the minority community. Watson is now cochairman of the Association of Black Faculty and Administrators, and helps to organize "racism awareness" programs for undergraduates at Harvard. He has played a leading role in past AWARE week programs.

Watson began our conversation on a pedagogical note, citing his advanced degrees from Cornell University, whose Africana Center is considered to be a beacon of Afro-American Studies. "It is widely perceived that people of color are inferior," Watson said, a belief he traced back to the famous three-fifths clause of the U.S. Constitution. "We were considered three-fifths of human beings," Watson said incredulously. Was it his impression that the American founders thought that is what blacks are worth? "Of course," Watson said. "It was a compromise, but that's what they concluded."

We have encountered similar moral indignation over the claim that the Constitution considered blacks as partial human beings in the words of activists at Stanford and Howard. While they are right that the founders compromised on the issue of slavery, permitting it to continue, it is especially important for them to address the truth about the widely misunderstood and distorted three-fifths clause. In fact, the argument was about political representation, not the intrinsic worth of blacks. The South wanted to count blacks as whole persons, in order to increase its political power. The North wanted blacks to count for zero, not because Northerners denied the humanity of blacks, but in order to preserve and strengthen the antislavery majority in Congress.[85] Thus reducing the percentage value of blacks was the antislavery position; paradoxically, black interests would have been best served had they counted for nothing. This complication bewildered Watson, who said "I really cannot recall the circumstances now. It's been a while since I read up on all that." If an academic dean specializing in issues of race is ignorant on this point, what does this say about the way history is being taught and learned in Afro-American programs?

According to Watson, the function of programs like Afro-American Studies is "to make some sense of the fact that we still live in a society that is blatantly racist." He would not agree to specify any incidents of racism, however, saying that would "compromise" the breadth of his indictment. Instead, citing "institutional racism," Watson argued that "if we [minorities] are not an integral part of the trustees, the administration, the faculty, the students, then we are talking about Harvard carrying on a tradition of racism."

Watson said it was important that "some great works be revised" because of their portrayal of women and minorities. "We've got to take the, quote, great works, unquote, and rewrite them, although in some instances this would be impractical," Watson said.

Asked about the usual complaint about "covert racism," Watson said racism was just as overt as ever. In fact, "We are still trying to abolish slavery," he paused, "both in the physical and the psychological sense." Drawing an analogy between the United States and South Africa, Watson said that the welfare system, homelessness, and drugs constituted "American apartheid." Citing the high murder rate in American cities, Watson said, "The conditions my brothers face in South Africa are similar to the conditions my brothers face in Boston and Washington, D.C." Even if American blacks did the killing, Watson said, "the question is not who is behind the gun, but the conditions that bring this about." The prison system in this country, he said, is a "plantation system" where "90 percent of inmates are black and 70 percent of the wardens are white."

These facts and ideas, he said, were "not well known in the white curriculum" and should be presented in the minority studies programs, "at least for the benefit of the students of color."

While few will disagree with Watson's recommendation to get out the facts about race relations in this country, it is questionable whether this is, in fact, Harvard's approach. For a university whose motto is *Veritas*, I found a surprising amount of deliberate prevarication that is sponsored, or at least encouraged, by the administration.

For instance, Harvard publishes an *Affirmative Action Newsletter*, whose fall 1989 issue contains a section called "Myths and Realities."

> Myth: Affirmative action means applying a double standard—one for white males and a somewhat lower standard for women and minorities.
>
> Reality: Double standards are inconsistent with the principle and spirit of affirmative action. One standard should be applied to all candidates applying for a position. This myth implies that women and minorities are inherently less qualified than white males, a proposition that is totally baseless.[86]

On affirmative action, as on other issues, people are entitled to their own opinions but they are not entitled to their own facts. As we saw in the case of Berkeley and other schools, it is unequivocally the case that affirmative action involves displacing and lowering academic standards in order to promote proportional representation for racial groups. Yet in the name of "sensitivity," Harvard seems not to be above distorting truth and disseminating information that is clearly false.

\* \* \*

Perhaps the impact of the race and gender pedagogy is best examined by asking students who take these courses what they learn from them. Tiya Miles is a bespectacled, soft-spoken student from Cincinnati, Ohio. Eva Nelson and Michelle Duncan are both from Detroit. While Duncan speaks with a slight drawl, however, Nelson speaks in short staccato outbursts, filled with passionate intensity. All three are majoring or double-majoring in Afro-American Studies at Harvard.

"I see white culture as deviant and I expect Afro-American Studies to take up that perspective," remarked Nelson. "In order to get into Harvard we have to show a white perspective. If someone had a truly Afro-American perspective they would not have gotten into Harvard and they would not have wanted to." Duncan agreed. "We're black on the outside, but a lot of us don't have the fortitude to be black on the inside." She said she was glad she left a private school she attended, because "if I stayed in private school, I would end up a brain-dead white person." She paused. "That's okay—if you're white."

Nelson argued, "If we lose our black cultural perspective, we have nothing left—only our murder rate, infant mortality, the bad stuff. Without our culture, all we are is a bunch of pathologies." What, then, was this distinctive black perspective? "My relatives down South are offended by the way I talk," Nelson suggested. "But now I refuse to talk nice. I say what I think. White people are more genteel and fake than black people." Blacks have traditionally had a different sense of humor than whites, Nelson said. For example, a white person may walk in from the cold and say: boy, it sure is hot out there. "Now a white person will think that's funny. Ha, ha, ha. A black person will think that's stupid. We're not into the little white sarcasms. I find that smart-alecky stuff sickening myself."

Nelson and Duncan admitted that there was a price to be paid for abandoning white etiquette. "My roommates last year were put off because I would talk in black cultural language," Nelson said. Duncan added, "My roommates can't stand me. In fact, I am always getting into fights. All my friends now are black women from the sorority. You know, Alpha Kappa Alpha, the black sorority."

Both Nelson and Duncan complained about discrimination, not only at Harvard, but within Afro-American Studies. "My instructor once used the term 'subculture,'" Duncan said. "Can you believe it? That offended me." Nelson added, "There is a juxtaposition of blacks and other ethnic groups. This is very offensive. When we see that other groups have done better, the conclusion is that we haven't done anything, so we're inferior. By the way, I just hate it when the Jews start comparing themselves to us. The other day I heard a very offensive remark about how Jews have done more for themselves than blacks."

Since they spoke frequently of Harvard as "institutionally racist," it seemed reasonable to inquire: what was the worst instance of bigotry the women had experienced at Harvard? "I once heard a white man say he could never go out with a black girl," Tiya Miles said. There was a long pause. "Look," Nelson chipped in. "Whites hide their racism very well. This is the problem with being genteel."

The students talked about why they were choosing to concentrate in Afro-American Studies. "At first, my parents were livid," Tiya Miles said. "They said I would never find a job. They said it would make me viewed as a militant." As for her friends at Harvard, "My white friends say: do it. But my black friends aren't so sure." Miles is going ahead because, as a young black from a middle-class background in the Midwest, she feels it is important to "get in touch with myself, who I really am." Down deep, she is convinced, she is not just a well-spoken, well-adjusted, middle-class woman from Cincinnati.

For Duncan and Nelson, who are both from poorer families in inner-city Detroit, the major means something quite different. "For me, it's been very liberating," said Duncan. "I have learned how racist and sexist I can be against my own people." For example, while crossing the street late at night, Duncan reported that she saw three large black men "and my first reaction was, oh shit."

Nelson pounced on that. "If they were white men, you would not have had that reaction."

"Exactly," Duncan said.

Nelson added that Afro-American Studies helped her realize how myths of black inferiority have sapped black self-confidence. Reflecting an element of hostility to Jews, she said, "Now I realize why I was insecure about some Steinberg." Duncan said Afro-American Studies majors learned to think critically. "In school you hear: I pledge allegiance to the flag. In Afro-Am you learn: it ain't my flag." Nelson said that she had learned that, even though he freed the slaves, Abraham Lincoln was a racist. "He was a joke," she said. "He himself said that if he could save the union without freeing the slaves, he would do it."

Tiya Miles hesitated. "Well, I'm not sure."

But the other two broke in. "Come on," Duncan said. "Lincoln was a mess." Nelson looked at Miles as if she wondered what had gotten into her.

Miles backed down. "Well, I haven't studied it that well."

On Jefferson the three were agreed: he was, in various descriptions, a "hypocrite," a "rapist" (an apparent reference to Jefferson's alleged relationship with a dark-skinned woman), and a "total racist."

None of the three students appeared to distinguish comments and personal practices of Jefferson and Lincoln from their principles and public acts. Miles occasionally edged in that direction, but inevitability retreated when disciplined by her more radical friends.

Nelson finally gave some credence to the argument that the American founders advanced principles of equality that were ahead of their time. The abolitionist Frederick Douglass had argued that slavery was only the "scaffolding" of the founders' work, "to be removed as soon as the building was completed. . . . These masters knew that they were writing the texts in which the slaves would learn their rights."[87] Lincoln had maintained that the Declaration of Independence announced the *right* to equality whose *enforcement* would follow as soon as circumstances permitted.[88] Without the principles of equality enshrined in the founding documents, I suggested, Lincoln would have had no ground to stand on against the South, and Martin Luther King would have had to look elsewhere for a moral basis for the civil rights struggle. Thus by articulating progressive principles, even though failing to live up to them in practice, an argument can be made that Jefferson and Madison were champions of human liberty and equality.

The matter is more serious than the reputations of the American founders: during the infamous *Dred Scott* case, Justice Taney argued that the American founding was proslavery, that proslavery principles were inherent in the document. Against these arguments the abolitionist movement put up stern resistance. Ironically, a century later, young black students were defending a view of history put forward by Taney to justify a constitutional right to own slaves.[89]

The more Nelson thought about it, the more she saw something there. She said, however, that she had never heard this argument made before. "Did you think of it yourself?" she asked. "You know, I too believe in those principles. I really do. I guess that's what makes us Americans." She laughed. "Really, we're pitifully American, if you think about it."

Although I left the three young women thinking that Harvard was not helping them find what they desperately sought—a principled ground on which to pattern their lives as self-conscious blacks—nevertheless there was a refreshing sharpness and candor in their views.

Nelson, for instance, freely denounced her "bearded, dashiki-wearing, flip-flop wearing liberal jerk of an instructor. He thinks that by dressing like this, and using South African pronunciations, he gets to be thought of as black." Duncan said, "I resent white feminists jumping on our back, taking the benefits, and then taking off." Nelson said. "I resent black people being compared to gays. Don't lump us all together, please, in your book."

I could not help liking, and even admiring, these students, whose very intensity of indignation, if somewhat overblown, commanded respect. It seemed hard to see how the well-meaning appeasement of their demands, by Harvard students and administrators, would diminish their outrage, which resembled a typhoon in search of targets to destroy. Somewhere after college, one hoped, these young women would, through experience and continued reflection, find a better understanding of themselves, their heritage, and their country than they were receiving at Harvard.

* * *

The *Harvard Salient* is a conservative campus newspaper whose editor for 1989–90 was a Cuban American, Alex Acosta. Acosta protested the level of race and gender indoctrination which he said occurs both inside and outside the classroom.

Each year Harvard has a "minority orientation week" which is separate from general class orientation. Acosta attended because he is considered Hispanic. "You were assigned to someone of your own racial background," Acosta said. "Blacks were assigned to blacks, Asian freshmen to Asians, and so on." Ethnic separatism was a constant theme, especially separatism between minority groups and the larger white culture. At the end of the week, Acosta said, "everyone on campus who had gone to the mainstream orientation knew everyone else, but I didn't know anyone who was not a minority."

Another newspaper staffer, Marie Delci, said she feels constant pressure from the university-funded Hispanic group on campus, RAZA, to participate in events to demonstrate "ethnic solidarity." Although her given name is Marie, and she likes to be called that, "the RAZA people insist on calling me Maria, because that to them is Hispanic. A friend of mine is Alex, but they insist on calling him Alejandro. He doesn't want to be called Alejandro."

Barrie Greene, a female physics major who is white, remarked that "I have never encountered sexism here." A campus group called Women in Science, however, operates under the premise that the field is paradigmatically inhospitable to women, Greene said. "They are always asking me if it's tough to be a woman in science. I tell them it is tougher to be a white person in science. Many of my classmates are Asian." The feminist premise that science is a masculine field "because it is cold and empirical," Greene said, confirms stereotypes about women that "feminism is supposed to be fighting."

All three students said that while Harvard did ensure that free speech was permitted, the norms of acceptable behavior on campus outlaw open or critical expression of views on questions of race, feminism, or homosexuality. Delci said that administrators, professors, and teaching assistants constantly badgered students to use gender-neutral language. "French is considered a very backward language here, because it has masculine and feminine words," Delci explained. Whenever she sees ads now, Delci said, "I have been trained by Harvard to look for racist and sexist implications. You know, I'm not really into that. But whenever I ignore it, they tell me that I am a person of color and a woman—someone of my background should know better."

Acosta said, "The gay students here are especially powerful. That's probably because there are so many of them, and also because they're very vocal, very political. It's not as bad as Yale, but it's still pretty bad. If you are insensitive to gay rights, that really gets you into trouble at Harvard." Acosta seemed to reflect a widespread sentiment that, to avoid ostracism, students need to go along with the campus orthodoxies, although Acosta said that if the situation is implausible or absurd, "I go back and tell my roommates and we laugh about it for half an hour."

\* \* \*

Harvard political scientist Harvey Mansfield, the villain of AWARE week, dismissed Dean Hernandez-Gravelle's description of him as a "crazy extremist"; he regards it as unworthy of comment. The problem at most universities, Mansfield said, is that sensitivity education constitutes institutional cover for preferential treatment and double standards. Mansfield maintained that these policies have reinforced, among both blacks and whites, the old stereotypes about black inadequacy; thus the "unspoken theme" of AWARE week was black inferiority. "The blacks were saying: we are not inferior, and the whites were saying: don't worry, we don't think so. The main target was not blue-collar bigots but people at Harvard like E. O. Wilson and Richard Herrnstein."

Wilson is a world-famous sociobiologist who explores the connections between nature and the environment; Herrnstein has published comparative data on intelligence tests. Both have been the object of vilification for their scholarly findings. So has Harvard political scientist Edward Banfield, author of *The Unheavenly City,* who has written frankly and critically of urban policy.

A couple of years ago, a group of Harvard scholars including

Mansfield, Wilson, Herrnstein, sociologist Nathan Glazer, philosopher Willard van Orman Quine, and economist Glenn Loury had meetings to discuss the university taboos, and how to deal with academic questions that were essentially beyond debate. "If the atmosphere was bad then," Mansfield said, "it is even worse now." Mansfield himself has become something of a pariah on the Harvard campus, but he is not unhappy about that; curiously, he argues, it exempts him from asphyxiating social pressures and gives him a certain intellectual freedom to speak his mind.

Commenting on the Thernstrom incident, Glenn Loury said "if this had happened fifteen years ago, there would have been an uproar." In fact, Afro-American Studies scholars such as Martin Kilson, W. Arthur Lewis, and Orlando Patterson used to address much more controversial material, Loury argued. A former professor of Afro-American Studies at Harvard, Loury requested to be transferred to the Kennedy School of Government in part because he found the Afro-American Studies atmosphere too restrictive and intolerant.

Similarly, Orlando Patterson, the eminent sociologist and author of *Ethnic Chauvinism*, left Harvard's Afro-American Studies department some years ago. He was initially lured to Harvard from the University of the West Indies, but according to one of his colleagues, "when he got here he had no idea of what to expect. It was only here that he saw the politicization of scholarship, and it shocked him. He got in touch with people like St Clair Drake and they confirmed his fears. Finally he just didn't want the stigma. He decided to teach in a real department." Patterson now teaches in the sociology department, but does not have a joint appointment with Afro-American Studies. He would not deny his colleague's account, saying only that he wished to pursue his academic interests without embroiling himself in political controversy.

David Riesman, professor emeritus of sociology at Harvard and author of *The Lonely Crowd*, commented that "it is very sad for me to see so many people from the sixties' cohort become enemies of true diversity. What we have now in universities is a kind of liberal closed-mindedness, a leveling impulse. Everybody is supposed to go along with the so-called virtuous position. At Harvard I have met a number of devoutly religious students—evangelical Christians, many of them—who find the atmosphere very intolerant."

Stephan Thernstrom and his wife Abigail, a political scientist who has taught at Harvard and Boston College, have concluded that Harvard and many other universities have generated a provincial and oppressive milieu which penalizes critical thought and stimulates deep if inarticulate resentment on the part of white students. Affirmative action causes "incredible touchiness," Stephan Thernstrom said. "Minority students come to class looking for put-downs. This cuts different ways, though. If a black professor quotes from racist tracts, the students shout: More, more. But the so-called studies programs and sensitivity sessions by and large produce unchecked extremism." Abigail Thernstrom added, "Look at the world around us, and how it is changing. Our university campuses are now islands of repression in a sea of freedom."

The documented ideologically imposed intolerance seems to run directly counter to Harvard president Derek Bok's stated goal for the university: "All students at Harvard should have an equal opportunity to gain as much from their experience here as their interests and talents permit. We should endeavor to build an atmosphere in which all students feel welcome and accepted. We should encourage the fullest interchange among all students as a means of furthering their own education, mutual understanding and personal development."[90]

Meanwhile, both inside and outside the classroom, the sensitivity indoctrination project proceeds at full pace, and its strongest effects are felt by the students who are the primary target. As the contempt of students such as Acosta suggests, undergraduates at Harvard and other colleges are growing weary of the intellectual double standards and social browbeating to which they are routinely subjected. Even politically progressive students who begin by adopting and promoting stated minority demands find that they have failed to assuage the seemingly insatiable anger of the activists. Consequently their initial sympathy decays into, at best, a half-hearted acquiescence; at worst, a new impatience and hostility.

Universities are making a big mistake by treating entire classes of students as bigots, Mansfield said. After all, he pointed out, no successful accusation of racism can be brought against anyone without significant support from the community. Thus the very charge that students are racist presumes that the majority are *not*. Minority activists greatly overstate their case, he said, and badly underestimate the real progress that has been made on these issues. In support of this assertion, Mansfield cited "the goodwill most white students have for blacks, the admiration for their courage and endurance, [and the] genuine longing for community with them."

But now, Mansfield added, voicing a widely held but taboo sentiment,

The victims of affirmative action are being forced to admit their guilt so the beneficiaries of affirmative action don't have to admit their inadequacy. After being accused time and again, people become weary of being scapegoats. Their patience cannot last forever. You can only get people to collaborate in the accusations against themselves for so long, and then you begin to lose their goodwill, and your accusation becomes a self-fulfilling prophecy.

Every few weeks, another American campus is cast into turmoil because of allegations of bigotry. Racial harassment is getting so bad that for the first time, the *Wall Street Journal* reports, many black students are avoiding troubled institutions and applying to safe—often historically black—universities.[91] Because universities have exhausted the patience of the most sympathetic advocates of the victim's revolution, the backlash against preferential treatment and sensitivity education will continue to get worse. Nobody will say so, but the truth is that a large number of students and faculty have simply *had it* with minority double standards and intimidation. Until they change their policies, universities are likely to see a dramatic increase in racial tension and racial incidents, with a corresponding upsurge of violence. The worst is yet to come.

# 8

# Illiberal Education

Each fall some 13 million students, 2.5 million of them minorities, enroll in American colleges.[1] Most of these students are living away from home for the first time. Yet their apprehension is mixed with excitement and anticipation. At the university, they hope to shape themselves as whole human beings, both intellectually and morally. Brimming with idealism, they wish to prepare themselves for full and independent lives in the workplace, at home, and as citizens who are shared rulers of a democratic society. In short, what they seek is liberal education.

By the time these students graduate, very few colleges have met their need for all-round development. Instead, by precept and example, universities have taught them that "all rules are unjust" and "all preferences are principled"; that justice is simply the will of the stronger party; that standards and values are arbitrary, and the ideal of the educated person is largely a figment of bourgeois white male ideology, which should be cast aside; that individual rights are a red flag signaling social privilege, and should be subordinated to the claims of group interest; that all knowledge can be reduced to politics and should be pursued not for its own sake but for the political end of power; that convenient myths and benign lies can substitute for truth; that double standards are acceptable as long as they are enforced to the benefit of minority victims; that debates are best conducted not by rational and civil exchange of ideas, but by accusation, intimidation, and official prosecution; that the university stands for nothing in particular and has no claim to be exempt from outside pressures; and that the multiracial society cannot be based on fair rules that apply to every person, but must rather be constructed through a forced rationing of power among separatist racial groups. In short, instead of liberal education, what American students are getting is its diametrical opposite, an education in closed-mindedness and intolerance, which is to say, illiberal education.

Ironically the young blacks, Hispanics, and other certified minorities in whose name the victim's revolution is conducted are the ones least served by the American university's abandonment of liberal ideals. Instead of treating them as individuals, colleges typically consider minorities as members of a group, important only insofar as their collective numbers satisfy the formulas of diversity. Since many of these students depend on a college degree to enhance their career opportunities, their high dropout rate brings tremendous suffering and a sense of betrayal. Even more than others, minority students arrive on campus searching for principles of personal identity and social justice; thus they are particularly disillusioned when they leave empty-handed. Moreover, most minority graduates will admit, when pressed, that if their experience in college is any indication, the prospects for race relations in the country at large are gloomy. If the university model is replicated in society at large, far from bringing ethnic harmony, it will reproduce and magnify the lurid bigotry, intolerance, and balkanization of campus life in the broader culture.

## WHAT'S WRONG WITH DIVERSITY

Although university leaders speak of the self-evident virtues of diversity, it is not at all obvious why it is necessary to a first-rate education. Universities such as Brandeis, Notre Dame, and Mount Holyoke, which were founded on principles of religious or gender homogeneity, still manage to provide an excellent education. Similarly, foreign institutions such as Oxford, Cambridge, Bologna, Salamanca, Paris, and Tokyo display considerable cultural singularity, yet they are regarded as among the best in the world.

The question is not whether universities should seek diversity, but what kind of diversity. It seems that the primary form of diversity which universities should try to foster is diversity of mind. Such diversity would enrich academic discourse, widen its parameters, multiply its objects of inquiry, and increase the probability of obscure and unlikely terrain being investigated. Abroad one typically encounters such diversity of opinion even on basic questions such as how society should be organized. In my high school in Bombay, for example, I could identify students who considered themselves monarchists, Fabian socialists, Christian democrats, Hindu advocates of a caste-based society, agrarians, centralized planners, theocrats, liberals, and Communists. In European universities, one finds a similar smorgasbord of philosophical convictions.

By contrast, most American students seem to display striking agreement on all the basic questions of life. Indeed, they appear to regard a true difference of opinion, based upon convictions that are firmly and intensely held, as dangerously dogmatic and an offense against the social etiquette of tolerance. Far from challenging these conventional prejudices, college leaders tend to encourage their uncritical continuation. "Universities show no interest whatsoever in fostering intellectual diversity," John Bunzel, former president of San Jose State University, says bluntly. Evidence suggests that the philosophical composition of the American faculty is remarkably homogenous,[2] yet Bunzel says that universities are not concerned. "When I raise the problem with leaders in academe, their usual response is that [the imbalance] is irrelevant, or that there cannot be litmus tests for recruitment."

But universities do take very seriously the issue of *racial* under-representation. Here they are quite willing to consider goals, quotas, litmus tests, whatever will rectify the tabulated disproportion. "What we're hoping," said Malcolm Gillis, a senior official at Duke, "is that racial diversity will ultimately lead to intellectual diversity."

The problem begins with a deep sense of embarrassment over the small number of minorities—blacks in particular—on campuses. University officials speak of themselves as more enlightened and progressive than the general population, so they feel guilty if the proportion of minorities at their institutions is smaller than in surrounding society. Moreover, they are often pressured by politicians who control appropriations at state schools, and by student and faculty activists on campus. As a consequence, universities agree to make herculean efforts to attract as many blacks, Hispanics, and other certified minorities as possible to their institutions.

As we have seen, the number of minority applicants who would normally qualify for acceptance at selective universities is very small; therefore, in order to meet ambitious recruitment targets, affirmative action must entail fairly drastic compromises in admissions requirements. University leaders are willing to use unjust means to achieve their goal of equal representation. In one of the more radical steps in this direction, the California legislature is considering measures to *require* all state colleges to accept black, Hispanic, white, and Asian students in proportion with their level in the population, regardless of the disparity in academic preparation or qualifications among such groups.[3]

The first consequence of such misguided policies is a general misplacement of minority students throughout higher education. Thus a student whose grades and qualifications are good enough to get him into Rutgers or Penn State finds himself at Williams or Bowdoin, and the student who meets Williams' and Bowdoin's more demanding requirements finds himself at Yale or Berkeley. Many selective universities are so famished for minority students that they will accept virtually anyone of the right color who applies. In order to fulfill affirmative action objectives, university admissions officers cannot afford to pay too much attention to the probability of a student succeeding at the university.

For many black, Hispanic, and American Indian students who may have struggled hard to get through high school, the courtship of selective universities comes as a welcome surprise. As we have seen, they receive expenses-paid trips to various colleges, where they are chaperoned around campus, introduced to deans and senior faculty, and most of all assured that their presence is avidly desired, indeed that the university would be a poorer place if they chose to go somewhere else. These blandishments naturally enhance the expectations of minority students. These expectations are reinforced by such focused events as the minority freshmen orientation, where black, Hispanic, American Indian, and foreign students are given to understand that they are walking embodiments of the university's commitment to multiculturalism and diversity. Universities emphasize that they are making no accommodations or compromises to enroll affirmative action students; on the contrary, they insist that these students will make a special contribution that the university could not obtain elsewhere.

Their lofty hopes, however, are not realized for most affirmative action students. During the first few weeks of class, many recognize the degree to which they are academically unprepared, relative to other students. At Berkeley, for instance, admissions office data show that the average black freshman's GPA and test scores fall in the 6th percentile of scores for whites and Asians; anthropology professor Vincent Sarich remarks, "As we get more and more selective among Asians and whites, the competitive gap necessarily increases."[4] Yet once these students get to class, professors at demanding schools such as Berkeley take for granted that they know who wrote *Paradise Lost*, that they are capable of understanding Shakespearean English, that they have heard of Max Weber and the Protestant ethic, that they can solve algebraic equations, that they know something about the cell and the amoeba. Students are expected to read several hundred pages of literature, history, biology, and other subjects every week, and produce analytical papers, appropriately footnoted, on short notice.

Unfortunately the basic ingredients of what E. D. Hirsch terms "cultural literacy" are by no means uniformly transmitted in American high schools, nor are regular intellectual habits of concentration and discipline. Thus in the first part of freshman year, affirmative action students with relatively weak preparation often encounter a bewildering array of unfamiliar terms and works. Coping with them, says William Banks, professor of Afro-American Studies at Berkeley, "can be very confusing and frustrating." While they wrestle with the work load, affirmative action students also notice that their peers seem much more comfortable in this academic environment, quicker in absorbing the reading, more confident and fluent in their speech and writing. Even if affirmative action students work that much harder, they discover that it is not easy to keep pace, since the better prepared students also work very hard.

For many minority students, especially those from disadvantaged backgrounds, these problems are often complicated by a difficult personal adjustment to a new environment. It is not easy going from an inner-city high school to a college town with entirely new social routines, or settling into a dormitory where roommates have a great deal more money to spend, or cultivating the general university lifestyle that is familiar to prep schoolers and sons and daughters of alumni but alien to many minority and foreign students.

University leaders have discovered how displaced and unsettled minority freshmen can be, and typically respond by setting up counseling services and remedial education programs intended to assure blacks and Hispanics that they do belong, and that they can "catch up" with other students. Neither of these university resources is well used, however. Students who are struggling to keep up with course work hardly have time to attend additional classes in reading comprehension and algebra. If they do enroll in these programs, they run the risk of falling further behind in class. Relatively few minority students attend counseling because they correctly reject the idea that there is something wrong with them. Nor would the therapeutic assurances of freshman counselors do much to solve their academic difficulties. For many minority undergraduates, therefore, the university's quest for racial equality produces a conspicuous academic inequality.

## SEPARATE AND UNEQUAL

As at Berkeley, Michigan, and elsewhere, many minority students seek comfort and security among their peers who are in a similar situation. Thus many sign up for their campus Afro-American Society or Hispanic Students Association or ethnic theme house or fraternity, where they can share their hopes and frustrations in a relaxed and candid atmosphere, and get guidance from older students who have traveled these strange paths. The impulse to retreat into exclusive enclaves is a familiar one for minority groups who have suffered a history of persecution; they feel there is strength and safety in numbers, and tend to develop group consciousness and collective orientation partly as a protective strategy.[5]

But when minority students demand that the college recognize and subsidize separatist institutions, the administration is placed in a dilemma.[6] The deans know that to accede to these demands is problematic, given their public commitment to integration of students from different backgrounds—indeed the promise of such interaction is one of the main justifications for the goal of diversity sought through affirmative action. At the same time, university leaders realize how dislocated many minority students feel, and how little the university itself can do to help them. Further, the administration does not know how it could possibly say no to these students, and harbors vague and horrific fears of the consequences.

As we have seen, virtually every administration ends by putting aside its qualms and permitting minority institutions to flourish. The logical extreme may be witnessed at California State University at Sacramento, which has announced a new plan to establish an entirely separate "college within a college" for blacks.[7] To justify this separatist subsidy, university leaders have developed a model of "pluralism," which they insist is not the same thing as integration. Since integration implies the merging of various ethnic groups into a common whole, it does not really contribute to diversity. By contrast, pluralism implies the enhancement of distinct ethnic subcultures—a black culture, Hispanic culture, American Indian culture, and a (residual) white culture—which it is hoped will interact in a harmonious and mutually enriching manner.

There is a good deal of camaraderie and social activity at the distinctive minority organizations. Most of them, especially ethnic residence halls and fraternities, help to give newly arrived minority students a sense of belonging. They do not, however, offer any solution to the dilemma facing those students who are inadequately prepared for the challenges of the curriculum. Virtually none of the minority organizations offers study programs or tutorials for affirmative action students. Indeed, some separatist institutions encourage anti-intellectualism, viewing it as an authentic black cultural trait. As researchers Signithia Fordham of Rutgers and John Ogbu of Berkeley describe it, "What appears to have emerged in some segments of the black community is a kind of cultural orientation which defines academic learning as 'acting white,' and academic success as the prerogative of white Americans."[8] Thus many minority freshmen who are struggling academically find no practical remedy in the separate culture of minority institutions.

What they do often find is a novel explanation for their difficulties. Older students tell the newcomers that they should be aware of the pervasive atmosphere of bigotry on campus. Although such racism may not be obvious at first, minority freshmen should not be deceived by appearances. Racism is vastly more subtle than in the past, and operates in various guises, some of them as elusive as baleful looks, uncorrected mental stereotypes, and the various forms of deceptively "polite" behavior.[9] In addition to looking out for such nuances, minority freshmen and sophomores are further warned not to expect much support from the university, where "overt racism" has given way to "institutional racism," evident in the disproportionately small numbers of minorities reflected on the faculty and among the deans and trustees.[10] Everywhere, forces of bigotry are said to conspire against permitting minority students the "racism-free environment" they need to succeed.

Typically, minority beneficiaries are strong supporters of preferential treatment, although their natural pride requires that its nature be disguised. They may speak more freely about it among themselves, but among white students and in the mainstream campus discussion, they understandably refrain from admitting that academic standards were adjusted to make their enrollment possible. Instead, these students assert, often under the banner of their minority organization, that the view that blacks, Hispanics, and American Indians benefit at the expense of overrepresented students is itself evidence of pervasive bigotry. Consequently, in the minds of minority students, affirmative action is not a cause of their academic difficulties, but an excuse for white racism which is the real source of their problems.

Once racism is held accountable for minority unrest, it is now up to students to find, expose, and extirpate it. Here the university leadership steps in with offers of assistance. Eager to deflect frustration and anger from the president's office, the administration seeks to convince minority activists that the real enemy is latent bigotry among their fellow students and professors, and that their energies are best invested in combating white prejudice.

Meanwhile, feminists and homosexual activists typically seek to exploit the moral momentum of the race issue. Just as blacks and Hispanics are victimized by arbitrary race discrimination, they assert, women are subjugated by gender bigotry and homosexuals are tyrannized by similar prejudice in the area of sexual orientation. Feminists, for instance, associate themselves with the black cause by insisting that marriage has always been a form of "domestic slavery." These groups promote the idea that they suffer the oppression of a common enemy. Many administrators believe in their cause and agree to link it with the campaign against white racism. Thus while women comprise between 40 and 60 percent of most university populations, they are routinely classified as vulnerable "minorities." Seeking to eradicate the various species of bigotry, the university's reeducation effort narrows to target the white, male, heterosexual element. As at Penn State, Wisconsin, and Michigan, universities set up committees and task forces to investigate the problem of latent and subtle bigotry. Minority students and faculty typically dominate these committees. Surveys are drawn up. Hearings are scheduled. In a Kafkaesque turn of events, the academic inequality of minority students is blamed on the social prejudices of their white male peers.

## THE NEW RACISM

Most white students do not take gender and homosexuality very seriously as political issues. Even the most sympathetic find it hard to believe that the female condition has historically been the moral equivalent of Negro slavery, nor do they equate ethnicity, which is an arbitrary characteristic, with homosexuality, which is a sexual preference. The race question, however, places white students in a very uncomfortable situation. Many of them arrive on campus with tolerant, but generally uninformed, views. They may not have known many blacks or Hispanics in the past, yet they are generally committed to equal rights regardless of race or background, and they seem open to building friendships and associations with people who they know have been wronged through history.

Since the time they applied to college, many students know that certain minorities have benefited from preferential treatment in admission. It is possible that some minority classmates did not need affirmative action to get in, but it is not possible to know which ones, and the question seems somewhat superfluous anyway. Even students who support the concept of affirmative action in theory are discomfitted when they see that it is now more difficult for them to get into the universities for which they have studied hard to prepare. Moreover, even if they win admission, many have friends who they believe were denied admission to places like Berkeley in order to make room for minority students with weaker scores and grades.

This seems unfair to many white and Asian students, and it is little solace to tell them that they must subordinate their individual rights to the greater good of group equality via proportional representation. Asian American students, unembarrassed by any traditional group advantages in American society, vehemently reject the idea that they should suffer in order to create space for underrepresented black and Hispanic groups who suffered no maltreatment or disadvantage at the hands of Asians. At Berkeley, recall the poignant contrast between Thuy Nguyen and Melanie Lewis.

White and Asian students are reminded of these concerns when they see the obvious differences in preparation and performance among various groups in the classroom. Black and Hispanic academic difficulties confirm the suspicion that universities are admitting students based on different sets of standards—a sort of multiple-track acceptance process. Yet this may not be stated in public, partly because most universities continue to deny that they lower admissions requirements for select minorities, and partly because favored minorities would take offense at such "insensitivity." Consequently, white and Asian students talk about affirmative action only in private. But since students live and study in close quarters, it is impossible to conceal these sentiments for long, and soon affirmative action students begin to suspect that people are talking behind closed doors about the issue that is most sensitive to them. White and Asian students frequently attempt to prevent confrontation with blacks and Hispanics by making passionate public proclamations of their fidelity to the causes of civil rights, feminism, and gay rights. But for many, a gap opens up between their personal and public views.

When minority students develop separatist cultures on the campus, white students tend to have a mixed response. For those who are actually prejudiced, minority self-segregation comes as a relief, because it removes blacks and Hispanics from the mainstream of campus life, and because it reinforces bigoted attitudes of racial inferiority. Many whites, however, are merely puzzled at minority separatism, because it goes so sharply against what they have heard from the university about integration and cultural interaction. As students at Berkeley, Michigan, and Harvard asked earlier, where is the "diversity" that is supposed to result from the interaction of racial and gender "perspectives"? What affirmative action seems to produce instead is group isolation. Eleanor Holmes Norton, former head of the Equal Employment Opportunity Commission under President Carter and now a professor at Georgetown Law School, complains that the new separatism is "exactly what we were fighting against—it is antithetical to what the civil rights movement was all about. It sets groups apart, and it prevents blacks from partaking of the larger culture." Historian Arthur Schlesinger adds that "the melting pot has yielded to the Tower of Babel," and with the loss of a common multiracial identity, "We invite the fragmentation of our culture into a quarrelsome spatter of enclaves, ghettos and tribes."[11] Somehow the intended symphony has become a cacophony.

White students generally have no desire to set up their own racially exclusive unions, clubs, or residence halls. But, as we have repeatedly heard, they cannot help feeling that the university is practicing a double standard by supporting minority institutions to which whites may not belong, and many agree with *Washington Post* columnist William Raspberry that "you cannot claim both full equality and special dispensation."[12] Separatist institutions irritate many whites on campus not because they are separate, but because in most cases they become institutional grievance factories. Many of these groups are quick to make accusations of bigotry, to the point where any disagreement with the agenda of the Afro-American Society or the Third World Alliance is automatic evidence of racism. Antiwhite rhetoric goes unchecked on campus, evoking at best an eerie silence. Thus, while it is possible to ignore minority self-segregation in principle, such indifference becomes harder when the groups serve as base camps for mounting ideological assaults against everyone else. "Pluralism" becomes a framework for racial browbeating and intimidation.

When they discover resentment among students over preferential treatment and minority separatism, university administrators conclude that they have discovered the latent bigotry for which they have been searching. Consequently, many universities institute "sensitivity" training programs, such as Harvard's notorious AWARE week, to cure white students of their prejudice. As at Michigan, the University of Connecticut, Stanford, and Emory, some schools go so far as to outlaw racially or sexually "stigmatizing" remarks—even "misdirected laughter" and "exclusion from conversation"—which are said to make learning for minorities impossible. On virtually every campus, there is a de facto taboo against a free discussion of affirmative action or minority self-segregation, and efforts to open such a discussion are considered presumptively racist. Thus measures taken to enhance diversity have instead created a new regime of intellectual conformity.[13]

S. Frederick Starr, president of Oberlin College, remarks that "diversity should not be the prerogative of any particular ideological agenda. But now it means subscribing to a set of political views." Donald Kagan, dean of arts and sciences at Yale, concurs. "It is common in universities today to hear talk of politically correct opinions, or PC for short. These are questions that are not really open to argument. It takes real courage to oppose the campus orthodoxy. To tell you the truth, I was a student during the days of McCarthy, and there is less freedom now than there was then."

One of the saddest effects of the divisiveness of campus life—remarked on by professors and students across the spectrum—is that few true friendships are formed between white and black students. Perhaps the main reason is that, as Aristotle said, friendship presumes equality between people who share common interests and goals. Many white and black students find that, socially and intellectually, they have little in common with each other. As Berkeley professor Duster's research shows, these differences are not reduced, but heightened, over time. Indeed they are converted into group differences, and these groups view each other across chasms that are virtually impossible to cross. Relations between white and minority groups are usually hostile since they are defined by allegations of white oppression and minority victimization: consequently, whites are forced into a defensive posture against political irredentism from highly self-conscious minority groups.

Campus browbeating and balkanization come to public attention by way of the outcomes they produce—the racial joke and the racial incident. Both represent white exasperation with perceived unfairness, double standards, and suppression of independent thought on the American campus. Jokes are ways for malcontents to express feelings which lack a respectable outlet. As with David Makled and Andrew Milot at Michigan, and the editors of the *Harvard Salient,* many whites whose prejudices should have been challenged and diminished through their human interaction with minorities find their stereotypes partially confirmed. Yet they know the risk of speaking their mind, so their views burrow underground, and sometimes resurface in the form of crude pranks and humor.

In one of his speeches, Malcolm X implied the omnipresence of white racism by asking: What do you call a black man with a PhD? Answer: Nigger. What was intended with passionate seriousness by

Malcolm X, I was surprised to discover, is now part of the culture of racial humor on campus. Something that was a cause of soul-searching, two decades ago, is today the occasion for laughter. The reason for the amusement is preferential treatment: who knows what the black man with the PhD is really capable of doing? The PhD has been placed, by affirmative action, into invisible quotation marks. The humor comes from the recognition of this fact, combined with the necessity not only of denying it in public, but of appearing appropriately shocked when such a suggestion is raised.

Similarly, racial incidents represent the uncorking of a very tightly sealed bottle. A careful examination of these incidents, at Michigan and Stanford and Temple and elsewhere, reveals that most of them are connected to preferential treatment and minority double standards. At Bryn Mawr, for example, a freshman found an anonymous note slipped under her door. "Hey Spic," it read, "If you and your kind can't handle the work here, don't blame it on the racial thing. Why don't you just get out? We'd all be a lot happier."[14] At George Washington University in 1987, students countered Black History Month by announcing a "White History Week Party."[15] And, as we have seen, for the first time the American campus now has university-sponsored white student unions. It is impossible to separate this "new racism" on campus from the old racism, because the bigotry which results from preferential treatment strengthens and reinforces the old bigotry which preferential policies were instituted to fight.

In one sense, the new racism is different, however. The old racism was based on prejudice, whereas the new racism is based on conclusions. Prejudice, of course, means prejudgment, judgment in the absence of information. This was an accurate way to describe many of the old racists of the earlier part of this century: they knew little about blacks, encountered few in the course of life, and disliked them based on the fear that stems from ignorance. The solutions for the old racism were education, enlightenment, and consciousness-raising. American society began an experiment in integration. By meeting blacks, living alongside them, eating with them, befriending them, the expectation was that whites would recognize common human interests which surpassed group differences, and that they would quickly lose their stereotypes. And to a considerable extent, this project has worked. The old racism is not dead, by any means, but it is truly powerful only in small pockets of society, and it is discredited morally and politically in all sectors of public life.

The new bigotry is not derived from ignorance, but from experience. It is harbored not by ignoramuses, but by students who have direct and first-hand experience with minorities in the close proximity of university settings. The "new racists" do not believe they have anything to learn about minorities; quite the contrary, they believe they are the only ones who are willing to face the truth about them. Consequently, they are not uncomfortable about their views, believing them to be based on evidence. They feel they occupy the high ground, while everyone else is performing pirouettes and somersaults to avoid the obvious.

Both university leaders and minority activists sense the durability of the new racism, and its resistance to correction by means of liberal reeducation. Even sensitivity sessions and other awareness requirements, backed by censorship codes, do not seem able to penetrate the inner reaches of human conviction; at best, they only regulate its outward expression.

But in fact, many administrators are privately ambivalent about combating these private suspicions about minorities, because they share them. Most of them, too, are among the new racists on the American campus. Their attitude toward minority students, however optimistic it might once have been, has turned to resigned condescension. They do not believe that they can afford to apply mainstream standards to minority students, because they are certain that minorities would fare badly, causing the institution to suffer serious embarrassment. Nor do they feel able to resist minority demands, however unreasonable they appear, lest these students react in some terrible and irrational way. Therefore, like presidents Donald Kennedy of Stanford, Lattie Coor of the University of Vermont, and Joseph Duffey of the University of Massachusetts at Amherst, they consistently acquiesce in these demands, abdicating their responsibility to both the students and the institution itself.[16]

The university leadership generally holds not that minorities are inferior, but that they must be treated *as though* they are inferior. The old racists sought to prove inferiority through ridiculous methods such as craniology; the new racists in the dean's office take inferiority for granted. The new racism among university leaders differs from its counterpart among undergraduates only in the sense that imprudent undergraduates, sometimes inadvertently, say what they think; by contrast, university leaders only act on those presumptions, confining their personal communication to meaningful glances, rolling eyes, and the rest of the insignia of administrative tact and prudence. In this sense, minority students are entirely correct in their frustrated belief that there exists in the establishment a subtle racism that is virtually impossible to document.

Whenever racial incidents occur, as we saw at Michigan and elsewhere, university leaders solemnly proclaim that these demonstrate how bad the problems of racism, sexism, and homophobia continue to be, and how "more needs to be done" in the form of redoubled preferential treatment programs, minority cultural centers, sensitivity training, and so on.[17] But the new racism cannot be fought with the more vehement application of preferential treatment, teach-ins, reeducation seminars, and censorship; indeed these tactics, which are tailored to address the old racism, only add to the new problem. In fact, to a considerable extent they are the problem because they legitimize a regime of double standards that divides and balkanizes the campus. However well-intended, university policies generally supply the oxygen with which the new racism breathes and thrives. This is why incidents of bigotry are confined predominantly to northern progressive campuses.

## VICTIM STATUS

Neither the hostility of white students nor the condescension of the administration goes unnoticed by minority students. Their awareness only intensifies their insecurity, because now they find it impossible to distinguish their friends from their enemies. Being intelligent people, they sense that some of their harshest critics might be uttering truths which they must face, while some of their most obsequious flatterers are not really friends with their best interests at heart. For many, therefore, it is hard to trust anyone outside the separatist enclave.

With the encouragement of the university administration and activist faculty, many minority students begin to think of themselves as victims. Indeed, they aspire to victim status. They do not yearn to be oppressed, of course; rather, they seek the moral capital of victimhood.[18] Like Rigoberta Menchu, they tend to see their lives collectively as a historical melodrama involving the forces of good and evil, in which they are cast as secular saints and martyrs. These roles allow them to recover the sense of meaning, and of place, which otherwise seems so elusive.

Many campuses have witnessed the somewhat strange phenomenon of various minority groups—blacks, Hispanics, American Indians, foreign students, feminists, homosexuals, and so on—climbing aboard the victim bandwagon. Even as they work in concert on some issues, these groups compete to establish themselves as the most oppressed of all. Everybody races to seize the lowest rung of the ladder. By converting victimhood into a certificate of virtue, minorities acquire a powerful moral claim that renders their opponents defensive and apologetic, and immunizes themselves from criticism and sanction. Ultimately, victimhood becomes a truncheon with which minority activists may intimidate nonminorities—thus the victim becomes a victimizer while continuing to enjoy superior moral credentials.[19]

Victimhood may provoke sympathy, but it does not, by itself, produce admiration. Being historically oppressed is nothing to be ashamed of, but neither is it an intrinsic measure of social status or moral worth. What evokes admiration is the spectacle of oppressed victims struggling against their circumstances, heroically, despite the odds. In this way victimhood can pave the way for greatness.[20] Yet the current victim psychology makes it impossible for them to be relieved of their oppression. Most university administrators understand this and cynically play along. A few, however, genuinely hope that in meeting minority demands, eventually the old wounds will heal, and they will settle down and become part of the academic culture. This philanthropic enterprise seems bound to fail, because it misses the central irony: even as they rail against their oppressors, minority activists cannot afford to lose their victim status.

When resistance to sometimes outrageous minority demands surfaces among students, these activists often express indignation and outrage. Sometimes they are entirely justified in so responding to gross racial incidents, which are calculated to inflame black and Hispanic sentiments and advertise white resentment. But minority sensibilities have become so touchy that any criticism of the activist agenda is automatically termed racist, and as we saw with Professor Farley at Michigan and Professor Thernstrom at Harvard, even narrative descriptions of controversial policies such as preferential treatment are regarded as improper. Through protest, many minority activists rediscover the power and prestige that they felt denied in the classroom, since accusations and takeovers typically put white students on the defensive and bring immediate concessions and accommodations from the administration.

Minority group sensibility and group activism are very strong on most campuses, and it is difficult for black students who are not part of the affirmative action crowd, and who wish to integrate with white students and focus on their studies, to do so without abuse and ostracism. Politically uncooperative students are sometimes called "Oreos" or

"Incognegroes"—black on the outside and white on the inside. Most intelligent black students who succeed in college maintain a shrewd tactical alliance with the local Afro-American Society or ethnic club, but give themselves enough flexibility to pursue independent intellectual and social activities as well.

## DOWN WITH ARISTOTLE

Although minority activists dominate race relations on campus, their original troubles began in the classroom, and it is to the classroom that their political energy ultimately returns. This phase of the struggle begins with a new recognition. Usually within the atmosphere of their separate enclaves, and often under the tutelage of an activist professor, minority students learn that extensive though their experience has been with campus bigotry, the subtlest and yet most pervasive form of racism thrives undiscovered, right in front of their eyes. The curriculum, they are told at Stanford and Duke and other colleges, reflects a "white perspective." Specifically, as Stanford Professor Clayborne Carson said earlier, it reflects a predominant white, male, European, and heterosexual mentality which, by its very nature, is inescapably racist, indisputably sexist, and manifestly homophobic.

This realization comes as something of an epiphany. Many minority students can now explain why they had such a hard time with Milton and Publius and Heisenberg. Those men reflected white aesthetics, white philosophy, white science. Obviously minority students would fare much better if the university assigned black or Latino or Third World thought. Then the roles would be reversed: they would perform well, and other students would have trouble. Thus the current curriculum reveals itself as the hidden core of academic bigotry.

At first minority students may find such allegations hard to credit, since it is unclear how differential equations or the measurement of electron orbits embody racial and gender prejudices. Nevertheless, in humanities and social science disciplines, younger scholar-advocates of the *au courant* stripe are on hand to explain that the cultural framework for literature or history or sociology inevitably reflects a bias in the selection or application of scholarly material. Restive with the traditional curriculum, progressive academics such as Edward Said at Colombia and Stanley Fish and Henry Gates at Duke seek a program which integrates scholarship and political commitment, and they form a tacit partnership with minority activists in order to achieve this goal. Since all knowledge is political, these scholar-advocates assert, minorities have a right to demand that their distinct perspectives be "represented" in the course readings. Ethnic Studies professor Ronald Takaki of Berkeley unabashedly calls this "intellectual affirmative action."[21]

Tempted by these arguments, many minority leaders make actual head-counts of the authors and authorities in the curriculum, and they find accusations of white male predominance to be proven right. Why are Plato and Locke and Madison assigned in philosophy class but no black thinkers? How come so few Hispanics are credited with great inventions or discoveries? Feminists ask: Why is only a small percentage of the literature readings by women? These protests sometimes extend beyond the humanities and social sciences; at a recent symposium, mathematics professor Marilyn Frankenstein of the University of Massachusetts at Boston accused her field of harboring "Eurocentric bias" and called for "ethno-mathematics" which would analyze numerical models in terms of workforce inequalities and discrimination quotients.[22]

Few minority students believe that democratic principles of "equal representation" should be rigorously applied to curricular content. Feminists make this argument because they want to replace alleged sexists like Aquinas and Milton with Simone de Beauvoir and Gloria Steinem. Blacks, Hispanics, and American Indians generally assent to this proposition because it provides an immediate explanation for the awkward gaps in academic performance. Not only are these differences evident in classroom discussion, grades, and prizes, but also in suspension and dropout statistics. Minority students must face the disquieting fact that many of their peers at places like Berkeley fail to graduate, if indeed they even stay through freshman year. It seems irresistible to adopt the view that if only the curriculum were broadened or revised to reflect black (or female, or Third World) perspectives, these academic gaps would close or possibly reverse themselves.

But it seems insufficient merely to agitate for a more "diverse" reading list, since the other apparatus of institutional racism would still be in place. In particular, it has not escaped the attention of minority activists that on all the indices of academic merit, from SAT scores to grades to law review seats and annual prizes, their groups do disproportionately poorly. Since democratic principle presumes that equality is the natural condition of mankind, what possible reason can there be for this inequality, other than discrimination of some sort? Consequently, as we saw in the case of Berkeley, the tests are said to be racially and perhaps sexually biased. Prima facie evidence of such bias is that all groups do not score evenly. Thus, minority student groups demand that the tests be abandoned or revised to allow "equal opportunity," which is defined as an outcome in which all groups perform equally well. Yet this does not eliminate group differences; it merely renders them invisible.[23]

## PROFILES IN COWARDICE

Many university presidents are not intellectual leaders but bureaucrats and managers; their interest therefore is not in meeting the activist argument but in deflecting it, by making the appropriate adjustments in the interest of stability. When a debate over the canon erupts, university heads typically take refuge in silence or incomprehensibility; thus one Ivy League president responded to Allan Bloom's book by saying that the purpose of liberal education was to "address the need for students to develop both a private self and a public self, and to find a way to have those selves converse with each other."[24] Earlier incidents reveal the posture of presidents Heyman of Berkeley, Kennedy of Stanford, Cheek of Howard, Duderstadt of Michigan, Brodie of Duke, and Bok of Harvard to be a curious mixture of pusillanimity, ideology, and opportunism.

As we saw at Stanford, Duke, and Harvard, when minority groups, assisted by activist professors, urge the transformation of the curriculum toward a "race and gender" agenda, they face potential opposition from a large segment of faculty who may be sympathetic to minority causes but at the same time believe that the curriculum should not be ideologically apportioned. These dissenters are branded as bigots, sexists, and homophobes, regardless of their previous political bona fides. If minority faculty and student activists are not a numerical majority, they inevitably are a kind of Moral Majority, and they wield the formidable power to affix scarlet letters to their enemies. Few dare to frontally oppose the alliance between minority groups and faculty activists; like Stanford's Linda Paulson, most wrestle with their conscience and win and even professors with qualms end up supporting curricular transformation with the view that change is inevitable.

The reason that most people in authority at the university have such a difficult time with the canon lobby is that, while championing the principle of "representation" in admissions, they have acknowledged the indeterminacy of merit standards, the unreliability of standardized tests, the need to reform tests so that different groups fare equally, the inevitability of political considerations entering into the assignment of merit, and so on. It seems a bit late in the day for college presidents, deans, and professors to assert that the curriculum should be exempt from this egalitarian critique.

Moreover, most university leaders have no answer to the charge that the curriculum reflects a white male culture, and consequently embodies all the hateful prejudices that whites have leveled against other peoples throughout history. Nor can they explain why, if not for discrimination, minority students aren't doing as well as other students. As we saw with Harvard's "Myths and Realities" letter, universities have insisted from the outset that standards have not been lowered, so why do black and Hispanic students fall behind if not for curricular racism? And won't the rationing of books among different ethnic "perspectives" make an indispensable contribution to "diversity"?

Thus begins the process, already far advanced, of downplaying or expelling the core curriculum of Western classics in favor of a non-Western and minority-oriented agenda. Universities like Stanford, Berkeley, and Harvard establish ethnic studies requirements, multicultural offerings, Afro-American Studies and Women's Studies departments. The typical rationale is that white professors cannot effectively communicate with, or provide role models for, minority students. This argument is somewhat transparent, since it relies on the premise that interracial identification is impossible, and no one has ever alleged that minority professors are racially or culturally disabled from teaching white students. College administrators will privately admit that "minority perspectives" is a pretext for meeting affirmative action goals. The so-called "studies" programs also serve the purpose of attracting minority students who are having a difficult time with the "white" curriculum, but who, like Harvard's Tiya Miles, Eva Nelson, and Michelle Duncan, feel psychologically at home in a department like Afro-American Studies.

What transpires in the "race and gender" curriculum is anything but "diverse." As we saw at Harvard, typically these programs promulgate rigid political views about civil rights, feminism, homosexual rights, and other issues pressed by the activists who got these departments set up in the first place. Thomas Short, a professor of philosophy at Kenyon College, observes that "ideological dogmatism is the norm, not the exception, in the 'studies' programs, especially Women's Studies. Intimidation of nonfeminists in the classroom is routine." Short adds that, curiously, ideologues in these programs practice the very exclusion that they claim to have suffered in the past.

Even if some faculty in the "race and gender" curriculum seek to promote authentic debate or intellectual diversity, this is difficult in an atmosphere where activist students profess to be deeply offended by views which fall outside the ideological circumference of their victim's revolution. Once a professor finds himself the object of vilification and abuse for tackling a political taboo—the fate of Farley, Thernstrom, and Macneil—others absorb the message and ensure that their own classes are appropriately deferential.

Eugene Genovese, a Marxist historian and one of the nation's most distinguished scholars on slavery, admits that "there is just too much dogmatism in the field of race and gender scholarship." Whatever diversity obtains, Genovese argues, is frequently "a diversity of radical positions." As a result, "Good scholars [who] are increasingly at risk are starting to run away, and this is how our programs become ghettoized."

The new awareness of racially and sexually biased perspectives is not confined to the "studies" programs, however; minority activists inevitably bring their challenging political consciousness into other courses as well, although this usually does not happen until junior or senior year. At this point, the students begin to function as sensitivity monitors, vigilant in pointing out instances of racism and sexism in the course readings or among student comments. Other students may inwardly resent such political surveillance, but seldom do professors resist it: indeed they often praise it as precisely the sort of "diversity" that minority students can bring to the classroom.

Minority students are often given latitude to do papers on race or gender victimization, even if only tangentially related to course material: thus some write about latent bigotry in Jane Austen, or tabulate black underrepresentation in the university administration. Minority activists can be offended when they do not receive passing grades on such papers, because they believe that their consciousness of oppression is far more advanced than that of any white professor. Further, they know how reluctant most professors are to get involved in an incident with a black or Hispanic student; hence they can extract virtually any price from faculty anxious to avoid "racial incidents."

University administrations and faculty also permit, and sometimes encourage, minority students to develop myths about their own culture and history, such as the "black Egypt" industry evident at Howard and elsewhere. This cultural distortion is routine in multicultural and Third World studies—the case of Stanford is typical. Bernard Lewis, professor of Near Eastern studies at Princeton, describes what he calls "a new culture of deceit on the campus," and adds, "It is very dangerous to give in to these ideas, or more accurately, to these pressures. It makes a mockery of scholarship to say: my nonsense is as good as your science." But even university officials who agree with Lewis say they aren't sure what they can do to counter these distortions, since the ideological forces behind them are so strong.

Although curricular and extracurricular concessions by the university greatly increase the power of minority activists, it is not clear that they help minority students use knowledge and truth as weapons against ignorance and prejudice, nor that they assuage the problems of low morale and low self-esteem which propelled them in this direction to begin with. Nor does an apparently more even "balance of power" between minority and nonminority students produce greater ethnic harmony. In fact, like Michigan activists Kimberly Smith and Tracye Matthews, many minority students find themselves increasingly embittered and estranged during their college years, so that by the time they graduate they may be virtually isolated in a separatist culture, and espouse openly hostile sentiments against other groups.

At graduation time, it turns out that only a fraction of the minority students enrolled four years earlier are still around, and even among them the academic record is mixed: a good number (most are probably not affirmative action beneficiaries) have performed well, but a majority conspicuously lag behind their colleagues, and a sizable group has only finished by concentrating in congenial fields such as Afro-American or Ethnic Studies, under the direction of tolerant faculty advisers. Relatively few of these students have developed to their full potential over the past four years, or have emerged ready to assume positions of responsibility and leadership in the new multiracial society.

## PRINCIPLES OF REFORM

No community can be built on the basis of preferential treatment and double standards, and their existence belies university rhetoric about equality. Conflicting standards of excellence and justice are the root of the bitter and divisive controversies over admissions, curricular content, and race relations on campus. In each case, the university administration is directly responsible for betraying student idealism and replacing it with cynicism and resentment. To remedy the problem, it is necessary to return to fundamental principles; as G. K. Chesterton said, we cannot discuss reform without reference to form.

First, liberal education is education for rulers. In ancient times, princes, aristocrats, and gentry sought liberal education to prepare them for the responsibilities of government. We do not share this elitist conception of liberal education, but this does not imply that we should change the definition. In a democratic society, every citizen is a ruler, who joins in exercising the duties of government. Consequently, instead of abandoning the highest ideals of liberal learning, we should extend them beyond previously confined social enclaves. In this modern view, liberal education is an opportunity for all citizens in a democratic society. Contrary to what some activists allege, liberal education is consistent with democracy; indeed it enables democratic rule to reach its pinnacle.

Second, democracy is not based on the premise of equal endowments, but of equal rights. It does not guarantee success, but it does aspire to equal opportunity. This opportunity is extended not to groups as such, but to individuals, because democracy respects the moral integrity of the human person, whose rights may not be casually subordinated to collective interests. Democracy requires representation, but in no sense does it mandate proportional representation based on race. Consequently it is entirely consistent with democracy for liberal education to treat students equally, as individuals.

Third, there is no conflict between equal opportunity for individuals in education, and the pursuit of the highest standards of academic and extracurricular excellence. After all, equal opportunity means opportunity to achieve, and we achieve more when more is expected of us. Test scores and grade point averages are mere measurements of achievement, which are necessary to register how much intellectual progress is being made. They provide a common index for all who seek to improve themselves, regardless of race, sex, or background. High standards do not discriminate against anyone except those who fail to meet them. Such discrimination is entirely just and ought not to be blamed for our individual differences.

Fourth, liberal education settles issues in terms of idealism, not interest; in terms of right, not force. There is nothing wrong with universities confronting controversial contemporary issues, especially those involving human difference that are both timely and timeless. Nor is radicalism itself the problem; if radical solutions may not be contemplated in the university, where else should they be considered? Because they are sanctuary institutions, universities can be a philosophical testing ground for programs of revolutionary transformation which, if improperly executed, might lead to lawlessness, violence, or anarchy. "The university sponsors moral combat in an atmosphere where ideas can be tested short of mortal combat," in the words of sociologist Manfred Stanley of Syracuse University.[25]

Fifth, liberal education in a multicultural society means global education. Provincialism has always been the enemy of that broad-minded
outlook which is the very essence of liberal learning. Today's liberally
educated student must be conversant with some of the classic formulations of other cultures, and with the grand political and social currents
which bring these cultures into increased interaction with the West.
Such education is best pursued when students are taught to search
for universal standards of judgment which transcend particularities of
race, gender, and culture; this gives them the intellectual and moral
criteria to evaluate both their own society and others. There is much
in both to affirm and to criticize.

## THREE MODEST PROPOSALS

### Nonracial Affirmative Action

Universities should retain their policies of preferential treatment,
but alter their criteria of application from race to socioeconomic disadvantage. This means that, in admissions decisions, universities would take
into account such factors as the applicant's family background, financial
condition, and primary and secondary school environment, giving preference to disadvantaged students as long as it is clear that these students
can be reasonably expected to meet the academic challenges of the
selective college. Race or ethnicity, however, would cease to count
either for or against any applicant.

Ordinarily the admissions policy of selective universities should
be based on academic and extracurricular merit. Preferential treatment
is justified, however, when it is obvious that measurable indices of
merit do not accurately reflect a student's learning and growth potential.
Every admissions officer knows that a 1,200 SAT score by a student
from Harlem or Anacostia, who comes from a broken family and has
struggled against peer pressure and a terrible school system, means
something entirely different from a 1,200 score from a student from
Scarsdale or Georgetown, whose privileges include private tutors and
SAT prep courses.

Universities seem entirely justified in giving a break to students
who may not have registered the highest scores, but whose record
suggests that this failure is not due to lack of ability or application but
rather to demonstrated disadvantage. Universities are right to see
the academic potential in these students, whose future performance
may well outdistance that of better-prepared seventeen-year-olds whose
path to success has been relatively smooth.

The greatest virtue of preferences based on socioeconomic factors is that such an approach restores to the admissions process the principle of treating people as individuals and not simply as members of ethnic groups. Each applicant is assessed as a person, whose achievements are measured in the context of individual circumstances. Skin color no longer makes a dubious claim to be an index of merit, or an automatic justification for compensation. No longer will a black or Hispanic doctor's son, who has enjoyed the advantages of comfort and affluence, receive preference over the daughter of an Appalachian coal miner or a Vietnamese street vendor. Regardless of pigment, any student who can make a genuine case that his grades or scores do not reflect his true potential has a chance to substantiate this claim in a tangible and measurable way.

Ordinarily it might seem an extraordinarily complex calculus to weigh such factors as family background, income, and school atmosphere. Fortunately, colleges already have access to, and in many cases use, this data. The application forms give applicants ample opportunity to register this information, and the financial aid office assiduously tabulates family assets and income. By integrating admissions and financial aid information, universities are in a good position to make intelligent determinations about socioeconomic factors that advanced, or impeded, a student's opportunities.

Since minorities are disproportionately represented among the disadvantaged, there is little question that they would benefit disproportionately from such a program. The disadvantages imposed by slavery, segregation, and past discrimination would still count as a plus, if they could be shown to translate into socioeconomic disadvantage currently suffered by the student applicant.

It is true that affirmative action seats must necessarily be limited, and any expansion of the program beyond its current beneficiary groups means that the number of blacks and Hispanics who benefit will necessarily be reduced. But this does not mean that fewer blacks and Hispanics will be enrolled in American universities—only that fewer will gain admission to the most selective colleges. In other words, a black student who cannot demonstrate socioeconomic disadvantage, whose credentials qualify him for Temple University, but who under preferential treatment could be admitted to Columbia, will probably now have to attend Temple. This outcome does not appear to be unjust.

Moreover, black and Hispanic graduation rates are likely to increase, because only students whose potential is hidden due to previous disadvantage would enjoy preferential treatment, in the reasonable expectation that they will be able to realize their capabilities and compete effectively with other students. All other students, whether white or black or Asian, would be admitted to colleges whose criteria correspond to their measured capabilities. Thus they would compete in a free and fair academic environment, and would not be subject to the undue pressures of intellectual mismatch. Placed in an appropriate university setting, these students would have every opportunity for graduation and academic success commensurate with effort.

Additionally, this kind of affirmative action loses the special stigma that is attached to racial preference. No longer would universities be forced to explain the anomaly of enforcing racial discrimination as a means to combat racial discrimination. The euphemism and mendacity currently employed to justify preferential treatment can stop—the new program can be explicitly stated and defended. The rationale for racial grievance among groups dissolves. Nobody gets to feel privileged, or injured, on account of race. Nobody may infer that members of other races are collectively inadequate to the standards of the institution. Whether or not they benefit from preferential treatment, all minority students are liberated from the raised eyebrow that currently belittles their achievements.

## Choice Without Separatism

Universities should discourage the practice of minority self-segregation on campus by refusing to recognize and fund any group which is racially separatist and excludes students based on skin color. Universities should, however, sanction groups based on a shared intellectual or cultural interest, even if these groups appeal predominantly or exclusively to minority students.

What this means is that universities would not permit a Black Students Association, but they would permit a W. E. B. Du Bois Society based on interest in the writings of the early twentieth-century author. Colleges would refuse to suppòrt a Latino Political Club but they would permit a Sandino Club based on interest in the thought of the Nicaraguan revolutionary hero. This principle could extend beyond race, so that universities would decline to fund a homosexual association but would fund a Sappho Society.

In all cases, university-funded groups should be built around intellectual and cultural interests, not skin color or sexual proclivity. This seems congruent with the purpose of a liberal education, which is to foster the development and exchange of ideas. Thought and expression are the currency in which universities trade and specialize. The consolidation of identity based on race or sexuality may be a project that some students ardently seek, but it falls outside the province of universities, which in fact have a declared interest in breaking down barriers based on accidental features.

If this solution is adopted, no longer will universities have to justify double standards in which they profess allegiance to cultural exchange, and then foster minority subcultures on campus; nor will they need to account for encouraging minority-pride groups but not white-pride groups such as the ones at Temple and Florida State. The new approach has the advantage of permitting both honesty and consistency.

Also, the idea of funding groups based on shared interests has the benefits of free association as well as inclusiveness: all students attracted to the principles embodied by the organization may join; nobody may be turned away on grounds of race or sex. There is no reason to think a Malcolm X Society, for instance, would not attract any white or Hispanic or Asian students, but if only blacks happen to join, at least others would have been extended the opportunity. In some cases, perhaps, groups will be formed on the mere pretext of a shared idea, but inevitably this pretense will be challenged by some persistent outsider who insists on signing up and who cannot be refused membership.

## Equality and the Classics

Universities can address their curricular problems by devising a required course or sequence for entering freshmen which exposes them to the basic issues of equality and human difference, through a carefully chosen set of classic texts that deal powerfully with those issues. Needless to say, non-Western classics belong in this list when they address questions relevant to the subject matter. Such a solution would retain what Matthew Arnold termed "the best that has been thought and said," but at the same time engage the contemporary questions of ethnocentrism and prejudice in bold and provocative fashion.

It seems that currently both the teaching of Western classics as well as the desire to study other cultures have encountered serious difficulties in the curriculum. As the case of Stanford illustrates, an uncritical examination of non-Western cultures, in order to favorably contrast them with the West, ends up as a new form of cultural imperialism, in which Western intellectuals project their own domestic prejudices onto faraway countries, distorting them beyond recognition to serve political ends.[26] Even where universities make a serious effort to avoid this trap, it remains questionable whether they have the academic expertise in the general undergraduate program to teach students about the history, religion, and literature of Asia, Africa, and the Arab world.

The study of other cultures can never compensate for a lack of thorough familiarity with the founding principles of one's own culture.[27] Just as it would be embarrassing to encounter an educated Chinese who had never heard of Confucius, however well versed he may be in Jefferson, so also it would be a failure of liberal education to teach Americans about the Far East without immersing them in their own philosophical and literary tradition "from Homer to the present." Universal in scope, these works prepare Westerners to experience both their own, as well as other, ideas and civilizations.[28]

The problem is that many of the younger generation of faculty in the universities express lack of interest, if not contempt, for the Western classics. Either they regard the books as flawed for their failure to endorse the full emancipation of approved minorities, or they reject their metaphysical questions as outdated and irrelevant. Naturally, young people will not investigate these texts, which are often complex and sometimes written in archaic language, if they do not believe their efforts will be repaid. Unfortunately, many undergraduates today seem disinclined to read the classics, but not because they oppose or detest them. Their alienation is more radical: they are indifferent to them. For them the classics have retreated into what Lovejoy called "the pathos of time."

Yet a survey of these books immediately suggests that many of them are fully aware of, and treat with great subtlety, the problems of prejudice, ethnocentrism, and human difference. Long before Willie Horton raised, in American minds, the specter of a dark-skinned man sexually assaulting a white woman, Iago raised this possibility with Brabantio. Will he allow his "fair daughter" to fall into "the gross clasps of a lascivious Moor"? If he does not intervene, Iago warned, "You'll have your daughter covered with a Barbary horse." *Othello* and the *Merchant of Venice*, Shakespeare's Venetian plays, are both subtle examinations of nativism and ethnocentrism. Both engage issues of ethnic and sexual difference. They reflect a cosmopolitan society's struggle to accommodate the alien, while maintaining its cultural identity. Othello is the tragedy of a foreign warrior who depended on Desdemona's love to legitimate his full citizenship in his new country—when Iago casts that love into doubt, not just his marriage but his identity was fundamentally threatened. By contrast with Othello, Shylock is the outsider who refused to integrate, and pressed his principles into uncompromising conflict with those of Christian civilization.[29] These timeless examples of the tension between community and difference are precisely what young people today should confront, and respond to in terms of their own experience.

The relevance of the classical tradition to questions of beauty and equality and freedom has not gone unrecognized by perceptive black thinkers and writers. Traveling in Vienna, W. E. B. Du Bois wrote, "Here Marcus Aurelius, the Roman Caesar died; here Charlemagne placed the bounds of his empire that ruled the world five centuries. . . . Around Vienna the intrigues and victories of Napoleon centered. . . . And here, after the downfall of the great Tyrant, sat the famous congress which parcelled out the world and declared the African slave a stench in the nostrils of humanity."[30] Du Bois saw the grandeur and degradation in a single unifying thought—slavery was the West's tragic flaw; yet it was tragic precisely because of the greatness of the civilization that encompassed it.

Paul Robeson recalled that his father took him "page by page through Virgil and Homer and other classics."[31] As a result, Robeson says, "a love of learning, a ceaseless quest for truth in all its fulness—this my father taught." Robeson believed that the Latin and Greek classics were just as much the treasure of the American black as of the American white. When Robeson played Othello on Broadway, he created a national sensation. Audiences found *Othello,* in Robeson's words, "painfully immediate in its unfolding of evil, innocence, passion, dignity and nobility, and contemporary in its overtones of a clash of cultures, and of the partial acceptance and consequent effect upon one of a minority group." Othello's jealousy thus "becomes more credible, the blow to his pride more understandable, the final collapse of his individual world more inevitable."[32] In 1943–44 Robeson's *Othello* set a record for a Shakespearean play on Broadway, running for almost three hundred consecutive performances.

\* \* \*

For a variety of reasons, university presidents and deans will not implement even the most obvious and sensible reform proposals. First, being for the most part bureaucrats rather than intellectual leaders, they lack the vision and imagination to devise new and innovative policies, preferring to continue familiar programs and echo their accompanying bromides. Second, university officials feel physically and morally intimidated by minority activists; as a result, the activists set the agenda and timorous administrators usually go along. Third, and perhaps most serious, many no longer believe in the emancipation brought about by liberal education, and are quite willing to sacrifice liberal principles to achieve expedient ends.

The liberal university is a distinctive and fragile institution. It is not an all-purpose instrument for social change. Its function is indeed to serve the larger society which supports and sustains it, yet it does not best do this when it makes itself indistinguishable from the helter-skelter of pressure politics, what Professor Susan Shell of Boston College terms "the academic equivalent of Tammany Hall." Nothing in this book should be taken to deny the legitimate claim of minorities who have suffered unfairly, nor should reasonable aid and sympathy be withheld from them. But the current revolution of minority victims threatens to destroy the highest ideals of liberal education, and with them that enlightenment and understanding which hold out the only prospects for racial harmony, social justice, and minority advancement.

Many university leaders are supremely confident that nothing can jeopardize their position, and they regard any criticism with disdain.[33] As Professor Alan Kors of the University of Pennsylvania has remarked, "For the first time in the history of American higher education, the barbarians are running the place." Liberal education is too important to entrust to these self-styled revolutionaries. Reform, if it comes, requires the involvement of intelligent voices from both inside and outside the university—students who are willing to take on reigning orthodoxies, professors and administrators with the courage to resist the activist high tide, and parents, alumni, and civic leaders who are committed to applying genuine principles of liberal learning to the challenges of the emerging multicultural society.

# Notes

## 1. The Victim's Revolution on Campus

1. These data have been confirmed with the Office of Student Research, University of California at Berkeley. Koenigsburg's remarks are based on a personal interview with the author. Unless otherwise identified, all quotations not attributed to a printed source are from firsthand interviews.

2. This information was provided by officials who requested anonymity, and verified by alumni and members of judiciary committees with access to admissions data. While most admissions officers will privately admit its accuracy, they will not publicly release this sort of information "because we don't think it's anybody's business," in the words of a source at the Princeton admissions office.

3. Lawrence Feinberg, "Black Freshman Enrollment Rises 40 Percent at U-Va," *Washington Post*, December 26, 1988, p. C-1. For 1988 the SAT average for blacks was 1,004 out of a possible 1,600; for whites it was 1,244. For 1989 the black average was 1023; for whites it was 1,251. Figures supplied by University of Virginia admissions office.

4. "Black Incentive Grant," Office of Student Aid, Pennsylvania State University, 1989. See also Thomas DeLoughry, "At Penn State: Polarization of the Campus Persists amid Struggles to Ease Tensions," *Chronicle of Higher Education*, April 26, 1989, p. A-30. This program is currently administered by Robert W. Evans, assistant vice president for student financial aid.

5. Laura Parker, "Florida School to Offer Free Tuition to Blacks," *Washington Post*, March 9, 1990, p. A-7.

6. Dennis Kelly, "Miami College Offers Job Guarantee," *USA Today*, March 13, 1990, p. 4-D.

7. "Minority Update," *Chronicle of Higher Education*, February 7, 1990, p. A-39.

8. AP Report, "Conservatives Contest Florida, Nebraska Scholarship Plans for Blacks," *Black Issues in Higher Education*, June 7, 1990, p. 2.

9. Remarks based on personal interview with author.

10. Testimony by Michael Harris before Minority Task Force appointed by Chancellor Jack Reese of the University of Tennessee at Knoxville, October 28, 1987. See William Hawkins, "Letter from the Volunteer State," *Chronicles*, November 1988, p. 45–46.

11. Stephen Carter, "Racial Preferences: So What?" *Wall Street Journal*, September 13, 1989. Carter did attend Harvard and is now a professor at Yale Law School. For a fuller account of Carter's criticism of affirmative action stigmatization, see Stephen Carter, "The Best Black," *Reconstruction* 1, 1990, p. 6.

12. Stephen Labaton, "Law Review Is Entangled in Debate on Bias Plan," *New*

*York Times*, May 3, 1989. See also the editorial, "Brave New World at Columbia," *New York Post*, May 6, 1989.

13. This incident was witnessed by the author's research assistant, Wendy Adams, who was enrolled in Bergin's class and took written notes.

14. Houston Baker, paper delivered at conference on "Restoring American Education," Madison Center, Washington D.C., October 24–26, 1989. For an elaboration of these views, see Inga Saffron, "Putting the Rap on Plato," *Washington Post*, January 8, 1990, p. B-12.

15. For example, NWA's song "F—the Police" talks about shooting policemen, presumably white.

16. Fred Rueckher, "One Student Learns about Black Studies and White Values," *The Campus*, CCNY, April 15, 1988, p. 7; "Learning about the Sun and the Ice with Dr Jeffries," *The Campus*, CCNY, April 26, 1988, p. 13. See also, "Racism in Black Studies," *Campus Report*, June 1988, p. 1,8, where Professor Jeffries argues that "white folks are deficient in melanin" and consequently less "biologically proficient" than blacks; and Joseph Berger, "Professors' Theories on Race Stir Turmoil at City College," *New York Times*, April 20, 1990, where Jeffries alleges that "rich Jews who financed the development of Europe also financed the slave trade."

17. Benjamin Hopkins, letter to the editor, *Mother Jones*, December 1982.

18. Patricia Collins and Margaret Anderson, eds., *An Inclusive Curriculum: Race, Class and Gender in Sociological Instruction*, American Sociological Association, Washington D.C., 1987.

19. Resolution passed at Modern Language Association annual conference, 1987. Text supplied by the MLA.

20. "Faculty Statement Regarding Intellectual Freedom, Tolerance and Prohibited Harassment," State University of New York at Buffalo, 1988.

21. University of Connecticut, *Student Handbook*, 1989–90. See President's Policy on Harassment, p. 102; Statement by President John Casteen, February 19, 1988, p. 103; Privacy Rights, p. 73. The policy urges black, Hispanic, and female undergraduates to report derogatory remarks, and warns that "persons involved in advising complainants . . . must avoid comments that dissuade victims from pursuing their rights. . . . Such behavior is itself discriminatory and a violation of the policy." Casteen is now president of the University of Virginia.

22. Alan Kors, "It's Speech, Not Sex, the Dean Bans Now," *Wall Street Journal*, October 12, 1989.

23. Symposium, "Who Needs the Great Works?" *Harper's*, September 1989, p. 46.

24. Editorial, "Conservative Newspaper Moves to Independence, Banned Issue Causes Withdrawal of VSA Funding," Report of the Student Press Law Center, Winter 1988–89.

25. Malcolm Carson, "The White Conspiracy," *The Hilltop*, February 10, 1989, p. 5.

26. Kristen Asmus, "Blaming the Dress," *Colorado Daily*, October 27–29, 1989, p. 13.

27. Stanton Samuelson, "Stanford Lock-In Ends with Arrest of 52," *San Francisco Examiner*, May 16, 1989.

28. Steven Chin, "Stanford President Rips Protesters, But Supports Racial Proposals," *San Francisco Examiner*, May 19, 1989, p. A-8.

29. Statement by Lattie Coor, Office of Public Relations, University of Vermont, April 22, 1988. Coor is now president of Arizona State University.

30. "Minority Student Organizations," Office of Minority Educational Affairs, Cornell University. List supplied by Malinda Smith, associate director of minority affairs, January 1990.

31. In Brief, "UCLA Gives Recognition to First Lesbian Sorority," *Chronicle of Higher Education*, March 9, 1988, p. A-2.

32. Julie Iovine, "Lipsticks and Lords: Yale's New Look," *Wall Street Journal*, August 4, 1987.

33. Jerry Adler, "Have Gays Taken Over Yale?" *Newsweek*, October 12, 1987, p. 96.

34. Iovine, "Lipsticks and Lords."

35. Nick Ravo, "Yale President Rebuts Story That Depicted School as 'Gay'," *New York Times*, September 29, 1987, p. B-1.

36. Adler, "Have Gays Taken Over Yale?"

37. Ibid.

38. According to the 1987 *Statistical Yearbook of the Immigration and Naturalization Service*, Asian immigration increased from 7.7 percent between 1955 and 1964 to over 40 percent between 1975 and 1987. Central and South American immigration rose from 7.6 percent between 1955 and 1964 to around 12 percent between 1975 and 1987. Caribbean immigration climbed from 7.1 percent between 1955 and 64 to around 15 percent between 1975 and 1987. Washington, D.C., 1988, pp. i–ix.

39. Ibid.

40. William Henry III, "America's Changing Colors," *Time*, April 9, 1990, p. 28. At current rates of reproduction and immigration, by the end of the century, the Hispanic population will have increased by 21 percent, the Asian population by 22 percent, blacks by 12 percent, and whites by 2 percent.

41. Symposium, "The Now and Future University," *Columbia*, Summer 1990, p. 20. Available from the Office of Public Affairs, Columbia University.

42. *A Survey of College Seniors: Knowledge of History and Literature*, conducted by the Gallup Organization for the National Endowment for the Humanities, Washington, D.C., 1989, pp. 33–56.

43. "The Condition of the Professoriate: Attitudes and Trends, 1989," Carnegie Foundation for the Advancement of Teaching, Washington, D.C.

44. Thomas DeLoughry, "Student of Transcripts Finds Little Structure in the Liberal Arts," *Chronicle of Higher Education*, January 18, 1989, pp. A-1, A-32.

45. Lynne Cheney, *Humanities in America*, National Endowment for the Humanities, Washington D.C., 1988, p. 5.

46. Three of them are Boston University president John Silber; S. Frederick Starr, president of Oberlin College, who has written favorably about Allan Bloom's *The Closing of the American Mind;* and Bard College President Leon Botstein, who has advanced a case for transmitting a common culture to white and minority students alike. See, e.g., Scott Heller, "Colleges Told to Stress Tradition and Shared Values Even as They Bring More Diversity into Curricula," *Chronicle of Higher Education*, October 4, 1989, p. A-1.

47. Letter from James Duderstadt to University of Michigan community, March 31, 1989.

48. Ibid.

49. Chin, "Stanford President Rips Protesters."

50. Reprinted in Duke *Dialogue,* September 1, 1989, pp. 4–5.

51. *The Smith Design for Institutional Diversity,* Office of the President, Smith College, March 1989.

52. *Final Report of the University Committee on Minority Issues,* Office of the President, Stanford University, March 1989.

53. *Ohio State University Action Plan,* Office of the Vice President for Academic Affairs and Provost, Ohio State University, October 1987.

54. *The Madison Plan,* Office of the Chancellor, University of Wisconsin at Madison, February 9, 1988.

55. *The Michigan Mandate: A Strategic Linking of Academic Excellence and Social Diversity,* Office of the President, University of Michigan, March 1990: see "Highlights of the First Two Years," p. vii, "Strategic Process," p. 14, and Appendix A, "A Two Year Status Report," p. 1.

56. Richard Bernstein, "Academia's Liberals Defend Their Carnival of Canons against Bloom's 'Killer B's,'" *New York Times,* September 25, 1988.

57. Henry Louis Gates, "Whose Canon Is It Anyway?" *New York Times Book Review,* February 26, 1989, p. 44.

58. Jay Parini, "Academic Conservatives Who Decry Politicization Show Staggering Naivete about Their Own Biases," *Chronicle of Higher Education,* December 7, 1988, p. B-1.

59. Alvin Sanoff, "'60s Protesters, 80s Professors," *U.S. News & World Report,* January 16, 1989, p. 54.

60. See, e.g., Barbara Vobejda, "New Orthodoxy on Campus Assailed: Conservative Academicians Fault Studies of Pop Culture," *Washington Post,* November 14, 1988, p. 18; Carolyn Mooney, "Conservative Scholars Call for a Movement to 'Reclaim' Academy," *Chronicle of Higher Education,* November 23, 1988, p. A-1.

61. See, e.g., Bernard Davis, M.D., *Storm Over Biology,* Prometheus Press, New York, 1986. Davis repeated this contention in an interview with the author.

## 2. More Equal Than Others

1. Linda Matthews, "When Being Best Isn't Good Enough: Why Yat-pang Au Won't Be Going to Berkeley," *Los Angeles Times Magazine,* July 19, 1987, pp. 23–28. The subsequent account of this incident is drawn from this article.

2. Office of Student Research, UC-Berkeley.

3. Tamara Henry, "Admissions Fight Highlights Inequity," *Orange County Register,* November 12, 1989, p. A-4.

4. See Ira Michael Heyman, "Don't Regress to Educational Apartheid," *Wall Street Journal,* July 19, 1989, Letters page. See also Larry Gordon, "UC Berkeley Will Require Course on Ethnic Studies," *Los Angeles Times,* April 26, 1989, p. 12.

5. "Berkeley should actively seek diversity—socioeconomic, cultural, ethnic, racial, and geographic—in its student body. It should do so for the sound educational reason that a broad diversity of backgrounds, values and viewpoints is an integral part of a stimulating intellectual and cultural environment in which students educate one another. In addition, Berkeley should seek a diverse student body in recognition of its responsibility to train the leadership of a racially, ethnically and culturally pluralistic society."
*Freshmen Admissions at Berkeley: A Policy for the 1990s and Beyond,* Report by the Committee on Admissions and Enrollment, Berkeley Academic Senate, May 19, 1989. Professor Jerome Karabel, chair, p. 30. This report has been endorsed as official policy by the university.

6. In 1988 the legislature approved a revision of the education Master Plan which recommended that "each segment of California public higher education shall strive to approximate by the year 2000 the general ethnic, sexual and economic composition of the recent high school graduates, both in first year classes and subsequent college and university graduating classes." Joint Committee for Review of the Master Plan for Higher Education, California Legislature, *California Faces . . . California's Future,* 1988, p. 19.

7. "The long-range goal of our efforts in student affirmative action is to have the Berkeley campus minority student enrollments represent the proportion of minority students enrolled in the high schools in California." Berkeley Five-year Plan, 1983–1988, Office of the Vice-Chancellor, p. 7. Vice-Chancellor Roderic Park has said that the plan continues to be in effect. See also University of California Five-year Plan, 1985–1990, which seeks to give ethnic groups admitted to the UC-system "parity" with their proportion in the state population. Issued June 1988 by UC-president David Gardner. See also Gardner's comment, "We want a mix of students in any given campus in any given year that is a rough approximation of what our society represents." "Gardner Gives Admissions Talk on KALX Radio," *Daily Californian,* December 1, 1987, p. 1.

8. See *Freshman Admissions at Berkeley, California Faces . . . California's Future,* and "Gardner Gives Admissions Talk."

9. Only 4.5 percent of black and 5 percent of Hispanic high school graduates meet the basic academic entrance requirements of the University of California system, compared with 15.8 percent of white students and 32.8 percent of Asian students. See California Postsecondary Education Commission, "Eligibility of California's High School Graduates for Admission to its Public Universities: A Report of the 1986 High School Eligibility Study," February 1988, agenda item 16.

10. Ira Heyman, "UC Berkeley Admissions: The Best of the Balance," *Los Angeles Times,* February 7, 1989.

11. Stephen Goode, "On the Outs Over Who Gets In," *Insight,* Oct. 9, 1989, p. 9.

12. See notes 5–7 above.

13. Cited by Matthews, "When Being Best Isn't Good Enough," p. 24.

14. Berkeley internal memorandum, 1984, information obtained from office of Rep. Dana Rohrabacher.

15. See Ronald Takaki, *Strangers from A Different Shore,* Oxford: Oxford University Press, and Little, Brown: Boston, 1989.

16. *Statistical Yearbook of the Immigration and Naturalization Service,* U.S. Department of Justice, 1987, see esp. Table 16, p. 32.

17. *Freshmen Admissions at Berkeley.*

18. Cited in Goode, "On the Outs Over Who Gets In," p. 13.

19. John Bunzel, "Affirmative Action: How It 'Works' at UC-Berkeley," *The Public Interest,* Fall 1988, p. 22. As late as 1968 only 2.8 percent of Berkeley students were black and 1.3 percent Hispanic; this climbed very slowly through the 1970s, reaching 3.9 percent black and 4 percent Hispanic by 1979; then it galloped in the 1980s, to a 1988 level of 10.8 percent black and 18.6 percent Hispanic. *Freshmen Admissions at Berkeley,* Table 3, "Ethnic Distribution of New Freshmen at Berkeley."

20. Whites who composed 57.9 percent of the student body in 1981 fell to only 37 percent in 1988; this was a smaller proportion than the white population in California. Figures supplied by the Office of Student Research, UC-Berkeley.

21. The number of white students admitted to Berkeley in 1989 dropped 16 percent

from 1988. Meanwhile, black admissions rose to 11.4 percent of the student body, and Hispanic admissions to 21.8 percent. Figures obtained from the Office of Student Research, UC-Berkeley.

22. Carl Irving, "UC-Berkeley's Radical Affirmative Action Fuels Race Debate," *Washington Times*, August 22, 1989, p. A-5.

23. Matthews, "When Being Best Isn't Good Enough," p. 23.

24. See, e.g., Karen Dewitt, "Harvard Cleared in Inquiry on Bias," *New York Times*, October 7, 1990; Larry Gordon, "Anti-Asian Bias Found in UCLA Program," *Los Angeles Times*, October 2, 1990.

At Harvard in 1982 Asian Americans who were offered admission had a combined SAT average of 1,467; for whites, the average was only 1,355. Thus Asians typically had to score more than 100 points higher than whites to be admitted to Harvard. Further, although Asian American application rates climbed rapidly between 1982 and 1987, Harvard continued to accept between 11 and 15 percent of Asians in each freshmen class, an "upper limit quota" in the minds of Asian activists. Robert Klitgaard, *Choosing Elites*, Basic Books, New York, 1985, pp. 134–41. See also John Bunzel and Jeffrey Au, "Diversity or Discrimination: Asian-Americans in College," *The Public Interest*, Spring 1987, p. 55.

Data from UCLA from 1987, released in a university admissions report, show that Asians had a 41 percent acceptance rate to the university, compared with 89 percent for American Indians, 85 percent for Hispanics, 73 percent for blacks, and 62 percent for a special category of "affirmative action" Asians, Filipino Americans. This was the case even though Asian applicants were stronger academically than any other minority group. Julie Johnson, "Asian-Americans Press Fight for Wider Top-College Door," *New York Times*, September 9, 1989, p. 1. See also T. Nhan, "U.S. Officials Investigate Alleged UCLA Racial Bias," *The Daily Bruin*, UCLA, April 12, 1989, p. 1.

25. Stanford's Committee on Undergraduate Admissions and Financial Aid discovered, after an inquiry, that between 1982 and 1985 Asian Americans were one-third less likely than whites to be offered admission, even though they were on average better prepared academically than white applicants. Annual Report of CUAFA, Stanford University, 1986, reprinted in *Campus Report*, November 12, 1986.

Some admissions officials have complained that Asian Americans tend to be lacking in extracurricular and personal qualities, which universities consider along with grades to ensure that they get well-rounded individuals. But there is no systematic evidence of this; indeed a report by the Corporation Committee on Minority Affairs (CCMI) at Brown, established to investigate charges of anti-Asian discrimination, found such assumptions to be the result of "cultural bias and stereotypes which prevail in the admissions office." In the early 1980s, these attitudes contributed to a 14 percent acceptance rate for Asians, who are on average the best-qualified applicants to Brown, compared with other students who averaged an acceptance rate of 20 percent. See Report of CCMI, Brown University, February 1984. Between 1978 and 1986, there was a 430 percent increase of Asian Americans applying to Brown, but the number of these students admitted remained fairly constant. Grace Tsuang, "Equal Access of Asian-Americans," *Yale Law Journal*, January 1989, pp. 659–78.

26. Berkeley Office of the Chancellor, *Report on 1984 Enrollments of Chinese Students*, December 5, 1984.

27. M. Aoki, "Asians Question UC Admissions Policy," *California Journal*, June 1988, p. 259.

28. Cited by Rep. Dana Rohrabacher, "Evidence of Asian-American Discrimination in College and University Admissions," Fact Sheet, June 1989.

29. Diane Curtis, "UC-Berkeley Chancellor Assailed for Bias," *San Francisco Chronicle*, March 4, 1989. Torres convened a Senate Special Committee which held hearings on discrimination in UC admissions policies.

30. "UC Berkeley Apologizes for Policy That Limited Asians," *Los Angeles Times*, April 7, 1989, part 1, p. 3.

31. James Gibney, "The Berkeley Squeeze," *New Republic*, April 11, 1988, p. 15.

32. In 1974, only 4,706 students applied to Berkeley, and 3,908 were admitted. By 1988 applications were up to 22,439 and 7,731 were offered admission. Berkeley enrolls approximately 3,500 freshmen each year. *Freshmen Admission at Berkeley*, p. 2.

33. Ibid., p. 15.

34. Joseph Sullivan, "College Leaders Focus on Enmity between Races," *New York Times*, April 23, 1988, p. 34.

35. Figure from the Office of Student Research, UC-Berkeley.

36. See California Postsecondary Commission, "Eligibility of California's High School Graduates"; see also Gibney, "The Berkeley Squeeze" p. 15.

37. Bunzel, "Affirmative Action," p. 16.

38. Larry Gordon, "Law Schools Weigh Value of Waiting Lists for Minorities," *Los Angeles Times*, February 26, 1989, part 1, p. 3. Berkeley denies using separate ethnic tracks for admission and has now discontinued the practice of informing students about which racial waiting list they are on. Nevertheless, the university still maintains internal race-specific waiting lists. See letter from William Smith, acting assistant secretary for civil rights, Department of Education, to Rep. Dana Rohrabacher, April 4, 1990.

39. Analysis by Berkeley's Office of Budget and Planning, cited in *Freshmen Admissions at Berkeley*, p. 22.

40. Randall Kennedy, "Persuasion and Distrust: A Comment on the Affirmative Action Debate," *Harvard Law Review*, April 1986, pp. 1327, 1330, 1336.

41. At Berkeley in 1986, for example, the mean SAT score for affirmative action freshmen was 952 for blacks, 1,014 for Hispanics, and 1,082 for native Americans. For whites it was 1,232; for Asians, it was 1,254. See Bunzel, "Affirmative Action," p. 20. For the term *academic mismatch*, which I use to describe this difference, I am indebted to Thomas Sowell, "The New Racism on Campus," *Fortune*, February 13, 1989.

42. Among "special admit" categories, 38 percent of Hispanics and 46 percent of blacks at Berkeley maintained grade averages below 2.0 during the 1985–86 academic year. Bunzel, "Affirmative Action," p. 21.

43. Office of Student Research, UC-Berkeley. See also Gibney, "The Berkeley Squeeze," p. 15.

44. Figure from Office of Admissions, UC-Berkeley. A study of "special action" students who entered Berkeley between 1978 and 1982 showed that 31 percent graduated in five years, compared to 61 percent for regularly admitted students. "Retention Rates by Admissions Status," Office of Student Research, June 20, 1988.

45. Confidential statement by Professor Stephen Barnett, "Fairness to Asian-Americans in Affirmative Action for Other Minority Groups," February 21, 1989, prepared with information supplied by the university, p. 27-A.

46. Ibid., pp. 28-A, 29-A. See table, "One Year Retention Rates for Freshmen Entering Berkeley in Fall Terms 1978 to 1986, Divided Between Regular and Special Action Admits."

47. Bunzel, "Affirmative Action," p. 21.

48. This was the conclusion reached by Professor Andrew Hacker of Queens College, who has studied the Berkeley admissions data. Hacker writes,

> Leaving ethnicity aside, we can simply say that some students are better prepared for college than others. Indeed, quite a gulf can separate those ready for demanding college work and those who will have difficulty grasping much of what is going on. In fact, many in the latter group can adapt to college. But for that to happen, they would be better advised to start in a setting where they will not be overwhelmed by better-prepared classmates. Nor is it clear that remedial courses can equip less-prepared students for the level of performance expected by professors at a university like Berkeley. Hence I fear that all too many may feel so frustrated that they drop out. And that would be an awful loss, since I am sure most of them could have made it on a less intense campus.

See Andrew Hacker's response to letters, *New York Review of Books*, December 7, 1989, p. 53. Hacker's original article, "Asians, Blacks and Whites Struggle for College," appeared in *New York Review of Books*, October 12, 1989, p. 63.

49. John Bunzel, "Boost Black Students the Old Fashioned Way," *Wall Street Journal*, June 21, 1989, citing 1986 U.S. Census Data. The black high school graduation rate was 75.1 percent in 1988, down from 76.4 percent in 1986. See Reginald Wilson and Deborah Carter, *Eighth Annual Report on Minorities in Higher Education*, Office of Minority Concerns, American Council on Education, 1989.

50. Bunzel, "Affirmative Action," citing National Association of Education progress report.

51. Between 1984 and 1986 total minority enrollment rose 6 percent, but black enrollment declined slightly from 617,000 to 615,000. Fortunately, black enrollment rose somewhat between 1986 and 1988, with private colleges registering a 7.1 percent increase but public colleges only a 0.2 percent increase. Despite the modest growth of the past two years, today only about 26–28 percent of black high school graduates go on to college, compared with 34 percent in 1976. These trends are particularly pronounced among black males. See "More Young Black Men, Worried by Higher Education's Costs and a Shaky Economy, Are Choosing Not to Go to College," *Chronicle of Higher Education*, December 9, 1987, p. A-1; Susan Tifft, "The Search for Minorities," *Time*, August 21, 1989, p. 22; "After Years of Decline, Black Enrollment at Colleges Rises," *Washington Times*, based on AP reports, March 29, 1990, p. A-10.

52. John Bunzel, "Boost Black Students," citing a 1988 Department of Education study.

53. *1988 Profile of SAT and Achievement Test Takers*, College Entrance Examination Board, Princeton, N.J., 1989. Updated figures for 1989 obtained from College Board. Surprisingly, Asians who declared that English was not their first language scored 10 points higher on the verbal SAT than blacks. Students of all groups who came from families with incomes under $10,000 a year scored above the black SAT average by 44 points in the aggregate.

54. *Profiles of College Bound Seniors,* College Entrance Examination Board, Princeton, N.J., 1989.

55. Ibid. Figures for 1988 show that fewer than 1,500 blacks scored over 599 on the verbal section of the SAT, and fewer than 3,000 scored over 599 on the math section.

56. The average SAT score at Harvard is approximately 1,370, at Yale 1,360, at Princeton 1,340, at Dartmouth 1,300. These averages take into account the scores of affirmative action students, so the mean score for students accepted on academic merit is considerably higher. Figures obtained from admissions office at respective schools. See also "America's Best Colleges 1990," *U.S. News and World Report,* Fall 1989 (special issue).

57. Michele Collison, "Colleges Try New Techniques in Fierce Competition for Black Students," *Chronicle of Higher Education,* June 10, 1987, p. A-1.

58. See chapter 1, notes 4–8.

59. Robert Klitgaard, *Choosing Elites,* Basic Books, New York, 1985, p. 154.

60. Sowell, "The New Racism on Campus," p. 115–16.

61. Donald Werner, "College Admissions: Shaky Ethics," *New York Times,* June 4, 1988.

62. Walter Allen, *Campus Gender and Race Differences in Black Student Academic Performance,* Southern Educational Foundation, Atlanta, 1986, pp. 33, 47.

63. Jacqueline Fleming, *Blacks in College,* Jossey-Bass, San Francisco, 1988, pp. 142–43. Fleming writes, "Black men on white campuses respond to feelings of competitive rejection that have consequences for their capacity to muster intellectual motivation. . . . The developmental profiles of black males in white colleges can be described as depressed. They become unhappy with college life. . . . They display academic unmotivation and think less of their abilities. They profess loss of energy and cease to be able to enjoy competitive activities." Although some resort to such diversions as political action, "these developments are defensive and do little to remedy their plight."

64. At the University of Wisconsin at Madison, 28 percent of all students, but 43 percent of minorities, fail to graduate. Since "all students" include minority students, the gap between the minority and nonminority dropout rate was even more pronounced. University of Wisconsin at Madison, *The Madison Plan,* Office of the Chancellor, February 9, 1988, p. 14.

At Oberlin College, 30 percent of all students, but 50 percent of blacks, drop out. Interestingly, an Oberlin study found that "components of the financial aid package only poorly predict differences in persistence to graduation." See Executive Summary, Report of the Dean's Research Group, Oberlin College, May 1988, Patrick Penn, chairman.

At Ohio State University, 47 percent of all students who enrolled as freshmen in 1980, but 79 percent of black students, had not graduated after six years. See *Action Plan: Recruitment and Retention of Black Students at Ohio State University,* Office of Academic Affairs, Ohio State University, 1987, see Executive Summary, p. 1.

65. During a 1986 court trial involving preferential treatment for college athletes, it emerged that only around fifteen of the two hundred blacks who played sports for the University of Georgia since 1969 ended up graduating. Memphis State University had the questionable honor of graduating not a single black athlete in twelve years. Nationwide, the graduation rate for black athletes is less than 25 percent, and most of those degrees are in physical education. See Malcolm Gladwell, "Dunk and Flunk," *New Republic,* May 19, 1986, p. 13.

66. A Department of Education study of 1980 high school graduates found that 52 percent of whites who entered four-year colleges graduated by 1986, compared with 26 percent of black and Hispanic students. See Denise Magner, "Colleges Try New Ways to Insure Minority Students Make It to Graduation," *Chronicle of Higher Education*, November 29, 1989, p. A-1.

Recently the education secretary reported that despite the existence of remedial and retention programs, 55 percent of black students and 51 percent of Hispanic students who enter higher education do not earn any degrees, even after twelve years. Only 33 percent of other students suffer this predicament. See Lauro Cavazos, Remarks at the 72nd Annual Meeting of the American Council on Education, January 1990, Department of Education transcript, p. 3.

67. Magner, *ibid.* "Colleges Try New Ways."

68. Barbara Ransby, "Black Students Fight Back," *The Nation*, March 26, 1988, p. 411.

69. Cited by James Fallows, "The Tests and the Brightest," *The Atlantic*, February 1980, p. 38.

70. Cited in Elizabeth Greene, "SAT Scores Fail to Help Admissions Officers Make Better Decisions, Analysts Contend," *Chronicle of Higher Education*, July 27, 1988, p. A-20.

71. See Jean Evangelauf, "Reliance on Multiple-Choice Tests Said to Harm Minorities and Hinder Reform," *Chronicle of Higher Education*, May 30, 1990, p. A-1; see also John Weiss, Barbara Beckwith, and Bob Schaeffer, *Standing Up to the SAT*, Arco Books, New York, 1989.

FairTest has petitioned the National Merit Scholarship Corporation to stop using the SAT as a criterion for awards. Co-signers of the petition include a broad coalition of minority organizations, such as the NAACP, the National Organization for Women, the National Congress of American Indians, the Puerto Rican Legal Defense and Education Fund, the League of United Latin American Citizens, Mexican American Legal Defense and Education Fund, and National Political Congress of Black Women. See FairTest petition, November 10, 1988, obtained from the National Center for Fair and Open Testing.

72. For a sober and detailed review of the data, see Thomas Donlon, ed., *The College Board Technical Handbook for the Scholastic Aptitude Test and Achievement Tests*, College Entrance Examination Board, New York, 1984.

73. Klitgaard, *Choosing Elites*, p. 15.

74. Donlon, *The College Board*, pp. 154–59.

75. Pat Ordovensky, "SAT under Assault as Admissions Tool," *USA Today*, September 11, 1989, p. D-1.

76. Cited by Fallows, "The Tests and the Brightest," p. 46.

77. For a sophisticated critique of the testing process, see James Fallows, "What's Wrong with Testing," *Washington Monthly*, May 1989, pp. 12–24.

78. Elizabeth Greene, "San Francisco State's Woo: No Time to Lament," *Chronicle of Higher Education*, November 18, 1987, p. A-39.

79. Dornbush found that Asian high school students spend an average of 11.7 hours a week doing homework, compared with 8.6 for whites and even less for blacks and Hispanics. "My bottom line is that these Asians work a heck of a lot harder." Cited by John Bunzel and Jeffrey Au, "Diversity or Discrimination: Asian-Americans in College," *The Public Interest*, Spring 1987, p. 55.

80. "New Controversy over the SAT," *College Bound*, March 1989, p. 1. U.S.

District Court judge John Walker observed that the probability that men would consistently perform better than women on the SAT, absent discrimination, was "nearly zero," and therefore the tests must embody a sexist bias.

81. Bates has made submission of SAT scores optional for applicants, the admissions office confirms.

82. For example, Harvard reduced its Jewish enrollment from about 25 percent to about 12 percent in 1926. Ironically, a common justification, which President Lowell of Harvard cited, was the fear that accepting too many Jews would lead to anti-Semitism. See M. Synott, *The Half-Opened Door: Discrimination and Admissions at Harvard, Yale and Princeton, 1900–1970*, Greenwood Press, Westport, Conn., 1979. See also George Will, "Prejudice against Excellence," *Washington Post*, April 16, 1989, p. B-7.

83. Learned Hand, *The Spirit of Liberty*, collected and edited by Irving Dilliard, University of Chicago Press, Chicago, 1977, pp. 20–23.

84. Richard Bernstein, "Black and White on Campus," *New York Times*, May 26, 1988.

85. See chapter 5, note 43.

86. Stephen Goode, "On the Outs Over Who Gets In," *Insight*, October 9, 1989, p. 14.

87. Among Berkeley's officially recognized minority groups are: African Descendants Valuing and Nurturing Community Empowerment, African Students Association, Association for Raza Talent, Association of Black Students in Sociology, Association of Graduate Muslim Students, Berkeley Women's Law Journal, Black Freshman Alliance, Black Women Support Group, Black Women's Network Association, Brothers of African Descent, Chicano Architecture Student Association, Chicanos in Health Education, Graduate English Women's Caucus, La Raza Law Students Association, Law Students of African Descent, MeChA, Minority Pre-Law Coalition, Minority Undergraduate Students of English, Multicultural Lesbian Bisexual Gay Alliance, Multicultural Multiracial Women's Coalition, Scientists of Color, Third World Voice, and United People of Color. For a complete list, see "Student Group List, April 1990," UC-Berkeley.

88. Cited by Goode, "On the Outs Over Who Gets In," p. 14.

89. Ibid., p. 9.

90. Shelby Steele, "The Recoloring of Campus Life," *Harper's*, February 1989, p. 51.

91. Bernstein, "Black and White on Campus."

92. Elizabeth Greene, "At Oberlin, Liberal Traditions, Intentions Are No Guarantee of Racial Harmony," *Chronicle of Higher Education*, April 26, 1989, p. A-31.

93. Veronice Woolridge, "Race Relations on Campus," *New York Times*, April 5, 1989.

94. Notebook, *Chronicle of Higher Education*, January 20, 1988, p. A-31. "White students are practically assured that they will be in the room with other white students because they are such an overwhelming majority," remarked Dollicia Floyd, the black organizer of the protest.

95. Michele Collison, "At Greensboro, Blacks Chafe at Stereotyping, White Students Assail Emphasis on Race," *Chronicle of Higher Education*, April 26, 1989, p. A-28.

96. Michele Collison, "A Seldom Aired Issue," *Chronicle of Higher Education*, October 5, 1988, p. A-39.

97. Donald Kennedy, response to Rainbow Coalition demands, *Campus Report*, Stanford University, February 17, 1988, p. 8.

98. "Black Students Get a Yearbook of Their Own," *New York Times,* July 23, 1989, p. 35.

99. Arnold Hence, "How to Make Effective Presentations to Minority Student Groups," *The Admissions Strategist,* College Entrance Examination Board, 1987, pp. 50–53.

100. See *Carolina: A Black Perspective,* University of North Carolina at Chapel Hill, 1989, p. 7.

101. "In Box," *Chronicle of Higher Education,* March 30, 1988, p. A-14.

102. "Many black and Hispanic students . . . find themselves making constant external and internal adjustments as they maneuver between a predominantly white, affluent environment at school and a working-class atmosphere at home. For some the transition produces confusion, frustration, pain and a loneliness that stems from the belief that few experience or understand their plight." See Crystal Nix, "Inner City, Elite Campus: How 2 Worlds Jar," *New York Times,* January 4, 1986, p. 1.

103. George Stuteville, "I.U. Blacks Testify Racism Continues in Newer Forms," *Indianapolis Star,* April 14, 1989, p. 1.

104. Cited by Michael Rezendes, "Campus Minorities: Confronting Racism with Mature Methods," *Washington Post,* April 19, 1988, p. 11.

105. Notebook, *Chronicle of Higher Education,* May 11, 1988, p. A-26.

106. William Raspberry, "Affirmative Action That Hurts Blacks," *Washington Post,* February 23, 1987.

107. Cited by Michele Collison, "Oberlin's New Admissions Director Is Used to Being First," *Chronicle of Higher Education,* September 9, 1987, p. A-3.

108. See Robin Wilson, "New White Student Unions on Some Campuses Are Sparking Outrage and Worry," *Chronicle of Higher Education,* April 18, 1990, p. A-1.

Temple University's White Students Union was set up in 1988. The university was forced to recognize it because it already recognized a host of all-minority institutions. See In Brief, "White Pride Group Recognized by Temple U," *Chronicle of Higher Education,* December 14, 1988, p. A-2.

Florida State set up its White Students Union in 1989, amidst an enormous campus outcry. See Boyd Hambleton, "Race vs. Race at UF," *Florida Review,* January 1990, p. 1. See also letter by Mark Wright, organizer of White Student Union, *Alligator,* January 22, 1990, p. 7. Wright comments, "Members of the Black Student Union oppose the White Student Union—unbelievable. The double standard in black-white relations is so bad. When whites decide to stand up for issues that are important to them, they are labelled racist. When blacks do so, they are labelled civil rights activists."

109. Collison, "A Seldom Aired Issue," p. A-39.

110. For anecdotal evidence of the stigma created by affirmative action in the workplace, see Sonia Nazario, "Many Minorities Feel Torn by Experience of Affirmative Action," *Wall Street Journal,* June 27, 1989, p. 1.

111. William Beer, "Resolute Ignorance: Social Science and Affirmative Action," *Society,* May–June 1987, pp. 63–69. See also William Beer, "Real-Life Costs of Affirmative Action," Op-Ed Page, *Wall Street Journal,* August 7, 1986, Beer remarks,

> Twenty years after the enactment of the Civil Rights Act of 1964, there has been no systematic inquiry into the effects of affirmative action on American society, neither its costs to the nation's economy nor its impact on our country's morale. In an age of program evaluation, when most

other social experiments are studied almost to death, our profession has
shown a resolute ignorance about an extraordinarily controversial policy
that has been in place for over two decades. It is as if affirmative action
has assumed the status of a religious article of faith, and professionals
choose to avoid studying its effects for fear of what they might find.

112. For example, making the case for affirmative action, Harvard President Derek
Bok cited as proof that preferential treatment does not exacerbate significant white
hostility a Harvard poll of 1,200 undergraduates, in which 60 percent of whites said
they did not question the ability of blacks or think them inferior, but a majority suspected
that *others* have such doubts. Bok completely misses the significance of this, which
is that, reluctant to confess to sentiments which may be interpreted as bigoted, white
students project their own opinions onto "others," reserving progressive views for
themselves. This certainly seems a more likely interpretation than Bok's, which is
that students are owning up to their own moral rectitude. See Derek Bok, "Admitting
Success: The Case for Racial Preferences," *New Republic,* February 4, 1985, p. 15.

113. For a penetrating analysis of student insecurity, see Martin Meyerson, "The
Ethos of the American College Student," in Robert Goldwin, ed., *Higher Education
and Modern Democracy,* Rand McNally, Chicago, 1965, pp. 7–8. Meyerson observes,

> The status which came from college attendance has been diluted. The
> college student is no longer one of the happy few—he is one of the
> frustrated many. . . . Today's student is neither one of the elect nor
> part of the electorate. . . . Students are on the fringe of the adult world,
> but not in it. They are in limbo. Many are grateful for the deferral because
> they can test themselves in different ways and so find their identity.
> Others are resentful of the deferral: they sense more keenly than they
> did in high school that students do not have inalienable rights, or indeed,
> many rights at all.

114. "Oppose Discrimination in University Admissions," Statement by Rep. Dana
Rohrabacher in conjunction with H. Con. Res. 147.

115. *Freshmen Admissions at Berkeley: A Policy for the 1990s and Beyond,* Report
by the Committee on Admissions for Enrollment, Berkeley Academic Senate, May
19, 1989. Professor Jerome Karabel, chair, p. 30.

116. In 1988, 63 percent of minorities went this route, compared with 59 percent
of whites.

117. Boalt Hall, Employment Reports—Class of 1986, 1987, 1988. Obtained from
the Berkeley Law School.

118. See Thomas Sowell, "Affirmative Action: A Worldwide Disaster," *Commentary,*
December 1989, pp. 21–41.

119. Currently American Jews number around 6 million and yet 31 members of
the House of Representatives and seven senators are Jewish. American blacks number
30 million, yet only 24 House members and no senators are black. Does this prove
that American voters discriminate against blacks and in favor of Jews? See Seymour
Martin Lipset, "Jewish Fear, Black Insensitivity," *New York Times,* March 9, 1990.

120. Tamara Henry, "Admissions Fight Highlights Inequity" *Orange County Register,*
November 12, 1989, p. A-4.

121. Currently it is Berkeley policy to give preferential treatment to Hispanics,
who are defined as Mexican Americans, Cuban Americans, Haitians, and natives of

Latin America, but not Spanish citizens. Although the term "Asian American" usually covers individuals of Chinese, Japanese, Korean, Filipino, Vietnamese, Cambodian, Laotian, Asian Indian, Pacific Islander, and Thai descent, Berkeley has decided that Filipinos are disadvantaged and continue to deserve preferential treatment, while other Asians are adequately or excessively represented and undeserving of special consideration. The UC-plan, which covers Berkeley, extends admissions preference to "underrepresented students," defined as "any student from a group whose proportion among university undergraduates is now, or has been in the last five years, lower than its proportion among California high school students." See Report of the Special Committee on Asian-American Admissions, Academic Senate, University of California at Berkeley, February 1989, pp. 11–12.

122. CUNY has added Italian Americans to its list of "protected classes" for affirmative action. See "Notification of Policy of Non-Discrimination," City University of New York, obtained from Sylvia Miranda, director of affirmative action, CUNY, 1990.

123. Jack McCurdy, "Asian American Is Appointed Chancellor of U. of California at Berkeley," *Chronicle of Higher Education*, February 21, 1990, p. A-2.

124. Carol Innerst and Jerry Seper, "Asian-Americans Cry Foul over College Enrollment Limits," *Washington Times*, May 10, 1989, p. 1.

125. When Congressman Dana Rohrabacher of California introduced a resolution in 1989 calling for institutions of higher education to review their policies and stop illegal discrimination against Asian Americans, he found to his surprise that several Asian groups, such as the Organization of Chinese Americans and the Japanese-American Citizens League, refused to support him and even denounced him because they feared that he sought to challenge the principle of preferential treatment. See Scott Jaschik, "Conservative Lawmaker Attracts Interest and Ire with Crusade for Asian-American Students," *Chronicle of Higher Education*, November 15, 1989, p. A-1; Letter from Robert Matsui, *Pacific Citizen*, November 17, 1989, p. 5; Dana Rohrabacher, "Why Are People Afraid of House Concurrent Resolution 1477?" *Congressional Record*, September 26, 1989, no. 125.

126. "Each and every change in the Berkeley admissions policy that we have considered would benefit some groups at the same time it would disadvantage others. The idea of a neutral admissions policy is thus a chimerical one, for any selection criterion that one might imagine favors some qualities over others and has, as a consequence, a disproportionately negative impact on some other group." *Freshmen Admissions at Berkeley*, p. 29.

127. Ibid., p. 26.

128. Allen Lue, "University Charged with Reverse Discrimination," *The Daily Californian*, January 19, 1990, p. 1; Barry Gordon, "University to Investigate White, Asian Bias Charge at Berkeley," *Los Angeles Times*, January 18, 1990, p. A-32.

Ironically, the complaint that Berkeley is discriminating against whites came from Arthur Hu, an Asian American graduate of MIT, who submitted statistics to the Department of Education suggesting that Berkeley has imposed quota ceilings for whites. "I'm trying to reform affirmative action the way Gorbachev is reforming socialism," Hu says. "You can't do the wrong thing for the right reasons." Mark Osmun, "Asian Says Whites Are Hurt by Quotas," *USA Today*, February 6, 1990, p. 2-A.

129. See University of California at Berkeley, *General Catalog 1989–90*, Vol. 83, April 1989.

## 3. Travels with Rigoberta

1. Bob Beyers and Eileen Walsh, "Bennett Charges Intimidation in CIV Decision," *Campus Report,* Stanford University, p. 14.

2. Richard Bernstein, "In Dispute on Bias, Stanford Is Likely to Alter Western Culture Program," *New York Times,* January 19, 1988, p. A-12.

3. Stephen Goode, "Studied Furor in Required Reading," *Insight,* March 7, 1988, pp. 58–60.

4. "Students Positive about Western Requirement," *Campus Report,* Stanford University, January 20, 1988, p. 8.

5. Carolyn Mooney, "Sweeping Curricular Change Is Under Way at Stanford," *Chronicle of Higher Education,* December 14, 1988, p. A-11.

6. Cited in Goode, "Studied Furor," p. 60.

7. Ibid.

8. Ibid.

9. Joseph Green, "Western Culture Is Racist," *Stanford Daily,* April 22, 1988.

10. Bernstein, "In Dispute on Bias."

11. "Area One Must Also Reflect the Values of the Younger Faculty, Robinson Says," *Campus Report,* Stanford University, January 27, 1988, p. 10.

12. "The Great Debate III," *Campus Report,* Stanford University, February 24, 1988, p. 13.

13. Larry Gordon, "Stanford Debates Its View of Western Culture," *Los Angeles Times,* February 3, 1988.

14. Office of Public Information, Stanford University.

15. Ibid.

16. This scene is vividly, although somewhat hyperbolically, described in William Bennett, "Why the West?" *National Review,* May 27, 1988, p. 37.

17. Office of Public Information, Stanford University.

18. Goode, "Studied Furor," p. 60.

19. "The Great Debate III," p. 14.

20. "The Great Debate II," *Campus Report,* Stanford University, February 10, 1988, p. 13.

21. "Raubitschek Aims to Promote Solution 'Acceptable to All,'" *Campus Report,* Stanford University, February 24, 1988, p. 16.

22. "The Great Debate III," pp. 13, 15.

23. Raymond Giraud, "Widen Western Culture," *Stanford Daily,* May 9, 1988.

24. "Western, Non-Western Culture Programs are 'Hopelessly Mixed Up': J. M. Evans," *Campus Report,* Stanford University, February 10, 1988, p. 21.

25. "'Don't Compromise on Proposal,' BSU Spokesman Says," *Campus Report,* Stanford University, February 10, 1988, p. 14.

26. There is no evidence that Socrates, Pythagoras, Herodotus, and Solon studied in Egypt although Herodotus may have traveled there. The Moors are dark-skinned but not wooly-haired. Toussaint L'Ouverture's defeat of Napoleon's troops, led by Napoleon's brother-in-law General Leclerc, occurred in 1801–1802. The French Revolution was in 1789. Thus it is not the case that Toussaint influenced the revolution. Since Saint Augustine is not present in the Bible, and in fact lived three hundred years after Christ, it is no surprise that he is omitted from Scripture. Reviewing Bill King's speech at my request, Bernard Lewis, an expert on Islamic culture at Princeton University, described it as "a few scraps of truth amidst a great deal of nonsense."

27. "'Don't Compromise on Proposal,' BSU Spokesman Says."

28. See, e.g., Carolyn Mooney, "Sweeping Curricular Change Is Under Way at Stanford," *Chronicle of Higher Education*, December 14, 1988, p. A-11; Bill Workman, "Stanford Puts an End to Western Civilization," *San Francisco Chronicle*, April 1, 1988.

29. Mooney, "Sweeping Curricular Change."

30. Thomas Wasow and Charles Junkerman, "The Process and the Product: The Inside Story on the Western Culture Debate," Office of the Dean of Undergraduate Studies, Stanford University, Fall 1988.

31. James Rosse, "Stanford and the Marketplace of Ideas," *Wall Street Journal*, February 24, 1989, p. A-17.

32. Ohio State's program gives an indication of how sweeping this enterprise can be. "All new course proposals will be reviewed to assess the extent to which they adequately address issues of race, ethnicity and gender. . . . Special efforts will be made to assess the curriculum to determine its influence on the education of blacks and other minority students. Faculty will be encouraged to include in their syllabi contributions of minority scholars, women and men, in their respective fields. . . . Faculty will be encouraged to conduct research on minority issues and race relations. Other contexts will be reviewed, such as freshmen orientation, student life programming, college-sponsored programs, and programs sponsored through the offices of Human Relations, International Affairs, Minority Affairs, Continuing Education, and the Graduate School. An assessment will be made of the extent to which publications by black and other minority authors are part of the university's libraries and bookstores. . . . We will begin to designate scholarships, fellowships, and chairs after prominent black heroes and heroines and black alumni. . . . The university will name buildings, rooms, and lecture series in honor of black leaders, and include black leaders as commencement speakers." See *Action Plan: Recruitment and Retention of Black Students at Ohio State University*, Office of Academic Affairs, Ohio State University, pp. 48–50.

33. Lynne Cheney, *Fifty Hours: A Core Curriculum for College Students*, National Endowment for the Humanities, Washington, D.C., 1989.

34. David Brooks, "From Western Lit to Westerns as Lit," *Wall Street Journal*, February 2, 1988.

35. Cited by William Bennett, speech to American Council on Education, January 19, 1988.

36. Jack McCurdy, "Bennett Calls Stanford Curriculum Revision Capitulation to Pressure," *Chronicle of Higher Education*, April 27, 1988, p. A-2.

37. Ibid.

38. Ibid., p. A-59.

39. William Chace, "There Was No Battle to Lose at Stanford," *Washington Post*, May 9, 1988, p. A-15.

40. This formulation is by Henry Louis Gates of Duke University, but it is very apt here. Perhaps the most frequently cited argument against a Western great books requirement at Stanford was that, while it claimed to be a course of the greatest thoughts ever, in fact it reflected the narrow interests of white males. See Henry Louis Gates, Jr., "Whose Canon Is It Anyway?" *New York Times Book Review*, February 26, 1989, p. 1.

41. Chace, "There Was No Battle."

42. "Stanford Slights the Great Books for Not-So-Greats," *Wall Street Journal*, December 22, 1988.

Although this outline was developed prior to the initiation of CIV, it is fairly typical of the texts actually assigned so far. In the "Europe and the Americas" track assignments for 1989, Stanford had its undergraduates read Augustine's *Confessions,* Shakespeare's *Tempest,* Rousseau's *Discourse on Inequality,* Marx's *Communist Manifesto,* and Max Weber's *The Protestant Ethic and the Spirit of Capitalism,* in addition to such non-Western offerings as the anonymous *Son of Old Man Hat,* Juan Rulfo's *The Burning Plain,* Aime Cesaire's *A Tempest* and *Return to My Native Land,* Alejo Carpentier's *The Kingdom of This World,* Carmen Taffola's *La Malinche,* Esteban Echeverria's *The Slaughterhouse,* and Maxine Kingston's *The Woman Warrior.*

For book listings from all eight tracks, see "The Freshman Experience in Books: Tracing Roots of Culture," *Campus Report,* Stanford University, May 17, 1989.

43. Ibid.

44. Ibid.

45. *I, Rigoberta Menchu: An Indian Woman in Guatemala,* edited and introduced by Elisabeth Burgos-Debray, translated by Ann Wright, Verso, New York, 1983.

46. See "Stanford Slights the Great Books for Not-So-Greats."

47. Cited in Robert Marquand, "Stanford's CIV Course Sparks Controversy," *Christian Science Monitor,* January 25, 1989, p. 13.

48. *I, Rigoberta Menchu,* p. 43.

49. Ibid., p. 220.

50. Ibid., p. xi.

51. Ibid., p. xiv.

52. Ibid., pp. 220–34.

53. Ibid., pp. xi–xxi.

54.

Where the mind is without fear and the head is held high;
Where knowledge is free;
Where the world has not been broken up into fragments by narrow domestic
    walls;
Where words come out of the depth of truth;
Where tireless striving stretches its arms toward perfection;
Where the clear stream of reason has not lost its way into the dreary desert
    sand of dead habit;
Where the mind is led forward by Thee into ever-widening thought and action;
Into that heaven of freedom, my Father, let my country awake.

55. Rabindranath Tagore, *Gitanjali,* with an introduction by W. B. Yeats, Macmillan Press, New Delhi division, 1913. See introduction, pp. xii–xiii.

56. Marquand, "Stanford's CIV Course Sparks Controversy," p. 13.

57. "The Koran? Pravda? Confucius' *Analects?* One Man's Criteria for Cultural Readings," *Campus Report,* Stanford University, June 8, 1988, p. 6.

58. Cited in Carolyn Mooney, "Sweeping Curricular Change Is Under Way at Stanford," *Chronicle of Higher Education,* December 14, 1988, p. A-11.

59. Rick Simonson and Scott Walker, *Multicultural Literacy,* Graywolf Press, Saint Paul, 1988.

60. Basil Davidson, *The African Slave Trade,* Little, Brown, Boston, 1980, pp. 42, 164, 208.

61. Walter Rodney, *How Europe Underdeveloped Africa*, Howard University Press, Washington, D.C., 1982, pp. 79–80. See Carol Innerst, "Plato and Dante Fight to Survive at Stanford," *Washington Times*, January 21, 1988.

62. Charles Johnson, *Bitter Canaan*, Transaction Books, Rutgers University Press, New Brunswick, N.J., 1988, with an introduction by John Stanfield.

63. "Footnotes," *Chronicle of Higher Education*, January 6, 1988, p. A-4.

64. Frantz Fanon, *The Wretched of the Earth*, Grove Press, New York, 1963, p. 37.

65. Ibid., preface, p. 22.

66. For example, Iraqi writer Ibn al-Faqih writes, "The people of Iraq have sound minds, commendable passions, balanced natures, and high proficiency in every art, together with well-proportioned limbs, well-compounded humors, and a pale brown color, which is the most apt and proper color. They are the ones who are done to a turn in the womb. They do not come out with something in between blond, blanched and leprous coloring, such as the infants dropped from the wombs of the women of the Slavs and others of similar light complexion. Nor are they overdone in the womb until they are burned, so that the child comes out something between black, murky, malodorous, stinking and crinkly-haired, with uneven limbs, deficient minds, and depraved passions, such as the Ethiopians and other blacks who resemble them. The Iraqis are neither half-baked dough nor burned crust, but between the two." See Ibn Taymiyya, *Al-Siyasa al-Shariyya*, cited in Bernard Lewis, ed., *Islam: From the Prophet Muhammad to the Capture of Constantinople*, Oxford University Press, New York, 1987, p. 209.

Practical violations of equality are widespread in non-Western countries, including the caste system in India, tribal hierarchies in Africa, and a continuation of slavery in parts of China and the Arab world. See, e.g., "Chinese Cracking Down on Thriving Slave Trade," *Washington Times*, February 8, 1990, for reports on the traffic in women and children in Anhui province in Eastern China; Murray Gordon, *Slavery in the Arab World*, New Amsterdam Books, New York, 1989.

67. Ibn Taymiyya, *Al-Siyasa al-Shariyya*, p. 39.

68. See, e.g., Hanny Lightfoot-Klein, *Prisoners of Ritual: An Odyssey into Female Genital Circumcision in Africa*, Haworth Press, Binghamton, N.Y., 1990; Jane Perlez, "Puberty Rite for Girls Is Bitter Issue across Africa," *New York Times*, January 15, 1990. According to the United Nations, 20 million African women have suffered this fate.

69. See, e.g., *Amnesty International Report 1990*, New York, 1990.

70. Basil Davidson, *The African Genius*, Little Brown, Boston, 1970, p. 73.

71. Edward Said, *Orientalism*, Pantheon Books, New York, 1978, p. 1.

72. Isaac Barchas, "What Really Happened at Stanford," *Academic Questions* 3, no. 1, (1990), pp. 24–34.

73. Ralph Waldo Emerson, "An Address in the Court-House in Concord, Massachusetts, on 1st August, 1844, on the Anniversary of the Emancipation of the Negroes in the British West Indies," Boston, 1844.

74. Bernard Lewis, "Western Culture Must Go," *Wall Street Journal*, May 2, 1988.

75. See Michael Thorpe, "Some Thoughts on Cultural Imperialism," *Encounter*, December 1989, pp. 40–44, where the author quotes Jomo Kenyatta praising clitoridectomy as a beautiful rite of passage, and a spokesman for the Indian Brotherhood

proclaiming, "It is our tradition and our culture if we want to discriminate against women."

76. Jacob Neusner, "It Is Time to Stop Apologizing for Western Civilization and to Start Analyzing Why It Defines World Culture," *Chronicle of Higher Education*, February 15, 1989, p. B-1.

77. The well-known Indian writer Nirad Chaudhuri remarks that British rule, for all its hardship, "emancipated Indian minds" so they could protest against all forms of "blatant oppression. . . . The awareness that happiness had a claim on human beings came to the Bengalis first from their reading of English literature and their observation of English life." Yet when Chaudhuri lectures in Western academic quarters, he finds that audiences demand unmitigated castigation of European ways and nothing short of fulsome praise of the Third World. See Nirad Chaudhuri, *Thy Hand, Great Anarch: India 1921–1952*, Chatto & Windus, London, 1987, pp. 861–62; Nirad Chaudhuri, *The Continent of Circe*, Macmillan, New York, 1967, p. 26.

78. Marx and Engels, *Collected Works*, vol. I, International Publishers, New York, 1975; cited by Nathaniel Weyl, *Karl Marx: Racist*, Arlington House, New York, 1979, p. 37.

79. Letter from Marx to Engels, August 7, 1866. Marx and Engels, *Collected Works*, vol. 42, International Publishers, New York, 1987, pp. 304–5.

80. Letter from Marx to Eleanor Marx, September 5, 1866. Ibid., p. 315.

81. Karl Marx, "The British Rule In India," *New York Daily Tribune*, June 24, 1853.

82. Walter Lippmann, "Education vs. Western Civilization," in *The Essential Lippmann*, ed. Clinton Rossiter and James Lare (New York: Random House, 1963), p. 421.

83. Gary Kates, "The Classics of Western Civilization Do Not Belong to Conservatives Alone," *Chronicle of Higher Education*, July 5, 1989, p. A-46.

84. Hayden writes:

> I find myself in agreement with those, including conservatives, who want to return to a core curriculum. The great books should be at the center of any general education. A core curriculum assumes that there are cultural traditions every American should be familiar with because we need a democratic society, not a passive elitist society, and democracy is a discipline and habit that needs to be cultivated. Each generation of students needs to review the arguments that have been made over centuries about the purpose of life, about the role of human beings in public affairs, about why citizenship has value. . . . The basic arguments about these propositions are, for example, in Thucydides' *Peloponnesian War*. When Thucydides said he was writing a book that would have value for all time, he was correct.

Tom Hayden, "Our Finest Moment," *New Perspectives Quarterly* 4, no. 4, Winter 1988, pp. 20–25.

85. Shylock says:

> I am a Jew. Hath not a Jew eyes? Hath not a Jew hands, organs, dimensions, senses, affections, passions?—fed with the same food, hurt with the same weapons, subject to the same diseases, healed by the same means, warmed and cooled by the same winter and summer as a Christian is? If you

prick us, do we not bleed? If you tickle us, do we not laugh? If you poison us, do we not die? And if you wrong us, shall we not revenge? If we are like you in the rest, we will resemble you in that. (Act 3, sc. 1)

86. "Head of Stanford News Service at Stanford U. Resigns in Policy Dispute," *Chronicle of Higher Education*, January 10, 1990, p. A-15.

87. Toni Long, "A Call to Action: Racism Runs Rampant," *The Real News*, Stanford University, May 1989, p. 2.

88. Steven Chin, "Stanford President Rips Protesters, But Supports Racial Proposals," *San Francisco Gemirer*, May 19, 1989, p. A-8.

## 4. In Search of Black Pharaohs

1. Lee Atwater, speech at Center for Nonviolent Social Change, Ebenezer Baptist Church, Atlanta, Ga., January 15, 1989. Transcript obtained from Republican National Committee (RNC).

2. Lee Atwater, speech to Republican National Committee, Washington, D.C., January 18, 1989. Transcript obtained from RNC.

3. Eric Alterman, "Playing Hardball," *New York Times Magazine*, April 30, 1989, p. 31.

4. Susan Estrich, "The Hidden Politics of Race," *Washington Post Magazine*, April 23, 1989, pp. 23–24.

5. Ibid., p. 24.

6. Anne Simpson, "Atwater's Election as Howard University Trustee Sparks Dissension," *Washington Post*, February 23, 1989.

7. *Howard University Bulletin*, 1987–89, Howard University, Washington, D.C.

8. Ibid.

9. Cited by Simpson, "Atwater's Election."

10. Ibid.

11. Eric Smith and Stacey Phillips, "Protest Slated for Today," *The Hilltop*, March 3, 1989.

12. Jacqueline Trescott, "Howard Protesters Take Over Ceremony," *Washington Post*, March 4, 1989.

13. See Liz McMillen, "Bill Cosby, Urging Support for Black Colleges, Gives $20 Million to Spelman," *Chronicle of Higher Education*, September 16, 1988, p. A-29.

14. Trescott, "Howard Protesters."

15. Office of Public Affairs, National Endowment for the Arts. Baraka received a creative writing award in 1981.

16. Ras Baraka, "Black Power Means Self-Rule," *The Hilltop*, October 21, 1988.

17. Trescott, "Howard Protesters."

18. Keith Alexander and Tina Travers, "Protesters Show There's Strength in Numbers," *The Hilltop*, March 10, 1989.

19. Trescott, "Howard Protesters."

20. Jacqueline Trescott, "We Stood Up Because We Love This Black School," *Washington Post*, March 10, 1989.

21. Trescott, "Howard Protesters."

22. Ibid.

23. Ibid.

24. Keith Alexander, "Students Prevail in Three-Day Takeover," *The Hilltop*, March 10, 1989.

25. "Editor's Notebook," *New Directions,* published by Howard University, April 1989.

26. James Walker and Kellye Lynne, "Q & A: Cheek Says Job Lacks Prestige," *The Hilltop,* March 10, 1989.

27. See also Susanne Alexander, "Local Businessmen Offer Support for Cause," *The Hilltop,* March 10, 1989.

28. Shrona Foreman, "HU Security Calls in Sick," *The Hilltop,* March 10, 1989.

29. Jerry Rubin, *Do It: A Revolutionary Manifesto,* Simon and Schuster, New York, 1970.

30. Trescott, "We Stood Up."

31. Philip Shenon, "Howard University President Threatens to Arrest Student Protesters," *New York Times,* March 9, 1989.

32. Sari Horwitz and Jeffrey Goldberg, "Atwater Resigns from Howard Board," *Washington Post,* March 18, 1989, p. 1.

33. George Curry, "Howard Protesters Follow in Parents' Footsteps," *Chicago Tribune,* March 9, 1989.

34. Eric Smith, "Jackson Visit Aids in Negotiations," *The Hilltop,* March 10, 1989.

35. Curry, "Howard Protesters."

36. Shenon, "Howard University President."

37. Rene Sanchez and Patrice Carter, "Howard U. Building Becomes a Nest for Student Demonstrators," *Washington Post,* March 8, 1989.

38. Michael Abramowitz and Lawrence Feinberg, "Howard Protesters Tighten Hold on Campus Building," *Washington Post,* March 7, 1989.

39. Ibid.

40. Glenda Fauntleroy, "Silver Exemplifies Strength, Modesty," *The Hilltop,* March 10, 1989.

41. Fauntleroy, "Silver Exemplifies Strength."

42. Horwitz and Goldberg, "Atwater Resigns."

43. Ibid.

44. Lee Atwater, "What I Would Have Told the Howard Students," *Washington Post,* March 10, 1989.

45. Paul Hendrickson, "Behind the Howard Barricades," *Washington Post,* March 8, 1989.

46. Keith Alexander, "Students Prevail in Three-Day Takeover," *The Hilltop,* March 10, 1989.

47. Jeffrey Goldberg and Rene Sanchez, "Howard Students Continue Disruption," *Washington Post,* March 9, 1989.

48. Ibid.

49. Jeffrey Goldberg and Lawrence Feinberg, "Victorious Howard Students End Seige of Building," *Washington Post,* March 10, 1989.

50. Ibid.

51. Ibid.

52. Ibid.

53. Ibid.

54. "President Cheek Issues Open Letter," *The Capstone,* Howard University, March 20, 1989.

55. Carol Randolph, "Howard Gave a Refresher Course in Activism," *Washington Times,* March 10, 1989.

56. Joyce Price, "Howard Dormitories Appalling, Students Say," *Washington Times*, March 10, 1989.

57. Jacqueline Trescott, "We Stood Up Because We Love This Black School," *Washington Post*, March 10, 1989.

58. Eric Smith, "AIDS Rapist Gets 81–243 Year Prison Term," *The Hilltop*, April 7, 1989.

59. Ibid.

60. Sandra Boodman, "Howard Parley Leaves Dispute Unresolved," *Washington Post*, March 5, 1989.

61. *Annual Report to the Dean of Admissions*, prepared by the Office of Planning, Analysis and Institutional Research, Howard University, 1987–88.

62. Ibid.

63. Paul Hendrickson, "Behind the Howard Barricades," *Washington Post*, March 8, 1989.

64. Yvonne Bonner, "Here We Go Again," *The Hilltop*, March 3, 1989.

65. Jacqueline Fleming, *Blacks in College*, Jossey-Bass, San Francisco, 1984, p. 2.

66. Elias Canetti, *Crowds and Power*, Farrar, Straus and Giroux, New York, 1962, p. 17.

67. Booker T. Washington, *Up From Slavery*, edited by John Hope Franklin, Avon Books, New York, 1963, p. 41.

68. Sojourner Truth, *Narrative and Book of Life*, Johnson, Chicago, 1970, pp. 126–27.

69. W. E. B. Du Bois, *The Seventh Son*, Little, Brown, Boston, 1971, pp. 12–13.

70. Ron Harris, "Black Youth: Assertive New Pride," *Los Angeles Times*, March 9, 1989, p. 1.

71. David Mills, "The Return of Malcolm X," *Washington Times*, August 1, 1989, p. C-1. Gerald Fraser, "The Voice of Malcolm X Has an Audience Again," *New York Times*, February 20, 1990, p. B-3.

72. Mills, "The Return of Malcolm X" and Fraser, "The Voice of Malcolm X." See also Michele Collison, "Fight the Power: Rap Music Pounds Out a New Anthem for Many Black Students," *Chronicle of Higher Education*, February 14, 1990, p. A-1. "Rap music is going to be the music of our movement," Stanford activist Louis Jackson said. " 'Fight the Power' galvanized people. These songs are like the freedom songs of the 1960s." Elizabeth Walter, president of the NAACP chapter at Penn State, invoked Malcolm X to argue, "African American students have gone from a more passive attitude to a more radical attitude. We have learned that we have to adopt a more radical approach to get what we want."

73. "The only way black people caught up in this society can be saved is not to integrate into this corrupt society, but to separate from it, to a land of our own, where we can reform ourselves." See *The Autobiography of Malcolm X*, as told to Alex Haley, Ballantine Books, New York, 1964, p. 246.

74. *Howard University Bulletin*, 1987–89, Howard University.

75. Abiodun Adepoji, "Awoko Talks," *The Hilltop*, April 7, 1989.

76. Frank Snowden, *Blacks in Antiquity*, Harvard University Press, Cambridge, Mass., 1970, Preface p. ix.

77. Ibid., p. 147.

78. Ibid., p. 170.

79. Ibid., p. 169.

80. Ibid., p. 195.

81. See, e.g., Carol Innerst, "Some Scholars Dispute 'Black' Egypt Theory," *Washington Times*, February 26, 1990; Michael Specter, "Was Nefertiti Black? Bitter Debate Erupts," *Washington Post*, February 26, 1990, p. A-3.

82. Martin Bernal, *Black Athena: The Afroasiatic Roots of Classical Civilization*, vol. 1: *The Fabrication of Ancient Greece, 1785–1985*, Rutgers University Press, New Brunswick, N.J., 1989, pp. 73, 242.

83. For a critical evaluation of Bernal's scholarship, see Molly Levine, ed., "The Challenge of *Black Athena*," a symposium published in the fall 1989 issue of *Arethusa*. In particular, see essays by Frank Turner, "Martin Bernal's *Black Athena*: A Dissent," and Frank Snowden, "Bernal's 'Blacks,' Herodotus and Other Classical Evidence."

84. Bernal, *Black Athena*, p. 9.

85. Jasper Griffin, "Who Are These Coming to the Sacrifice?" *New York Review of Books*, June 15, 1989, pp. 25–28.

86. Cited in Ellen Coughlin, "Scholars Work to Refine Africa-centered View of the Life and History of Black Americans," *Chronicle of Higher Education*, October 28, 1987, p. A-6.

87. Ibid.

88. Ivan Van Sertima, ed., *Black Women in Antiquity*, Transaction Books, New Brunswick, N.J., 1984, essay by John Clarke, "African Warrior Queens," pp. 126–27.

89. David Brion Davis, *The Problem of Slavery in Western Culture*, Oxford University Press, New York, 1966, p. 50.

90. Murray Gordon, *Slavery in the Arab World*, New Amsterdam Books, New York, 1989, p. ix. See also Jonas Bernstein, "New Study Sweeps Arab Slaving out from under Carpet," *Washington Times*, July 3, 1989, p. D-7.

91. "Egypt Says Ramses II Wasn't Black," *Washington Post*, based on AP Report, March 23, 1989.

92. Cited in Specter, "Was Nefertiti Black?"

93. Robert Hill, ed., *The Marcus Garvey and Universal Negro Improvement Association Papers*, University of California Press, Berkeley, 1987, p. 194.

94. Although hundreds of thousands of blacks joined the "Back to Africa" movements of the late nineteenth and early twentieth century, only 25,000 or so blacks migrated to Africa between 1816 and 1940. See Molefi Kete Asante, *The Afrocentric Idea*, Temple University Press, Philadelphia, 1987, p. 155. See also A. J. Garvey, ed., *The Philosophy and Opinions of Marcus Garvey*, Universal Publishing, Encino, Calif., 1923, vol. 1, pp. 73–78.

95. Jerry Seper, "Leader Urges Black Exodus," *Washington Times*, February 28, 1990, p. 1. Farrakhan argues, "Separatio . to us is a last resort. If all that we have here in America does not work to produce justice for all, then we as a people have to think about . . . separation." Farrakhan wishes the U.S. government to release all blacks from U.S. prisons to be rehabilitated by his Nation of Islam, and to pay unspecified sums in resettlement reparations for the historical crime of slavery.

96. See, e.g., Rousseau, *Confessions*, E. P. Dutton, New York, 1931; see also Rousseau, *The Discourse on the Origin and Foundations of Inequality Among Men*, edited by Roger Masters, St. Martin's Press, New York, 1964.

97. James Baldwin, *The Fire Next Time*, Dial Press, New York, 1963, p. 95.

98. Martin Luther King, Jr., "Pilgrimage to Nonviolence," *Stride toward Freedom*, Harper and Row, New York, 1958, p. 102.

99. Denise Magner, "Howard U., a Year after a Tense Campus Sit-In, Awaits the Arrival of a New President Who Faces Myriad Tough, Unresolved Issues," *Chronicle of Higher Education*, March 7, 1990, p. A-18.

## 5. The New Censorship

1. Stephen Gregory, "Ex DJ Apologizes for Racial Slurs," *Michigan Daily*, March 4, 1987.

2. Isabel Wilkerson, "Campus Race Incident Disquiets U. of Michigan," *New York Times*, March 9, 1987, p. A-12.

3. Cited in Stephen Franklin, "Is Racism on Campus Increasing?", *Chicago Tribune*, March 13, 1988.

4. Ibid.

5. Cited by Isabel Wilkerson, "Campus Blacks Feel Racism's Nuances," *New York Times*, April 17, 1988.

6. Cited by Wilkerson, "Campus Race Incident."

7. Michele Collison, "For Many Freshmen, Orientation Now Includes Efforts to Promote Racial Understanding," *Chronicle of Higher Education*, September 7, 1988, p. A-29.

8. Jim Poniewozik, "Complaint Lodged over Flier," *Michigan Daily*, March 3, 1988.

9. Jessica Strick, "Racist Fliers Surface Again on Campus," *Michigan Daily*, April 3, 1989.

10. See, e.g., "Wrong Message from Academe," *Time*, April 6, 1987, p. 57; Susan Tifft, "Bigots in the Ivory Tower," *Time*, January 23, 1989; Allan Gold, "Campus Racial Tensions and Violence Appear on Rise," *New York Times*, February 21, 1988; Thomas Short, "A New Racism on Campus?" *Commentary*, August 1988; Shelby Steele, "The Recoloring of Campus Life," *Harper's*, February 1989; Deb Reichmann, "Colleges Tackle Increase in Racism on Campus," *Los Angeles Times*, April 30, 1989; Art Levine, "America's Youthful Bigots," *Newsweek*, May 7, 1990, p. 59. See also Ernest Boyer, *Campus Report: In Search of Community*, Carnegie Foundation, Washington, D.C., 1990.

11. See Haynes Johnson, "Racism Still Smolders on Campus," *USA Today*, May 10, 1988.

12. "On Campus, Civil Rights and Wrongs," *Washington Post*, March 23, 1987.

13. Joseph Berger, "Deep Racial Divisions Persist in New Generation at College," *New York Times*, May 22, 1989, p. 1.

14. Cited by Charles Farrell, "Black Students Seen Facing a New Racism on Many Campuses," *Chronicle of Higher Education*, January 27, 1988, p. A-1.

15. Editorial, "Racial Tension on Campus," *Washington Post*, March 23, 1987, p. C-2.

16. This is based on a geographical classification of schools at which racial incidents occurred. A fairly comprehensive list can be obtained from the National Institute Against Prejudice and Violence, Baltimore, Maryland.

17. Ibid.

18. Ibid.

19. Walter Massey, "If We Want Racially Tolerant Students, We Must Have

More Minority Professors," *Chronicle of Higher Education*, July 15, 1987, p. A-76.

20. "Efforts Under Way to Contain Aftermath of October Brawl," *Chronicle of Higher Education*, March 18, 1987, p. A-41.

21. Cited by Wilkerson, "Campus Race Incident."

22. Cited by Thomas Sowell, "The New Racism on Campus," *Fortune*, February 13, 1989, p. 115.

23. Notebook, *Chronicle of Higher Education*, April 5, 1989, p. A-31.

24. Tifft, "Bigots in the Ivory Tower."

25. "WFU Fraternity Drops Rebel Symbols," AP Press Release, January 7, 1988, Winston-Salem, N.C.

26. In a recent survey, Schuman et al. synthesize data gathered over time from the National Opinion Research Center, Gallup, and the Institute for Social Research. They found "a remarkably large, wide ranging and generally consistent movement toward white acceptance of integration." Despite "short term stresses and opposition, there is no longer an attempt by any significant number of Americans to justify segregation." In fact, "norms in the United States have changed radically over the past 40 years, so that anti-black speech and action that were once acceptable and common are now almost completely taboo in the public arena." See Howard Schuman, Charlotte Steeh, and Lawrence Bobo, *Racial Attitudes in America*, Harvard University Press, Cambridge, Mass., 1985, pp. 86, 171, 181.

27. Ibid., pp. 74–75, 118–19.

28. Ibid.

29. Ibid., pp. 104–10.

30. Ibid., pp. 74–76, 106–8.

31. Ibid., pp. 127–36. This research indicates white attitudes toward goals. Perhaps understandably, there are sharp differences of opinion on the best means to achieve shared goals. Whites are much more ambivalent about federal handouts, preferential treatment, and busing. Schuman et al. worry that these data may reflect contradictions and even schizophrenia in white attitudes toward race, but they concede that unanimity on objectives such as legal equality, equal opportunity, and social integration are quite compatible with divergent strategies of enforcement and realization. Ibid., pp. 88–90.

32. See Reginald Wilson, "Letter to the Editor," *Chronicle of Higher Education*, October 12, 1988, p. B-3.

33. For further comment, see William Beer, "Preferential Treatment for Blacks Is Likely to Exacerbate Racial Hostilities on Campus," *Chronicle of Higher Education*, April 27, 1988, p. B-2.

34. Stephen Johnson, "Reverse Discrimination and Aggressive Behavior," *Journal of Psychology* 104, 1980, pp. 11–19. See also Stephen Johnson, "Consequences of Reverse Discrimination," *Psychological Reports* 47, 1980, pp. 1035–38. Johnson tested 64 white subjects (32 male, 32 female) who were measured for level of aggression in their responses on account of being defeated by white and black opponents, whose victories were attributed (a) to superior ability or (b) to preference on account of deprivation. Johnson found that most whites did not mind losing to blacks on account of ability, but registered the highest resentment when they perceived themselves as victims of reverse discrimination.

35. Stephen Franklin, "Is Racism on Campus Increasing?" *Chicago Tribune*, March 13, 1988.

36. Ibid.

37. Ibid. See also Deb Reichmann, "Colleges Tackle Increase in Racism on Campus," *Los Angeles Times*, April 30, 1989.

38. Phil McDade, "Seeds of Student Protests Planted in Fear and Frustration," *Centre Daily Times*, February 18, 1988.

39. "Wrong Message from Academe," *Time*, April 6, 1987.

40. Ibid.

41. "Black Students in Ohio Boycott Classes," *Washington Post*, Around the Nation, April 12, 1988.

42. Matthew Wald, "Racism Blamed for Brawl at U. of Mass.," *New York Times*, February 6, 1987, p. A-12.

43. See Haynes Johnson, "Racism Still Smolders on Campus," *USA Today*, May 10, 1988; also Elizabeth Greene, "Racial Incidents at Four Universities Spark Protests," *Chronicle of Higher Education*, April 20, 1988, p. A-14.

44. Robert Barr, "Racial Incidents Spark Protests on College Campuses Nationwide," *The Atlanta Journal*, April 20, 1988.

45. "Having been raised in a conservative cultural background, I was feeling very uncomfortable performing without my shirt because it is not something my cultural heritage has accepted," Manish Mishra said. The director's request that he perform without a shirt "showed insensitivity to my cultural heritage," Mishra added. See Vivek Mehta, "Cast Member Leaves 'Promises': Actor Walks Out of Theater Production over Racial Dispute," *The Hoya*, March 6, 1990, p. 1.

46. Jared Taylor, "Racism at Stanford?" *Chronicles*, January 1990, pp. 51–53. See also the report on the Beethoven poster incident, available from the Office of the President, Stanford University.

47. "Campus Minorities: Confronting Racism with Mature Methods," *Washington Post*, April 19, 1988.

48. Taylor, "Racism at Stanford?"

49. "School Colors: Uneasy Gray between Black and White," *Christian Science Monitor*, June 14, 1988.

50. In fact Brown president Vartan Gregorian issued a statement saying, "We are treating [the incidents] as what, in all cases, they clearly were—assaults or assault and battery." See Pete Hamill, "Black and White at Brown," *Esquire*, April 1990, p. 68.

51. "Tufts Mulls Charges of Racial Harassment," *Boston Herald*, February 20, 1987.

52. Ibid.

53. Cited by Patricia Wen, "Tufts University Rally Attacks Racism," *Boston Globe*, February 20, 1987.

54. See Patricia Wen, "Questions Raised on Tufts Attack: Police Say Pieces of Story Don't Fit," *Boston Globe*, February 24, 1987. Kremer brought a suit against Tufts, the *Tufts Daily*, and several university officials alleging that they defamed him and violated his civil rights. But Kremer dropped the suit and the parties issued a joint public statement expressing "satisfaction with the resolution of this matter without acknowledging the merit of the other side's position." He transferred to another school.

55. Thomas Short, "A New Racism on Campus?" *Commentary*, August 1988.

56. Although the university found that both direct and circumstantial evidence, including fingerprint and handwriting analysis, pointed to Sabrina Collins as the guilty party, the administration said it would not charge Collins with any offense. Indeed Jan Gleason, spokesman for Emory, said the university would go ahead with programs

to combat campus racism, such as the creation of a new multicultural center, which were agreed to in the aftermath of the alleged crime. In another strange twist, Otis Smith, president of the Atlanta chapter of the NAACP, said, "It doesn't matter to me whether she did it or not, because of all the pressure these black students are under at these predominantly white schools. If this [incident] will bring that to the attention of the public, I have no problem with it." See Peter Applebome, "Hoax Suspected over Allegation of Racial Crime," *New York Times,* June 1, 1990; also Denise Magner, "Emory Will Not Prosecute Black Student Who Said She Was Victim of Harassment," *Chronicle of Higher Education,* June 13, 1990, p. A-26.

57. James Feron, "Jewish Student Accused of Faking Anti-Semitism," *New York Times,* September 15, 1989.

58. Charles Farrell, "Students Protesting Racial Bias at U. of Massachusetts End Occupation of Campus Building after Five Days," *Chronicle of Higher Education,* February 24, 1988, p. A-41.

59. Allan Gold, "Students End Takeover at U. of Massachusetts," *New York Times,* February 18, 1988, p. 1.

60. "Blacks on Campus Learn Nuances of Bigotry," *New York Times,* April 17, 1988.

61. Denise Magner, "Hotline Targets Racism," *Chronicle of Higher Education,* June 7, 1989, p. A-33.

62. "Charges against Students Dropped," *Washington Post,* April 19, 1988.

63. Phil McDade, "Seeds of Student Protests Planted in Fear and Frustration," *Centre Daily Times,* February 13, 1989. See also Robert Barr, "Racial Incidents Spark Protests on College Campuses Nationwide," *The Atlanta Journal,* April 20, 1988.

64. Barr, "Racial Incidents Spark Protests."

65. Cited in Joseph Sullivan, "College Leaders Focus on Enmity between Races," *New York Times,* April 23, 1988, p. 34.

66. Information obtained from United Coalition Against Racism, University of Michigan.

67. Ibid.

68. Ibid. See also *The Michigan Mandate: The Strategic Linking of Academic Excellence and Social Diversity,* Office of the President, University of Michigan, March 1990.

69. Statement of Concerned Faculty, "Faculty Responds to Fleming," *Michigan Daily,* April 12, 1988.

70. *University Record,* University of Michigan, March 17, 1988.

71. "University of Michigan," *Detroit Free Press,* October 16, 1988.

72. Isabel Wilkerson, "U. of Michigan Fights Its Legacy of Racial Trouble," *New York Times,* January 15, 1990.

73. "Michigan," *Chronicle of Higher Education,* April 1, 1987, p. A-27.

74. "Nineteen New Black Faculty Welcomed to Campus," *University Record,* September 26, 1988.

75. Out of 904 PhDs awarded to blacks in 1987, 425 were in the fields of education, sociology, and physical education. See *Summary Report 1987: Doctorate Recipients from United States Universities,* survey conducted by U.S. Department of Education et al., National Academy Press, Washington D.C., 1989.

76. Tom Rogers, "U-M Minority Enrollment Increases," *Ann Arbor News,* October 27, 1988.

77. "University of Michigan," *Detroit Free Press,* October 16, 1988.

78. Cited by Lisa Pollack, "Black Faculty Challenge Steiner," *Michigan Daily,* January 13, 1988.

79. Ken Weine, "Fleming Fails on Institutional Racism," *Michigan Daily,* March 14, 1988.

80. *University Record,* March 17, 1988.

81. Letter to Michigan students from James Duderstadt, March 31, 1989, Office of the President, University of Michigan.

82. Jane Elgass, "Assembly Endorses Bias Concept," *University Record,* September 26, 1988.

83. Cited by ibid.

84. Ibid.

85. Concerned Faculty, "Faculty Responds to Fleming," *Michigan Daily,* April 12, 1988.

86. Indeed, in overturning a federal law making it a crime to deface the American flag, the Supreme Court, in an opinion written by Justice Brennan, noted, "While flag desecration—like virulent ethnic and religious epithets, vulgar repudiations of the draft, and scurrilous caricatures—is deeply offensive to many, the government may not prohibit the expression of an idea simply because society finds the idea itself offensive or disagreeable." As the *Chronicle of Higher Education* recognized, this ruling poses a serious challenge to public institutions which seek to regulate racist and sexist speech. See Robin Wilson, "Court's Flag Ruling Could Affect Policies Against Harassment," *Chronicle of Higher Education,* June 20, 1990, p. A-33.

87. "Discrimination and Discriminatory Harassment by Students in the University Environment," Office of the President, University of Michigan.

88. *John Doe* v. *University of Michigan,* Eastern District Court, Detroit, Michigan, Civil Action No. 89–71683, September 22, 1989.

89. Ibid.

90. Alan Dershowitz, "Campus Speech Control," *Washington Times,* May 4, 1989, p. F-4.

91. Carol Innerst, "ACLU, Meese Condemn College's Anti-Conservatism," *Washington Times,* May 17, 1989, p. 1.

92. Cited in Dirk Johnson, "Censoring the Campus News," *New York Times,* November 6, 1988, Section 4A.

93. Ibid.

94. Nick Ravo, "Campus Slur Alters a Code against Bias," *New York Times,* December 11, 1989, pp. B-1, 3.

95. Statement of Student Press Law Center, July 27, 1988.

96. Ibid.

97. "Racism Charges Prompt Student Editor's Firing," *Chronicle of Higher Education,* December 13, 1989, p. A-3.

98. In recent years, foreign policy speakers such as Jeane Kirkpatrick, Caspar Weinberger, and Adolfo Calero have been heckled and booed off the campus podium. See, e.g., Jeane Kirkpatrick, "My Experience with Academic Intolerance," *Academic Questions,* Fall 1989, pp. 21–29.

At Northwestern University in 1985, English professor Barbara Foley urged a campus audience to "shout down" Nicaraguan resistance leader Calero; indeed Calero was prevented from speaking. Foley remarked that Calero "should feel lucky to get out of here alive." Red liquid was hurled at Calero to symbolize what Foley said was blood on his hands. This was not an ill-considered judgment which Foley subsequently regretted; in a subsequent letter to the university provost, she stood by her heckling as morally justified. After a protracted dispute, Foley was denied tenure and moved on to another academic post. See letter from Foley to Provost Mack, Northwestern University, May 22, 1985. For a full account of this controversy, see "Decision in the Matter of Professor Barbara C. Foley," opinion by Northwestern President Arnold Weber, reprinted in *Academic Questions*, Winter 1987–88.

99. Robin Wilson, "Colleges' Anti-Harassment Policies Bring Controversy over Free Speech Issues," *Chronicle of Higher Education*, October 4, 1989, p. A-38.

For example, Middlebury's censorship rules are contained in its racial and sexual harassment policy, which says: "Harassment includes derogatory comments that express racial, ethnic, or religious prejudice such as slurs, jokes, or taunts and disparaging references to racial, ethnic or religious stereotypes." See *Concerning Racial/Ethnic/Religious Harassment*, Office of the President, Middlebury College, Vermont.

100. Ibid.

101. *Putting an End to Harassment: A Guide for the Students, Staff and Faculty*, University of Pennsylvania, February 1988.

102. Hackney wrote that art is "inherently unsettling . . . reordering the world for us, perhaps challenging our assumptions and beliefs. . . . The price of a vibrant artistic scene is the risk of occasional offense to someone's sense of what is appropriate to display or say in public." Sheldon Hackney, "The Helms Amendment Imperils the Basis of Intellectual Freedom," *Chronicle of Higher Education*, September 6, 1989, p. A-48.

103. Melissa Russo, "Free Speech at Tufts: Zoned Out," *New York Times*, September 27, 1989.

104. James Laney, "Why Tolerate Campus Bigots?" *New York Times*, April 6, 1990.

105. Richard Delgado, "Words that Wound: A Tort Action for Racial Insults, Epithets and Name-Calling," *Harvard Law Review* 17, 1982, p. 133; Mari Matsuda, "Public Response to Racist Speech: Considering the Victim's Story," *Michigan Law Review* 87, 1989, pp. 2320, 2356.

106. Cited by Stephen Holmes, "Debating Art: Censorship or Protest?" *New York Times*, December 6, 1989, pp. B-1, B-2.

107. Cited by Felicity Barringer, "Drives by Campuses to Curb Race Slurs Pose a Speech Issue," *New York Times*, April 25, 1989, p. 1.

108. Sharon Gwyn, "Muzzle the Stanford Bigots," *New York Times*, May 12, 1989, p. A-31.

109. See Nat Hentoff, "Stanford and the Speech Police," *Washington Post*, July 30, 1990.

110. Steve Marmel, "Trying to Eliminate Racism from Campus Is Worth Any Risk," *USA Today*, April 17, 1989.

111. Stanford Law School Forum, April 5, 1989.

112. Ibid.

113. Denise Magner, "Update on Minority Groups," *Chronicle of Higher Education*, August 1, 1990, p. A-26.

114. Nat Hentoff, "Watching What You Say on Campus," *Washington Post*, September 14, 1989, p. A-23. See also Robin Wilson, "Colleges Anti-Harassment Policies

Bring Controversy over Free Speech Issues," *Chronicle of Higher Education*, October 4, 1989, p. A-38.

115. Wilson, "Colleges' Anti-Harassment Policies Bring Controversy over Free Speech Issues."

116. See Joseph Grano, "Free Speech v. the University of Michigan," *Academic Questions*, Spring 1990, pp. 13–14.

117. Reynolds Farley, *Blacks and Whites: Narrowing the Gap*, Harvard University Press, Cambridge, Mass., 1984, Farley, *The Color Line and the Quality of Life*, Oxford University Press, New York, 1987.

118. Cited in David Schwartz, "Students Criticize Soc. 303 Prof," *Michigan Daily*, January 11, 1989.

119. Ibid.

120. Ibid.

121. Herbert Marcuse, "Repressive Tolerance," in his *Critique of Pure Tolerance*, Beacon Press, Boston, 1965, p. 100.

122. See David Sears, "Symbolic Racism," in Phyllis Katz and D. Taylor, eds., *Eliminating Racism: Profiles in Controversy*, Plenum Press, New York, 1988, pp. 53–84. Sears identifies opposition to reverse discrimination or handouts as a "new form" of racism, no less insidious than the old, and perhaps even worse for being camouflaged in "the finest and proudest of traditional American values, particularly individualism."

123. Lincoln sympathized with the goals of the prohibitionists, but faulted their methods. Instead of attempting to persuade the alcohol peddlers and drinkers, the prohibitionists instead insisted that

> they were the manufacturers and material of all the thieves and robbers and murderers that infested the earth; that their houses were the work-shops of the devil; and that their persons should be shunned by all the good and the virtuous, as moral pestilences—I say, when they were told all this, and in this way, it is not wonderful that they were slow, very slow, to acknowledge the truth of such denunciations and to join ranks with their denouncers in a hue and cry against themselves.

Abraham Lincoln, *Selected Speeches*, edited by Harry Williams, Holt, Rinehart & Winston, New York, 1957, p. 18.

124. Cited by Jim Poniewozik, "Prof.: Competition Spurs Racism," *Michigan Daily*, January 29, 1988.

## 6. The Last Shall Be First

1. Maya Angelou, "Journey to the Heartland," Address to the National Assembly of Local Arts Agencies, Cedar Rapids, Iowa, June 12, 1985.

2. *The Madison Plan*, University of Wisconsin at Madison, Office of the Chancellor, February 9, 1988, p. 11.

3. Robert Marquand, "Holes in the College Safety Net," *Christian Science Monitor*, June 15, 1988, p. 18.

4. Announcement by President Steven Beering, reported in press release, Purdue University, February 9, 1988.

5. Edwin Darden, "Northern Illinois University Starts Minority Hiring Incentive," *Education Daily*, October 13, 1988.

6. Edward B. Fiske, "Lessons," *New York Times*, May 24, 1989, p. B-8.

7. Scott Heller, "Some English Departments Are Giving Undergraduates Grounding in New Literary and Critical Theory," *Chronicle of Higher Education*, August 3, 1988, p. A-15.

8. Sacvan Bercovitch, "America as Canon and Context: Literary History in a Time of Dissensus," prospectus for forthcoming textbook, cited by James W. Tuttleton, "Rewriting the History of American Literature," *The New Criterion*, November 1986, p. 8.

9. George Levine, Peter Brooks, Jonathan Culler, Majorie Garber, E. Ann Kaplan, Catharine Stimpson, "Speaking for the Humanities," American Council on Learned Societies, Occasional Paper No. 7, 1989, p. 10.

10. Charles Truehart, "Profs, Dons and Icons," *Washington Post*, December 29, 1989, pp. D-1, D-9.

11. Scott Heller, "A Constellation of Recently Hired Professors Illuminates the English Department at Duke," *Chronicle of Higher Education*, May 27, 1987, pp. A-12–14.

12. Cited by Robert Bliwise, "Putting Life into Literature," *Duke Magazine*, May–June 1988, Duke University, p. 4.

13. Ibid., p. 7.

14. Ibid.

15. Heller, "A Constellation of Recently Hired Professors," p. A-12.

16. Bliwise, "Putting Life into Literature," p. 2.

17. Ibid., p. 4.

18. See John Spencer Bassett, "Stirring Up the Fires of Race Antipathy," *South Atlantic Quarterly*, October 1903.

19. Bliwise, "Putting Life into Literature," p. 4.

20. Heller, "A Constellation of Recently Hired Professors," p. A-12.

21. Ibid.

22. Duke University, *Catalog of Undergraduate Courses*, vol. 32, no. 5-A, pp. 72–76. Supplied by archivist, Duke University.

23. David Brooks, "From Western Lit to Westerns as Lit," *Wall Street Journal*, February 2, 1988.

24. Ibid.

25. Ibid.

26. Ellen Coughlin, "In Face of Growing Success and Conservatives' Attacks, Cultural Studies Scholars Ponder Future Directions," *Chronicle of Higher Education*, January 18, 1989, p. A-4.

27. Janice Radway, *Reading the Romance*, University of North Carolina Press, Chapel Hill, 1984, pp. 9, 217.

28. Scott Heller, "Duke Professors Back Plan to Require Each Academic Unit to Hire at Least One Black Faculty Member by 1993," *Chronicle of Higher Education*, April 27, 1988, p. A-17.

29. Donald Patterson, "Duke Vote on Hiring Reversed," *Greensboro News and Record*, April 22, 1988.

30. David Newton, "Protesters Call for More Blacks at Duke," *Durham Morning Herald*, April 16, 1988.

31. Ibid.

32. Editorial, "An Eye for Color," *The Chronicle*, March 23, 1988, p. 8.

33. Scott Lehrer, "Council Approves Hiring Plan," *The Chronicle*, March 18, 1988, p. 6.

34. Scott Lehrer, "Black Faculty Recruitment Plan Sparks Protests," *The Chronicle*, April 11, 1988, p. 4.

35. Ibid.

36. Cited in Rocky Rosen, "Black Faculty Hiring Debate Escalates," *The Chronicle*, April 14, 1988, p. 9.

37. Newton, "Protesters Call for More Blacks."

38. Rosen, "Black Faculty Hiring Debate," p. 4.

39. Ibid., p. 1.

40. Phil Pitchford, "Duke Students Stage Rally for More Black Faculty," *Raleigh News and Observer*, April 16, 1988, p. 2-C.

41. Kathleen Sullivan, "Council to Decide Black Hiring Policy Today," *The Chronicle*, April 21, 1988, p. 1.

42. Pitchford, "Duke Students Stage Rally."

43. Rae Terry, "ASDU Supports Black Faculty," *The Chronicle*, March 22, 1988, p. 9.

44. Heller, "Duke Professors Back Plan."

45. Patterson, "Duke Vote on Hiring Reversed."

46. Bert Fraser-Reid, "Small Applicant Pools Make Required Hiring Implausible," *The Chronicle*, April 21, 1988, p. 12.

47. Jacqueline Johnson Jackson, "Black Faculty Proposals Don't Address the Real Problems," *The Chronicle*, April 18, 1988, p. 7.

48. "Duke Requires All Departments to Hire Blacks," *New York Times*, April 22, 1988. Compiled from news reports.

49. Dan Berger and Kathleen Sullivan, "Academic Council Votes to Require More Black Faculty," *The Chronicle*, April 22, 1988, p. 1.

50. Cited by Rocky Rosen, "Rally for Black Faculty Hiring Attracts 300," *The Chronicle*, April 18, 1988, p. 1.

51. Pitchford, "Duke Students Stage Rally."

52. David Newton, "Protesters Call for More Blacks at Duke," *Durham Morning Herald*, April 16, 1988.

53. Geoffrey Mock, "Council Approves Black Faculty Hiring Resolution," *Duke Dialogue*, April 29, 1988, p. 1-A. Special Section.

54. In 1979, there were 1,056 blacks who received their PhD; by 1987, this number was down to 780. Of 32,000 doctorates awarded in 1987, black men earned only 332, and black women 448. For black men, the drop in PhDs was precipitous: a 54 percent decline from the 684 awarded ten years earlier. In 1987, every other ethnic group—American Indians, Hispanics, Asians—increased their percentage of doctoral recipients, but blacks did not. Estimates for 1988 and 1989 show a persistence of this trend: the total number of minority doctorates continues to increase, but largely because of growth in foreign student PhDs. See "Doctorate Recipients from United States Universities," *Summary Report 1987*, Survey conducted by the U.S. Department of Education, National Institutes for Health, National Endowment for the Humanities, U.S. Department of Agriculture. National Academy Press, Washington, D.C., 1989. See also Denise Magner, "Decline in Doctorates Earned by Black and White Men Persists, Study Finds," *Chronicle of Higher Education*, March 1, 1989, p. A-11; Carolyn Mooney, "Universities Awarded Record Number of Doctorates Last Year; Foreign

Students Thought to Account for Much of the Increase," *Chronicle of Higher Education*, April 25, 1990, p. A-1.

55. "Doctorate Recipients from United States Universities."

56. See Abigail Thernstrom, "On the Scarcity of Black Professors," *Commentary*, July 1990, p. 23.

57. Carolyn Mooney, "Only Four Black Americans Said to Have Earned Math Ph.D.s in 1987–88," *Chronicle of Higher Education*, August 2, 1989, p. A-11.

58. Ibid., p. A-12.

59. According to the American Council on Education (ACE), between 1977 and 1983 the number of black faculty fell by 4 percent, from 19,674 to 18,827. Meanwhile, the number for whites increased by 5 percent, to 473,787.

60. See "Minority Group Members in Academe," *Chronicle of Higher Education*, August 2, 1989, p. A-10.

61. Michael Hirschorn, "The Doctorate Dilemma," *New Republic*, June 6, 1988, p. 26.

62. Mark Reisler, "Colleges Need Aggressive, Inspiring Leadership If They Are to Achieve Genuine Integration," *Chronicle of Higher Education*, January 20, 1988, p. A-52.

63. Debra Blum, "Big Faculty Shortages Seen in Humanities and Social Sciences," *Chronicle of Higher Education*, September 20, 1989, p. A-1.

64. Carolyn Mooney, "Affirmative Action Goals, Coupled with Tiny Number of Minority Ph.D.s, Set Off Faculty Recruiting Frenzy," *Chronicle of Higher Education*, August 2, 1989, p. A-1.

65. Robert Marquand, "Holes in the College Safety Net," *Christian Science Monitor*, June 15, 1988, p. 18.

66. Elizabeth Kolbert, "The Scramble for Black Professors," *New York Times*, Education Section, January 8, 1989, p. 65.

67. Cited in Mooney, "Affirmative Action Goals," p. A-11.

68. Alison Gendar, "Minority Students Seek Reform," *The Berkshire Eagle*, April 23, 1988, p. 23.

69. Kolbert, "The Scramble for Black Professors."

70. Mooney, "Affirmative Action Goals," p. A-10.

71. Ibid.

72. Ibid.

73. Cited by John Bunzel, "Exclusive Opportunities," *The American Enterprise*, March–April 1990, p. 48.

74. Ibid., p. 49.

75. Ibid.

76. Ibid.

77. Geoffrey Mock, "Faculty, Administration Track Progress in Goals on Minority Faculty Hiring," *Duke Dialogue*, August 11, 1989.

78. Among the projects that Gates has supervised or edited: "The Schomburg Library of 19th Century Women Writers," "The Norton Anthology of Afro-American Literature," Perennial Library's Zora Neale Hurston series, and "The Oxford Companion to Afro-American Literature." See Adam Begley, "Henry Louis Gates, Jr.: Black Studies' New Star," *New York Times Magazine*, April 1, 1990, p. 25; "In Box," *Chronicle of Higher Education*, August 9, 1989, p. A-9.

79. Stanley Fish, *Doing What Comes Naturally: Change, Rhetoric and the Practice*

*of Theory in Literary and Legal Studies,* Duke University Press, Durham, N.C., 1989, p. 11.

80. Wimsatt and Beardsley, "The Affective Fallacy," originally from *The Sewanee Review* 57, 1949. Reprinted in David Lodge, ed., *20th Century Literary Criticism,* Longman, London, 1972, p. 345.

81. Stanley Fish, "Literature in the Reader: Affective Stylistics," *New Literary History,* Autumn 1970, pp. 123–62.

82. Critics have pointed out that Fish assumes an especially naive, even moronic, reader who, surprised by syntax, must constantly revise his understanding of language as he reads. See, e.g., Roger Kimball, *Tenured Radicals,* Harper and Row, New York, 1990, p. 148.

83. Stanley Fish, "Interpreting the Variorum," *Critical Inquiry,* Spring 1976, pp. 465–85.

84. Fish, *Doing What Comes Naturally,* pp. 10–11.

85. Elizabeth Greene, "Under Seige, Advocates of a More Diverse Curriculum Prepare for Continued Struggle in the Coming Year," *Chronicle of Higher Education,* September 28, 1988, p. A-13.

86. The term "common sense" is not intended to refer to the most popular or obvious reading, but rather to the "sense" or critical intelligence that human beings have "in common." Obviously some have a sharper and more penetrating sense than others. See Jeffrey Hart, *Acts of Recovery,* University of New England Press, Biddeford, Maine, 1989.

87. Jacques Lacan, *Ecrits,* translated by Alan Sheridan, Tavistock, London, 1977, p. 65.

88. Terry Eagleton, *Literary Theory,* University of Minnesota Press, Minneapolis, 1983, p. 55.

89. Austin Warren and René Wellek, *A Theory of Literature,* revised edition, Harcourt Brace Jovanovich, New York, 1964.

90. For a popular introduction, see Eagleton, *Literary Theory.*

91. See Lee Lemon and Marion Reis, eds., *Russian Formalist Criticism: Four Essays,* University of Nebraska Press, Lincoln, Neb., 1965.

92. Hans-Georg Gadamer, *Truth and Method,* Seabury Press, San Francisco, 1975.

93. Tzvetan Todorov, *Grammaire du Decameron,* Humanities Press International, Atlantic Highlands, N.J., 1969.

94. Norman Holland, *The Dynamics of Literary Response,* Oxford University Press, New York, 1968.

95. See, e.g., Frederic Jameson, *Marxism and Form,* Princeton University Press, Princeton, 1971; Raymond Williams, *Marxism and Literature,* Oxford University Press, New York, 1977; Cliff Slaughter, *Marxism, Ideology and Literature,* Humanities Press International, Atlantic Highlands, N.J., 1979.

96. H. Bruce Franklin, *Prison Literature in America,* Oxford University Press, New York, 1989, p. xv.

97. For an introduction to deconstruction, see Jonathan Culler, *On Deconstructionism,* Cornell University Press, Ithaca, N.Y., 1982; Paul de Man, *Blindness and Insight: Essays in the Rhetoric of Contemporary Criticism,* University of Minnesota Press, Minneapolis, 1983; Jonathan Arac, Wlad Godzich, and Wallace Martin, *The Yale Critics: Deconstructionism in America,* University of Minnesota Press, Minneapolis, 1983;

Vincent Leitch, *Deconstructive Criticism*, Columbia University Press, New York, 1982; Christopher Norris, *Deconstruction: Theory and Practice*, Routledge, Chapman and Hall, New York, 1982.

98. Eagleton, *Literary Theory*, p. 204.

99. René Wellek, "Destroying Literary Studies," *The New Criterion*, December 1983, p. 4. Wellek argues that although literary criticism is a complex process, "there are patently absurd and wrong interpretations, for example, that Hamlet is a woman in disguise, or that Hamlet is in reality King James I." Wellek charges that Stanley Fish's notion of "interpretive communities" doesn't restore meaning and protect against anarchy; it merely establishes the triumphalism of the professional literary class. "Great critics have fortunately eluded interpretive communities, resisted or contradicted them." Wellek accuses Fish of making "far-fetched, forced and sometimes demonstrably mistaken readings of texts."

100. Edward Shils, *The Academic Ethic*, University of Chicago Press, Chicago, 1984, p. 3.

101. Stanley Fish, *Is There a Text in This Class? The Authority of Interpretive Communities*, Harvard University Press, Cambridge, Mass., 1980, p. 368.

102. Geoffrey Hartman, *Saving the Text: Literature/Derrida/Philosophy*, Johns Hopkins University Press, Baltimore, 1984, pp. 60–61.

103. For a discussion of this point in connection with Shakespeare studies, see Gary Taylor, *Reinventing Shakespeare: A Cultural History from the Restoration to the Present*, Weidenfeld & Nicolson, London 1989.

104. Cited by Roger Kimball, "The Contemporary Sophist," *The New Criterion*, October 1989, p. 6.

105. See Roger Kimball, *Tenured Radicals*, Harper and Row, New York, 1990.

106. Cited by Colin Campbell, "The Tyranny of the Yale Critics," *New York Times Magazine*, February 9, 1986, p. 25.

107. Geoffrey Hartman, "Criticism and Restitution," *Tikkun* 4, no. 1, 1989, p. 31.

108. Cited by Charles Sykes, *Profscam*, Regnery-Gateway, Washington, D.C., 1988, p. 192.

109. Michael Ryan, *Marxism and Deconstruction*, Johns Hopkins University Press, Baltimore, 1982, p. 8.

110. Cited in Karen Winkler, "Post-Structuralism: An Often Abstruse Fresh Import Profoundly Affects Research in the United States," *Chronicle of Higher Education*, November 25, 1987, p. A-6.

111. Jane Tompkins, "An Introduction to Reader Response Criticism," in *Reader Response Criticism: From Formalism to Poststructuralism*, edited by Jane Tompkins, Johns Hopkins University Press, Baltimore, 1980, from the introduction, p. xxv.

112. James Atlas, "The Battle of the Books," *New York Times Magazine*, June 5, 1988, p. 74.

113. Daniel Farber, "Down by Law," *New Republic*, January 4, 1988, p. 36.

114. Jacques Derrida, "Like the Sound of the Sea Deep within a Shell: Paul de Man's War," *Critical Inquiry*, Spring 1988, pp. 590–652.

115. Michele Collison, "Black Professors Create Nationwide Organization to Promote Their Interests," *Chronicle of Higher Education*, November 4, 1987, p. A-19.

116. Cited by ibid.

117. Hitler reportedly refused to approve research projects in physics on the grounds

that they constituted "Jewish science." The result, reports Arthur Weitzman of Northeastern University, is that German universities suffered a blow from which it was not easy to recover. See Arthur Weitzman, "Autonomy of Ideas," *New York Times*, May 15, 1988, p. E-27.

118. Report of the Commission on the Humanities, *The Humanities in American Life*, University of California Press, Berkeley, 1980, p. 11.

119. Cited by Edward B. Fiske, "Lessons," *New York Times*, May 24, 1989, p. B-8.

120. Carolyn Mooney, "Conservative Scholars Call for a Movement to Reclaim Academy," *Chronicle of Higher Education*, November 23, 1988, p. A-1.

121. Denise Magner, "Minority Graduate Students Say the Path to the Professoriate Can Be Rocky," *Chronicle of Higher Education*, November 15, 1989, p. A-19.

122. This was the case with Michelle Wallace, a professor of Women's Studies and Afro-American Studies at SUNY-Buffalo. As a result of the late 1960s' graduate curriculum at the City College of New York that focused mainly on "minority perspectives," Wallace dabbled in a fashionable potpourri of Eastern verse, African and Caribbean radical tracts, and counterculture propaganda. When she became a book reviewer at *Newsweek*, Wallace found that "there were words commonly used by writers and fellow researchers that I neither knew how to pronounce nor how to use in a sentence." When she subsequently entered a PhD program in American studies at Yale, Wallace further realized that "I was lost before I started. I had never heard of Cotton Mather, Jonathan Edwards, Max Weber, Veblen, John Dewey or C. Wright Mills." Her previous emphasis on writers such as Alice Walker and James Baldwin seemed to "count for nothing." As a consequence of her inadequate preparation, Wallace said, "I came to loathe the superbly well-educated, articulate white males who shared my classes." Only through enormous effort in later life did Wallace overcome the deficiencies of her college education—an education designed to make life easier for minorities that ended up making things tougher, after all. See Michelle Wallace, *The Graywolf Annual Five: Multicultural Literacy*, edited by Rick Simonson and Scott Walker, Graywolf Press, St. Paul, Minn., 1988, pp. 166–69.

123. In 1980, when minority teacher candidates from Grambling State University showed very poor results on the Louisiana certification exam, university officials decided that instead of combating the test, as they had for several years, they would combat the lack of preparation that produced the low scores. Programs were revised, new personnel were hired, higher standards were implemented, outside funds were raised. As a result, Grambling's pass rate went up from around 5 percent to 85 percent. See John Bunzel, "Minority Faculty Hiring," *The American Scholar*, Winter 1990, pp. 49.

124. Jeff Howard and Ray Hammond, "Rumors of Inferiority," *New Republic*, September 9, 1985, p. 17.

125. Cited in Joseph Perkins, "A Survival Plan for Black Colleges," *Wall Street Journal*, June 7, 1987.

126. Jacqueline Fleming, *Blacks in College*, Jossey-Bass, San Francisco, 1984.

127. Victor Farias, *Heidegger and Nazism*, Temple University Press, Philadelphia, 1989. For a discussion of this controversy, see also Mark Lilla, "What Heidegger Wrought," *Commentary*, January 1990, pp. 41–51.

128. See Paul de Man, *Wartime Journalism, 1939–1943*, edited by Werner Hamacher, Neil Hertz, and Thomas Keenan, University of Nebraska Press, Lincoln,

Nebr., 1989. See also Denis Donoghue, "The Strange Case of Paul de Man," *New York Review of Books,* June 29, 1989, pp. 32–37.

129. See, for example, Jonathan Culler, "It's Time to Set the Record Straight about Paul de Man and His Wartime Articles for a Pro-fascist Newspaper," *Chronicle of Higher Education,* July 13, 1988, p. B-1. "What makes Nazism the worst excess of Western civilization is the fact that it took to an appalling extreme the process of constituting a group by opposing it to something else and attempting to exterminate what it falsely defined as a corrupting element. . . . Deconstruction seeks to undo oppositions that in the name of unity, purity, order and hierarchy try to eliminate difference."

130. J. Hillis Miller, "NB" Column, *Times Literary Supplement,* June 17–23, 1988, p. 685.

131. Geoffrey Hartman, "Blindness and Insight," *New Republic,* March 7, 1988.

132. Derrida, "Like the Sound of the Sea."

133. Jon Weiner, "Deconstructing de Man," *The Nation,* January 9, 1988, p. 23.

134. Ibid.

135. Jane Tompkins, "The Reader in History," in *Reader Response Criticism: From Formalism to Poststructuralism,* edited by Jane Tompkins, Johns Hopkins University Press, Baltimore, 1980, p. 225.

136. See exchange between Griswold and Donoghue, "Deconstruction, the Nazis and Paul de Man," *New York Review of Books,* October 12, 1989, p. 69.

137. Ibid.

## 7. Tyranny of the Minority

1. Heather McLeod, "Students Criticize Class as Racially Insensitive," *Harvard Crimson,* February 9, 1988, p. 1.

2. Chrystia Freeland, "Thernstrom und Drang," *Perspective,* March 1988, p. 15.

3. See, e.g., *Poverty and Progress: Social Mobility in a Nineteenth Century City,* Harvard University Press, Cambridge, Mass., 1964; *Nineteenth Century Cities: Essays in the New Urban History,* Yale University Press, New Haven, Conn., 1969; and *The Other Bostonians: Poverty and Progress in the American Metropolis,* Harvard University Press, Cambridge, Mass., 1973.

4. Letter from Stephan Thernstrom to the *Harvard Crimson,* February 9, 1988.

5. Wendi Grantham, "Course Displayed Racial Insensivity," *Harvard Crimson,* February 17, 1988.

6. McLeod, "Students Criticize Class."

7. Cited by Kenny Schultz, "Speak No Evil?" *Harvard Independent,* March 10, 1988, pp. 1, 3.

8. Fred Jewett, "College Reacts to Racism," *Harvard Independent,* February 18, 1988.

9. "Procedures for Dealing with Concerns of Racial Harassment," Office of the Dean, Harvard College, February 1988.

10. Although Spence praised Thernstrom's accusers for not taking their case to the press, by this time the incident was already widely publicized. "Text of Spence's Remarks," *Harvard Crimson,* March 10, 1988, p. 6.

11. Susan Glasser, "Spence Says Thernstrom Heard Racial Complaint," *Harvard Crimson,* March 23, 1988, p. 1.

12. Letter from Bonnie Savage, Harvard Women's Law Association, March 23, 1989.

13. Letter from Ian Macneil to Bonnie Savage, April 3, 1989.

14. Tara Nayak, "Law Prof Denies Sexism Charge," *Harvard Crimson*, April 11, 1989, p. 1.

15. "WLA Makes No Apologies," Harvard Women's Law Association Newsletter, May 12, 1989, p. 1.

16. "Sexual Harassment and Unprofessional Conduct: Guidelines in the Faculty of Arts and Sciences," Office of the Dean, Harvard University, September 1989.

17. Letter from Ian Macneil, *Commentary*, March 1990, pp. 10–11.

18. Grantham, "Course Displayed Racial Insensitivity."

19. Ibid.

20. Cited by Susan Glasser, "Sensitive Issues," *Harvard Crimson*, April 9, 1988, p. 3.

21. Cited by Freeland, "Thernstrom und Drang."

22. Ibid.

23. Nathan Glazer, "Taking Racial Issues Seriously," speech to regional conference of student journalists sponsored by the Institute for Educational Affairs, reprinted in *Newslink*, April–May 1988, Washington, D.C., p. 1.

24. Cited by Connie Leslie, "Lessons from Bigotry 101," *Newsweek*, Spetember 25, 1989, p. 49.

25. See Nat Hentoff, "Campus Court Martial," *Washington Post*, December 15, 1988. See also Hentoff, "Whose Freedom of Speech?" *The Jewish Journal*, July 7–July 13, 1989, p. 21. This account has been confirmed by Dolfman and university officials. Dolfman's reaction to the incident is from an interview with the author.

26. Timothy Egan, "Challenge in Women's Course Roils Washington U. Campus," *New York Times*, April 6, 1988. For a fuller account, see Nicholas Davidson, "Who Is Pete Schaub?" *Chronicles*, January 1989, pp. 46–48.

27. Cited by Debra Blum, "Black Professor Accuses His Colleagues of Censorship and Anti-Semitism," *Chronicle of Higher Education*, June 8, 1988, p. A-13. See also editorial, "Ambush at Amherst," *New Republic*, June 27, 1988, pp. 9–10.

28. *EEOC* v. *Sears, Roebuck and Company*, Decision of U.S. District Court for Northern Illinois, in *Daily Labor Report*, February 2, 1986, pp. D1–D-43. See also Jon Weiner, "Women's History on Trial," *The Nation*, September 7, 1985, pp. 176–80; Karen Winkler, "Two Scholars Conflict in Sears Sex Bias Case Sets Off War in Women's History," *Chronicle of Higher Education*, February 5, 1986, p. A-8; Rosalind Rosenberg, "From the Witness Stand: Previously Unpublished Testimony in the Sex Discrimination Case against Sears," *Academic Questions*, Winter 1987–88, pp. 16–34; Coordinating Committee of Women in the History Profession Newsletter, February 1986, p. 8.

29. Report of the Committee on the Status of Women in the Academic Profession, American Association of University Professors, May 1989, reprinted in *Academe*, July–August 1989, pp. 35–39.

30. Christopher John Farley, "African Culture Resurges on Campus," *USA Today*, November 21, 1989 (citing a figure supplied by the National Council for Black Studies).

31. At Cornell, black students carrying guns took over the administration building for two days before the university capitulated and agreed, among other things, to

establish the Africana Studies and Research Center. At Berkeley, a similar program was established because of fear of riots following Martin Luther King's assassination in 1968. In 1969 at Harvard, student protesters occupied University Hall, and the *Harvard Crimson* frightened the administration with a picture of a black student with a meat cleaver. The university agreed to set up an Afro-American Studies department, whose first chairman, Ewart Guinier, was a labor activist with no academic credentials. For a review of the origins of Afro-American Studies, see Henry Louis Gates, "Academe Must Give Black Studies Programs Their Due," *Chronicle of Higher Education*, September 20, 1989, p. A-56. See also Seymour Martin Lipset and David Riesman, *Education and Politics at Harvard*, McGraw-Hill, New York, 1975, pp. 222–24. For an account of Women's Studies and a survey of scholarship on the women's movement, see "Feminism in America," *The Wilson Quarterly*, Fall 1986.

32. Cited by Tom Sowell, "The New Racism on Campus," *Fortune*, February 13, 1989, p. 118.

33. Ibid.

34. Ibid.

35. Gates, "Academe Must Give Black Studies Programs Their Due."

36. Eugene Genovese wrote *Roll, Jordan, Roll* as a member of the history department at the University of Rochester. Nathan Huggins was in the Harvard history department when he wrote *Harlem Renaissance*. Harvard had no Women's Studies program when Carol Gilligan wrote *In a Different Voice*.

37. See Bayard Rustin, ed., *Black Studies: Myths and Realities*, A. Phillip Randolph Educational Fund, New York, 1969, p. 13.

38. Cited by Michele Collison, "Enhanced by New Scholarship, Afro-American Studies Enjoy a Renaissance on University Campuses," *Chronicle of Higher Education*, January 4, 1989, p. A-9.

39. Houston Baker, "Generational Shifts and the Recent Criticism of Afro-American Literature," *Black American Literature Forum* 15, Spring 1981, p. 9.

40. Bell Hooks, *Talking Back: Thinking Feminist, Thinking Black*, South End Press, Boston, 1989, p. 20.

41. University of Illinois professor Thomas Kochman argues that

> Blacks do not believe that emotions interfere with their capacity to reason. . . . [In debate] opponents are viewed as antagonists, givers and receivers of abuse, not simply contenders in a struggle to produce a more valid thought or idea. . . . Whites believe that the truth or merits of an idea are intrinsic to the idea itself; blacks admit that they deal from a point of view, and are disinclined to believe whites who claim not to have a point of view. . . . The requirement to behave calmly, rationally and logically when negotiating is looked upon by blacks as a political requirement, and to accede to it in advance is considered as a political defeat. . . . In black culture it is customary for black men to approach black women in a manner that openly expresses sexual interest.

Thomas Kochman, *Black and White: Styles in Conflict*, University of Chicago Press, Chicago, 1981, pp. 19, 21, 38, 40, 75.

42. Molefi Kete Asante, *The Afrocentric Idea*, Temple University Press, Philadelphia, 1987, p. 56.

43. Cited by Roger Kimball, "The Academy Debates the Canon," *The New Criterion*, September 1987, p. 38.

44. Phyllis Rosser, *The SAT Gender Gap: Identifying the Causes*, Center for Women Policy Studies, Washington, D.C., 1989. See also Jean Evangelauf, "SAT Is Called a Defective Product That Is Biased against Women," *Chronicle of Higher Education*, May 3, 1989, p. A-3.

45. Feminists have criticized science for the "master molecule" theory of DNA functioning; for the notion that forces act upon objects, thus creating an active-passive relationship; for thinking of evolution as a "struggle for survival," giving strength a significant role in human development; for advancing the theory of scarcity of resources generating "competition" among animals, another male trait. In summary, most scientific notions that imply force, violence, or hierarchy are denounced as chauvinist. See, e.g., Margarita Levin, "Feminists and Science," *The American Scholar*, Winter 1988, pp. 100–106. Levin's critical analysis focuses on two well-known texts, Sandra Harding's *The Science Question in Feminism* and Evelyn Fox-Keller's *Reflections on Gender and Science*.

46. Ruth Hubbard, *The Politics of Women's Biology*, Rutgers University Press, New Brunswick, N.J., 1990, p. 32.

47. See, e.g., Richard Delgado, "The Imperial Scholar: Reflections on a Review of Civil Rights Literature," *University of Pennsylvania Law Review* 132, 1984, p. 561, and "When a Story Is Just a Story: Does Voice Really Matter?" *University of Virginia Law Review* 76, 1990, p. 95; Mari Matsuda, "Affirmative Action and Legal Knowledge," *Harvard Women's Law Journal* 11, 1988.

48. Cited by Tamar Lewin, "For Feminist Scholars, Second Thoughts on Law and Order," *New York Times*, September 30, 1988.

49. Allan Gold, "Blacks Hold Sit-in on Harvard Hiring," *New York Times*, May 11, 1988.

50. See, e.g., Fox Butterfield, "Harvard Law School Torn by Race Issue," *New York Times*, April 26, 1990, p. A-20; Butterfield, "Old Rights Campaigner Leads a Harvard Battle," *New York Times*, May 21, 1990, p. A-18; Abigail Thernstrom, "On the Scarcity of Black Professors," *Commentary*, July 1990, pp. 22–26.

51. Randall Kennedy, "Racial Critiques of Legal Academia," *Harvard Law Review* 102, 1989, pp. 1745, 1749. Kennedy's article criticizes the work of Richard Delgado of the University of Wisconsin Law School and Mari Matsuda of the Hawaii Law School. For a discussion of the debate see Charles Rothfeld, "Minority Critic Stirs Debate on Minority Writing," *New York Times*, January 5, 1990.

52. Michael O'Brien, "A Paradox of Intellectual Life Since the 60s: We Are Cosmopolitan, Our Scholarship Is Not," *Chronicle of Higher Education*, November 30, 1988, pp. B-1, B-2.

53. Cited by Ellen Coughlin, "Scholars Work to Refine Africa-Centered View of the Life and History of Black Americans," *Chronicle of Higher Education*, October 28, 1987, p. A-6.

54. Asante, *The Afrocentric Idea*, p. 169.

55. Cited by Alan Dershowitz, "Weighted Scale of Diversity," *Washington Times*, May 10, 1990, p. F-1.

56. "The days are gone," Kochman writes, when scholars can "work with minority groups simply to demonstrate the methods and procedures of their discipline or to

obtain interesting comparative data." Today "they will only be able to serve . . . . their career goals insofar as these are compatible with the social needs and goals of the minority groups with whom they work." Kochman, *Black and White,* p. 3.

57. Cited by Karen Winkler, "Scholars Nourished on the 60s Question the Impact of Their Research on Public Policy and Law," *Chronicle of Higher Education,* November 9, 1988, p. A-5.

58. Linda Kerber, "Despite Its Focus on Diversity, American Studies Has Remained Too Much a Part of the Status Quo," *Chronicle of Higher Education,* March 29, 1989, p. B-2.

59. Cited by Elaine Showalter, *The New Feminist Criticism,* Pantheon Books, New York, 1985, p. 5.

60. "Scholars Seek Wider Reach for Women's Studies," *New York Times,* May 17, 1989, p. B-6.

61. Cited by Patricia Hill Collins and Margaret Anderson, eds., *An Inclusive Curriculum: Race, Class and Gender in Sociological Instruction,* American Sociological Association, Washington, D.C., 1987, p. 153.

62. Report of the Committee on the Status of Women in the Academic Profession, May 1989, AAUP, reprinted in *Academe,* July–August 1989, p. 38.

63. Bell Hooks, *Feminist Theory: From Margin to Center,* South End Press, Boston, 1984, p. 110.

64. See, e.g., Ellen Berg, "Feminist Theory: Moving Sociology from the Male-stream," *Footnotes,* March 1987, p. 5.

65. A fairly exhaustive list of feminist neologisms can be found in Casey Miller and Kate Swift, *The Handbook of Nonsexist Writing,* Harper and Row, New York, 1980.

66. Cited in Christina Hoff Summers, unpublished manuscript on Women's Studies, available from the author, Department of Philosophy, Clark University.

67. Guidelines of Women's Committee, McGill University. Available from McGill Faculty Senate.

68. Testimony of James Freedman, *Dartmouth Review* v. *Dartmouth College,* Grafton County Superior Court, December 21–23, 1988.

69. Cited by T. R. Reid, "Shootout in Academia over History of U.S. West," *Washington Post,* October 10, 1989.

70. In fact, only 33 percent of women identify with a feminist label, with 58 percent rejecting it; survey by Yankelovich, Clancy, Schulman for *Time*/CNN, December 1981.

71. Collins and Anderson, *An Inclusive Curriculum.* A sampling of recommended texts: Sylvia Walby, *Patriarchy at Work;* Cherrie Moraga and Gloria Anzaldua, *This Bridge Called My Back: Writings by Radical Women of Color;* Maxine Kingston, *This Woman Warrior;* Manning Marable, *How Capitalism Underdeveloped Black America;* Ginny Vida, ed., *Our Right to Love: A Lesbian Resource Book;* Bell Hooks, *Ain't I a Woman: Black Women and Feminism;* Kathleen Barry, *Female Sexual Slavery;* Barrie Thorne and M. Yalom, *Rethinking the Family;* Ruth Zambrana, ed., *Latina Women in Transition;* Margarita Melville, *Twice a Minority: Mexican-American Women.*

72. Proceedings of the Eleventh Annual Great Lakes College Association's Women's Studies Conference, "Looking Forward: Women's Strategies for Survival," 1985, p. 14.

73. Cited by Christina Hoff Summers, "Feminism and the College Curriculum," *Imprimis* 19, No. 6, 1990, p. 2.

74. See letter to Harvard faculty from Harvard Gay, Lesbian and Bisexual Issues Network, signed by Robert Kiely, English department; Warren Goldfarb, philosophy department; and William Ira Bennett and Joanna Rohrbaugh, Harvard Medical School, May 9, 1989. See also brochure of Curriculum Committee of the Lesbian and Gay Studies Center, Yale University, 1989.

75. Statement by group chairman Aaron Bismo. See "Group Helps Men to Rethink of Women's Issues," *New York Times*, Campus Life, March 11, 1990, p. 43.

76. "The white, male, heterosexual, able-bodied, Christian, middle-class norm has served as a definition for men and all of humanity, and that's been the problem," says Harry Brod, coordinator of Men's Studies at Kenyon. "We need to break down the monolithic model of what it is to be a real man."

Some outside the university have misunderstood Men's Studies to agitate for "male" concerns in the same way that Women's Studies is activist on behalf of feminism. In practice, however, Men's Studies appears to be a framework for marketing feminism to men who might otherwise stay away from programs labeled "Women's Studies."

See Ginny Wiegand, "His-tory Lessons: Men's Studies Gaining Favor on Campus," *Washington Post*, November 27, 1989, p. B-5.

77. See Curriculum Outline, "The Politics of Reproduction," San Francisco State University, Spring 1990.

78. See, e.g., *Federalist 10* and *Federalist 51*, where Publius discusses the dangers of majority faction. Publius hoped that, by enlarging the sphere, and setting faction against faction, the hope of assembling majority factions to tyrannize over others would be thwarted. "In an extended republic of the U.S., and among the great variety of interests, parties and sects which it embraces, a coalition of a majority of the whole society could seldom take place on any other principles than those of justice and the general good." Clinton Rossiter, ed., *The Federalist*, Mentor Books, New York, 1961.

79. William Damon, "Learning How to Deal with the New American Dilemma," *Chronicle of Higher Education*, May 3, 1989, p. B-1.

80. Robert Detlefsen, "White Like Me," *New Republic*, April 10, 1989, pp. 18–20.

81. "Take Care," *The Economist*, February 10, 1990.

82. Philip Rubin, "Students Discuss Montreal Massacre," *Harvard Crimson*, December 13, 1989, p. 1.

83. Valerie Batts and Joyce Brown, "Assumptions and Definitions," Visions, Inc., Cambridge, Mass., 1989.

84. Nancy Brown, "Conditions under Which Racial Learning Occurs," NTL Reading Book for Human Relations Training, NTL Institute, 1989.

85. For a fuller treatment, see Robert Goldwin, "Why Blacks, Women and Jews Are Not Mentioned in the Constitution," *Commentary*, May 1987, pp. 28–33.

86. *Affirmative Action Newsletter*, Harvard University, Office of the Assistant to the President, Fall 1989.

87. Frederick Douglass, "Address for the Promotion of Colored Enlistments," reprinted in *The Life and Writings of Frederick Douglass*, edited by Philip S. Foner, International Publishers, New York, 1950, vol. 3, p. 365.

88. The authors of the Declaration, Lincoln said, "did not mean to assert the obvious untruth, that all were then actually enjoying that equality. They meant simply to declare the right, so that the enforcement of it might follow as fast as circumstances should permit." Roy Basler, ed., *The Collected Works of Abraham Lincoln*, Rutgers University Press, New Brunswick, N.J., 1953, p. 406.

89. See, e.g., Harry V. Jaffa, *Crisis of the House Divided*, University of Chicago Press, Chicago, 1959.

90. Derek Bok, "Open Letter on Issues of Race at Harvard," Office of the President, Harvard University, February 27, 1981.

91. Suzanne Alexander, "Freshmen Flood Black Colleges, Defying Trend," *Wall Street Journal*, July 9, 1990.

## 8. Illiberal Education

1. In 1988, there were 10.3 million whites, 1.1 million blacks, 680,000 Hispanics, 497,000 Asian Americans, 93,000 American Indians, and 361,000 foreign students enrolled in American colleges. See "1988 College Enrollment," U.S. Department of Education, table reprinted in *Chronicle of Higher Education*, April 11, 1990, p. A-1.

2. A recent Carnegie Foundation report shows that the number of philosophically liberal professors is more than double the number of conservative professors. In humanities departments, where presumably ideology is most likely to manifest itself in the classroom, the ratio is almost four to one. For faculty under the age of forty, the ratio is almost three to one, suggesting that the imbalance is likely to become greater in the future. See *The Condition of the Professoriate*, Carnegie Foundation, Washington, D.C., 1989, p. 143.

3. See Assembly Bill 462, introduced by member Tom Hayden (February 2, 1989) and Assembly Bill 3993, introduced by member Willie Brown (March 2, 1990) in the California legislature, 1989–90 session. Copies obtained from office of Assemblyman Hayden. Although the wording of these bills is somewhat ambiguous, some critics believe that their effect will be to require not only admission, but also passing grades, promotion, and graduation, at the same rate for all racial groups. See John Bunzel, "Inequitable Equality on Campus," *Wall Street Journal*, July 25, 1990; Abigail Thernstrom, "On the Scarcity of Black Professors," *Commentary*, July 1990.

4. See Bunzel, "Inequitable Equality on Campus."

5. The long history of segregation and discrimination has produced a "heightened sense of group consciousness" among blacks, and a "stronger orientation toward collective values and behavior" than exists among whites. See Gerald Jaynes and Robin Wiliams, eds., *A Common Destiny: Blacks and American Society*, National Academy Press, Washington, D.C., 1989, p. 13.

6. For example, Cornell president Frank Rhodes remarks, "We face an unresolved conflict between the natural impulse toward proud, separate racial and ethnic identity on the one hand and the genuine desire, on the other, for meaningful integration that transcends differences of background." See Frances Dinkelspiel, "In Rift at Cornell, Racial Issues of the 60s Remain," *New York Times*, May 3, 1989.

7. California State University officials, led by faculty member Otis Scott, are planning to establish Cooper-Woodson College as a special adjunct to the university. "Is it separatist?" Scott asked. "No more than the separation that already exists between [black] students and the institution. We are committed to creating a comprehensive support network for African-American students." Cited by Karen O'Hara, "Sacramento

State May Try Black University Structure," *Black Issues in Higher Education,* May 10, 1990, p. 13.

8. Seth Mydans, "Black Identity vs. Success and Seeming White," *New York Times,* April 25, 1990, p. B-9. Although the study by Fordham and Ogbu focused on black high schools, Fordham said in an interview that her findings also apply to black culture on college campuses.

9. This view even claims some scholarly support. One study concluded that "research on nonverbal behavior shows that white college students often sit further away, use a less friendly voice tone, make less eye contact, and more speech errors, and terminate the interview faster when interacting with a black rather than a white." See Thomas Pettigrew, "New Patterns of Racism: The Different Worlds of 1984 and 1964," *Rutgers Law Review* 37, 1985, pp. 673, 689.

10. At the University of Virginia, for instance, minority students demanded to know why a larger proportion of blacks than whites were charged with honor code violations, and many called for the abolition of the allegedly bigoted and discriminatory honor system. See Darryl Brown, "Racism and Race Relations in the University," *University of Virginia Law Review* 76, 1989, pp. 295, 334. See also Editorial, "Dishonorable Schoolboys," *Washington Times,* April 9, 1990.

11. Arthur Schlesinger, "When Ethnic Studies Are Un-American," *Wall Street Journal,* April 23, 1990.

12. William Raspberry, "Why the Racial Slogans?" *Washington Post,* September 20, 1989.

13. A vivid recent example of this is the case of Linda Chavez, former staff director of the U.S. Civil Rights Commission, who was invited to be the commencement speaker at the University of Northern Colorado in May 1990. When a campus Hispanic group and several other students and faculty protested, however, President Robert Dickeson rescinded Chavez's invitation. "The intent of the university in inviting Linda Chavez was to be sensitive to cultural diversity and the committee making the decision intended to communicate the importance of cultural pluralism," the university explained in a press release. "It is clear that the decision was both uninformed and gave the appearance of being grossly insensitive." Although Chavez's role as a prominent Hispanic woman apparently accounted for her selection, the problem turned out to be her conservative views, in particular, her opposition to preferential treatment and bilingualism. As Chavez herself observed in the *Chronicle of Higher Education,* "The problem with the cultural pluralist model is that not all blacks, Hispanics or women think alike." Diversity, Chavez charged, was invoked in this instance "to keep out certain ideas and certain people, to foreclose debate, to substitute ideological catechism for the free inquiry usually associated with a university." See "The Importance of Cultural Pluralism," press release by University of Northern Colorado, reprinted in *Wall Street Journal,* May 9, 1990; Linda Chavez, "The Real Aim of the Promoters of Cultural Diversity Is to Exclude Certain People and to Foreclose Debate," *Chronicle of Higher Education,* July 18, 1990, p. B-1; Carol Innerst, "Chavez Encounters Big Chill," *Washington Times,* May 4, 1990, p. 1.

14. Nancy Gibbs, "Bigots in the Ivory Tower," *Time,* May 7, 1990, p. 104.

15. Sari Horwitz, "Black Students Protest GWU Party," *Washington Post,* February 8, 1987, p. A-15.

16. In a somewhat comical recent episode, after instituting a series of multicultural measures on campus, President William Gerberding of the University of Washington

at Seattle was denounced by activist groups for making a joke about illegal immigration, which protesters branded an "ethnic slur." Before a rally of 250 students, Gerberding apologized and agreed to enroll *himself* in a "multiracial awareness" course aimed at curing bigoted tendencies. See Michael Park, "Gerberding Issues Public Apology," *Daily Campus Newspaper,* University of Washington at Seattle, May 16, 1990, p. 1.

17. All signs point to the multicultural revolution on campus expanding its reach.

• Recently the Middle States Association of Colleges postponed accreditation for Baruch College in New York City, citing insufficient progress in preferential recruitment of faculty and students. Both the Middle States Association and the Western Association of Schools and Colleges have announced that institutional commitment to diversity will now constitute an essential criterion for accreditation.

• Proportional representation has extended to some cases of campus discipline, for example, when a firebomb exploded on the Wesleyan campus in May 1990, minority activists insisted, and university investigators agreed, that regardless of where circumstantial evidence pointed, white and black students should be interrogated in roughly the same proportion as their group representation in the student body, to avoid the appearance of prejudicial inquiry.

• As censorship codes have grown more expansive, previously innocuous conduct is now prosecuted—thus at Southern Methodist University, the judicial committee recently punished one student for referring to Martin Luther King, Jr., as a communist and singing "We Shall Overcome" in a "sarcastic manner," and another student for calling a classmate a Mexican "in a derogatory manner" even though the student immediately apologized for the perceived slight.

• Finally, group classification based on ethnicity has become increasingly nuanced at the University of California at Davis, where Latino activists have organized hunger strikes to protest the Spanish department's alleged bias toward the Castilian language, spoken in Spain, over colloquial Spanish, spoken in Mexico.

See Ed Wiley, "Agencies Likely to Incorporate Diversity Standards," *Black Issues in Higher Education,* May 24, 1990, p. 4; Kirk Johnson, "Racial Graffiti Found on Walls at Wesleyan," *New York Times,* May 5, 1990; "Three Bias Incidents Provide Lessons for Class on Race," *New York Times,* May 6, 1990, Campus Life, pp. 53–54; Eric Brazil, "Irked Latino Students Castigate Castilians at California College," *Washington Times,* May 17, 1990.

18. I believe that the moral power of the idea of victimhood derives from Christianity. The Greeks elevated the heroic virtues, while Christianity elevated the sacrificial virtues. It was Christianity which invented the doctrine of the sanctified victim. Previously victims were, for the most part, despised and degraded. Christ, however, was the victim who, even in defeat, emerged triumphant. Modern racial and gender politics seems to be a new version of this *tableau,* without Christian themes of penance and regeneration.

19. Thomas Sowell argues that deep-seated cultural grievance often manifests itself in repressive ways. White Afrikaners in South Africa nurtured a profound isolation and "seige mentality" that they used to justify their policies of apartheid. Similarly, Hitler exploited a German sense of grievance and humiliation, engendered by the defeat in World War I and the Treaty of Versailles, to justify the irredentism and mass brutality of World War II.

Shelby Steele finds that some blacks on campus "badger white people about race almost on principle. It's kind of a power move for them."

This perception is shared by writers entirely sympathetic to the causes of minority victims. Frantz Fanon writes that the historical victim "is overpowered but not tamed . . . he is patiently waiting until the settler is off his guard to fly at him. The native is an oppressed person whose permanent dream is to become the persecutor."

Albert Memmi observes, "The oppressed want to forge ahead by themselves, to find their own particular and individual path, entirely cut off from their former overlords, and at first in direct opposition to them—from now on, they will acquiesce in the ugliness of their own reactions, which they will no longer attempt to disguise; indeed they will make use of them, inducing in themselves hideous paroxyms of hate."

Thomas Sowell, "Affirmative Action: A Worldwide Disaster," *Commentary*, December 1989; Shelby Steele, "I'm Black, You're White, Who's Innocent?" *Harper's*, June 1988, pp. 45–52; Frantz Fanon, *The Wretched of the Earth*, Grove Press, New York, 1963, p. 53; Albert Memmi, *Dominated Man*, Beacon Press, Boston, 1969, p. 9.

20. "I have learned that success is to be measured not so much by the position that one has reached in life, as by the obstacles which [one] has overcome while trying to succeed." Booker T. Washington, *Up from Slavery*, reprinted in John Hope Franklin, ed., *Three Negro Classics*, Avon Books, New York, p. 50.

21. See John Leo, "The Class That Deserves Cutting," *U.S. News & World Report*, May 29, 1989, p. 58.

22. Cited in Glenn Ricketts, "Multiculturalism Mobilizes," *Academic Questions*, Summer 1990, p. 57.

23. Harvard Law School professor Randall Kennedy says that it is possible to find cases where tests and standards are biased, but "the proper response is not to scrap the meritocratic ideal" but rather "to abjure all practices that exploit the trappings of meritocracy to advance interests that have nothing to do with the intellectual characteristics of the subject being judged." See Randall Kennedy, "Racial Critiques of Legal Academia," *Harvard Law Review* 102, 1989, pp. 1745–1807.

24. Comment of President James Freedman of Dartmouth College, cited by Edward Fiske, "Redefining Dartmouth New President's Quest for 'Private Selves,'" *New York Times*, August 23, 1988, p. E-24.

25. Manfred Stanley, "The American University as a Civic Institution," *Civic Arts Review*, Spring 1989, p. 6.

26. See, e.g., Edward Said, *Orientalism*, Pantheon Books, New York, 1978.

Delusions about other cultures are not simply an ancient phenomenon but are evident in this century. Disgruntled with race relations in America, Paul Robeson visited the Soviet Union in the early 1930s, and returned with high praise for Stalin's ethnic policies. "The Soviet Union is the only place where ethnology is seriously considered and applied." See Paul Robeson, "I Breathe Freely," *New Theater*, July 1935, p. 5.

More recently, in 1979, Richard Falk of Princeton University found in the Ayatollah Khomeini a progressive alternative to the Shah of Iran. Embittered by U.S. support for the Shah, Falk was certain that Khomeini would champion the progressive cause.

The depiction of Khomeini as a fanatical reactionary and the bearer of crude prejudices seems certainly and happily false. What is also encouraging is that his entourage of close advisers is uniformly composed of moderate, progressive individuals [who] share a notable record of concern for human rights. In Iran, the Shiite tradition is flexible in its approach to the Koran. . . . Khomeini's Islamic republic can be expected to have a doctrine of social justice at its core. Iran may yet provide us with a desperately needed model of humane governance for a Third World country.

See Richard Falk, "Trusting Khomeini," *New York Times*, February 6, 1979; Richard Falk, "Khomeini's Promise," *Foreign Policy*, Spring 1979, pp. 28–34.

Paul Hollander of the University of Massachusetts at Amherst argues that Western intellectuals have since the 1930s searched for a peasant paradise abroad. The quest began with Stalin's Russia, then Mao's China, Castro's Cuba, and most recently Ortega's Nicaragua. Every time irrefutable evidence surfaced showing how bloodthirsty were the regimes that Westerners revered, the Western fantasy moved on to the next destination. Hollander argues that foreign countries are often experienced by Western intellectuals as a projection of their own domestic alienation and self-hatred. See Paul Hollander, *Political Pilgrims*, Oxford University Press, New York, 1981.

27. Even a careful reading of the Vedas or Analects will not transplant young Americans into the culture of which those important works are a part. It would take years, perhaps a lifetime, of experience and study for an outsider to penetrate the inner reaches of another culture—as difficult as it would be for a Chinese to become an expert on Mark Twain or Henry James. This is not only beyond the capacity of most students, but also of most faculty. There are only a handful of teachers who could even approach such comprehension, and probably none of them teaches general undergraduate courses. Consequently, non-Western study is better aimed at the narrower but more practical goals of widening the Western scope of familiarity, preparing the Westerner for travel and cultural exchange, and learning how to empathize with others who are very different from oneself.

28. Michael Novak at the American Enterprise Institute points out that most Western classics aim at the production of universal knowledge. Adam Smith did not write "The Wealth of Scotland" but rather *An Inquiry into the Nature and Causes of the Wealth of Nations*. The Declaration of Independence does not state that "all Americans" but rather that "all men are created equal and endowed by their creator with certain inalienable rights." Again, the founders intended to make a universal statement, even if they neglected to use gender-inclusive language. The Western tradition, at its best, teaches self-criticism toward itself and openness to other cultures.

29. See Allan Bloom with Harry Jaffa, *Shakespeare's Politics*, Basic Books, New York, 1964.

30. W. E. B. Du Bois, "The Spirit of Modern Europe," cited by Herbert Aptheker, ed., *Against Racism*, Amherst College Press, Amherst, Mass., 1985, pp. 52–54.

31. Paul Robeson, *Here I Stand*, Beacon Press, Boston, 1957, p. 26.

32. Paul Robeson, "Reflections on Othello and the Nature of Our Times," *The American Scholar*, Autumn 1945, p. 390.

33. For example, while the number of humanities majors plummets, the American Council of Learned Societies boasts, "Precisely those things now identified as failings in the humanities indicate enlivening transformation." See "Speaking for the Humanities," American Council of Learned Societies, Paper No. 7, New York, 1989, p. 3.

# Index